the BiG ⚛ BANG THEORY

the BiG BANG THEORY

THE DEFINITIVE, INSIDE STORY OF THE EPIC HIT SERIES

JESSICA RADLOFF

GRAND CENTRAL
PUBLISHING

NEW YORK   BOSTON

Grand Central Publishing
Hachette Book Group
1290 Avenue of the Americas, New York, NY 10104
grandcentralpublishing.com
twitter.com/grandcentralpub
First Edition: October 2022

Grand Central Publishing is a division of Hachette Book Group, Inc. The Grand Central Publishing name and logo is a trademark of Hachette Book Group, Inc.

The publisher is not responsible for websites (or their content) that are not owned by the publisher.

The Hachette Speakers Bureau provides a wide range of authors for speaking events. To find out more, go to www.hachettespeakersbureau.com or call (866) 376-6591.

Library of Congress Cataloging-in-Publication Data
Names: Radloff, Jessica, author.
Title: The big bang theory : the definitive, inside story of the epic hit series / Jessica Radloff.
Description: New York : Grand Central Publishing, 2022. | Includes index.
Identifiers: LCCN 2022019470 | ISBN 9781538708491 (hardcover) | ISBN 9781538708514 (ebook)
Subjects: LCSH: Big bang theory (Television program)
Classification: LCC PN1992.77.B485 R33 2022 | DDC 791.45/72—dc23/eng/20220511
LC record available at https://lccn.loc.gov/2022019470

ISBNs: 978-1-5387-0849-1 (hardcover), 978-1-5387-0851-4 (ebook)

Printed in the United States of America

LSC-C

Printing 1, 2022

CONTENTS

LIST OF CONTRIBUTORS

MAIN CAST

Johnny Galecki: "Leonard Hofstadter"
Jim Parsons: "Sheldon Cooper"
Kaley Cuoco: "Penny Hofstadter"
Simon Helberg: "Howard Wolowitz"
Kunal Nayyar: "Rajesh Koothrappali"
Mayim Bialik: "Amy Farrah Fowler"
Melissa Rauch: "Bernadette Rostenkowski Wolowitz"
Kevin Sussman: "Stuart Bloom"

GUEST CAST

Christine Baranski: "Beverly Hofstadter"
Lance Barber: "Jimmy Speckerman"/"George Cooper," *Young Sheldon*
John Ross Bowie: "Barry Kripke"
Mark Hamill: "Himself"
Laurie Metcalf: "Mary Cooper"
Bob Newhart: "Arthur Jeffries/Professor Proton"
Adam Nimoy: Leonard Nimoy's son/"Himself"
Amanda Walsh: "Katie"
Wil Wheaton: "Wil Wheaton"

CREATORS/PRODUCERS/WRITERS/ETC.

Chuck Lorre: co-creator, executive producer
Bill Prady: co-creator, executive producer
Steve Molaro: executive producer, showrunner
Steve Holland: executive producer, showrunner

Lee Aronsohn: co-creator, *Two and a Half Men*; executive producer, *The Big Bang Theory*

James Burrows: director (both pilots)

Mark Cendrowski: director

Peter Chakos: editor/co-executive producer

Maria Ferrari: executive producer/writer

Dave Goetsch: executive producer/writer

Andy Gordon: co-executive producer/writer

Eddie Gorodetsky: co-executive producer, *The Big Bang Theory*; co-creator, *Mom*

Tara Hernandez: co-executive producer/writer

Eric Kaplan: executive producer/writer

Scott London: prop master

Nikki Lorre: 2nd assistant director/director

Ken Miller: casting director

Mary T. Quigley: costume designer; co-producer

Anthony Rich: 1st assistant director/director

Professor David Saltzberg: science consultant

Nikki Valko: casting director

EXECUTIVES

Peter Roth: president, Warner Bros. Television, 1999–2013; president and chief content officer, Warner Bros. Television Group, 2013–2020; chairman, Warner Bros. Television Group, 2020–2021

Nina Tassler: president of entertainment, CBS, 2004–2014; chairman of entertainment, CBS, 2014–2015

Wendi Trilling: executive vice president, comedy development, CBS, 2004–2015

EXTENDED FAMILY

Judy Parsons: Jim Parsons's mother

Zoe Perry: "Mary Cooper," *Young Sheldon*

CHUCK LORRE PRODUCTIONS

Hindsight is not twenty-twenty. At least that's what I kept thinking while being interviewed for this book. For me, hindsight is myopic, color-blind, and suffering from a mild concussion. But I like to believe there's a good reason for that (other than the dementia slip 'n' slide ride at LorreLand). In order to effectively participate in the writing, casting, directing, performing, and producing of a TV series, our brains have to download everything nonessential in order to focus on the work at hand. A running joke at many Wednesday morning table reads was to ask an actor or a writer what the episode was about that we had shot just the night before. Twelve hours ago. Their universal blank stare was confirmation that the information was nowhere to be found. Everyone was unconsciously creating mental space for the next episode. And this went on for 279 episodes. Twelve mostly joyful but always laugh-filled years.

There's an old saying that "history is written by the winners." I believe *The Big Bang Theory* won, and this book represents our history. I hope you enjoy what is the culmination of years of hard work by the amazing Jessica Radloff. I would just suggest that as you read our recollections and anecdotes, you keep in mind one thing: On most Wednesday mornings, the "winners" struggled to remember Tuesday night.

HOW THE REUNION CAME TO BE

Two years. One hundred and twenty hours of brand-new interviews over ten months. Thousands of pages of transcripts. One hundred and fourteen pages of notes from rewatching 280 episodes (279 that aired, plus the original pilot that didn't). I could keep going with statistics, though most likely that's not why you picked up this book. But they do matter. Those staggering numbers only happened because the creators, cast, producers, writers, studio and network executives, guest stars, etc. of *The Big Bang Theory* put together a show of such brilliance and magnitude that anything less could not do it justice.

For hours on end, they all thoughtfully answered the longest list of questions they've ever been asked. They watched iconic moments with me, texted and emailed me an endless amount of photos (prop master Scott London even dug up the *Star Trek* transporter room boxes and Penny's old résumé and driver's license during our Zoom), and dug up scripts and documents from that first, unaired pilot. And while there was plenty of laughter and joy and tears, no one shied away from going deep when it came to discussing the more difficult moments over the years, whether it be contract negotiations, pay cuts, divorce, miscarriage and loss, to the tumultuous few days when it was decided the show's twelfth season would be its last. If you're going to tell the full story of why *The Big Bang Theory* became one of the most successful, popular, and beloved shows of all time, then it has to be told from all angles and all perspectives. And it is. Thanks to them.

But perhaps even more remarkable was the time and access they gave of themselves to do that. It's not like they weren't busy with other projects; all of them have numerous TV shows or films going on, but it was continued proof just how important *Big Bang* was *and is* to their lives. Bill Prady got on Zoom for a follow-up interview (after doing hours of interviews as it was) the day before leaving for his wedding in New York. Melissa Rauch and I did interviews often while she was doing the dishes at 11 p.m. after working on new scripts for *Night Court* and getting her kids to bed. Kaley Cuoco had me over to her home to go through pictures for this book, which just happened to be the same day she was nominated for her first Emmy award (you know, casual). Truthfully, I blame executive producer Steve Molaro for setting the tone when he did a nearly four-hour interview for our first session, which I ended only because I got hungry. And that's just scratching the surface of what everyone from Chuck Lorre to Mark Hamill did to make this book come to life.

I'll never forget what Jim Parsons said on the first of what would be over twenty hours of interviews: "I'm reading Mike Nichols's biography right now and you just love to go back and hear the stories about how it was made, because you felt something for the work. It moved you. It changed you in some way. And that's a real honor. It's one of the reasons I was so glad to say we should do these conversations, however many we're going to do, because if it's worth looking into, it's worth getting new and interesting facts out there. When stuff is good, it celebrates humanity, and I think that feeling is what's hard to ignore and not be moved by."

Here's the thing: I was never going to be a scientist (full disclosure: I never wanted to), but *The Big Bang Theory* resonated with me as a viewer—and impacted me as a journalist—more than any other show I've covered. As *Glamour*'s senior West Coast editor, I wrote more than 150 features / articles / think pieces on the series. I also met many of you throughout the years, whether through social media or in person, and have been forever touched by the stories of what *Big Bang* meant to you.

And I got it. As a kid and young adult who always felt different and socially behind—three learning "disabilities" will do that to you—I related to Amy's desire for a best friend; I understood Sheldon's habits, work ethic, and OCD; I got Raj's desire to find the love of a lifetime—as well as his doubts about when or if it would ever happen. If my fantasy was to be just as cool as the characters I saw on *Friends*, the truth is that I—and I think most of us—relate a hell of a lot more to who we saw on *The Big Bang Theory*.

A show that started as four "nerds" and the hot but ditzy female neighbor became a smart, socially relevant blockbuster of a sitcom that tackled topics like intimacy, consent, motherhood, marriage, career, and money with humor, poignancy, and heart. And as a result, it became one of the greatest sitcoms of our time.

the BiG BANG THEORY

Chapter 1

WHERE IT ALL STARTED

A show like *The Big Bang Theory* is not supposed to be a mainstream success. Not when the two lead characters are a theoretical physicist and an experimental physicist. Or when episodes involve the Born-Oppenheimer approximation and Schrödinger's Cat. Or when a lot of attention is paid to whiteboards and theorems. It's just not. And it probably wouldn't have gone further than the idea bin if it weren't for the power and respect that creator Chuck Lorre commanded, when in 2006, he—along with Bill Prady—went to CBS with an idea for a new series built on that very concept. In almost any other setting, it wouldn't have made it through the door, and then if it had, it would have been greeted with a "Thanks, we'll get back to you." But Lorre had a plan—albeit a risky one. And to understand how it came together, you have to go back to childhood obsessions, computer programming days, and a determined television executive by the name of Peter Roth.

Chuck Lorre (co-creator, *The Big Bang Theory*, co-creator *Two and a Half Men*): Growing up, I devoured all things DC Comics, and then Marvel came along and elevated the whole genre. Everything changed when I read Ray Bradbury's *The Martian Chronicles* as a kid. That changed my life. I became obsessed with devouring every book by every sci-fi author I stumbled upon. And that led to Robert A. Heinlein, and Isaac Asimov, and Frank Herbert's *Dune*, which led to Roger Zelazny. I was an enormous fan of *Star Trek* in the '60s, so much so that when it got canceled after three seasons—the same year *The Smothers Brothers* got canceled—I said, "That's it for television. I'm through with television! Any medium that would cancel *Star Trek* and *Smothers Brothers* is not worth my time!" I would tell anybody that would listen that television was a stupid medium and we need not spend any time with it. And then during the next decade, I didn't even own a TV. Unless I was dating a woman with a television, I didn't watch it. I was also stupid poor, so any money I made certainly wasn't going to be spent on buying a TV.

Ironically, the man who declared himself "through with television," is now one of the most prolific and successful television producers in history, having been called "the king of comedy." And while Lorre has proven himself to be a hitmaker again and again, he will be the first to tell you that no successful comedy is a solo effort.

Peter Roth (former chairman, Warner Bros. Television Group): In 1994, I was at 20th Network Television (now 20th Century Fox Television Productions). My boss, Peter Chernin, said to me, "Peter, you do a great job in drama, but frankly, you suck in comedy." [*Laughs*] And he was right. That led to my team and I putting together a list of what we considered to be the seven greatest comedy creators and showrunners in the business. Number one on that list: Chuck Lorre. Number two on that list was Danny Jacobson, who created *Mad About You*, followed by five others who will remain anonymous because none of them succeeded. I brought that list to Mr. Chernin, who said, "How much do you think it's going to cost to [get those people]?" It was going to cost an extraordinary amount of money, especially in those days. The next week we went to see [then chairman and CEO of News Corporation] Rupert Murdoch about why we should be investing this money. Rupert just looked at us and said, "Do it!" I walked out of the office, my knees buckling, thinking, *Oh my God, I can't believe this man just committed this amount of money. More importantly, I can't believe the onus is now on me and I have to execute all of this.*

Roth, who was responsible for hit dramas like *The X-Files*, *Picket Fences*, *21 Jump Street*, and more, had never met Chuck Lorre, but he sure knew of his work and read his material. For that reason and more, Roth was relentless in his pursuit to sign him. And it worked. In the end, Roth made deals with all seven comedy creators on his list.

Peter Roth: But only two of those deals actually worked out well. And only one of them paid for the entire investment and literally quintupled the original amount—and that was Chuck Lorre, with one show—*Dharma & Greg*.

Chuck Lorre: It was a very low point in my life when Peter walked in. I created *Grace Under Fire* and ended up quitting the show because it was a very toxic environment. I wasn't capable of sustaining any kind of sanity there. I went to producers Marcy Carsey and Tom Werner, and wept in their office. I told them I couldn't do this anymore. It was just an emotional battering that was involved in working with a very unhappy lead actress (Brett Butler). They said, "Well, just finish the season, and then we'll find someone else." And I agreed, but for reasons that should probably be kept between me and a therapist, I agreed to develop a show for Cybill Shepherd. But the gold of that was that I became friends with Christine Baranski. *Cybill* was a runaway hit immediately, which was exciting as hell, but going into the second season, everything changed. Cybill was no longer my biggest fan or supporter. She wanted me to rewrite a script, and I didn't think it needed to be. As a result, I got fired. So enter Peter Roth saying, "Let's talk." I wasn't feeling really good about myself. I had somehow stumbled into creating two hit shows and now I was on neither one of them.

Christine Baranski ("Maryann Thorpe," *Cybill*; "Beverly Hofstadter," *The Big Bang Theory*): I did *Cybill* because of Chuck Lorre's writing. After winning the Emmy, I thought to myself, *Damn, girl! You made the right decision, and here we are!* And then the next season he was fired. I actually went to Les Moonves's office and asked to be let out of that show. I said, "I did the show because of Chuck Lorre, and because of the writing. I don't know what I'm in for now, but I don't think this is good and I'm really unhappy!" And Les said to me: "I need you. Sorry, but I need you." And I stuck it out for three and a half years. But I saw Chuck slumped in a chair the day he was fired. He was at a very, very low point. So the fact that he then went on to become one of *the* most successful television writers-producers of all time, to me, is just a tribute to his ability to pull himself up and say, "I'm just going to keep going."

Chuck Lorre: I was definitely a little lost. But then Peter made me an unbelievable offer, which was overwhelming. He had more faith in me than I did. And that faith was contagious. I got a little cocky. [*Laughs*] I was like,

Maybe they're right! Maybe I can do this again! It was a clumsy start, but creating *Dharma & Greg* in 1997 was an effort on my part to create an alternative approach to a female-driven comedy. And it worked. It gave me a great deal of confidence that I didn't necessarily have at that moment in time.

Although Peter Roth was a tremendous ally and supporter of Lorre's, he left 20th Network Television in March 1999 to become president at Warner Bros. Television. Lorre couldn't believe it.

Chuck Lorre: I was only a year into my deal when he left. I went, "Wait a minute, where are you going?! I came here because of you! And now you're leaving!" But in 2000, towards the end of my four-year deal at Fox, I went to Warner Bros. Peter was confident I could make something happen again. And I certainly didn't. I proceeded to let him down for three years.

And then, in September 2003, Lorre created *Two and a Half Men* with Lee Aronsohn, which not only became one of the most successful series ever produced by Warner Bros. Television, but would change Lorre's life forever.

Wendi Trilling (executive vice president, comedy development, CBS, 2004–2015): *Two and A Half Men* was a perfect pilot. It felt like a hit show that would be on the air for ten years. That's not usually the case, and it doesn't usually feel that way. *The Big Bang Theory* didn't feel that way. We had to do two pilots. It was a process.

Chuck Lorre: There's no *Big Bang* without *Two and a Half Men*. I just didn't have the horsepower to get CBS on board with a show about theoretical physicists without *Two and a Half Men* being a rip-roaring success. I truly think that gave CBS the patience and a willingness to let us grow.

Peter Roth: But it must be said that Chuck is the most brilliant comedy creator I've ever worked with in my forty-six and a half years. He simply is. He has an eye and ear for story, especially in half-hour form. People don't think you can tell a good story in twenty-two minutes. The fact is, you must. And no one does that better than Chuck Lorre.

While *Two and a Half Men* was killing it in the ratings, producer-writer Bill Prady (who was an executive producer on Lorre's *Dharma & Greg*, and

had begun his career at Jim Henson Productions) was looking for his next project.

Bill Prady (*The Big Bang Theory* co-creator): I was doing a show on the WB called *Related*, from Liz Tuccillo, who co-wrote *He's Just Not That Into You*, and executive-produced by *Friends* co-creator Marta Kauffman. It was a job that I was *so* ill-suited for. I was hired to be the number two person in charge, but I ultimately quit because I was so unhappy doing it. I was just simply the wrong person for it; it was a drama about four sisters.

Chuck Lorre: Bill was a dear friend—we're still very close—so we knocked around all sorts of ideas for months. We were circling around this idea about a young woman who moved to Los Angeles trying to find her way in the world. We actually met with some actresses to play this lead role, but we never really could put that into a coherent form that we were happy with. But one weekend, Bill was telling me about his computer programming days back in the '80s, and these wonderful characters that he worked with who were beyond brilliant, but entirely inept in the real world. They could figure out Pi to eighty decimals but couldn't figure out a tip in a restaurant because there were too many variables. And I recall saying, "Well, *that's* the show! *That's* the show we should be doing! That's fantastic! These are great characters."

Bill Prady: That specific conversation happened in his office in Burbank, where we started talking about the guys I worked with at our software company. The specific calculations one guy could do in his head were remarkable. He was a mathematical savant. He also had selective mutism around women. We broke those two qualities off [between Sheldon and Raj], because although it was based on an actual person, it would have seemed unbelievable on a show at the time, even though this person really did suffer in that way. Now we look at these things and have a better understanding of people who are neuro-atypical and who process the world differently, but at the time, he was just that dude! And he did that stuff!

Chuck Lorre: But I didn't want to do the computer "nerd," the guy with the pocket protectors and the pens and the glasses with the tape in the middle. It felt like a cliché, which I was eventually wrong about because *Silicon Valley* did something similar [in concept] and it was a terrific show. [*Laughs*]

Bill Prady: Chuck also said it's hard to show people at computers in a multicam because they're hunched over a computer. I just remember thinking out loud, "What's smart that you do standing up?" And then as I was writing, I said, "Oh, I'm writing on a whiteboard," which quickly became, "Oh, scientists!" It was more shootable [to show a whiteboard versus a computer screen].

Chuck Lorre: I recall suggesting that these characters were not interested in getting rich, but unraveling the secrets of the universe. I didn't even know what that meant. *A Beautiful Mind* with Russell Crowe had already been out, which was a little darker than we wanted to go. We decided to go for brilliant minds without the psychosis. [*Laughs*] And then our abandoned idea that the young woman who comes to Los Angeles to find her way in the world suddenly made sense because if we could put her in the world of these physicists, she would be the audience. She would be us. They'd have to explain to her, thus explaining to us—the audience—what the hell is going on. And so the two elements kind of came together very quickly.

Bill Prady: Early on, I would do a draft of a scene and then send it to Chuck, and he would tell me why it was terrible. [*Laughs*] And then we'd work some more at his house and then go out to lunch. There was this bookstore nearby, and I really wanted Chuck to read the memoirs of the physicist Richard Feynman, so I bought him the works of Feynman.

Chuck Lorre: By the way, there was a moment where I thought perhaps the female character was an android that the guys built. We wrote a test scene and had a couple actors read the scene for us. And they were halfway through the scene when I went, "Never mind." [*Laughs*] It was terrible. It was just terrible. But I needed to get it out of my system and move on. Looking back, you can't regret any of those initial ideas because they were all necessary to get where we got.

Once Lorre and Prady abandoned the idea of a female android and settled on something a bit more realistic, they invited Peter Roth, and Warner Bros. Television's head of comedy, Len Goldstein, to Lorre's office for a private reading of this new show, which didn't have a title.

Peter Roth: It was around the fall of 2005, and I remember Bill and Chuck just wanted to hear our thoughts. Mark Roberts, who went on to co-create *Mike & Molly*, played one of the roles in the script, along with actor J. D. Walsh, who was in a pilot of Chuck's called *Nathan's Choice* that never made it to series. And it was there that they read us two early scenes from what would be *The Big Bang Theory*. There were too many 'Sheldon is a genius' jokes, but I remember thinking, *Boy, these characters are really cool.* The character of Penny as we know her did not exist. The female character that they had written was hardly the girl next door—she was a hardened character from the streets, which made the contrast of Sheldon and Leonard even more pronounced. And supposedly comedic. But it didn't really work. I said, "I think you're on to something," but Chuck and Bill knew the script needed additional work, and the characters needed greater definition.

Although Roth and Warner Bros. Television were on board with developing what would become *The Big Bang Theory*, none of that matters if you don't have a network that's interested as well. Enter CBS.

Chuck Lorre: We put on a little play at CBS with folding chairs, bringing in actors who came in as a favor to me and read a sample scene of what we were doing.

Bill Prady: Yeah, it was this weird little reading. [*Laughs*]

Makeshift plays for the heads of a studio or network aren't the norm, just in case you're wondering.

Chuck Lorre: I can't tell you what got into me that I decided that was the way to present it. It might have been my concern that walking into any office, either at Warner Bros. or CBS, and saying, "Hey, we want to do a show about theoretical physicists!" might have been a hard sell. It might have gotten an immediate no. I was hoping to maybe override that immediate rejection by showing this relationship between two scientists had a place on television. So it was a little bit of Barnum & Bailey—we put on a little circus act.

Bill Prady: We just knew you had to hear the voices of these guys instead of reading the words on paper.

Chuck Lorre: Amazingly enough, it worked, and we got a green light to make a pilot.

Wendi Trilling: My team and I would hear about three hundred pitches a season. Of those three hundred pitches, we would buy fifty projects—basically pay for a script. But a lot of the time if it's a producer like Chuck Lorre, you know you're going to commit to making a pilot. If Joe Blow came in off the street and said, "We want to do a staged reading of a pilot in front of you," we might say, "No thank you," or "Let us read it first." But if Chuck—the creator and executive producer of a very big hit show at the time [*Two and a Half Men* on CBS]—requests to come in and do a pilot reading, we say, "Yes, when would you like to do that?" [*Laughs*] So we were all sitting—in folding chairs—in the CBS executive dining room watching a couple actors read a script out loud. I thought the two guys and their dynamic was funny and unique—and not like other characters on television. We were intrigued by the fact that these characters weren't traditional sitcom leading men.

James Burrows (director, both pilots): It was a very unusual script. I usually end up doing shows that have ordinary characters who are only a little bit different. And this was nerds. It was a high-concept show for me. The only real high-concept show I ever did was *3rd Rock from the Sun*, because I wanted to work with John Lithgow. So I read the script, and as with Chuck, they're always wonderful. And I knew Billy [Prady] from *Caroline in the City*. So, we talked and hashed out a few things.

While the character traits of the two leading men were established early, the names "Sheldon" and "Leonard" came later in the development process.

Bill Prady: *Lenny, Penny, and Kenny* was the original placeholder title of the show, so Lenny was the Leonard character, and Kenny was the Sheldon character. That title lasted for about five minutes. In fact, my contract says "'Lenny, Penny and Kenny' a/k/a 'Big Bang Theory.'"

Chuck Lorre: Those were the names of the characters originally. But we wanted to pay homage to TV producer-director-actor Sheldon Leonard [the Emmy-winning producer and director of shows like *The Danny Thomas Show*, *The Andy Griffith Show*, *The Dick Van Dyke Show*, and more], so that's where Sheldon and Leonard came from.

LICHTER, GROSSMAN, NICHOLS & ADLER, INC.

ATTORNEYS AT LAW

FILE

*ALSO ADMITTED IN NEW YORK

OF COUNSEL
CYNTHIA FARRELLY GESNER
A PROFESSIONAL CORPORATION

June 25, 2007

File No. 1601.21

<u>VIA U.S. MAIL</u>

Bill Prady

Re: "Lenny Penny and Kenny" a/k/a "Big Bang Theory"
        Amalgamated Show Business, Inc. f/s/o Bill Prady
        Script Agreement and Amendment

Dear Bill:

Enclosed for your files please find a fully-executed copy of each of the above-referenced agreements between you and Warner Bros. Television Production, a division of WB Studio Enterprises Inc. regarding your services in connection with the above-referenced project currently entitled "Lenny Penny and Kenny" a/k/a "Big Bang Theory."

Of course, if you have any questions regarding the enclosed, please do not hesitate to call me. Thank you.

Best regards.

Very truly yours,

Jonathan E. Shikora

JES/cg
Enclosures

cc: Robb Rothman (w/encl.)
       Linda Lichter, Esq. (w/o encl.)

The cover letter that contained the agreement between Bill Prady and Warner Bros. Television Production to begin work on *Lenny Penny and Kenny* a/k/a *Big Bang Theory. Courtesy of Bill Prady personal archive.*

Bill Prady: And we needed the guys' last names right away for set dressing with their diplomas. Hofstadter I liked, because Douglas Hofstadter had written a book of philosophy of math and physics called *Gödel, Escher, Bach:*

An Eternal Golden Braid, which is a book I'd read a zillion times, and I assumed these guys would've read it, too. And I like the name "Hofstadter."

The eventual title—*The Big Bang Theory*—was actually influenced by *Two and a Half Men*'s humor.

Chuck Lorre: I emailed Bill and said, "Let's take a look at various scientific phrases and see if there's anything in any of them." One of the titles on the list was *The Big Bang Theory*...something you learn studying sciences. Looking back, this is somewhat embarrassing, but given how much the success of *Two and a Half Men* impacted me, the title *The Big Bang Theory* had in it the inkling of a sexual innuendo. And I was crass enough to grasp on to that. I also liked the idea of co-opting something that was already part of the culture. I remember some Nobel Prize–winning scientist once mentioned in an interview—to his horror—that when you Google "the Big Bang Theory," the show came up first. [*Laughs*] Not the theory of how the universe began! So I remember looking at the list and going, "Well, it's obvious! *The Big Bang Theory*! It's kind of got a little humor built into it." I never thought twice whether the audience would understand what we were doing or not. I just thought, *What a cool name. Let's make it ours.*

Johnny Galecki ("Leonard Hofstadter"): Yeah, I never got that; I just literally never made the connection. I don't get the double entendre there, I sincerely don't. But it takes a while for a show to find itself...and I think it took a while for Chuck to realize, understand, and appreciate that the show he was doing next door—*Two and a Half Men*—was a very different show than where *Big Bang* thrived, and where *Big Bang* was meant to live.

Bill Prady: There's an early promo for the show once it was picked up to series where the double entendre is acknowledged. It said something like, "A new comedy from Chuck Lorre, the creator of *Two and a Half Men*," and somebody says *The Big Bang Theory*, and then Kaley Cuoco says, "Oh, I think he means the other kind of bang." Then Jim Parsons says, "Well, maybe I don't care for this Chuck Lorre," or something like that. I will say for the record, I'm a prude, and I'm from Michigan, and I did express some very prudish objections to Mr. Lorre. I recall him sending that list to me by email, and in my pearl-clutching way, I absolutely lodged an objection.

Problem was, I didn't have a good alternative. And the only way you can get rid of a thing you don't like is with something better. [*Pause*] I had nothing better. [*Laughs*] So I did not fight too hard. But I did lodge a formal objection with whatever mechanism people lodge with each other!

And with that, casting began on what would be the first pilot for *The Big Bang Theory.*

Chuck Lorre: It was a train wreck.

Chapter 2

CASTING LEONARD, SHELDON...
AND KATIE

With the green light from CBS to make a pilot, the veteran casting team of
Nikki Valko and Ken Miller began the search for Sheldon and Leonard...and
Katie, as well as Gilda.

Ken Miller (casting director, *The Big Bang Theory*): We knew the characters
had to be scientists and not great socially. It really helped us focus, because
often when we're handed a script, the roles could be anybody.

Bill Prady: Even though I had run shows, this was the first time I was sitting in casting sessions and network sessions for series regulars. I don't think I'd
really internalized the notion of...*perfect*. When you're casting for guest stars,
you cast the best person that comes in. But this was the first time I'd been in the
process where it has to be just the right one. As the naive person, there had been
many people who'd come in, and I'd say, "Oh, he's good! He's good! Do we
have it?" And obviously Chuck, who had cast series regulars, knew what he was
looking for. It's not just "This person is going to be good in this role," it's "This is
the person who's going to *be* this character." That was an eye-opening moment.

At the time, a relatively unknown actor by the name of Jim Parsons was
flying back and forth from New York to Los Angeles for pilot season. He
had already been in some well-known projects (the indie film *Garden State*;
CBS's *Judging Amy*), but like all actors, he was looking for that breakout role.

Jim Parsons ("Sheldon Cooper"): I auditioned for Jim or for Dwight on
The Office, but I didn't make it past the first casting director on tape. That

doesn't mean they didn't send it somewhere and it wasn't rejected further down the line, but I don't know that it ever made it out of the local NBC office in New York. However, the role I thought I was going to be a shoo-in for but never heard another word again was Kenneth on *30 Rock*. And years later, Jack McBrayer, who is one of the sweetest people, and who got the role, ended up playing Penny's brother on *Big Bang*. I also auditioned—and got called back a couple times—for the role of Barney on *How I Met Your Mother*. But I didn't want to audition for it because they described him in the casting breakdown as a "big lug of a guy." I was like, *What are they fucking thinking?! I'm not a big lug of a guy!* [*Laughs*] And then when Neil Patrick Harris got it, I was like, *Oh, talk about a lesson!* Not that we're the same at all, but he's not a big lug of a guy, let me say that. And I thought, *Don't read that crap in the breakdown anymore. Just forget all of that. Go in and do what you want to do with the material.*

But when Parsons first got the audition for *The Big Bang Theory*, he thought he was auditioning for a series from game show host Chuck Woolery, not Chuck Lorre.

Jim Parsons: I will never forget my agent saying they had an audition for me for the new Chuck Lorre show, and after I got off the phone, I said to [my now-husband] Todd, "they're really excited about this. I didn't even know that guy from *Love Connection* was making TV! And sitcoms!" I just couldn't put it together. I knew I had something wrong, but I didn't know what we were getting at. And then it all made a lot more sense to me. I think it was another example of ignorance is bliss. It's a lot less nerve-wracking to think you're going in to do a favor for the guy from *Love Connection*. Not that he needed my favor, but you know what I'm saying.

Parsons's *Big Bang* costar, Simon Helberg, didn't come on board until the second pilot (more on that later), but Helberg remembers seeing the audition pages for Sheldon in the first incarnation and not envying whoever had to do the scene.

Simon Helberg ("Howard Wolowitz"): I very vividly remember thinking, *Oh my God, the actor that has to go in for this role*... because it was a two-page monologue about sitting at the right position where the cross-ventilation is.

Jim Parsons: I had several days to prepare for the audition, and I have always used little note cards as flash cards to learn my lines. I used to do this trick during my first few seasons of *Big Bang* where I'd put a pencil in my mouth, bite down with my teeth and articulate through that because it forced my tongue to overarticulate. That way when I took it out, all these strings of words with all their syllables floated out with more of an ease. It was an oddly physical process. And I really just drilled it into my brain. I was excited to present their material to them because I liked it, regardless of whether I ended up getting the part. But I was also nervous that the adrenaline would be too much to the point where you cannot relax into doing the dance that you know so well.

Judy Parsons (Jim's mother): He called me on the phone when he got the audition papers, and said, "You know what? I can do this guy. I can play Sheldon if they'll only give me the opportunity." And I think it was right around the Oscars, and he was invited to parties or events, but he said, "I just can't go because I've got to know this part. I've got to know it perfectly." He did nothing but work on it until it was time to go to his audition. His dad was like that—very focused and dedicated to what he was doing.

Jim Parsons: Sheldon was the kind of character I enjoyed, which was borderline idiot savant. He was both exceptionally bright and completely clueless. And that was territory I was and am very comfortable with. I also remember I wore some sort of blue Izod or Polo shirt with a long-sleeve, pale blue shirt underneath it, because I had an actor friend who always said make sure you wear something blue for your eyes. So an undershirt under the main shirt came from me.

Nikki Valko (casting director, *The Big Bang Theory*): It wasn't like he came in with a bow tie or looked real nerdy. But boy, when he opened his mouth I couldn't believe what came out of it, just all that science. As far as Ken and I were concerned, once Jim read for Sheldon, we knew. He just understood the character from day one.

Jim Parsons: There were two scenes, and after the first one, I felt good about what I did. I could see and hear and feel that they were reacting well. But then they said, "OK, do the next one." I might have said "Shit" or something. And they were like, "Do you need a moment?" And I was like, "No, no, if I take time, I'll get in my head about it." I guess I was hoping I wouldn't have to do the second scene since the first one went so well. [*Laughs*]

Chuck Lorre: He didn't just come in and read the lines. He had prepared a fully realized character. He had prepared the material so his dialogue had a rhythm, intonation, syntax, the pauses, everything was calculated. He had decided how this character handles his body, how he occupies space, or is uncomfortable occupying space. It was a whole other level of audition. And it was not the character that I envisioned. Frankly, I don't remember what kind of character I envisioned, but that wasn't it! I was thrown off in a good way. Ken, Nikki, Bill, and I were laughing our asses off. I said, "I need to see it again." I wanted to know if he could create that performance again. And he did it perfectly, as if he had never done it before. This is why the man's got like nineteen Emmys.

Bill Prady: It was obvious he was Sheldon right away. I remember thinking, *Oh my God, this transcends doing a good job with the material. This is what it means to create a character.*

Eddie Gorodetsky (co–executive producer, *The Big Bang Theory*; co-creator, *Mom*): Jim was just a force of nature. I was thinking, *Are we really seeing this?* And then later that night, my wife and I were driving down Santa Monica Blvd. and I saw Jim Parsons pulling into a store, and I rolled down the window, and I yelled, "Jim Parsons, you're a genius!" I knew it was going to happen a lot, so I wanted to be the first person to tell him that.

Jim Parsons: I vaguely remember that, but I also have been one not to get too excited when I book a role or a project gets green-lit. It's always been the way I am. When I get a role, my feeling is that it means nothing until I get on the set for the first day because it could fall apart before then. And secondly, not quite so pessimistically, I feel very aware of the work ahead of me. I'm just a very low-key receiver of good career news.

But casting Sheldon was a breeze compared to the rest of the characters, especially Leonard.

Nikki Valko: Kevin Sussman was in the mix, originally, for Leonard. And he was wonderful but it wasn't right.

Eddie Gorodetsky: Kevin was wrong for the role, but I remember Chuck saying, "He's right for *something*." It was obvious. We knew he was a great comedic tool.

Ken Miller: Macaulay Culkin was also someone we pursued for Leonard in the first pilot.

Nikki Valko: Chuck was a fan of Macaulay. It was so early on, even before Johnny came in. He was just someone that Chuck really liked in the very beginning.

Chuck Lorre: There's a special ethereal quality to that actor that I thought might be great.

Bill Prady: We had a terrific meeting with Macaulay . . . and then we heard that he had decided he wasn't interested.

Ken Miller: But from the minute Nikki read the script, she was like, "Johnny Galecki is Leonard."

Nikki Valko: We wanted Johnny to come in and read, but he wasn't interested in the role at the time. He just felt like he wasn't really that role of that nerdy scientist.

Ken Miller: He had gotten very fit and was doing a very sexy role on Broadway in *The Little Dog Laughed*. He starred opposite Julie White and played the gay lover of a closeted movie star. He was phenomenal, but he just felt like he had moved on from the nerdier roles. That's what we had heard from his agent. Nikki called him like three times saying, "Please, please," but we kept hearing "It's a pass." And then later on, his agent called and said, "What about Johnny?" Nikki's like, "He passed three times! What are we supposed to do?!" I guess his agent just really believed in the show and the role, too.

Johnny Galecki: I was in New York when I got a call out of the blue from Chuck, who I knew from when he was writing on *Roseanne*. He said he and Bill Prady had an idea for a show and were thinking of me for it. They hadn't written much of anything yet, but started faxing pages to the theater for me to read once they did. I was really struggling with how to understand the premise, the tone, the characters, because I was just getting a page here and there. And at the time, they were talking to me about the Sheldon role but I just couldn't make sense of it. I was also very happy being in New York [*The Big Bang Theory* would shoot in Los Angeles]. *The Little Dog Laughed* was about to go to Broadway, and I was in love with a beautiful Belarusian woman. And the original material wasn't exciting enough for me to leave my life in New York to do this sitcom that I only had nine pages of.

This was so early on in the process that it was before casting had begun or even the casting directors had seen a script. Galecki was also hesitant because *The Little Dog Laughed* provided a chance for him to play a role he wasn't always offered: the object of someone's affection.

Johnny Galecki: I was usually cast as a character's comic relief best friend or gay assistant, so I was riding pretty high on my ego in this role. But then, the more material I got from Chuck and Bill, the more I was drawn to the Leonard role, especially since it seemed like Leonard might have a better chance at romantic relationships on the show. I thought they would say, "Go fuck yourself, end of conversation," but Chuck just said, "Well, great, play that guy." [*Laughs*] But I was not easy on them. I was a difficult piece of casting.

Even when Lorre gave Galecki the green light to play Leonard, the actor was still very hesitant to join the sitcom world again, especially after appearing in almost one hundred episodes of the original *Roseanne*.

Johnny Galecki: My longtime agent said, "Why do you keep turning this down? Are you afraid that it's going to get picked up to series and then you'll have to sign another seven-year contract and not be able to go back to New York full-time?" And I said, "No, I don't know if it's going to get picked up or be successful." And he said, "Well then, go do it! Go do the pilot, make some money—more than you're making onstage—and if it doesn't get picked up, then you go back to New York and keep doing what you're loving right now." And I thought, you know, if I do that, it would give my understudy, Brian Henderson, his Broadway debut credit. So I flew out Brian's parents so they could see him in the play, and I flew out to LA for the pilot of *Big Bang*. And I can confess this now because it only illustrates what an idiot I am, but I did turn down the role five times before eventually saying yes.

Although technically the role was his, Galecki still needed to have a chemistry read with Parsons for the studio and network.

Johnny Galecki: I realized at a certain point that they could have pulled the plug on me if they didn't like what I was doing. Because I'm so naive to such things, I didn't realize it until after the fact, that the producers or my representatives said, "They need to see you and Jim together."

Jim Parsons: These characters are supposed to be an odd couple and see the world differently from each other. There was an innate tension there, and that was the chemistry. I read with so many different Leonards at the start of this process, but the second I read with Johnny, I was like, *That's who it is*. And it wasn't because he was a "good" Leonard, or the way he was saying his lines, although I'm sure that was part of it, but it was just a feeling. We were able to be these two orbs that bumped up against each other. It was very freeing to me, which made the scene come alive.

Johnny Galecki: Jim was so honest and unique and driven. He knew the result that he wanted from his performance, which is very different from just performing and inhabiting a character. And as soon as I saw him doing what his take on Sheldon was, I was immediately proud of myself for having the intuition that I should not have done that character. I mean, who else can play that role but Jim?

Now that the roles of Sheldon and Leonard were in place, it was time to cast the female lead, Katie. The character's name was originally Penny ("Sheldon and Leonard encounter this woman on the street; she's a lucky penny," Prady explains), but at the time, CBS had another pilot in contention with a character called Penny, and asked Lorre and Prady to change it to something else. They obliged. But even with a new name, the character of Katie was nothing like the character of Penny that audiences would come to know and love. Penny was bubbly with a Midwestern innocence and optimism; Katie was cynical, down on her luck, and off-putting.

Ken Miller: Kaley Cuoco went to the network and tested for the first pilot of *Big Bang*. She's so sunny and bubbly, and they just loved her, but she just didn't bring the dark qualities. She just wasn't the essence of Penny in that first incarnation.

At twenty years old, Cuoco looked a bit too young for the more experienced Katie, who first appears sitting on a curb, crying over a breakup as she talks on her cell phone.

Kaley Cuoco ("Penny Hofstadter"): I loved the role, and I loved Chuck. I had worked with him when I was fourteen or fifteen on a pilot called *Nathan's Choice*. I know Chuck really wanted me for the role of Katie, and I was definitely bummed when I didn't get it, but I kind of have a way of moving on because you have to.

In fact, in the very early days, Marisa Tomei was considered for the series, and actually auditioned with Jim Parsons.

Jim Parsons: I had the part of Sheldon for a long time before everything was settled. I read with Marisa Tomei. Johnny was cast by then, but he was doing a play in New York. I had come back to read with her. I remember going to the snack room after we were done, and telling Ken and Nikki, "I've never been in someone else's audition before!" And they said, "Well, she was kind of really auditioning you." And I went, "Oh, that makes sense." But oh my gosh what a different world that would have been.

Bill Prady: Tara Reid also came in for the role of Katie, and I think Elizabeth Berkeley went to network for the role, too. She was terrific.

Amanda Walsh, a Canadian actress who was starring as Jenna Halbert on the short-lived ABC dramedy *Sons & Daughters*, was also brought in for the first round of casting.

Amanda Walsh ("Katie"): *Sons & Daughters* was on the bubble for a possible second season, but it wasn't looking good. I went in for the role of Katie for *Big Bang*, and had a really positive first audition and I loved the script. But I wasn't cast.

Jodi Lyn O'Keefe, best known at the time for movies like *She's All That* and *Whatever It Takes*, auditioned for Katie, and got the role. Iris Bahr, who had

credits ranging from *Friends* to *Curb Your Enthusiasm*, was cast as the secondary female character, Gilda, a fellow scientist who harbored a crush on Leonard, and who also had sex with Sheldon at a *Star Trek* convention.

Bill Prady: Jodi is just a terrific actress, and she later appeared on the show as a prostitute that Wolowitz meets in Vegas. Jodi is who you want if you want somebody who can give you a tough, street-hardened woman who plays that character real. She's just a remarkable woman, and I love everything that she does. And Iris Bahr is a wonderful woman, and I'm still in touch with her.

Jodi Lyn O'Keefe was cast as the original female lead in *Big Bang*'s first pilot. Years later, she would appear as a woman named Mikayla in season two, episode twenty-one, titled "The Vegas Renormalization." (Pictured here with Johnny Galecki as Leonard and Kunal Nayyar as Raj) *Photo™ & © Warner Bros. Entertainment Inc.*

With the cast now in place, Johnny Galecki thought it would be helpful to spend time bonding with Jim Parsons ahead of the table read and tape night. Although Katie and Gilda were featured prominently in the pilot episode, the show's premise was really centered around Sheldon and Leonard.

Johnny Galecki: I asked Jim to come meet me the afternoon before the first table read because we didn't know each other that well yet. It's always an odd thing when you have no history with someone and all the sudden you're playing their best friend. I like to do what's called accelerated bonding, where you just share a lot with each other. That often requires some wine to open up and be that honest with one another within, like, six hours. [*Laughs*] And so, we did. We had many bottles of wine and learned we had so many things in common, including that our grandfathers worked for the railroad, and both of our fathers had passed away at a very early age. I think we both passed out on my living room couch at one point. And then we woke up and went to the first reading. Apparently it went well. [*Laughs*]

The cast, producers, writers, and executives gathered that next day for the show's first table read. It seemed to go well, but unbeknownst to the actors, the producers felt something wasn't clicking.

Jim Parsons: We did that table read, and I thought Jodi was great. Afterward, me, Johnny, Jodi, and Iris were going to meet at some restaurant. I was new to LA and got lost trying to find the place when Johnny texted me and said, "Hurry up, Jodi got fired." I mean, we had just done the table read thirty minutes earlier. Johnny, Iris, and Jodi were already there when Jodi got a call from her agent saying she was being let go. I hadn't done a ton of table reads in my career by that point, but I'm not an idiot—I know when someone's not good. And Jodi was *great*. I was stunned. But they realized during that table read that the character's approach to the other characters was too harsh, too whatever, even though Jodi, in my opinion, nailed what they had written.

Johnny Galecki: We were at a Mexican restaurant and I got there first, and then Jodi walked in and told me she had been fired. I thought she was kidding. She was like, "No, I'm *not* kidding." I was like, "You're a really good actress, because there's just no way." She finally convinced me that she was being honest, and I was like, "Shit, let's get you a margarita." And she said, "I don't drink." I was like, "I'm so sorry! I just poured salt into the wound."

Nikki Valko: Jodi Lyn O'Keefe was so good in the original pilot as Katie, but it was just a totally different character. [Jodi] brought a darkness, which just didn't work, so she was replaced after the table read. We had to recast in three days, so I remember holding auditions Easter Sunday.

Reenter Amanda Walsh, who had auditioned already, but didn't get the role, and was still waiting on the fate of ABC's *Sons & Daughters.* **Walsh had a very different look than O'Keefe, and the casting directors hoped it might be a better fit for the character.**

Amanda Walsh: I got this call from Nikki and Ken's office that they wanted to see me again on Sunday morning, which was rare. So I went and auditioned again, and they said they wanted to test me at Warner Bros. on Monday morning. It was very, very quick. Then on Monday, I went into Mary Buck's office, who was the head of casting at Warner Bros. Television, and all the other executives were there. The audition went really well and was a lot of fun, and then I went to wait in this little room. Not long after, Chuck came out, shook my hand, and said, "You got it." Usually you wait to hear from your reps, so this was an exceptional moment. And it happened so fast, I can't remember if they said, "You start tomorrow," or "You start this afternoon." Either way, we hit the ground running.

Jim Parsons: They brought in Amanda, with the assumption being that her mere presence would soften the character...which is just a tough position to be in because the role wasn't really written for her.

Amanda Walsh: Jim and Johnny were both really kind and welcoming. Johnny just had this very understated, natural ease. The way he hit the jokes really stuck out to me. And Jim just mastered his role from the get-go with all the science talk, and made it sing. But so much was shifting and changing. I remember going to Chuck's office one day and we talked about the character because I always felt like I was trying to hit exactly what they needed but the target kept moving. And I understand the process of making a pilot—it's such a pressure cooker. There was a lot being figured out and retooled as we were moving through it. I feel like on Monday the character was a party girl who picked the wrong guys, and by the end of the week I had blown up a car and was homeless! [*Laughs*] So I was just trying to keep up and do the best I could.

Johnny Galecki: I just remember Amanda being such a sweet person, and they kept pushing her to be harsher, because Katie was very street savvy. [Director Jimmy] Burrows had her work in the blue, which is what we call it when you, let's say, add a "fuck" to every line. So during rehearsals she would start talking like a sailor to make her feel more comfortable and kind of get her in that tone. Burrows asked her to work in the blue so that the lines would reverberate into that sharper, more kind of feral manner, so even when you took the filthy words out, you were in that mind frame. And that helped her an incredible amount. But ironically, the way they were pushing her—into that place of street-smart and maybe deceptive and duplicitous as a character—was what ended up being wrong with the character because the audience immediately felt so protective of Leonard and Sheldon.

Amanda Walsh: It was one of the hardest weeks professionally that I've gone through, but by the end I felt like we landed on something. And Chuck was incredibly supportive through it all.

(left to right) Iris Bahr as Gilda, Jim Parsons as Sheldon Cooper, Johnny Galecki as Leonard Hofstadter, and Amanda Walsh as Katie during filming for the unaired pilot of *The Big Bang Theory* in 2006. Ultimately the pilot wasn't picked up, but CBS would later give Chuck Lorre and Bill Prady a second chance. *Courtesy of Kaley Cuoco photo collection*

The pilot isn't available in its entirety online, but various scenes were downloaded to YouTube over the years. Compared to the show fans know now, the sets were originally completely different, and the aesthetic was much darker. Katie seemed like she could rob Sheldon and Leonard at any

moment, and Gilda was tightly wound. Sheldon's style largely remained the same from the first pilot to the second one, but Leonard wore oversized suits, a complete departure from the laid-back hoodie and jeans look. Still, there were plenty of elements that stuck, namely the essence of Sheldon's and Leonard's personalities, as well as a dedication to their love of science. In order to make that convincing, Lorre and Prady were steadfast in making sure they got the scientific references right.

Chuck Lorre: We had a physicist, Professor Peter Gorham from the University of Hawaii, come on board for the original pilot because we all agreed to make the science as real as we can. We didn't want to cut corners. He wasn't able to stay on, but he recommended David Saltzberg, who inextricably became the most valuable player for the rest of the series. And to think who we were able to get on our show because of how seriously we took the science—Professor Stephen Hawking, Bill Gates, Steve Wozniak, Nobel Prize–winning scientists—it was beyond anything we could have dreamt.

And long before the Barenaked Ladies agreed to record a theme song for *The Big Bang Theory*, Chuck Lorre used Thomas Dolby's "She Blinded Me with Science" as the temporary theme song for the first pilot.

Chuck Lorre: I didn't ask permission; it was just something to create a kind of ambiance for the pilot. We may have even used it to score the thing, too, along with little snippets of "Science!" between scenes because we didn't have the swirling atoms that came later.

There were a lot of great ingredients in the first pilot, but it was the equivalent of an undercooked dish.

Lee Aronsohn (co-creator, *Two and a Half Men*; executive producer, *The Big Bang Theory*, 2007–2011): *The Big Bang Theory* was another pilot, basically, to me. I didn't see the show as something that had legs, or that was particularly better than the other pilots we had done together that didn't go.

Nina Tassler (president of entertainment, CBS, 2004–2014; chairman of entertainment, CBS, 2014–2015): I remember most distinctly the chemistry and banter between Johnny and Jim. It was like watching two extraordinary artists-athletes. You really respected their level of professionalism and excellence. But the Katie character didn't really service Sheldon and Leonard's relationship. She was tougher and edgier, really down on her luck.

James Burrows: You need[ed someone like] Julia Roberts. Those are really hard things to find in a television show, because you need a hooker with a heart of gold. We just could never find the right fit. I liked the premise; it was just hard to make work.

Amanda Walsh: I don't even know how much I was thinking about the chances of it getting picked up because it was such a whirlwind week. I was so consumed with wanting to do the best job possible. After we had wrapped, we all went over to Johnny's house that night (April 25, 2006). I remember him saying, "If I had been through the week you had, I would've had a nervous breakdown." [*Laughs*] And that was really nice to be acknowledged. But it was a sense of, "Yeah, we did it," and then I think we were kind of excited to see what came next.

James Burrows: Chuck is a genius in what he does, and the more Chuck shows you can have on the air, the better, because he protects 'em. So I thought it would get picked up based on the relationship of the two guys. They had chemistry, like Debra Messing and Eric McCormack on *Will & Grace*. They could finish each other's sentences. And the same was true here.

What came next was certainly not the norm. Most pilots either make it or they don't, but an even smaller percentage get a second shot. Even more rare is when that second chance turns into something even remotely successful.

Chuck Lorre: It was May 2006, and I was in Australia on vacation when Nina Tassler called me and said, "We're not picking up the show. It didn't really come together." And then she said the most remarkable thing that no one had ever said to me up until that point, which was "Would you be willing to try again?"

Nina Tassler: I was extremely nervous! [*Laughs*] Pilots aren't perfect. Sometimes they're more perfect than others, but it's not dry cement. And so in this case, we were at a little bit of a crossroads, but there was more upside in trying to reshoot the pilot than letting it go.

Wendi Trilling: I was sitting across from Nina, and she was on speaker-phone when she called Chuck. It's always sensitive when you're not exactly giving someone the news that they want and asking them to do more work. And you're asking them to do more work *speculatively*, because we weren't saying we wanted to pick up the series with certain changes. We were saying, "We want to do another pilot." But Chuck felt the same way we did, fortunately. He wanted to do the work and make it great.

> Listen, no one sets out to make a mediocre pilot. You can have the best ingredients, but it's just a crapshoot. The unaired pilot of *Big Bang* was no different.

Chuck Lorre: It was one of the great gifts of my career to get that phone call. Nina also said, "You know, we think the casting of the female part was the problem," and I said, "No, the problem wasn't the casting, it was the *writing*. We wrote a bad script!" Nina and the people at CBS recognized that something special was happening with Jim and Johnny, but it wasn't realized to its full potential.

Nina Tassler: Chuck has a very strong personality, but he's immensely talented and really, really cares about the work, the actors, and the writing. He was the first to acknowledge that it didn't work and he and the team could do better and would do better. Bill was also very positive. They embraced it and gave us the shot.

Chuck Lorre: We didn't understand what we were doing when we wrote that first script, and we knew more as a result of having failed. I called Bill and said, "Let's throw out the plot. These characters are so wonderful, we don't really need a plot. And let's add some more of these guys! It's not about some romantic triangle, it's about these guys." So that's what led to the development of Wolowitz and Koothrappali. They played a very small role in the pilot, but now there was this community. I was truly determined if we were going to get another chance, we would not fail.

Peter Roth: Without Nina, who knows if *The Big Bang Theory* would have ever happened. It can't be said strongly enough... Nina was the champion. Most failed pilots just go the way of the detritus. I remember thinking to myself, *Boy, that is a bold and incredibly supportive thing to do.*

Johnny Galecki: I went back to New York and was back onstage when I heard we were going to do another pilot. Chuck told me that the ingredients that worked were Jim and I. And since I was under contract, I didn't really have a choice in the matter. [*Laughs*] I was like, "Oh, okay."

But while Galecki and Parsons were going to be moving forward on the new pilot, it was a different outcome for Amanda Walsh and Iris Bahr.

Kaley Cuoco: I think about Amanda because she was the original [lead actress]. And it wasn't her fault; it was totally rewritten and changed. And Jodi Lyn O'Keefe and I were friends for years, and she ended up being on *Big Bang* in season two.

Amanda Walsh: You're waiting to find out, to get that phone call, if the show gets picked up and if you'll be flying to New York. And when that phone call came in, it was a crazy twenty-four hours because I found out *Sons & Daughters* was not getting picked up. And then I found out that *Big Bang Theory* wasn't getting picked up, either, but it was going to be retooled—except with a new character, without me.

Bill Prady: I adored Amanda. She had a hard week when we did that pilot. And when we found out we needed to rewrite the character and recast it, I called Amanda, and I said, "I want to apologize. One of the qualities of this business is that remarkably unfair things happen to people in it. And if this is the first time an unfair thing is happening to you, I'm so sorry. And I'm sorry I was a part of it. And it will happen again. It is just the nature of the business." She took it well enough, but remember at that point, it was a busted pilot and we were going to try again. And who knows what was going to happen. The proof that the problem was in the writing and not the acting is that both Jodi Lyn O'Keefe and Amanda Walsh are terrific. So if two terrific women can't do this, the problem is not with the actors.

Amanda Walsh: It's never a call you wanna get as an actor, but Bill was as nice as possible about the whole thing. And then I was really fortunate that a year later, Burrows hired me for another pilot called *The Mastersons of Manhattan* with Molly Shannon and Natasha Richardson. For me, that really validated the notion of "It's not you," because as an actor, you always question that. So, to get rehired by the same people for another big project was very, very validating. And I've been brought in for other projects of Chuck's, and Nikki and Ken have always said that Chuck is a fan [of mine], which helps a lot.

Chuck Lorre: Amanda did exactly what was asked of her, and she did it beautifully. I certainly didn't understand that despite Sheldon and Leonard's intelligence, they were like children, and you couldn't put a toxic character next to them like that. It broke your heart. And again, I was very much under the influence of *Two and a Half Men*, and thought that edgy humor would carry over to *Big Bang*. It did not. And I had a lot to learn because of that.

Bill Prady: When we were doing the pilot a second time, Amanda's team asked if she could come in to audition again, but the network was not receptive to that. CBS knew that Katie had scored badly among test audiences. Chuck and I were very upfront in saying that the reason the character scored poorly was because the [role of] Katie was written badly. But we were not able to persuade them to see her again.

Amanda Walsh: Time is really the best helper for those things. I leaned on friends who had been in LA for a long time. They said, "Well, you've officially made it if you've been recast!" *[Laughs]* Even Jim Burrows said, "Remind me to tell you about Lisa Kudrow," because she had been in the pilot for *Frasier*. So leaning into the notion that now I have my Hollywood story helped. I became an actor because I love to act, so that's what I was going to keep on doing. *Big Bang* wasn't my path, and I'm at peace with that. For people outside of the industry, I could see how that could be hard to imagine. But as a writer as well, I understand you have to try things a few different ways to figure out what works. I was part of a process that resulted in a show that reached a lot of people, and that's cool. It's really cool, actually. And here's a fun fact that I didn't realize until I watched the *Friends* reunion, but we shot the first *Big Bang* pilot on the *Friends* stage, and I was told I was in Matthew Perry's old dressing room.

James Burrows: I had done a couple of shows on stage 24 [the *Friends* Stage] that were really successful, so I thought it was a good omen. But yes, I told Amanda that in the pilot for *Frasier*, Roz [eventually played by Peri Gilpin], who was Frasier's producer at the radio station, had to make this big, convincing speech to Frasier about allowing his dad to move in with him. And Lisa Kud-row's style was not forceful like that. Her style is more ethereal. So we let Lisa go. It happens. We also had to let Ray Romano go on the pilot of *NewsRadio*.

Just because it happens often doesn't mean it hurts any less. And it wasn't easy that *Big Bang* was the kind of series that felt like it was everywhere, especially once it started airing in syndication. Still, Walsh maintained a healthy perspective that she says has served her well throughout the years and made it easier to accept.

Amanda Walsh: It was such a huge success, I don't think you could avoid the show! And I think everyone's really talented who was involved. But it was a huge help that the show wasn't exactly the same as that first pilot. The fact that it wasn't immediately picked up and there was such retooling made it an easier pill to swallow.

But Walsh's story also didn't end there. She's still acting and writing, and was part of another successful sitcom you may have heard a thing or two about.

Amanda Walsh: I had a show in development with 20th Television and from that script, I got an interview for *Schitt's Creek*, where I wrote on the show for a couple seasons. It was really cool to be a part of it from the beginning, especially getting to write for Catherine O'Hara and having Eugene Levy in the writers room. I think being an actor makes me a better writer, and being a writer makes me a better actor. And I really trust that this was my path. Over the years I've been asked to do interviews about *Big Bang*, but I've always said no. It's the kind of thing if you haven't been through it, I didn't want people to project their idea of what I went through onto me. I didn't want them to say things like, "Oh, my God! What it must have been like!" or "You missed this thing!" It really was one week of my life. It was one pilot out of many. I never wanted that story to be taken out of context or seen in the wrong light. I was protective of it in that way, and all the people I worked with were so kind. The show went on to be great, and there's no real losers. And years later, I ran into Jim Parsons when I was going to a meeting by Warner Bros. and we had a nice hello. He's lovely. They really were all such wonderful people.

Chapter 3

THE PILOT—TAKE TWO

Once Chuck Lorre was back in Los Angeles, rewrites began on *The Big Bang Theory*. Lorre and Prady were informed they could use the name Penny again for the Katie character, since the other CBS pilot that was using that name didn't go forward. But that was about the only thing that seemed to go right.

Chuck Lorre: There were so many bumps along the way that I thought, *Maybe this isn't going to happen at all.* When we got a chance to do it again, Johnny was not eager. It was almost a year after we shot the first pilot, and I think his attitude towards it was pessimistic. It was a reasonable reaction given what we failed to accomplish on the first try. But he got there. Still, there were a couple of close calls where I was ready to throw in the towel on ever shooting that second pilot. It was just one thing after the other. We were struggling with casting Penny, Wolowitz, and Raj. It just seemed like there were so many obstacles and so many things that went wrong. I was *so close* to picking up the phone and saying, "I'm out. This is just too heartbreaking."

Ken Miller: When Chuck and Bill rewrote the character of Katie/Penny, we said, "What about Kaley?" [who had just come off of *8 Simple Rules* and *Charmed*]. And they said, "Let's get her in." And then she passed. She liked the darker role from the first pilot and didn't think the rewritten character was as interesting. Nikki spent the entire weekend saying to Kaley's agent, "She's gotta come back in for this, she's gotta do it."

Nikki Valko: We begged and we pleaded and we groveled. I mean, I was *groveling*. Ken, too. [*Laughs*]

Ken Miller: We've known Kaley since she was fourteen [when we cast her in the pilot *Nathan's Choice*]. In hindsight, the role of Katie was an [age] inappropriate role for her in the first pilot. But we really believed that she was the one for the second go-around. It was obvious it was her.

Peter Roth: I begged Kaley's team, too. [*Laughs*] Everything in the second pilot was timed to get Kaley to play Penny because she was exactly what we knew we needed.

Kaley Cuoco: I remember where I was sitting in my house when my agent, Ro, told me, "They really want you for this," and "It's probably going to go to series because it's a Chuck show." My team just wanted to make sure I wouldn't be stuck in anything that wasn't an exciting role since it seemed like a secondary character at first, but Nikki and Ken kept saying, "No, no, it's going to grow! The guys and this new girl are really going to blow each other's worlds up." And I knew when Chuck's name is next to something,

"BIG BANG THEORY"

Characters 9/28/06

PENNY. Early 20s, energetic and optimistic, Penny's a bit lost in the world. She's prone to bad decisions in men, etc. – things that in retrospect she feels she should have seen coming. She hasn't really made a life plan for herself. Currently, she's bartending, but she's also "working on a screenplay about a woman who came to Los Angeles to be an actress but failed." Her enthusiasm for popular and junk pseudo-science like astrology and "eating by your blood type" frustrates Leonard and Sheldon.

WOLOWITZ. Howie Wolowitz is a friend of Leonard and Sheldon. He works in the applied physics department of Cal Tech – he's one of the guys who design those things that explore the surface of Mars. Howie fancies himself a ladies' man despite no evidence whatsoever of any success in that department.

KOOTHRAPPALI. Dave Koothrappali (American-born to immigrant Indian parents) is arguably one of the most brilliant minds of the 21st Century. At the same time, however, his deep understanding of the universe seems to have contributed to a festival of neuroses. Knowing how much background microwave radiation we all experience, for example, has lead him to line his ever-present baseball cap with aluminum foil. He is also the most socially inept of the group – he is unable to speak in the presence of women.

KURT. Penny's ex-boyfriend is a gorilla of an ex-frat boy turned stock broker. He likes flat-screen TVs, leather couches and bar fights. He's a schoolyard bully wearing an expensive suit.

Once casting began on the second pilot for The Big Bang Theory, Katie was now Penny, and the characters of Howie Wolowitz, Dave Koothrappali (later, Raj) and Kurt were added.
Courtesy of Bill Prady personal archive and Warner Bros. Entertainment

you really don't question it. I laugh thinking about it now. And then, at every table read on Wednesdays, we always sat in the same place, and Ken and Nikki always sat behind me. And I would always yell out, "Thank you for hiring me!"

Peter Roth: Kaley's a brilliant comedic actress, and as good as anybody I've ever worked with. She is going to be one of the biggest stars of all time. So when we got Kaley, that changed everything. She was the catalyst for the success of the show.

> Now with Cuoco in place to round out the main trio of Leonard, Sheldon, and Penny, casting Wolowitz and Koothrappali should have been a breeze. In reality, it was anything but.

Nikki Valko: Kevin Sussman came back in, this time for the role of Wolowitz. At the time, he was starring in the first season of ABC's *Ugly Betty* as America Ferrera's boyfriend, Walter.

Bill Prady: The part of Wolowitz was written for Kevin. We loved him, especially after he first came in and auditioned for Leonard in the first pilot.

Kevin Sussman ("Stuart Bloom"): I auditioned for Chuck as well as James Burrows, and came in with my own version of a super-cocky, sex-obsessed guy...the polar opposite of who I would eventually play as Stuart. As soon as I was done reading for Wolowitz, James Burrows said, "Okay, yeah." And then I got a call saying I had booked it.

> That's right. For a matter of hours, Kevin Sussman was given a verbal commitment that he was going to play the role of Howard Wolowitz. What happened next is why they say you shouldn't become an actor unless you're sure you can't do anything else.

Kevin Sussman: That night, at my celebratory dinner at my manager's house, I got a call from my agent saying that the whole thing fell apart.

Bill Prady: [ABC] wouldn't let Kevin out of his contract, even though his arc on *Ugly Betty* was done at the time.

Ken Miller: ABC had an option on Kevin and wouldn't release him. And then the sad part is, he was never on *Ugly Betty* after that again. They kept him from getting that role on *Big Bang*.

Chuck Lorre: ABC made a very petty gesture because Kevin was maybe a recurring character on *Ugly Betty*—and we had been told they were writing the character out of the series. However, when they found out we were interested in him in a regular role on a CBS show, they decided not to write the character out of the series. And then after Simon got the role of Wolowitz, ABC let Kevin go anyway! I thought, *Are you kidding?! What's wrong with you?!* It really is a dick move. Now, I don't know this for a fact [that that's why, but] I am just surmising they did it to stop another show from having Kevin, but *really*?! As soon as they found out that we wanted him, they put a stop to it. And then they let him go shortly after.

Kevin Sussman: My role was basically to play the heel that Betty sheds after season one, and then she starts dating people that are acceptable. [*Laughs*] I had gotten [the *Ugly Betty* producers'] blessing to do *Big Bang*. But business affairs at ABC dropped the ball in terms of communicating what we needed in order to get me released from ABC. Now, at the time, *Big Bang* was just another show that was filming a pilot, so nobody knew it was going to be a big hit. I was just disappointed because it meant I wasn't going to get paid [had I done] the pilot, which is a big deal. It wasn't until a couple of years later when I was on the show as Stuart, just a guest star, that during a table read one morning they made an announcement that *Big Bang* was picked up for a couple more seasons. They guy's words were, "If you've been waiting on a mortgage or something, go ahead and sign the papers." And that's when I realized the extent of how crazy that was that I was that close to being a series regular at that point. [*Laughs*] But, hindsight's always twenty-twenty. I try not to drive myself crazy over that. I mean, my first job on TV was an episode of *Law & Order*, and I remember telling all my friends and family, "This is the big time!" It was just a scene in the cold open where I was one of the young kids that found a dead body. The day I was filming, I was waiting for hours and hours in my trailer when one of the producers knocked on my door and said, "We got some bad news. The episode's running long, so we're not going to be able to use you. We're just going to go straight into the episode and not shoot the cold open." I was devastated, but in a way it set the tone of this business, meaning nothing in this business happens until it really happens. With *Big Bang*, although I had a verbal commitment, until the deal is signed on the dotted line, it doesn't actually exist. You develop a thick skin.

Bill Prady: Years later, I ran into a writer who had been on the staff of *Ugly Betty*, and [that writer confirmed to me they] had finished Kevin's storyline on that show, and he was done. But then they were told to write him back in. That writer remembers it being an insane instruction and it was impossible to do because they had written the character off. So the inference from that was that it was just vindictive . . . that they were simply looking for a way to deny another show an actor.

Eventually, Lorre and Prady created the character of comic book store owner Stuart Bloom, which Sussman started playing at the end of season two.

Kevin Sussman: Chuck is a super-loyal guy, and incidentally he had no knowledge that I actually used to work in a comic book store for years. That was just a coincidence.

Chuck Lorre: It was such a great way to pull him back into the tent because he made the series better. He was a gift to us on our show, and it's strange how things worked out. We would have never gotten to Simon had ABC not blocked Kevin.

Ken Miller: It was unfair how it happened, but things work out how they're supposed to, and it's what we found out after all these years of casting. But Simon was the way to go.

Bill Prady: Looking back, Simon became that part in ways that are only him, and I think about the great aspects of that character, like his relationship with his mother, his relationship with Bernadette, all of that. Simon became that character, while Stuart was a creation that only could have come from Kevin. And Stuart evolved and was wonderful and was a fun character to write.

And for the entire run of *Big Bang*, Sussman chose to never tell Simon Helberg what had happened.

Kevin Sussman: I never mentioned it. I just didn't want to put that out in the ether because my relationship with him was so good. He was always so supportive and so amazing in his role. I feel like anything that actually winds up being good in the entertainment industry is through a series of mistakes, because the cards are so stacked against every project. We lucked out by getting a cast that all really enjoyed each other, so I never brought it up because I didn't want that to affect our working relationship.

It wasn't until the interview process for this book that Helberg learned every-thing that happened. Understandably, he was stunned.

Simon Helberg: Oh my God, I'm literally covered in goose bumps right now. I have always said, "I don't think [*Big Bang* producers] wanted me or certainly something happened, and I feel like it involved Kevin Sussman," because I knew that Kevin was a favorite of theirs from the first time he came in to audition for Leonard in the first pilot. And it was a week from my last test audition until I found out I got the role, and I remember thinking, *They're definitely not certain that I'm the guy.* Like, they haven't jumped into the ring with me yet, so there's some kind of deliberation that's going on, and that's usually not a great sign. My feeling was that the network or the studio was not fully on board, but I had *no idea* what really happened...and Kevin obviously never told me that. And now I know that Kevin tested with Jim Burrows, and what's weird is that I never read for Burrows.

Helberg is the first to acknowledge that these things happen all the time when it comes to casting, but the shock for him lies more in the fact that after all this time—fifteen years—it was never mentioned to him.

Simon Helberg: I've gone and played parts in movies that you're cast in at the last minute, and when you get there it's still got the other actor's name on the wardrobe. So, I don't have to feel like I was the number one guy or I was the only guy, but after twelve years on the show and in the years since, it is surprising. I've gotten a little more of a thick skin about the whole insane process that this business necessitates, and I feel like ultimately, if I get the role, that's the takeaway.

Kevin Sussman deserves a lot of respect for not wanting to tell Helberg, or any of the cast, really, what had happened, for fear it could make things awkward. And immediately after Helberg learned, he asked if it was OK to reach out to Sussman and let him know he knew.

Simon Helberg: It's kind of like when you get married and you find out your wife dated some guy and you didn't know that and you can obsess over it, like, *Would she have been happier with him?* In many ways we're past it, but also, at the same time, it's the nature of this whole thing. When you're an actor and you're rejected or swapped out, you can't help but internalize it as a slight against you personally. But at the same time, after doing it for so long, you do, for better or for worse, become a little bit immune to that. I'm the biggest Kevin fan in the world. I would have loved to see Kevin play my role, too. I'm happy I was ultimately the one who got to do it, but I love Kevin. I always thought everything he did on the show was just so spectacularly unique and brilliantly funny. Now, if I learned this when I was shooting the pilot or the second episode, or maybe the whole first season, it might've killed me, but I already felt like I was kind of trudging uphill and there was just a learning curve in regards to the communication styles of everybody. I think I always felt a little at odds with what Chuck wanted, and I wanted to accommodate that, but I also wanted to do things my way at times, so just developing that trust from both sides is something that did take time. And obviously hearing they wanted someone else first is an easier piece of information than hearing, "Oh, you almost got the role that would have gotten you on television for twelve years and set you up [for life]," and I realize that. It's just fascinating because you do something for so long with people…and I knew we would learn things in this book, but…wow. [*Laughs*]

> Let's go back to 2007, though, when Lorre and Prady were frustrated they couldn't get Sussman for the role of Wolowitz. They still had to cast the role, and unless ABC suddenly reversed course (which they didn't), they realized they needed a plan B.

Bill Prady: Simon's audition was wonderful. He was a very different kind of Wolowitz. The way in which Kevin has a flustered quality, Simon has an intensity to him, and it was a very different concept, but it worked great.

> Except there was one problem; Helberg was still on the fence about leaving Aaron Sorkin's *Studio 60 on the Sunset Strip*, starring Matthew Perry, Amanda Peet, Sarah Paulson, Bradley Whitford, and other high-profile names.

Simon Helberg: I had gotten a recurring role on *Studio 60 on the Sunset Strip*, which had a lot of anticipated acclaim because it was from Aaron Sorkin. But ultimately when it came out of the gate, it didn't quite do as well as everybody hoped. Regardless, when I got the audition for *Big Bang*, I had done so many pilots, had so many failed nerd characters under my belt, *and* I was having a great time on *Studio 60*, that I said, "I don't really want to play more nerds." But my agents convinced me to go in for an audition, which went great, and I actually really enjoyed it. After I finished, Chuck said, "Well, actor goes home knowing he killed." I don't even think he knows that he said that; it was like he was just speaking his subconscious. But when they asked me to test for it, I said no, because once you test for something, you're committed [whereas if you audition, you're doing it to see what happens, no strings attached]. I liked the material and knew I could do a good job, but I wanted to stay on *Studio 60*.

Bill Prady: If Simon took *Big Bang*, he'd be giving *Studio 60* up even though he was a recurring cast member at the time. It wasn't that he couldn't get out of it, but when you've got a job recurring on an Aaron Sorkin show, do you give that up?

Ken Miller: We were like, "Come on, Simon!"

Nikki Valko: We believed in him because Simon equals comedy genius. He is just so, so funny.

Simon Helberg: At that point, Chuck had made calls to my agent, and through a series of different conversations, I ultimately was like, *I think I gotta go test for this*. But I just wanted Aaron Sorkin and Chuck to have a boxing match over me. [*Laughs*] Eventually, I tested for Wolowitz. Then the next morning I read online that Kaley got the part of Penny, and I was like, *Oh, so they made a decision*. At the time, I knew Kevin auditioned for Wolowitz and they loved him. I get it. My hunch was always that they wanted him to play Wolowitz, and somewhere in that discussion, in that week of silence on my end after I tested, there was a big discussion, but it's how it goes. No surprise, but actors are riddled with insecurities. That whole process is such a grind.

Ultimately I did get the role, and then I wrote an email to Aaron where I asked him for time off from *Studio 60* to film the pilot for *Big Bang*. I assured him that given the sheer number of pilots I had done that didn't get picked up, the odds weren't that likely, but if it did, I would have to leave his show. I think I was also giving him an opportunity to say something along the lines of, "Well, hey, like, we'll make you a regular or something," because I was really inclined to stay on *Studio 60*. He wrote back and said, "You ungrateful little piece of sh——" followed by, "Just kidding! They will have to pry the pen out of my cold dead hands to get me to stop writing for you. Good luck!" And then, when I tested at CBS, Peter Roth was there, and Peter was having me do impressions for Chuck, because he knew I did all these impressions on *Studio 60*. I don't know if you can have a negative reaction to something like that, but I'd say this was pretty close to it. Chuck kinda stared at me…and then I got an endless amount of notes and adjustments, to the point where I wondered if they were thinking, *What is* this *that you're doing now? What happened to the other thing?* I just felt they weren't totally sold, whereas there had been a lot of excitement for me to come in and test. So I wasn't surprised that there was some hesitation because I felt it from that moment that I came back.

Chuck Lorre: It's strange how things worked out. We would have never gotten to Simon had ABC not blocked Kevin. And listen, if *Studio 60* had continued, it would have been a no-brainer. Simon would have correctly wanted to tie his future to Aaron Sorkin, and who wouldn't? He is the greatest playwright and screenwriter in our world for the last many years.

While Sussman is a talented actor who would surely have brought his own spin to Howard, one of the main reasons the show succeeded for twelve years was because of the chemistry Helberg had with the rest of the cast, specifically Kunal Nayyar as Raj and Melissa Rauch as Bernadette. From his piano skills to his impressions to the lovable father and husband that Wolowitz became, it was all because of Helberg.

And with the casting of Helberg now in place, it was time to focus on Raj.

Kunal Nayyar ("Rajesh Koothrappali"): I didn't have my own car when I got the audition. I wanted to rent whatever shit car the rental place had, but they didn't even have that, so they gave me a white Toyota Solara. It was a convertible, and it was the greatest day of my life! So, anyway, I was wearing khaki pants, an orange-and-blue-checked plaid shirt with the buttons all the way up, and a hat, because [the script] said Raj wore a hat. Ken or Nikki walked past me after the first audition and said, "Just lose a few more buttons and make it look a little more natural." I definitely was playing the caricature of the character as opposed to the character. The biggest note was to just relax into it. I hadn't done that much work in television, so everything I was doing, especially the physical stuff, was larger than it needed to be. I think it almost took three seasons to really understand what it means to let go and find the rhythm. When I look back at the earlier seasons, I'm just trying *so* hard. I can see it. The pressure for me to get this right was so great.

The role originally called for a first generation Indian-American, and the character's name was Dave.

Bill Prady: The original idea was that he was going to be an American-born son of immigrant parents. But when Kunal came in and we heard his accent, we said, "Let's say that he's Indian-born." He picked his first name because India has a lot of regions and ethnic groups, and we wanted to make sure that the last name and first name went together. Koothrappali is a Southern Indian name, and so he picked "Rajesh." I think he had a couple of choices, but we liked "Rajesh" because his nickname is almost the nickname for "Roger"—"Rog" and "Raj." We liked the sound of it. And when we needed a middle name for Raj, he gave Raj a middle name.

Kunal Nayyar: Yeah, Rajesh Ramayan Koothrappali. They came to me because I became the de facto Indian consultant since I spent most of my whole life in India. [*Laughs*] Don't ask me why I thought of Ramayan for his middle name...I guess I just thought it sounded great together. And I remember when I went in for the audition, I was auditioning against Asian actors, South Asian actors, so they were looking at all ethnicities, which was very true to reflect the diversity the university has.

But it was still a tough role to cast because Raj didn't have a lot of dialogue early on.

Ken Miller: Raj didn't speak. He was afraid to talk to women. But Kunal, who had just finished drama school in London, really was fantastic.

Nikki Valko: It was a huge stroke of luck to get Kunal, because as they gave him more to do, he was actually a great actor. But we didn't know that from casting him in the pilot necessarily because he didn't have very much to do. We just got real lucky on that.

There were still plenty of hurdles to come, but for now the cast was in place and they could get to know each other in the week leading up to the filming of the second pilot.

Simon Helberg: I first met Jim at my test reading at CBS when he was reading with Kaley. As you would expect, he was just soft-spoken and gentle and kind. Then, during the pilot, I remember being really impressed by his talent and the facility that he had in particular with those impenetrable speeches and just this "lightness" with which he could do that comedy.

Jim Parsons: Simon and I didn't necessarily have a lot in common, but once we were together more and had the chance to have private conversations, I realized we had so much overlap in the way we viewed the world and life. There was nothing that I could have been struggling with, whether it was the show or outside of that, that I couldn't talk to him about. Simon is also one of those people that makes you laugh more than most I've ever met in my life. And then when I met Kunal, I thought he was so good-looking. He knows this because I told him. [*Laughs*] There's also a musical quality about Kunal that's soothing to me. He could also be ridiculous and we'd make fun of him because of that. Well, not always. But very often.

Kunal Nayyar: I remember being quite intimidated the first time I met Jim. I was just in awe of him and his talent. I had seen him on *Judging Amy* and in *Garden State* as the guy who has "balls" written on his forehead. I know that's not the epitome of someone's acting career, but for me, I was just a kid out of graduate school and I was sitting in front of Johnny Galecki and Kaley Cuoco and Jim Parsons and Simon Helberg, all of whose shows I had seen. Back when I was in India, I was watching *8 Simple Rules* when it was in reruns. Same with *Roseanne*. I grew up watching these people and now, a year later, I was sitting in a room with them. I was full of enthusiasm and naive confidence. I thought I belonged in that room, yet I had no idea what I was doing. I overcompensated that nervous energy by acting like a cool, confident cat, which probably came across as just arrogant and obnoxious. We had a rehearsal before we did the first table read, and I remember seeing Simon and saying, "Wow, you're not six two. On your IMDbPro page it says you're six two. You're, like, not that tall." I'd never met him; how did I know? Does IMDb lie? [*Laughs*]

Simon Helberg: I don't know why he thought that, but the point of that story is that for twelve years he continued to always be wrong about everything.

But Helberg had actually met Cuoco years earlier when he was visiting the set of *8 Simple Rules*.

Simon Helberg: Jason Ritter has been one of my best friends since our NYU days. His dad, John Ritter, played Kaley's father on the show. I met Kaley again when we tested for our *Big Bang* roles.

Kaley Cuoco: Simon was such a great connection to John, so he loved John just as much as I did. That's why I was really excited when Billy Bob Thornton guest-starred on *Big Bang* because John was best friends with Billy Bob. I still remember sitting around the set of *8 Simple Rules* and John [was] telling stories about Billy Bob. I had never met him before he came on *Big Bang*, so when he came on the show, I was like "I have to talk to you about John." His whole face lit up, and we connected on this really sweet level of reminiscing about him. John has a way of bringing people together even from above. That's just so him!

Jim Parsons: And Kaley and I read together at her test, and I thought she was just so charming. She was twenty when we first started, and I remember being in the makeup room and watching her fingers slide across her phone to text like it was the easiest thing in the world. We're thirteen years apart. It made a big difference, but it quickly became evident that she and I worked really well together. Even after doing the show for twelve years, there was just something about Sheldon and Penny, and Kaley specifically. I don't know that anybody on the show has a greater ease with comedic timing than she does. And I never saw her with a script in her hands. I was like,

How are you doing this?! I mean, it was unbelievable to me! We'd be doing a scene to rehearse for a tape night and new pages would have come out, and she was like, "Oh, they did? Can I see them?" [*Laughs*] And she would learn the lines immediately! Meanwhile, I have been beating my head against the wall all week—and yes, I had different dialogue than she did—but even then, just from a sheer confidence standpoint, I could never have performed at her level going, "Yeah, I looked at it. I'm fine." [*Laughs*] I want to get there at some point in my career. And she's just brilliant in *The Flight Attendant*. There's just a confidence and a joy that comes together to give her this ease.

Kunal Nayyar: I remember meeting Kaley and thinking, *Wow, she's like an adult*. She was only twenty, but much more mature than I could ever be. [*Laughs*] She had a real unintimidating bubbliness about her. And Johnny, for me, was like the older brother. He played the role of de facto leader of the cast. I thought, *He's cool, he rides motorcycles, and smokes cigarettes. So, I'm just gonna watch this guy and learn from him.* [*Laughs*]

Johnny Galecki: It was also a reluctant position to be elected in, but I've been so blessed in having learned from the best about what to do, and learned from the worst about what not to do. I wouldn't want to keep such lessons to myself if I thought they might be helpful. I remember talking to the cast and relaying that a stage is an incredibly fragile ecosystem. I said, "It's okay to have a bad day but we don't take it out on each other. Let's be very protective of this stage." And we really did.

Kaley Cuoco: Johnny and I partnered up early on and took it upon ourselves to be the example. We just kind of stepped into that leadership role. And then throughout the series and our lives, we would always have each other's back. We were just kind of impenetrable.

Johnny Galecki: Kaley was my rock. I knew everything that we talked about was from the truest of our hearts.

Kaley Cuoco: We told our teams very early on, "What you hear from me, you'll hear from him, so we're doing everything the same." I didn't want them to think... *Well, we need to talk to Kaley*. No, if Johnny said it, then we're good.

Johnny Galecki: And once Jim, Kaley, Kunal, Simon, and myself did that first table read together, it felt like all the planets aligned and all the puzzle pieces fell into place. Everything that everyone did complemented the next line, and it just kept building like that. It was like playing music with a whole new band. It was really exciting. Simon would do something one way and it would tweak how I approached my next line even by two degrees. It just kept working like that with each line between all five of us, and that was a really inspiring day. And I knew that I could be there for a long time and be very happy.

Chapter 4

LAYING THE FOUNDATION... LITERALLY

It all started with a big bang—er, actually a sperm bank—and that's no bazinga. In the second pilot—the one that would eventually air on CBS—the first scene takes place in, yes, a high-IQ sperm bank with Sheldon and Leonard filling out paperwork to donate their sperm. There they encounter the receptionist, Althea (Vernee Watson), who will appear half a dozen times in various hospital roles before the series signs off, and now stars as Gloria on *Bob Hearts Abishola*. The scene with Sheldon, Leonard, and Althea does not appear in reruns on TBS, but can be seen in its entirety on HBO Max, where all *Big Bang* episodes now live.

Chuck Lorre: The scene was so wrong. In my mind, the show truly began with those awkward hellos between Penny, Sheldon, and Leonard when she's unpacking boxes in her apartment.

Jim Parsons: At the time, the sperm bank scene didn't bother me. It was just another scene that had to be done. Looking back, it was out of place, but there was no way for the producers to know, and that's where it wasn't a mistake. One of the glories about television is if you're able to do the same show for a while, the characters develop. But when you're making a pilot with a majority of people you've never met with people who are writing this, there's nothing wrong with the scene. Nobody knew who Sheldon was yet, so the live audience accepted it for what it was. But it is confusing information now, and I get why Chuck took it out in syndication, because the episode is much stronger and more special without it.

Bill Prady: Prior to broadcast when the pilot started airing on American Airlines flights, they basically said, "You can't show that scene." So we shot wonderful wraparounds with Johnny and Jim where they introduced the show and said, "We're not going to be able to show you the first scene, because it's a little grown-up and we don't know who's looking over your shoulder. We've had a discussion with American Airlines, and decided not to show it. But the story pretty much works without that scene, so we'll jump in starting with the second scene." Then Jim said, "As long as we have a few extra minutes, I'm going to explain how airplanes fly," and Johnny responds, "No one on an airplane wants to hear how airplanes fly!" It's a great little piece of footage. And then when there's a callback to the sperm bank scene later in the episode (Penny says, "What do you guys do for fun around here?" Sheldon says, "Well, today we tried masturbating for money"), Jim and Johnny interrupt out of character and say, "There's a joke here you won't get because it's about the first scene, but it's a pretty funny joke. Moving on." And then it goes back to the show.

As for what happens in the sperm bank scene...well, nothing really. Sheldon and Leonard come to the realization it's not for them—mainly because donating their sperm won't guarantee a genius child—and leave. In the next scene, they are seen walking up their apartment stairs, one of the many significant changes from the first pilot to the second.

Chuck Lorre: In the first pilot, we built this sidewalk-street thing on the set, and it looked terrible. When they met Katie, she was crying while sitting on the curb. It just did not work to build an outdoor set indoors. It didn't look real. So in the second pilot, I thought the stairwell could replace the street as a place where we could control the lighting, the sound, and not have fake cars going by. And by the way, there wouldn't even have been cars going by because we were on a soundstage! Even the footsteps on the pavement didn't sound right because it wasn't pavement—it was wood. So I thought it would be terrific to give the characters an opportunity to communicate minutiae. Not necessarily important stuff, but on occasion very important stuff. The stairway was a solution to that, but we had to blow through concrete foundation on stage 25 to create it. It was an expensive thing to request, because if the second pilot failed, Warner Bros. would have had to fill in that hole and repave it. I mean, we had guys with jackhammers blowing through the concrete foundation of the stage to put those steps down there so our characters could walk up flights of stairs. It was just a hunch that this was a better way to go than having them walk down the street. And it was an expensive hunch, but I think we paid off the hole!

When Sheldon and Leonard get to the landing of the fourth floor, they notice a young woman unpacking boxes across from their apartment. She's gorgeous, full of energy...and so clearly not of their world. In what is now an iconic scene, they exchange awkward "hi's" followed by multiple "greats," and then "byes."

Bill Prady: We wrote it, and then as with all good collaborative things, the actors made it better. We just knew, "This is clicking." It feels like the look and sound of a home run in baseball; you just know, *that's outta here*. And we all knew it.

Kaley Cuoco: That exchange got rewritten so many times, which is interesting on a show that had very few rewrites. But that scene set the tone for the show. And I remember Jimmy Burrows had a lot to do with the buoyancy of that scene, and all of the sudden we were bouncing off each other and it became kind of like music, the three of us. It was a song that came to life. It took a while to find, but once we did, it ended up being one one of the most adorable, remembered scenes on TV.

Jim Parsons: I don't think the full exchange of *hi*'s, *great*s, and *bye*s were in the script originally, which is, under these circumstances, kind of remarkable because that would have been an excessively rare moment in the history of *The Big Bang Theory*. Regardless, the scene still kind of tickles me when I think about it. It was something so beautifully odd and so simple that said so much.

After that awkward introduction, Sheldon and Leonard walk into their apartment where viewers see the first glimpse of their living space, complete with the brown leather couch, whiteboards, and the DNA molecular structure. It was in stark contrast to their apartment in the first pilot, which looked run-down and depressing—the opposite of the colorful, earth-toned, science playground that became instantly recognizable to viewers.

Professor David Saltzberg (*Big Bang* science consultant): The first pilot was very dark in its aesthetic and a little depressing, so for the second one, they wanted it a little more upbeat. I remember Chuck saying, "If you have a choice, make it more colorful and bright." And so I always tell my grad students that their real lives were too depressing for TV.

> Minutes after Sheldon and Leonard meet Penny for the first time, they head back over to her apartment, where another round of awkward "hi's" unfolds before Leonard invites Penny over for lunch. She excitedly accepts, which is both stunning and terrifying for Sheldon and Leonard. And then, with that, we hear *The Big Bang Theory* theme song for the first time.

Chuck Lorre: It never occurred to me to write *The Big Bang Theory* theme song even though I cowrote the theme for *Two and a Half Men*. Bill and I discussed who we might corral into giving it a try, and amazingly enough, I got Ed Robertson of the Barenaked Ladies on the phone. I said, "Here's my idea for the song in twenty-five to thirty seconds... it encapsulates the entire history of the universe from the big bang to the characters sitting on the couch eating Chinese food." The Barenaked Ladies had some serious commercial success with cramming a great deal of lyrics into a pop song, and Ed's ability to make music out of dense lyrics was already well established. But apparently he didn't want to do it. His wife made him rethink saying no, and so he did. He speculatively wrote the theme song pretty close to what it is, and sent an acoustic guitar and vocal demo to us. I thought it was perfect, but he said it had to be the whole band. I tried to talk him out of it, but I lost. And then he sent the band version, which is what we used for twelve years.

> The next scene is a prime example of why the *Big Bang Theory* pilot ultimately succeeded. Penny sits in Sheldon's spot, prompting Sheldon to spiral. His entire routine is interrupted, thereby giving viewers a deeper insight into just how complex the character is.

Bill Prady: The struggle that Jim creates, and the battle that Sheldon ultimately loses until he finally reclaims his spot is so fascinating to watch. Look at that struggle. That's the whole character. He *knows* it's rude to ask guests to move if they've seated themselves. He knows that. His mama raised him right. But he *can't* do it. And that's the struggle of that character encapsulated in a moment.

Jim Parsons: Sheldon basically has a breakdown when he can't get what he needs, and it makes his skin crawl and his muscles twitch. I am positive I was mimicking a thousand brilliant other performances that I had seen and absorbed in my entire life and stored away for the chance to use one day because I thought that they were magnificent. I just knew that this was *my* chance to do my tortured dance. [*Laughs*] And when Penny sits in Sheldon's spot, I'll never forget the words Jimmy Burrows said to me, which were, "When she sits in that spot, I want you on her like a cat! Like *meow*! As in, *Oh no you don't!*" And that one note, that one direction, launched that whole section for me. Once I knew that that's what he wanted my reaction to be, everything else unfolded from that.

Chuck Lorre: The audience went wild at that moment. They were in love with Sheldon's neuroses. I'm standing on the stage, and I look at Jimmy Burrows, who directed both of our pilots, and Jimmy looks at me, and we both look at each other with these big grins. We knew this was working. It was one of those goose bump moments you never forget. We got it right.

But while the moment defined Sheldon, the episode exposed character flaws in Penny.

Steve Molaro (executive producer, showrunner): She was the ditzy blonde girl in the pilot, which is one of the things that is not great about that pilot. It took a long time for her to become a person. There's an unfortunate joke about how she's a vegetarian but she loves steak. I didn't write the pilot, but those are moments where you wish you could undo a little bit of. Or you wish you had a little bit clearer picture of where we ended up going. But that's how pilots work. It's tough.

Chuck Lorre: One of the most underwritten characters in the show early on was Penny. It was really obvious immediately that we hadn't developed the character beyond the pretty girl next door, and Kaley was certainly capable of doing a great deal more than what was asked of her. We had to make the character more fully realized. Not just for an episode, but *always*. [Over time] Penny had an intelligence about people, about relationships, and about sussing out a situation and understanding the dynamics of what's going on in a room.

Bill Prady: Chuck was doing *Two and a Half Men* at the time, and that was very successful. I think his feeling was that something a little edgy would work, evidenced by the sperm bank scene, and Penny in the towel when she uses Sheldon and Leonard's shower. There are a couple of things in the pilot that I could live without.

Regrets aside, Penny's relationship to Sheldon and Leonard was crucial in those early episodes. She was both amused by the guys and protective of them.

Kaley Cuoco: There's zero judgment from the minute she meets them. What was interesting was they were judging *her*. I felt like they were judging her for a long time, and I actually loved that. She just wanted to hang out with them. She immediately included them. But it took them longer to include her.

Peter Roth: Penny found the guys hysterical and cute, but she didn't make fun of them. She thought they were endearing, but never to the point of you feeling like she was secretly mocking them behind their backs. That's why one of the most brilliant relationships was Penny and Sheldon. That was very special.

While Sheldon, Leonard, and Penny are having lunch, she tells the guys she's a waitress at The Cheesecake Factory.

Mary T. Quigley (costume designer; co-producer): I went to The Cheesecake Factory to look at the actual outfits that the servers wore. I wanted the outfit to be fitted but not look unrealistic.

Chuck Lorre: We wanted Penny to work somewhere that was pedestrian and wonderfully quotidian. Here are these guys who are trying to unravel the secrets of the universe, and Penny introduces herself by saying, "I work at The Cheesecake Factory." The juxtaposition of scientists working in the quantum field, perhaps changing the world with their work, and "I work at The Cheesecake Factory" seemed to be a funny dichotomy. And the cheesecake is great! I personally really love their chocolate chip cheesecake. And the menu went on for days—it was like a book! There was a lot going for it, and the company was very gracious about letting us use their name.

Surprisingly, the California Institute of Technology (abbreviated as Caltech) wasn't as enthusiastic when it came to establishing Sheldon and Leonard's workplace.

Chuck Lorre: Caltech wasn't keen on us using their name or likeness early on, so we obliged for a while, and then when the show took off, they communicated with us again and said something along the lines of, "Please feel free to use the word *Caltech* in your show," because it was a good promotion for Caltech! [*Laughs*] Someone over there recognized that being associated with this burgeoning hit show was not going to damage their reputation. If anything, it would make more young people aware of the school as a possible destination after high school. So yeah, they reversed course, pretty much saying, "Go ahead and use it as much as you want. In fact, if you wanna come over here and shoot on our campus, come on over." And we did. We shot the first scene that we did with Professor Stephen Hawking in the Caltech library.

But we're getting ahead of ourselves. Let's go back to the pilot, where at this point Penny has just revealed she's newly single after breaking up with her jerk of a boyfriend. She's emotionally and physically drained, noting she can't even take a shower because hers doesn't work yet. Leonard offers to let her use his, and while she's in the bathroom undressing, there's a knock at the door. It's Rajesh Koothrappali and Howard Wolowitz, who have arrived nearly two-thirds of the way through the pilot episode.

Simon Helberg: Kunal and I came in—two people the audience had never met—and we got an entrance applause from the audience. It was so surreal. And in that moment, I knew as much as anyone can know something, that that show was going to have some kind of future. I could feel from the moment we started the taping there was a really spectacularly rare confluence of people and material and energy that was going to lead to something special.

Kunal Nayyar: We were nobodies and the audience started applauding. I had no frame of reference, so I thought, *Oh, okay, this must be normal! This is the way it's supposed to be!*

Immediately upon entering the apartment, Wolowitz mentions a Stephen Hawking lecture from MIT and does his Hawking impression. He's wearing his signature alien pin on his dickie, and a Nintendo controller belt buckle (which Helberg himself took home as a memento after the series finale). But Leonard says he and Koothrappali can't stay because they have company. Howard mentions "coitus" for the first time, and as soon as Penny walks out in her towel, he starts hitting on her.

Lee Aronsohn: What Wolowitz was certainly doing in the first season could be called harassment today. I rewatched the pilot recently, and it did occur to me that the Wolowitz character was not 2021 friendly.

Simon Helberg: People were very unhappy with some of the things that Howard would do or say, and I was like, "Yeah, I agree." I didn't necessarily think that meant the character should be removed, but it certainly was more fun to play him as his heart got bigger and he shed his layer of sleaze.

Bill Prady: By the way, I have a friend named Howard Wolowitz. When I was in the computer business, Howie was my partner. He's in his seventies now, living in Connecticut, and nothing like Wolowitz; I just liked his name because there was this musicality to it. I asked him at one point if that was okay if we used his name and he thought it was fun and wouldn't really affect his life much. Of course, he then spent years putting down a credit card or a driver's license and people going, *"Really?* No, really, that's your name?" [*Laughs*] Howie and Simon got to meet, actually, and he was also an extra in an episode.

On the other hand, Raj had selective mutism and not only couldn't speak to Penny, but women in general.

Bill Prady: I worked with a fellow who had selective mutism and it wasn't to the extreme, but it was pretty close. And when you were talking and women came over, it was like a clockwork toy had wound down, and he simply couldn't speak. It was a very interesting thing to observe.

Later in the episode, Penny asks Leonard to get her TV back from her ex-boyfriend, Kurt. It doesn't work, and Leonard and Sheldon (who also came along) lose their pants in the process. It was the first of several times that Parsons was pantsless on the show.

Jim Parsons: I couldn't have cared less not to be in pants. Now, if they had asked me to be shirtless, that would have made me more uncomfortable. But I had never had an issue with my legs. I never minded being in my underwear. I'm certainly no exhibitionist, but there is something that takes over in my performer's brain when I am onstage, where I am capable of saying and doing things that I would never say or do ten minutes after I leave the stage. Never! And the pants fall in there, if you get my meaning.

In the pilot episode, Leonard (Johnny Galecki) and Sheldon (Jim Parsons) try to get Penny's television back from her ex-boyfriend, Kurt, and end up losing their pants in the process. *Courtesy of Kaley Cuoco photo collection*

By the time the episode ends, an appreciative Penny feels so bad for what the guys went through, so she says dinner is on her. When she goes to grab her wallet, Sheldon astutely observes that Leonard's not about to give up hope on being with Penny one day. Leonard, looking longingly at Penny from across the hall, says, "Our babies will be smart and beautiful," to which Sheldon replies, "Not to mention imaginary." Fade to black as the audience applauds.

Peter Roth: I remember hugging Chuck a lot that night. And Jimmy Burrows. And Nina Tassler. I think we knew we got it this time. And thank God we got it. That was a markedly different experience from the first pilot. Nobody said it out loud, but we knew the first one wasn't working. It was like watching a ball team that is not playing well together. A lot of individual stars but not a lot of chemistry between them.

Simon Helberg: After we wrapped, everyone literally left. Jim had to fly back to New York. Johnny was on Broadway, so he left. Kaley always left right after the show. And I don't know what happened to Kunal, but there was no one there. Usually you're like, "That was a good show, let's have a beer!" I said to my wife, "I kind of wish I got to hang out and say bye to everyone." But she and I went to the Smoke House in Burbank, where I had a delicious wedge salad and a martini, and I said, "I hate to talk about this kind of stuff, but I feel like this show is going to get picked up." And she was like, "Yeah, I feel that way, too."

Kunal Nayyar: I had like twenty people or something there for the pilot, so afterward I just went home and we hung out. Except for a few people, every single person who was in my audience for the pilot was in the audience for the series finale. My parents were there, too. And as a gift, my friend Brian Bitner gave me the program that they handed out to the audience from the pilot. He framed it and gave it to me on the final taping.

On May 14, 2007, CBS announced that it was picking up *The Big Bang Theory* for thirteen episodes for the 2007–2008 season. Nina Tassler's gamble to reshoot the pilot had paid off. Galecki and Parsons would both be relocating to Los Angeles, the stairwell on stage 25 could stay put, and a terrified Chuck Lorre decided he needed the advice of television's most prolific producer, the legendary Norman Lear.

Chuck Lorre: When we got picked up to series, I was immediately terrified of trying to be an executive producer–writer on two shows at the same time. So I thought, *Who might know anything about this and could help me?* Obviously Norman Lear. At one point he had seven shows on television. So I cold-called his office. I had never met the man. I told his assistant who I was and if there was an opportunity to speak with Mr. Lear, I would be so appreciative. I was invited to come meet with him in his office in Beverly Hills, and I said, "I have two shows on the network this fall, and I can barely do one. One is overwhelming, exhausting, horrifying, debilitating. I was hoping maybe you would have some insight as to ways to do it?" And he said, "Oh, you're going to be very disappointed in my answer!" [*Laughs*] He said, "Basically the trick is you go to where the fire is burning the brightest and try to put it out." That was his entire strategy for executive-producing multiple shows: Go to the show where the second act isn't working. Or go to the show where a guest part is miscast and you have to find a different actor. It was a memorable moment for me, just to be sitting there talking to Norman Lear. Like, *Norman Lear is giving me a half hour of his time! This is pretty exciting!* I've met with him a couple of times over the years, had dinner with him, been to his home, done some events and panels together...but talk about humbling. He's a remarkable fella.

Unbeknownst to Lorre, that crucial advice would come in handy sooner than he ever would have expected. Days after CBS ordered the sitcom to series, Lorre, Prady, Galecki, Parsons, Cuoco, and Helberg flew to New York City for the annual upfronts, where networks unveil their fall shows to advertisers. It's jam-packed days of press, red carpets, cocktail hours, and meet-and-greets. The only issue? A key member of the cast—Kunal Nayyar—was not included. What happened next proved just how loyal Lorre was to his cast, and just how important Lear's advice was to him.

Kunal Nayyar: When the show got picked up, I read about it on *Deadline Hollywood*. No one had called to tell me. I reached out to Simon and he said, "Listen, I don't know what's going on. The show's picked up. They've just booked my flight to New York. I leave tomorrow; I'm sure they'll be calling you." And that whole night, I waited and waited, and no one called. My agent was trying to find what was going on. CBS had flown all four cast members to New York for the upfronts except for me, and I thought, *Huh. I* *wonder if I'll just be recast.* At that time, CBS had not picked up my option on the show. They had until June 30, and it was only May. To make matters even more difficult, my visa was going to expire in two months. I didn't have a work visa; I didn't know what was going on. I was starting to think if this doesn't work out, I'll go home and work in India. That was the reality of the situation.

Chuck Lorre: When I landed in New York for the upfronts, I was informed that Kunal wasn't there. I was like, "What do you mean he isn't here? Why isn't he here?" Apparently while I was flying across the country, a CBS executive determined—unilaterally—that Kunal wasn't right for the role and we would recast that part. Well, I did not respond well. I was furious. They made this decision without consulting me. Plus, if you go back and watch the pilot, we didn't really give him much of a chance in that episode. It wasn't because Kunal didn't deliver, it was because we still hadn't quite landed on his character. I called the execs at CBS and said, "You can't fire him. I cast him, I believe in him, I'll take responsibility for this decision. He's my guy." If I'm going to fail, I'm going to fail on my own choices. I'm not going to fail on someone else's choices. I wasn't about to recast that part because *someone else* made a decision. It seemed so unfair to cut the actor from the series based on what—the two lines where he whispered to Wolowitz?

James Burrows: Good ol' CBS will find one sacrificial lamb in every pilot, just to put their stink on it. It got real bad for a while that way. Believe me, the number of pilots I did that got on the air and we had to replace a character is ridiculous.

Ken Miller: Chuck was steadfast in his support and said, "I'll prove all of you wrong." And boy, did he. He just stood his ground and said, "No, this is my guy."

Johnny Galecki: It felt very odd that we were missing a cast member at the upfronts. We all felt terribly awkward and frustrated and helpless because we didn't know what that meant for the show. But mostly we were really feeling for Kunal.

Chuck Lorre: I got on the phone with Kunal—who was distraught—and I said, "You're not here in New York, but that's okay because you're in the show!" I told him not to worry about it, we would get this figured out.

Kaley Cuoco, Jim Parsons, Johnny Galecki, and Simon Helberg attend the 2007 CBS Upfronts, where advertisers got their first look at *The Big Bang Theory*. Noticeably absent was Kunal Nayyar, who was back in Los Angeles waiting to hear if he would be on the series moving forward. *Courtesy of Ro Diamond*

We had a better handle on Sheldon and Leonard and Wolowitz, and so if anything, Kunal suffered not from his own inabilities, but from ours. We had to discover his character. And we did. Beyond our wildest dreams. He became a great, wonderful voice of the ensemble. You can't imagine the show without him

Kunal Nayyar: I remember that phone call vividly. Chuck said, "Look, I don't know why you're not here. I don't know what's going on, but this is *your* role. I'm going to talk to everyone because it's bullshit you're not here. I'm going to make sure this gets done." He really did fight for me. And I don't know the inside story of *how* Chuck fought for me, but I do know on June 30, 2007, I was packing up my flat when my agent said she just got papers faxed to her to pick up my option. And I remember falling on the floor in my apartment on my knees and weeping. Just *weeping*. Because it had been almost forty-five days of not knowing. And that's a very difficult place to be in.

Nina Tassler: To Chuck's credit, when he is an advocate for somebody, he's a fierce advocate. And he was incredibly respectful and very passionate about his cast.

Kunal Nayyar: Looking back, it's not personal. I was a kid out of graduate school. From the prospect of a network about to invest whatever they're about to invest into a project, I have no experience and they only know me from this one audition. Would you take a chance on someone? To me, it was just another thing that I had to prove myself. But Chuck fought for me. He believed in me.

To the outside world, the upfronts were a huge success. On May 9, 2007, *Slate* declared that CBS "has a hit on its hands, if the response of advertisers in Carnegie Hall is any gauge." Of the five new series that the network would be premiering that season, Kim Masters in *Slate* called *Big Bang* "the one that seemed to make the best impression," referring to the series as "sort of *Beauty and the Geek* meets *Three's Company*, with the same jiggle-and-giggle tone of *Two and a Half Men*: Two nerdy geniuses with a hot babe across the hall. The audience lapped it up."

Nina Tassler: There's this really interesting kind of serendipity that happens with regard to certain television shows coming along at the right time and in the right place. *Big Bang* was sort of right at the moment when conversations about geeks, nerds, scientists were happening [particularly as superhero comic book–inspired movies were becoming more mainstream]. You had the magic of Kaley on the cast, and you cannot overstate the specific spark she brought to the Sheldon and Leonard dynamic. Her addition to the cast, as well as Simon and Kunal, was the secret alchemy. Peter Roth was a huge champion for the show, and I can't say enough how great a partner he and Warner Bros. were. Plus, Chuck does multicam better than almost anybody by today's standards, and when you have a show that is hysterically funny, but with depth and character development, it's a real gift.

There was also another reason it worked.

James Burrows: *Mary Tyler Moore, Taxi, Cheers, Friends, Frasier, NewsRadio, Caroline in the City*... they're all shows where most of the cast, if not all of the cast, was unknown in the beginning. That's my wheelhouse. And so when an audience discovers an unknown actor and they become famous, the audience feels empowered that they made them famous, so they're much more apt to watch the show.

On September 24, 2007, *The Big Bang Theory* premiered to 9.52 million viewers. The *Washington Post* called it "the funniest new sitcom of the season," while *USA Today* noted that Lorre's shows "tend to get better after the pilot," adding that he "has produced a first episode that leaves you eager to try the second. These days, maybe that does count as genius." There were also reviews, like that of the *Detroit Free Press*, that called it the "least charming" of the new fall offerings, but for the most part, the pilot was well received.

Judy Parsons: Our family threw a great big party at my daughter's house. My friend brought specially designed *Big Bang* cookies—even ones with Jim's name on 'em. The show appealed to so many age groups...high schoolers, college kids, adults, seniors. So many people told me it was such a bonding thing they could all watch it together. And being a teacher, I loved that the theme was "smart is the new sexy." I loved that it focused on somebody that was different. And just because they're different, you can still be their friend, you can find ways to include them. We were just so proud.

TIME FOR A HOT BEVERAGE...

Stairway to 4A

The teal-green stairs that became its own plot device for twelve years on *Big Bang* did not exist in the original, unaired pilot. It came at the request of Lorre, who wanted a more authentic way to walk and talk in scenes instead of a makeshift street inside a soundstage. And by eliminating a working elevator and forcing the characters to use the stairs, "I just loved that the conversations were naturally broken by making the turn," Lorre says. "The dialogue could either continue or we could have laughter carry us through the turn as they were either going down or going up."

But because there was only one set of stairs, each time the characters walked to a new floor, the set dressers had to redress it to make it look different from the one before.

Mark Cendrowski (director): Early on it was more difficult because they would write these stair scenes but you needed to time them whenever a character turned the corner. Meaning you'd realize a line is so funny that you needed to move a couple lines to the next floor because the laugh was going to carry over to the next flight of stairs. But sometimes you couldn't have them walk that slow for the laugh, so it was a process. If we were really having trouble, we'd say to the writers, "This is really funny, but we may need to shorten this," or "Maybe we need them to start on the second floor instead of the third floor." And the set dressers had it down to a science. The numbers on the door changed, the tape went up, throw a bicycle out there. We also had a pipe on the second floor. I kept the cameras rolling usually when we'd go floor to floor because you didn't want to stop and cut and reslate and have to get the audience into it again. It was like, "Nope, keep the roll, change it, here we go, third floor," so they knew they were watching one scene.

Jim Parsons: I did enjoy the stairway scenes. They're so physical, they're so technical, but that's part of comedy, so when they work, they're a high point of the evening. They offer you entrances and exits and the chance to say something just as you've gone out of view, which can be exceptionally funny to get that last line with nobody's face on-screen. But the hard part would be that you would have to time these, and how fast you walk, the pace you walk, the placement... it was very technical. And then no matter how you planned for it, so often the audience reaction would fuck it all up. You could only prepare so much for where the laugh is going to be, how long it's going to be, what you're going to do. When you're walking downstairs, you have to find very specific reasons to completely stop and take a moment. It's just not natural otherwise. But I loved leaning that fully into *such* a theatrical device for a decade and two years. It's brilliant to me because there's a certain obnoxious quality to it, like, no we can't deliver good lines in an elevator that's closed. We have to have the stairs, so we're just going to

There's only one set of stairs on the set of *Big Bang*, but thanks to clever set dressing and Warner Bros. agreeing to blow through the concrete below the stage so the actors could have a flight of stairs to 'walk down,' they were able to create the illusion of several flights of stairs. *Courtesy of Jessica Radloff*

break the elevator and keep it broken. And we weren't living in a tenement! There was no logical reason that the elevator shouldn't have been put back together! But to me, that's an element of good comedy, and it allowed us to have the elevator fixed in the last episode, which was so nice.

The bottom of the stairs had a tiny holding area where all the actors would have to wait until they called action.

Jim Parsons: The funniest part was the little area downstairs before you walked up, and the little area upstairs. At least the one upstairs had a wooden staircase going down to craft services so you had space. The one down below…if there were four of us, you were full body against full body lined up waiting for the word *action*. It was very odd. Not horrible. But just very odd.

Mark Cendrowski: And the lobby set was off to the right of the audience and always had to be a preshoot because it was separate from the stairway set. There weren't that many scenes that had the lobby and all three floors. If we didn't have room for that set, and they wanted a stairs run, they knew they had to contain it on the three floors and they wouldn't be able to use the lobby.

Chapter 5

GROWING PAINS AND A MIRACLE DISGUISED AS A WRITERS' STRIKE

The second episode of *The Big Bang Theory* was monumental for several reasons. It was the first time the cast and most of the crew had reunited after filming the retooled pilot five months earlier. It was also the first of 278 complex—and nearly impossible to remember—episode names, starting with "The Big Bran Hypothesis." (The pilot episode was colorfully just called "Pilot.") Most important, episode two—which aired on October 1, 2007—marked the first of 244 episodes that eventual resident director Mark Cendrowski would helm, in addition to the first episode for Steve Molaro. But as long and exciting as the journey was about to be, the early years were about as rocky as Leonard's relationship with his mother.

Chuck Lorre: The first couple of years were a mad scramble to figure out what the show was, how to write it, produce it, and direct it. It was volatile, and on top of it, it was all happening while I was still writing and producing *Two and a Half Men*, and I had no experience at multitasking at that level. There was a lot of yelling and arguing in the *Big Bang* writers room, and rewriting and redoing things on the stage, changing the way things were being blocked and shot.

As a result, Lorre asked *Two and a Half Men* co-creator Lee Aronsohn and executive producers Eddie Gorodetsky, Mark Roberts, and Don Foster to help out in various consultant and writing-producing roles.

Chuck Lorre: They probably helped save the show from going off the rails and even being canceled, because in the beginning, there was no guarantee the show was going to become what it became.

Lee Aronsohn: I think Chuck also felt Bill could use an extra hand. My big contribution to the show was I was a nerd myself. I wasn't into physics, but I was a comic book and pop culture nerd—far more than Chuck was. So I think my biggest value to the show was just helping to keep the train running in the beginning.

Eddie Gorodetsky: I think people mistake Chuck for being harsh or hard because he's smart and cuts to the chase. But he's as hard on himself as he is on anyone else. He'll take a good idea from anyone, but doesn't want to hear a bad idea from anyone, including himself. And so if you come to him with a bad idea or an idea that's bullshit, he's not going to say, "Hey, that's great." There are no participation trophies in Chuck Lorre's world. In fact, one of my favorite Chuck quotes is, "If you're not scared, you're not paying attention." It's so true.

> But the show that *Big Bang* was in year one was certainly not the same show it was by year three or year four, and that was because of eventual showrunnner Steve Molaro. The second-generation Italian-American from Queens says growing up, he was a sedentary, lonely, only child, who found comfort in iconic sitcoms like *Happy Days*, *Laverne & Shirley*, and *Mork & Mindy*. But the real connection for Molaro in regards to *Big Bang* was "the emotions and feelings I had growing up and feeling like an outcast, which lent itself to a deeper understanding of these characters."

Steve Molaro: I was the only writer that got hired without actually meeting Chuck because he was in New York when I had my meeting with Bill in Los Angeles. Bill was excited to hear about my love of *Star Trek* conventions, and he responded strongly to my writing samples. Bill called Chuck and said, "Please meet him, because I want to hire him," and Chuck was like, "It's fine. If you're excited about him, hire him."

> Molaro was also dialed into the mindset and interests of a younger generation, having written for *Zoey 101*, *iCarly*, *Drake & Josh*, and *What I Like About You*.

Bill Prady: I said to Chuck, "We *absolutely* need this guy. We're gonna need this guy to make this show."

Steve Molaro: I was the lowest-level writer there in the beginning. In fact, I was often not even *in* the writers room. I was doing things like rewriting promos or trying to come up with story pitches. In a typical show, the writers room will break a story, make an outline, and then send one writer off with a fairly detailed outline. Then they'll come back days or a week later with a first draft. And then the showrunner will go through that script, and there'll be rewrites and all that kind of stuff. But Chuck's shows are all gang-written, which moves super fast and is intense. Everyone's writing together, so it was hard to find spots to pitch because it was basically being written live in front of you on the screen. There was a stretch of time where I was struggling to just get anything in. And, especially at my lower level—and already being very nervous—just being around these guys who were really funny and knew Chuck's rhythms was a crazy, intimidating game of trying to find my place and not getting in the way.

Lee Aronsohn: There's no security on the writing staff of a new sitcom, so I think it was very tough for the staff writers because they were trying to execute something that was also not clear. When the showrunners have a clear vision and can communicate that to the staff, then you're able to do it or not able to do it. When the showrunners aren't sure and are finding their footing or changing their minds a lot, then it drives the staff crazy because you can spend the morning writing something and then someone will come in and say, "No, this doesn't work, and start all over again." So I had a lot of sympathy for Steve and the other staff writers that first year, because trying to get a sitcom off the ground is one of the hardest things.

Steve Molaro: I remember Don Foster [an upper-level writer] said to me, "You know, if you want, pitch to me, and I'm happy to pitch it to Chuck. And if it goes in, I will give you credit. If it doesn't go in, I'll take the hit." That was a nice buffer while I was getting my feet under me, and Don was very nurturing. But it was a tough place to be early on, and Chuck and Bill will agree. We didn't quite know what the show was yet, and I felt like I was not being helpful or productive.

Those growing pains extended to the role of director as well. Although veteran Jimmy Burrows—best known for directing *Friends, Cheers, Taxi, Will & Grace*, etc.—had helmed both pilots, he went on to other projects afterward, leaving the role open for various directors.

Lee Aronsohn: For any director to succeed on a Chuck Lorre show, they have to be very collaborative, because basically television is the showrunner's medium, not the director's medium. Jimmy Burrows did both pilots of *Big Bang*, but Jimmy doesn't stick around. He just goes home and counts the money. [*Laughs*]

Mark Cendrowski, best known at the time for directing *Yes, Dear, According to Jim, The King of Queens*, and even a couple episodes of *8 Simple Rules*, was brought in for episode two.

Mark Cendrowski: Chuck had put out feelers for me prior to *Big Bang*, but I was doing another show. I had never met him; we just knew of each other. Eventually I interviewed for *Big Bang* and he mentioned he liked something I did on *King of Queens* because it was a little different. But what I think cemented that first interview was when Bill Prady—who is from Detroit—said, "You're from Detroit as well, right? Are you a Tigers fan?" And I said, "Oh yeah, I'm a big Tigers fan!" It was nice to have that personal connection in addition to the work one. And eventually they had me come on to do a few more episodes.

Still, the plan wasn't for Cendrowski—or really anyone—to become the "resident" director on *Big Bang*. It was only a few episodes later when another director—whom Cendrowski declines to name—was fired in the middle of the week that Cendrowski was asked to come in and take over the episode.

Mark Cendrowski: They called me up and said, "Are you available to come back and finish this episode?" I was doing *Rules of Engagement*, but we worked it out, and I came back and finished that episode. And they were like, "Oh, you saved the show!" And I was like, "Not really, I *finished* the show." But that sort of solidified it, like, "He's the guy, he's the director." And then I became *the* guy after that.

Lee Aronsohn: Mark was the perfect director for the show because he was good with the actors and very collaborative. If we knew what we wanted, he would give it to us, which a lot of directors can't. A lot of directors don't even know where the joke is. You have to tell them where to point the camera to get the joke.

Cendrowski directed thirteen out of the seventeen episodes in season one. It was evident from the series' second episode when Sheldon and Leonard had to move a huge piece of furniture up the stairs to Penny's apartment that he was the right fit.

Mark Cendrowski: All that was written in the script was "Montage of guys trying to get shelving unit in box up the stairs." That was it. So in rehearsals we came up with six bits on the stairs, or two bits on each landing. We did them in the run-through, and the writers loved it. We ended up using three of them—the idea that they got it up so far and then it slid down. It was just simple little stuff, but the actors were into it. I think that endeared me to Chuck and the writers.

Johnny Galecki: There was a great comedic moment there, but it was also the first moment where Jim and I looked at each other and heard the audience laughing and we felt like something special's going on here. We really connected.

Jim Parsons: It was our first episode to shoot in the regular season because it had been months since we had been on that stage to shoot the pilot. So, really, what I remember most of all is the sensation of going, "My God, we're starting this journey! This job has begun!"

Mark Cendrowski: I have done plenty of shows I don't think are that funny, and it's a paycheck, but this was different.

Of course, from the title of the episode alone—"The Big Bran Hypothesis"— one would have no clue what the episode was actually about (in this case it referenced Sheldon having Big Bran cereal), but that was also kind of the point.

Lee Aronsohn: The idea to name the episodes like that came from Bill Prady, even though you can't possibly remember them, which goes for most sitcoms. That's why with *Friends* they did "The One Where..." for every title, since that's how you talk about episodes.

Bill Prady: I wanted a naming scheme, and I pitched a few before suggesting that each episode's title sound like a scientific theory, law, or phenomenon. We had a giant list of "science-y" words that was tacked up on the wall in the writers room. We had a rule that we wouldn't reuse a word in the same season. Sometimes it would take as long as an hour to come up with a title. Chuck never stayed for that.

Steve Holland (executive producer, showrunner): We would sometimes play this game in the room of "Say an episode title" and be like, "What happened in it? Go!" We were not good at it.

Episodes three and four introduced two *Roseanne* fan favorites—Sara Gilbert (Darlene Conner) as scientist Leslie Winkle, and Laurie Metcalf (Jackie Harris) as Sheldon's religious mother from Texas, Mary Cooper. Although *Roseanne* had been off the air for nearly ten years, it marked a reunion of sorts for Lorre, who was a writer and co-executive producer on the series, and Galecki, who played David Healey, Darlene's boyfriend and eventual husband. While one could assume it was a bit of stunt casting to cast them on *Big Bang*, Lorre says that wasn't the case.

Chuck Lorre: I was just a fan of them and we wanted to work with them. When you're writing a part, say, for a love interest for Leonard, and you want Leonard to perhaps be dating a scientist who is as good as or better than him, and was a prickly character, you think, *Hmmm, who do we know?* [*Laughs*] And Sara was wonderful.

Kaley Cuoco: I knew Sara and Johnny were super close and they are still really good friends. He was so excited she was going to come on the show.

Johnny Galecki: It was amazing to have her on. I will say, it was weird because we were playing different characters than Darlene and David, but still there was a comfort level to it. The episode when we were playing the cello messed me up a little bit, though, because the writers had asked if I played an instrument, and I said, "Yeah, I play a lot of instruments!" In reality, I hadn't touched my cello in years. So I think they were expecting more. [*Laughs*] And that's fair!

Sara Gilbert—seen here with Kaley Cuoco during a break in filming—is best known for playing Darlene Conner on *Roseanne*, but was also a regular during *Big Bang Theory*'s early years as Dr. Leslie Winkle, an experimental physicist. She dated Leonard briefly before he got together with Penny. *Courtesy of Kaley Cuoco photo collection*

The writers wanted to see if a relationship between Leonard and Leslie might take off, but it kind of fizzled, especially since viewers were holding out for a Leonard-and-Penny pairing.

Steve Molaro: We wanted love interests for Leonard and we were just looking for stories. It was also a great way to add female scientists, because Leslie was at the university as well. And Chuck had a history with Sara from *Roseanne*. But we were never looking for a permanent, everlasting relationship for Leonard because we always thought he would date Penny on and off. We weren't looking to find a permanent girlfriend for him. We were adding characters and seeing what worked and what was leading to fun stories.

Lee Aronsohn: We tried a couple of women in love interest roles, social-interest roles, before we came up with Amy Farrah Fowler and Bernadette Rostenkowski, and Leslie Winkle was one of them. There was also Sara Rue. We were realizing that if we wanted the show to have longevity, we had to enlarge the family.

Steve Molaro: But we never planned too far ahead because we wanted things to unfold organically. We never arced ahead in anything, except in season twelve we were starting to plan ahead to an ending and Sheldon winning the Nobel Prize. But as far as relationships and adding characters, we really preferred to add them and see how it felt, and see how it grew naturally.

> **Laurie Metcalf made her first appearance in the fourth episode, titled "The Luminous Fish Effect," after Lorre, knowing that she was close to Galecki, asked him to see if she was interested. In the story, Mary comes to town when Leonard tells her that Sheldon's been fired from Caltech. Mary explains that Sheldon gets his temper from his dad, and all the science stuff "comes from Jesus."**

Laurie Metcalf ("Mary Cooper"): Johnny asked me if I would be interested in coming on. It was like old home week because there were so many people in the cast and crew and writers that knew each other from the *Roseanne* days. And I just remember being really impressed by everybody's work ethic. Even though it was early on it felt like an ensemble. And I kept coming back because the writing was incredible.

Johnny Galecki: Laurie and I had worked together a lot since the original *Roseanne*. I was asked to go on *The Norm Show*, which Laurie was on, and said I'll do it if I can kiss Laurie Metcalf, which I'm not sure if she knows about. So they wrote me in as a younger man that she was dating. [*Laughs*] I did two episodes, and Norm made fun of her for robbing the cradle.

Chuck Lorre: Laurie was just magical and hilarious as this deeply religious woman from Texas. She never parodied the character. She played the character with a great deal of affection. Those were some of my favorite episodes.

Laurie Metcalf: I give full credit to the writers for coming up with that brilliant combination of religion and science in the mom and the son. There

The *Roseanne* reunion continued on *Big Bang* with the addition of Laurie Metcalf as Sheldon's mother, Mary Cooper. (Also pictured: Costume designer Mary T. Quigley, Johnny Galecki, and *Big Bang* co-creator Chuck Lorre, who all worked together on *Roseanne* with Metcalf). *Courtesy of Kaley Cuoco photo collection*

were tenfold reasons for these two to butt heads during the course of the show.

Jim Parsons: It was—in the best way—really heavy having her on the show. It added even more weight if an actor like Laurie Metcalf was joining us. When I learned she was going to play my mother, it felt like an answered prayer that I hadn't even specifically prayed for. I was like, *This experience is going perhaps even better than I knew!* She may have been like, "You know what, I'd like a trip to Greece, I'm going to go on this show to get this paycheck!" But I don't think that's what she was doing, though. [*Laughs*] One of my favorite moments with Laurie was when we were doing a scene where she's tucking Sheldon into bed, and in between takes, she whispered into my ear a very intimate secret, almost a kind of gossipy story, until they'd say, "And action!" and she'd shut up and do her part. Then we'd cut, and in that real dim light of the bedroom, she'd whisper the rest to me. [*Laughs*]

Laurie Metcalf: Jim and I hit it off and bonded so quickly that he and I are still looking for something to do together, perhaps onstage. Jim takes the job seriously, while still being able to have fun. And I did *not* go on the show just for a paycheck! [*Laughs*] Sometimes it's just about who you want to work with. I'm always surprised fans know all my episodes because I was in so few of them in the big picture. I think they remember me being around more than I actually was.

> For the show's first Halloween-themed episode that year—titled "The Middle Earth Paradigm"—Penny's ex-boyfriend, Kurt, shows up at her costume party and bullies Leonard. For Galecki, it was an emotional moment, but not for the reasons viewers would have known.

Johnny Galecki: I very much remember that moment. It was a complex episode for me because I didn't feel a lot of personal connection with Leonard initially. And that episode—although I know it's not our best episode by any means—is where I felt I really met Leonard. He was bullied by Penny's ex-boyfriend, Kurt, and him picking me up as Leonard really affected me to the point where I think I cried after we shot the episode. I shared that with Kaley and Jim at the time because it really dug up some old schoolyard stuff for me. It didn't happen all week during rehearsal; it was only when we shot it that it really hit home—in a good way, though, because I had a way into Leonard and really began to understand him. Still, it kind of felt like an after-school special episode, which I hate, but we were still finding our footing.

> It also showed viewers the kind of guy Leonard was at his core. When a drunk Penny apologizes to Leonard on behalf of her ex, she starts to break down herself, upset for choosing guys like Kurt. And then, in her emotional state, she kisses him. Leonard is stunned, but before it goes any further, he asks how much she's had to drink, and if this moment is more a result of her being upset with what's happened with Kurt. When she says yes and commends Leonard for recognizing that, they both agree that she should leave.

Johnny Galecki: I hope I have carried some of Leonard's traits like that with me in real life. When you love a character, there's certain things you want to retain from them on a cellular level. And there are certain things about Leonard that I certainly hope is the case.

Bill Prady: The story for me was very personal. When Penny gets drunk and comes on to Leonard, he basically says, "That's not how I want this to happen." And here's the thing about writers rooms: If you're gonna write about pain, you've gotta be brave, and talk about painful, embarrassing, awful moments from your life. So I told the story of my life in my twenties when I had fallen for a girl who had a boyfriend, and there was a party, she'd had a lot to drink, and all the sudden she let me know she was an option. And I said no. That was not how I wanted to have that experience with a person who was drunk and angry and possibly doing it for revenge. Chuck mocked me mercilessly. [*Laughs*] And then we wrote the episode.

But the momentum that was building with episodes such as that soon ground to a halt. On November 5, 2007, twelve thousand film and television screenwriters of the American labor unions Writers Guild of America, East, and Writers Guild of America, West, went on strike. Productions were forced to shut down for the foreseeable future, which was difficult enough for established shows, but nearly unsurvivable for freshman series. On the same day that the strike began, *Big Bang* was airing its seventh episode, "The Dumpling Paradox." They only had one other episode completed—episode eight, "The Grasshopper Experiment"—which would air a week later, on November 12, 2007 (and interestingly was directed by Ted Wass, Mayim Bialik's father on *Blossom*).

Kaley Cuoco: I don't think I knew how serious the writers' strike was; just like with COVID-19 when we were shutting down in the middle of filming *The Flight Attendant*. I was like, "You guys, we'll be back in a few weeks. Everyone needs to calm down." This is what I was telling my poor crew. With the writers' strike, I was like, "Guys, this is going to be fine." Little did I know how long it would be.

Chuck Lorre: We were shut down for one hundred days. No one knew what was going to happen. No one knew if we were going to get canceled.

Kunal Nayyar: I remember driving to set the first day on *Big Bang* and seeing BMWs and Audis and Lexuses, and I was in this Nissan Altima that I had bought for $3,000 at a car auction. I mean, the side mirror was held together with Scotch tape. But when I saw the other cars parked in front of our stage, I was like, "I don't care if I spend all of my paycheck on a car, but I need to get out of this car." So I went and bought a nicer car. And of course, eight episodes into *Big Bang*'s run, the writers' strike happened, and now I had this beautiful Audi TT and was like, "Oh my God."

Johnny Galecki: I moved back to New York with my girlfriend at the time, and I was very emotional about it. And this was a show I had turned down five times! I'd even cry sometimes, telling my girlfriend, "They took my show away." One hundred days felt like such a long time. I don't think I ever gained a true gratefulness for being on the show until the writers' strike.

Big Bang wasn't an out-of-the-gate hit, but it was doing well enough prior to the strike. The producers were terrified that audiences would lose interest without new episodes on the air.

Lee Aronsohn: Chuck and I were very concerned that the early momentum and ratings success would dissipate over the course of the strike and the audience wouldn't come back for it. I know that affected Bill a lot. And Bill was a strike captain.

Bill Prady: Joel Murray was the director when we were shut down in the middle of the episode ("The Cooper-Hofstadter Polarization"), and I was beside myself. I believed in the issues of the strike, because the strike was about the emergence of streaming, and making sure that the Writers Guild had jurisdiction over streaming. It wasn't prescient to see—fifteen years ago—that the business was going to change into what it is right now. And if the Guild hadn't gotten jurisdiction over streaming, it would have been a terrible thing. One of the silver linings was that as a strike captain, it kept me from sitting at home. If I sat home during that, I don't know if I would have been able to cope with the emotion of the show shutting down. I was out there picketing five days a week. It gave me a place to go, something to focus on, and camaraderie and friends that I have to this day.

Steve Molaro: Personally, it was hard. My income stopped, and I had two kids and a mortgage. That's always a little scary. And it wasn't like we were hanging out at home, stockpiling scripts for when it was over. We were all out there picketing.

And then something unforeseen happened. CBS began repeating the first eight episodes over and over again, which not only created familiarity for

those who had already seen the show, but gave those who hadn't had a chance to watch something "new." And without streaming services like Netflix or Hulu at the time, choices were limited.

Jim Parsons: In my opinion, the strike was one of the most accidentally fortuitous things that could have happened to us because CBS re-aired our first eight episodes over and over.

Chuck Lorre: In a way, it was an early Netflix experiment. The show was always available to be seen.

Kaley Cuoco: Episodes were being shown on flights, and it got us a lot of traction. I started having people come up to me to say, "Oh my God, I watched some episodes on my flight home the other day and it was so funny!" People that wouldn't have looked twice kind of got forced to watch it in a way. [*Laughs*]

Jim Parsons: It was a really weird but magical time. We were in limbo and we didn't know what was going to happen, exactly, but we weren't necessarily down about it; we were just kind of running around town, and Simon and his wife, Jocelyn, was the first close friendship that Todd and I had in LA. We had the holidays through that writers' strike and we all bought each other way too many gifts. We even had a family Christmas Eve festival! We were all very much in love. The four of us played Mexican dominoes every night. I was also within walking distance enough to Simon that even if we were going to get together that night, we'd still get coffee earlier in the day and drive around or whatever. We just couldn't get enough of each other.

Simon Helberg: Jim and I were just eating our feelings, because we didn't know if or when the show was going to come back. We did start to hear that when CBS was rerunning the show, the ratings were going up, so that was exciting. But still, it took a while. The insecurity of getting canceled is just always there. I remember it taking me such a long time to put a nail on the wall of my dressing room and hang up a picture. Once we had some job security and the show was doing well, I hung up a picture of Jim and I eating. I'm kidding.

The strike ended on February 12, 2008. Chuck Lorre and Bill Prady hit the ground running, making it clear to the cast and crew that the next nine weeks would be crucial to the show's survival.

Steve Molaro: The strike helped make the show a hit, without a doubt. But many shows threw in the towel, like, "We'll just start again in season two." And Chuck said, "Nope, we're gonna come back and make as many episodes as we possibly can." Only two new shows came back—I believe ours and [the action-comedy series] *Chuck.* And since a lot of people watched us in reruns, they were excited to see us come back with new episodes, not to mention since there wasn't a lot else out there. That combination really kind of set the show's foundation with the audience.

Jim Parsons: And then we came back to even better ratings. We didn't jump from zero to eighty, so it was a gradual enough experience for me that by the time we were being noticed, we had done so much work already.

Bill Prady: The first season of a show is a whitewater raft ride down a river with no break. You do not get a moment to sit quietly on the banks of the river and think. But now we had that chance. When we went back to work, it was very clear that the show had marinated in everyone's mind. The things that ultimately would be hallmarks of the show had occurred to everybody, and how relationships would work among the characters, what kinds of stories worked better, etc., were evident. There was a very different energy to the writing of the show after the writers' strike.

Chuck Lorre: I was relentless. We weren't supposed to write during the writers' strike, so we couldn't stockpile scripts. That was against the rules. But I remember just being maniacal about it when we came back. We produced nine episodes in two months. My mantra was, "We. Are. Not. Going. To. Let. This. Thing. Fail."

And they didn't. On February 14, two days after the strike ended, CBS renewed *The Big Bang Theory* for a second season.

Bill Prady: Every renewal was a moment of pure joy, but that renewal came in very early. It was clearly related to the success CBS had re-airing those first eight episodes during the strike. There's no other logical explanation.

Nina Tassler: By the time we did come back, the fan base was beginning to build up and viewership had increased.

But the producers couldn't celebrate for too long; they had a show to make. Interestingly, one of the most memorable character traits to occur over the series happened by accident while filming the tenth episode—titled "The Loobenfeld Decay." It was there that the studio audience witnessed Sheldon walk over to Penny's apartment and knock three times before he entered.

Lee Aronsohn: It was just one of those things where the stage direction was *Sheldon knocks on the door, Penny answers.* And I just said, "What if he does this?" And I demonstrated that instead of one knock and Penny opens the door, it was three knocks. It showed Sheldon's obsessive compulsiveness. People like that like patterns and structure, so we had some fun with Sheldon once that got established. There was one time he knocked on her door twice, and on the second one she opened the door, and Sheldon could just not continue! He struggled and struggled and struggled and finally had to go back to the door and go, knock, knock, knock, Penny. [*Laughs*]

Peter Chakos (editor, co–executive producer): I was there when Lee did it. It was just a moment where Sheldon knocked once and Penny answered. I saw Lee acting it out in his head and thinking, *If Sheldon knocks three times, is that funny?* And then he pitched it, and that became fodder for the series.

Years later in season ten, the writers decided to reveal that Sheldon's reason for knocking three times wasn't quite because of his OCD tendencies after all. He tells Penny that when he was thirteen years old, he walked in on his father, George Sr., with another woman—and although his father saw Sheldon appear at the door, the two never talked about it again. Sheldon reveals that it's why he never opens a door without knocking three times. "The first is traditional, but two and three are for people to get their pants on," he says. Aronsohn, having departed in the middle of season four, was not aware of the development.

Lee Aronsohn: I was gone by the time they came up with that, but that's brilliant reverse engineering. Certainly from a story and character point of view, I love the explanation that he obviously was traumatized by walking in on his father. That's from the Molaro years. And I was gone by that time. So kudos.

Steve Holland: We came up with that reveal kind of in the moment, but I remember some crew people being upset by that revelation. One person said, "It's upsetting that that is why he does that. I don't like that his knock is from this darker place."

Tara Hernandez (co-executive producer, writer): We weren't looking for an opportunity to justify that behavior, but it came up really organically in the room, where he's talking to Penny and he says this is why I knock three times. It scared a lot of people because something that was played off as really silly and a joke was actually rooted in something kind of traumatic for Sheldon. Moments like that, that are kind of scary, are always my favorite in a writers room because people are going to react very strongly. We talked about it a lot, but ultimately we trusted that it felt real for Sheldon so it should go in the show, whether that brought up complicated feelings for people or not.

Steve Molaro: I think the real answer is, we were just trying to find a way to add some weight and importance to the scene when he said it, and that was a way to do it. Had I known it would end up having an impact on *Young Sheldon*, I might have thought twice about it. [*Laughs*]

The introduction of "Soft Kitty" was also a significant midway addition to season one. In episode eleven, "The Pancake Batter Anomaly," Sheldon is sick with a cold, and he makes Penny learn the childhood tune so she can sing it to him.

Bill Prady: When we were writing that episode, we were trying to think of specific things Sheldon's mother would have done for him. What happened in Sheldon's childhood was always a question because he carried most of those things forward into his adult life. I mentioned that when my daughter attended Sherman Oaks Nursery School, she loved when they would sing "Soft Kitty." As best I could figure out, one of the nursery school teachers was Australian or had worked in Australia because it's a children's song that's kind of known over there. There was a big kerfuffle with the rights to it, but the Warner Music people researched it and researched it and said they couldn't find any evidence of ownership, so they called it public domain. It eventually became a big legal thing, but ultimately I guess it worked out, because they use it in *Young Sheldon*. When it came time to teach it to people, I don't sing very well, and people couldn't get the melody, so I asked Scott London if he had a recorder. I played it for Jim on the recorder and that's how he learned it. Also, fun fact, but when Jim played "Greensleeves" on the recorder in season four, that's actually me playing.

Jim Parsons learned the melody for "Soft Kitty" thanks to co-creator Bill Prady playing it for him on the recorder. They also practiced "Greensleeves." Their tour has yet to be announced. *Courtesy of Dave Goetsch*

Perhaps even more important than the actual song was the sweetness that it brought out in Sheldon—well, usually. But when he had Penny sing it to him, it was just another example to the writers that perhaps the most important relationship in the series wasn't Leonard and Sheldon or Leonard and Penny, but Sheldon and Penny.

Ken Miller: The chemistry became so impactful between those two characters. The writers saw it helped soften Sheldon's edges even more by allowing Penny to be the one person that really got him.

Steve Holland: We found out early on that Sheldon and Penny were a powerhouse combination. There was something very funny and sweet about that relationship. I think some of our best scenes were those two. They were so opposite, and they frustrated each other, but there was this deep, deep love.

Jim Parsons: I've had people request the song a couple of times when they meet me, but it's really rare. I think I might have said to some people, "I only do that for money." [*Laughs*] Which I don't mean quite as rude as it sounds. I am not a freebie request for one-liners or one songs, no thank you!

> **Even though the characters were clicking and the writers were finding success by digging deeper into their quirks and personalities, things still weren't as smooth behind the scenes. With half a dozen episodes left to film in season one, Molaro was beginning to question whether the show was the right fit for him.**

Steve Molaro: I wasn't happy. I had an opportunity to go back to Nickelodeon, which is where I started my career, so at the end of season one, I made arrangements to quit. I actually did quit and was let out of my contract. Chuck was all right with it, but at the same time, he wanted me to stay.

Chuck Lorre: A tremendous amount of discovery had to happen in a really short amount of time, so I can understand looking back why Molaro needed to leave. It was not a happy place early on. There was a lot of fear that we were not going to succeed, and the writers' strike added to that fear.

Steve Molaro: Chuck was always very supportive of me. And while he could be intense to work with, it was more just a thing you feel in the air, rather than "at me." He was also doing *Two and a Half Men*, which was on fire at the time, so there was not a lot of time for goofin' around.

Lee Aronsohn: Chuck and I made the case to Steve that he really had a future if he stuck around, but of course, we had no idea at the time that *Big Bang* was going to become the biggest hit on television and run for twelve years. So he had a very difficult decision to make. He had a family and he was being offered a degree of security at Nickelodeon that could not be offered by Chuck at the time.

Steve Molaro: At the season one wrap party, Chuck said, "If you change your mind, I am holding the door open to you. Even if it's at the last minute, just come back." I really was wrestling with my decision, especially because once we got to the end of the season, I started to feel a bit more at ease. Chuck even said, "Well, maybe that's your subconscious telling you to stay. Listen to that." So we went into that hiatus, and the thought of leaving, which I basically had because I had resumed working at Nickelodeon, was really making me ill. I couldn't sleep. In fact, I didn't sleep for about two months. And finally, a day before the writers room was going to commence for season two, I couldn't take it anymore. The cells in my body were telling me, *You need to un-quit and go back.* So, I called Bill and said, "I think I want to come back." There was a moment of silence, and then he said, "Great! I'll see you on Monday!" And that was the first night I had slept in months.

Bill Prady: The first three years were hard. It was not an easy show to write. When the premise of the show is that the characters have a completely different outlook on the world, you spend a lot of time just trying to get into their mindset. There were people that I've known and loved and brought in who were not right. It was heartbreaking and very painful. I lost a friendship or two. It probably was around the fourth season where there was a rhythm and we knew the show we were making. It's growing pains. And it's a common experience when you're making a show. Everybody who came to work in the writers room in that show was remarkably talented.

Peter Chakos: If Molaro had left, it would have changed everything because Molaro put more heart and soul into the show. It became a much more emotional show. The characters grew.

Jim Parsons: A lot of people who are fans of the show wouldn't know Steve if they saw his picture, but if you take that piece out of the puzzle, I don't know how long we go for, and I certainly don't know the quality we go on with. It's a little harrowing to think what would have happened had he left the show.

Lorre and Prady were also faced with losing editor Peter Chakos, who would win five Emmys over the course of *Big Bang*'s run. In fact, he was so instrumental to the show that he had a co-executive producer credit as well. But there was friction with Lee Aronsohn, which escalated as the season came to a close.

Peter Chakos: I know the difference between making something better [in the editing room] and making something different, and sure, Lee made some things better. But 90 percent was making things different, and not always in a good way. And then Chuck would come in and undo it all. That's what drove me crazy, and that happened over and over and over again. When we came back from the writers' strike, I was editing the last episode of season one, and I told our producer, Faye Oshima Belyeu, that she should look for another editor. She told Bill, and then five minutes later, Chuck was in my room, and he's like, "You're leaving?" and I said, "Yes." He pretty much said, "I'll fire him," and I said, "You can't fire one of the showrunners because the editor doesn't like him," and he said, "Well, I'll tell him to back off." I said, "OK, that could work. But if he doesn't back off, then I'm gone again." And he did lay off. It was a lot better, but the first season was torturous.

Lee Aronsohn: I drove Peter Chakos absolutely nuts. He is a brilliant editor, but I would go in and have him make so many minute changes that I am sure in his eyes made no difference whatsoever, but to me improved a joke or improved a shot. I know it drove him insane. And Chuck will say I am kind of a control freak with actors. He'd say I'd shove my hand up their ass and move their mouth with my hands if I could. [*Laughs*]

Chuck Lorre: In all fairness, Lee drove everyone nuts. [*Laughs*] But he was a very powerful help in the early days in getting the show on its feet.

As the season one finale neared, the writers decided to take a major step forward in the possibility of a Penny and Leonard romance coming to life. Throughout the season, Penny was affectionate with Leonard, but never to the point where you believed she'd actually want to date him. That all changed in episode seventeen, "The Tangerine Factor" ("I don't think it should be called a finale; it was just the last episode of that season," Molaro says. "We didn't know how many we'd be making that first year."), when Penny breaks up with her latest guy of the month after he writes about their sex life on his blog. Thanks to the clever use and explanation of Schrödinger's Cat—and a vulnerable and fed-up Penny—she says yes when Leonard gets the courage to ask her out. The studio audience broke out in applause.

Chuck Lorre: It was one of the moments that led me to believe something special was happening, beyond what we'd ever imagined. People were even coming to the taping dressed in lab coats and things! The audience was totally invested in these two fictional characters. And the fact that there was hope for that relationship is why they were applauding, cheering. You know, "Oh, boy, Leonard's gonna have the dream date!" And when the audience cares about fictional characters, it's wonderful. I know it's make-believe, but you still get swept away.

Johnny Galecki: I remember it because in the first failed pilot the audience was not rooting for Leonard and Katie, so it felt great to have that enthusiasm for Leonard and Penny. That's exactly what I had hoped for when joining the show, to be in these stories involving matters of the heart. The audience went crazy. And in the same manner, when she said she's in love with him years later, the audience went crazy, too. I get very emotional even thinking about it now. It was really beautiful. You can't create that out of nothing. Those sentiments came from honesty and reality.

Bill Prady: Steve and I wrote that episode, and we were struggling because in the original outline he never asked her out at the end. The original version of the story was Leonard imagined going out with Penny, and he decides to rehearse the date with Sheldon playing the part of Penny. And the rehearsal goes so bad that he doesn't ask her out. We worked on it for hours and hours, until we finally called Chuck. He said, "This doesn't make sense; no matter how bad the rehearsal date goes, it's Sheldon's fault. It's not actually Penny there, it's Sheldon. See what happens if he asks her out." So we went back, and I think we got to the place where if he asked her out, we couldn't think of any reason why she wouldn't say yes. I think she would be curious. And even though Leonard found her very attractive, that wasn't the basis for his interest in her. He was a different kind of guy for her. All men start by being attracted to someone, and for some men, that's enough. But Leonard isn't that kind of person. He was a different kind of man for Penny than those she had previously encountered. It was the first of many, many times when we'd write ourselves into a corner at the end of the year, and hope that we or the other writers who showed up after a hiatus could figure a way out of it. [*Laughs*]

Mark Cendrowski: My daughter played softball, and one of her coaches, who is in construction, came up to me and said, "You're the director of *The Big Bang Theory*, aren't you?" I was shocked he even knew that, but also because he just didn't seem like the type of guy I expected to watch it. But he said, "What Leonard is going through…you don't have to be a nerd to understand what it's like to have trouble talking to a beautiful girl." And that's when I realized, *Oh, these stories are universal. This is not just for a specific audience.* I went home saying, "I feel very good about this show."

And in the hands of another creator, it might not have worked, but Chuck Lorre—even with all his fear, anxiety, and trepidation about failing—knew what he was doing.

Eddie Gorodetsky: People always talk about Chuck having all this hubris, but it's interesting that Chuck has always been willing to take a cold, hard look at things and see what doesn't work and adjust accordingly. The original pilot to *Big Bang* is a great example. Compare that to the current streaming model where they make ten episodes before they even put it on the air. You have no chance to be surprised by breakout characters—no matter how smart you think you are, the audience will surprise you. That's the reason Chuck keeps doing it and why he's so good at it. And that's why a lot of places are having a hard time delivering multicams. There is nothing wrong with the form—it's the way people have devalued it. You usually work six episodes ahead in multicam, but Chuck would never let us do more than three episodes, because no matter if you think you know what you're doing, you're always going to be surprised. It's kind of like Chuck is in the business of making unicorns now.

Chapter 6

THE COMIC-CON INITIATION

If the writers' strike helped make *Big Bang* a hit, then San Diego Comic-Con International was proof of that success. *Big Bang* finished sixty-eighth in the ratings following its first season and had already been renewed for season two, but without the advantage of social media as we know it, it was hard to pinpoint just how invested the fandom was. That all changed on Friday, July 25, 2008, at 10:15 a.m., when *The Big Bang Theory* made its Comic-Con debut to a standing-room-only crowd of about three thousand adoring fans. Formally billed as "positive proof that physics is funny," the audience watched a screening of "The Nerdvana Annihilation," the fourteenth episode of the series (where Leonard buys a full-size replica of the time machine from the film *The Time Machine*), before a Q&A with Lorre, Prady, Galecki, Parsons, Cuoco, Helberg, and Nayyar. What happened during that trip was proof that they were now bona fide stars.

Johnny Galecki: We were on the train from LA to San Diego, and I showed Chuck the schedule with shows like *Battlestar Galactica* on it. I said, "Nobody's going to show up, man. This is going to be a disaster. We should just get on the next train and turn around."

Kaley Cuoco: Johnny was making it like doomsday. He was like, "This is not going to go well, no one is going to come." It was very depressing.

Johnny Galecki: It's because we were a sitcom, and Comic-Con is about sci-fi. And they had one of the largest arenas reserved for us in that time slot, and I was like, "This is going to be a mess." And we tried to get out of it on the train while we were on the way there, but we couldn't.

Chuck Lorre: I thought going to Comic-Con was a horrible idea, even though I was game to go to San Diego. I thought there would be eleven people in an auditorium and it would be horribly embarrassing. I even prepped the cast. I said, "No matter how many people come, let's have a good time! Let's go for it. Don't be disheartened."

Johnny Galecki: So after we got off the train, we were in a shuttle bus headed to the hotel when we learned that people had camped out overnight.

Kaley Cuoco: We saw a line of people for miles. I said, "Oh my God! I wonder what that line is for?" And our driver says, "It's for you! It's for *The Big Bang Theory*!" We thought, *No, you have that wrong.*

Chuck Lorre: There were thousands of people in this convention center room. It was standing room only! And when the cast walked out on the stage, they went berserk! It was like the Beatles. It was staggering that those seventeen episodes meant so much to so many people. I remember my agent at the time talking to me about the success of *Two and a Half Men*, and I said, "You don't get it. That's *not* the show. *The Big Bang Theory* is *the* show that's going to eclipse *Two and a Half Men* by an extraordinary margin." I could only say that because I saw the kind of passion people had. I was always obsessed with our ratings because I was in a continual state of fear that we'd get canceled. It went away after that Comic-Con.

Kunal Nayyar: I was in absolute awe. There were so many people screaming that you could actually feel the vibration of energy on your skin. It was just a jaw-dropping experience, like I was living someone else's reality, not mine. And yet, there I was. It was really amazing.

Simon Helberg: People were dressed like us and grabbing us. It was very sweaty, and very loving. I guess that goes together. Passion. Passionate love. Comic-Con was a watershed moment and so was our press trip to Mexico City, which was a similar thing, only in Spanish. We were whisked through the airport and then we were on the cover of the newspaper the next day with the words "El Nerdos." Or some headline about how the nerds were invading Mexico. What's weird is that it just didn't feel that way in LA. We were the least popular kids there. I think that comes with being part of a mainstream hit, and there's stigmas that go along with it. But those two particular experiences were definitely where we realized that this show had a real specific and broad appeal.

Simon Helberg and Kunal Nayyar channeling their inner Rocky Balboa on top of the pyramids in Mexico. *Courtesy of Kunal Nayyar*

Jim Parsons: It was overwhelming in that I had never seen such a thing before. I had heard about it; I had even lived in San Diego since that's where I had gone to school. But I didn't understand what that was *at all*. It was just astounding to me to be absorbed in a mob of people that thick…I was being ushered in and out of hallways and little booths. And it seemed so otherworldly to see fans dressed like Sheldon…that's the best way I can put it. And to varying degrees, I still feel that. The thing that I used to get asked all the time was, "What is your favorite Sheldon T-shirt?" And I'd be like, "Oh, hell, I don't know! When I glance in the mirror before I run down onstage, it's to make sure the collar is lined up right!"

Lee Aronsohn: After that first year I felt there was no reason to go back to Comic-Con, because I've done it as well as anybody can ever do. And that's the last time I ever went.

At the inaugural Comic-Con panel, the audience asked the cast a wide range of questions, from who is most like their character to what is the geekiest thing they've ever done. Moderator Adam Savage (former cohost of *Mythbusters*) also used the opportunity to inquire about whether Sheldon has Asperger's. According to AutismSpeaks.org, Asperger's, which in 2013 became part of one umbrella diagnosis of autism spectrum disorder, or ASD, refers to a broad range of conditions characterized by challenges with social skills, repetitive behaviors, speech, and nonverbal communication. There is no one type of autism.

Parsons answered that he wasn't sure, even though he had previously asked the writers. The best answer he received was "that's just the way Sheldon is," and no formal diagnosis had been given. Looking back nearly fifteen years later, Lorre and the producers explain why they were hesitant to label Sheldon.

Chuck Lorre: We did not want to put a label on Sheldon, because with that comes a responsibility of authenticity... which should be respected. Our solution was the line, "I'm not crazy. My mother had me tested." And that put it to rest. Mary took Sheldon to a general practitioner in East Texas in 1990 who said, "Oh, he's fine! He's peculiar, but he's fine!" It was probably a doctor who was still smoking! I think not having a label gave Jim a great deal of more freedom to play the part as he wanted to play it, as opposed to how we might have been pressured to do for a very-real syndrome that can be difficult.

Steve Molaro: Sheldon was never diagnosed, and it was nice that he didn't have that label, because like anybody on the spectrum, they should be able to just be who they are.

Jim Parsons: I really took it as the writers wanting to celebrate and utilize certain aspects of someone on the spectrum, but were not interested in carrying the responsibility they would feel. I mean, just getting the science right was enough of a responsibility. But looking at where we are today in the world, would you have needed to then find somebody on the spectrum to play that part? Now, that being said, who's to say I'm not on the spectrum in some way? I'm not saying I am, but it's called the spectrum for a reason— I just may not be at a notable point on it! I don't know. That's the whole point in some ways. But at the time, the more I read up on Asperger's, I was like, *Well, the writers can say no, but Sheldon sure has a lot of the same traits!*

I think he was probably based on someone Bill Prady knew, who probably was on the spectrum, and many of the traits that this other individual had made them such a remarkable and unique person to base a character on. I don't think that most people—no matter what they are, or what disabilities they have—spend the majority of their time, if any, talking about it. But regardless, it was just such a gift that Sheldon had all these off-centered ways of looking at things and doing things, because it opened up so many possibilities for how he could react to any given situation.

Peter Roth: Sheldon was definitely on the spectrum, there's no question about it. And Steve Molaro wrote Sheldon with a wisdom and an insight and a compassion that really defined the character. My wife and I have an autistic daughter, and while Sheldon is very different from her, I've certainly found myself drawn to him, rooting for him, and loving him. The special needs of the character is something that enabled me to relate to and, or more importantly, to root for. It's one of the reasons I was always so touched by Sheldon and Penny's relationship. As annoying as Sheldon was, Penny accepted him and loved him.

Wendi Trilling: I remember thinking that it was cool that we had a character who was clearly on the spectrum. We weren't saying it, but we were kind of celebrating it and him, and making it okay to be different.

Bill Prady: I can't tell you how many times a parent would bring their son or daughter to set and say, "I'd love for you to meet him," followed by, almost as a warning, "He's a lot like Sheldon." I would always say, "Yeah, we get it! [*Laughs*] It's fine, really. We understand." There was never a conscious decision, as far as I'm aware, to not say what Sheldon's diagnosis is. It's clear that he's *not* neurotypical. I think there's a certain responsibility when you say, "This is *this* kind of diagnosis." We preferred that Sheldon was simply Sheldon. There were some things about him that would *seem* spectrum-y, but you would discover, in fact, a real and logical reason and warrant, and then some things that were not.

Several years after that Comic-Con panel, Prady had a discovery of his own: He, too, was on the spectrum.

Bill Prady: This was a discovery for me, around the fourth or fifth season. In doing the show, we all did a lot of reading about neuro-atypicality. I went, "Huh. That seems familiar." I was seeing a therapist, and there's a neat written test you can take, as well as other [tests] ... and it's eye-opening. To be able to say to my wife, "I miss things. I don't pick up on certain cues," has been a really terrific thing, as opposed to her getting mad with me. She'll say, "Do you know that the thing you said before was upsetting?" And I'll go, "Oh, no! Was it? I'm terribly sorry!" [*Laughs*] It's been really great to now know why.

But to me, the central question about *The Big Bang Theory* was always this debate of: Is it better to try to be in a world which is really scary? Or is it better to retreat into your own world of director's cuts, Blu-rays, and *Star Trek*, which is comforting? I always find the world terrifying. The notion of saying, "Let's do a *Lord of the Rings* rewatch"—I'm all in. Let's spend the next three days in the shire. On the other hand—and I really remember this from my twenties—I had that feeling that there's something going on out there and I'm not a part of it. And I wanna go, too. But in my youth, I was miserable in those places. My friends and I would wait forty-five minutes to get into some club, and then I'd get in there and it was loud and I had sensory overload and I was miserable. It's like, *I wanna go there!*, and then when I get there, I'd just want to go home and be Sheldon and pop the Blu-ray in and say, "All right, *Galaxy Quest*, here we are, my old friend." I related to that.

Chuck Lorre: And at Comic-Con that first year, I realized the show was touching people on a much deeper, emotional level than I could have possibly anticipated. It's why I never liked the word *nerd*, or *nerd comedy*, because I saw them as brilliant people who were feeling left out, feeling disenfranchised and alienated from the culture many people take for granted. I had no personal relationship with being a genius, but I did understand feeling left out and incapable of being able to participate socially. That was very hard for me all my life, and at Comic-Con I realized that is a universal feeling, no matter who you are. Even if you're the queen of the prom or president of the senior class or quarterback of the team, on some level, you're feeling not enough. Those who feel they were enough, God bless 'em. There are shows for them. I don't know what those shows are, but there are other shows that will address their successful socialization skills. But *Big Bang* spoke to a deeper issue, which is, on the simplest level, loneliness and feeling left out. It promised community. *Two and a Half Men* was pretty much about jokes. It was misogynistic nonsense. You could never make that show now. But here we were inexplicably stumbling into a show that was about something. It was not simply a situation comedy. It was a show that needed to be cherished, protected.

Adam Nimoy (Leonard Nimoy's son and *Big Bang* guest star): It's such a crazy, zany show, but then they have these incredible, powerful moments of connection between the characters and it's so endearing. It's so beautiful, it makes you want to cry. It's so comforting, even inspiring, to know it's OK to be different, to be outside the mainstream, and yet still be accepted and loved and have a place in the world. And that's what it's all about for Sheldon and for me. He's an exaggerated version of us who don't see ourselves as the popular one, the social one, the one who is comfortable in a lot of situations with people around.

The success of the panel led to ten more appearances by the cast and writers over the years, but 2008 would be the last time most of the cast could get around San Diego without 24/7 security.

Bill Prady: We did our Comic-Con panel on a Friday that year, and the next day there was some room in the schedule before the Warner Bros. party, so I said, "Let's get together for drinks." There were ten of us, and everyone enjoyed themselves. And by the last Comic-Con we did, it was a catered party by the pool with security and a guest list. Needless to say, it grew.

Peter Roth: One year we needed six security guards to literally get us from the elevator at the Warner Bros. party to the cars that took us to the airport. They were mobbed. It was by far the most popular of our panels as it was reflective of the most popular show on television. Seeing people moved to tears just to meet this cast…*that's* what it's all about. That's why you do this.

Chuck Lorre: And when the cast went into the autograph session after the panel, I watched as people came up to them and started crying. Seeing the emotional response was beyond anything I could have ever dreamed of. If you weren't there, it is hard to communicate that this was something I had never seen before. And listen, I spent two years on *Roseanne*, and that was the biggest show in the world at the time. But nobody cried! I've been in restaurants with Roseanne Barr when people would come over to get an autograph; nobody got teary-eyed. [*Laughs*] Nobody stood in line and started crying to get a picture signed by Jon Cryer. They were happy to meet him, believe me, but it didn't cause that emotional response that these *Big Bang* characters represented.

That first Comic-Con was also a very memorable one for Galecki and Cuoco. They had been secretly dating for a few months (which they'll go into in greater detail later in this book) but hadn't told anyone.

Kaley Cuoco: We all had different hotel rooms at Comic-Con. There were two giant buildings for this one hotel and Johnny and I weren't even in the same building. So we were like little mice in the night, running back and forth to each other's rooms, trying not to be noticed. I mean, who did we think we were? The couple from *Notting Hill*? That we were just *so* famous that we couldn't let anyone see the two of us together? [*Laughs*]

Johnny Galecki: And it was still so new that we hadn't told the rest of the cast that we were dating yet, and here they were our closest friends. So we would all be in the hotel lobby, and Kaley and I would give each other a hug and pretend to say good night, and go our separate ways.

On that same weekend, Cuoco impulsively decided to tell Lorre that she and Galecki were an item when he inquired about her dating life.

Chuck Lorre: This is charming looking back, but I was on a shuttle bus with the cast and I was sitting next to Kaley trying to strike up a conversation. The best I could come up with was, "So...what's going on with you? You got a fella? You seeing anybody?" Like, I'm her dad or something. And she starts giggling and says, "Oh my God, you don't know?" And I said, "I don't know what? What don't I know?" And she says, "I'm seeing Johnny." I felt the earth opening up beneath me and falling because my immediate thought—which I certainly didn't say to her—was, *What if they break up? What happens if they don't want to do scenes with each other? What happens if this doesn't go well? And what happens to their on-screen relationship?* But what I said was, "Oh! Well, that's great! Congratulations! That's wonderful!" And as it turns out, obviously, they handled their relationship with such dignity and grace, and there was never a concern. But I was quite oblivious.

Kaley Cuoco: When I said, "Oh, I'm seeing Johnny," he said, "Does he make you happy?" and I said, "Yeah." And Chuck does that nod where he's in agreement, but I'm sure in the moment he was thinking of all the horrible things that could go wrong. He probably blacked out. [*Laughs*] But it was really, really cute.

> **Molaro also found out that weekend that the two were an item, but his encounter was a bit different.**

Steve Molaro: One evening it was late when I was headed back to my hotel room, but as I was walking through the lobby, I saw Johnny at the bar. I was walking over to say hello, but as I got closer I realized I was walking into what felt like an uncomfortable situation. Kaley looked like maybe she had just been crying a little. I went from going, "Hey, guys!" to "Oh, no! I should go, right?" And Kaley's like, "No, stay." And I'm like, "So, what's going on? You guys having fun here?" [*Laughs*] I didn't know they were dating. I felt so awkward, but in a way it was a great bonding moment.

Johnny Galecki: Eventually, I think the three of us all took a walk by the marina. Kaley was still crying because she was mad at me about something, but yes, it was definitely a bonding moment, and lovely, too, in a weird way. [*Laughs*]

> **Something else the cast nearly kept from Lorre and Prady during that Comic-Con trip? Their perhaps ill-advised decision to rent a boat when no one really knew how to operate one.**

Johnny Galecki: For some reason, Simon and I had this thing where we have rented a lot of boats together, which makes no sense because neither of us are sailors. But every time we went to Comic-Con and we'd rent a boat, he'd buy a captain's hat, and we'd just endanger everyone's lives.

Bill Prady: When they told us the story of how they all chartered a boat but none of them knew what they were doing, I just remember thinking, *Well, this almost ended very badly*, and my stomach just *flipped*. I don't think I've had that feeling... other than when I got a phone call from my daughter

Captain Simon Helberg at your service, or at least for Johnny Galecki's amusement. *Courtesy of Johnny Galecki*

that began, "Everyone's all right…" when she was in a car accident. So to answer the question, nausea.

Jim Parsons: Chuck was also apoplectic about it when he heard. [*Laughs*] He was like, "Wait, what? They did *what*?! Do you know how much money and insurance is in that one boat?!" Now, for what it's worth, I don't remember getting on the boat or accepting the invitation/plan to be on the boat. It just happened. I remember being on it. But looking at it now, I'm like, "I don't know if I would have said yes to that. I don't know who that was that said, 'Yes!'" I guess I was like, "Well, somebody said we were going to do it, so let's do it!" Thank God I was sober at the time. I don't even know what body of water we were in. I mean, by the grace of God do I still walk on this earth after that.

Johnny Galecki: Jim is right. Si and I trailed off from the group and returned with a boat. [*Laughs*] Jim was *very* hesitant to come aboard. And absolutely refused to jump off into the water, which I think the rest of us did whenever or wherever Captain Helberg and I deemed our location a safe depth. We truly didn't understand the financial investment of billions of dollars at hand until we saw our bosses' reactions to such behaviors. And also started to notice how the studio would split us up into different cars while on press tours and such—"Oh, I see. So if this car rolls over a land mine only half the cast / their investment is dead. Got it." And then Kaley's accident with her horse years later. That really put in perspective how many people's livelihoods our actions affected. Before then, we just saw ourselves as a weirdo, ragtag bunch of scrappy actors who didn't think enough of ourselves to understand we were of value to many people we cared about deeply.

That Comic-Con trip was technically the first time that Lorre and Prady were with the group in a social setting that was more personal than business. While out to dinner with the cast one night, they noticed that fame might be going to Nayyar's head a bit more than they'd have liked.

Chuck Lorre: It became apparent at that Comic-Con panel that something remarkable was happening to this show and this cast. I got the impression on a couple of outings where we had dinner with the cast and everyone that success/fame was messing with Kunal. Fame is fast and furious; it's disorienting when that happens, let alone when you're young and it's your first job. I remember him saying during that dinner in San Diego that he could go to India during the hiatus and do movies and make millions of dollars. It just seemed inappropriate. [*Laughs*]

Kunal Nayyar: I was saying things which were just ridiculous and behaving in a way that was not really me. I was just a kid and way out of my depth. I remember feeling very uncomfortable in my own skin. I was so insecure that I was trying to pretend I was cool or something. Pretend that I belong. It just wasn't true to my nature and I think that probably worried them.

Bill Prady: Johnny and Kaley knew how to deal with success and fame; it was not new to them. But Jim and Kunal—wow. To go out in public and experience all that [adoration] for the first time...it's, you know, a lot.

At the time of that Comic-Con dinner, Lorre and Prady didn't say anything to Nayyar, instead choosing to have a discussion with him when they were back in Los Angeles and about to start season two.

Kunal Nayyar: I'll never forget getting a call from Chuck's assistant, Mona, saying, "Hey, Chuck and Bill want you to come in. Do you have time today?" I thought, *That's it. I'm getting fired.* Something in my heart knew it. So I walked into their office and said, "Just before you start anything, tell me if I'm getting fired." And they were like, "No! You're here because we love you." But the gist of the conversation was basically, "You think you know stuff, but you don't. And we're here to tell you, you're a year out of graduate school, and this could be a *huge* show. Who are the people—agents, managers, lawyers—representing you? Do you trust them? If anyone comes to you with a business deal, ask us and we'll vet it, or we'll ask our lawyers. Be very careful with the way in which you partake of your nightly activities and the crowds that you hang around with, because everyone's going to want a piece of you. We've done this for a long time, and we've seen actors lose everything. *Everything.*" Now, this was very, very nice of them, but I'll never forget what Chuck said to me next. He said, "Kunal, the only way to survive in this industry is humility." And not that I didn't know or understand those things; I'm very lucky to come from a close-knit family, but for them to extend their hand and say, "You have us if you feel like you're in a dilemma you can't get out of," I really was grateful for that. And I never forgot it. But, to be honest, my ego was bruised, too. I thought, *What do these people think of me? That I'm just this crazy party boy doing all these things and misbehaving? And I'm not like that; I'm a professional, I show up on time.* It took me a while to truly understand the message of that meeting, which was, *We're here for you.* But I was twenty-five. Wisdom does not come overnight.

Chuck Lorre: He just needed to be told, *Slow down, calm down.* There was no question about whether he was going to be on the show. That was never the point of the meeting. The point of the meeting was to say, *Breathe, slow down, don't make any big decisions right now.* And to remind him that the ensemble was *everything*. I said, "Listen, God willing, this is a long journey, and the journey is one that should be made as an ensemble, not as *here's my solo career*. Don't leave the band and go off on your solo career so quickly!" Everybody in the cast started doing things separate from the show as the years went by and that's fine, it's a given. People want to expand their horizons. But that conversation was a little bit of a come-to-Jesus talk, as they say.

In the end, they had nothing to worry about—with any of them. And Kunal, especially, never forgot any of their words.

Kunal Nayyar: The pressure that I put on myself every single day was to not fuck up. That's it. Because if I messed up, what would my country think of me? What would my parents think of me? I put a lot of responsibility on my shoulders, and it's not exactly a healthy way to live, but I was always so afraid to lose the gift that had been given to me.

A few years after *Big Bang*'s first Comic-Con, Mayim Bialik and Melissa Rauch experienced the fandom up close when they joined the rest of their castmates.

Mayim Bialik ("Amy Farrah Fowler"): Comic-Con was very overwhelming, but it was a really good bonding experience to be able to go with the cast. They had so much more experience going than Melissa and I, so they got to catch us up. They told us to stick together and don't get separated from the pack because it's madness. We all had to follow the security guards, but I was like, "I want to go to this booth!" and they're like, "No, you're not going anywhere. We just stick together!" I remember when I got there, I was like, "These are all my people! I want to go hang out with them! I want to go to the Pokemon thing!" [*Laughs*] So I had to kind of curtail my own personal interests in Comic-Con because it was like an ocean of people. You can't just walk the floor doing your own thing. We got to see the bowels of the convention center, and we were in golf carts at back doors where it was shrimp cocktail on trays and us walking through hallways.

Melissa Rauch ("Bernadette Rostenkowski Wolowitz"): My first Comic-Con, I went to the bathroom after the panel, and when I was in the stall a green Hulk hand reached underneath with some kind of photo for me to sign. It was terrifying and hilarious and just so 1,000 percent Comic-Con. And then at my last Comic-Con that I went to, I booked a hotel about thirty minutes outside of downtown San Diego, thinking that I would fly under the radar and be out of the craziness. My husband and I were riding down in the elevator and in walk two *Big Bang* cosplayers. I'm not sure if they were part of a larger group that had other characters, but it was an interesting pairing of Sheldon and Bernadette—complete with a blonde wig and cropped cardigan. As soon as they came into the elevator I was preparing for them to ask for a picture or something. They said "Excuse me." And I said, "Hello!" And cosplayer Bernadette said coldly, "Can you hit 'lobby'?" I did and we all rode down in silence until they got off. Afterwards, a family in the elevator with us said, "Well, that was weird. We weren't going to say anything, but we can't believe they didn't notice!" We all had a good laugh and "Hit the lobby" will forever be code to my husband and I for flying under the radar. [*Laughs*]

Kevin Sussman: I've gone to Comic-Cons all over the world, and it's one of those things you don't really understand until you walk into a giant convention center and get mobbed in a foreign country. That's when I realized, *Holy moly, the popularity is insane.* I remember when I was a kid, some of my happiest times were watching shows like *Cheers* and *Taxi*. It was part of the fabric of my growing up. So to now be in a position where I am taking part in something that's that meaningful to other families? That's very special to me. And so many people would tell me, "Oh, I'm such a Stuart" or "My boyfriend's such a Stuart." I was in Saudi Arabia and a woman in a burqa came over and said, "I'm such a Stuart!"

Chapter 7

ANYTHING BUT A SOPHOMORE SLUMP

On September 22, 2008, *The Big Bang Theory*, which had finished sixty-eighth in the ratings at the end of the first season, returned for its second season with an additional two million viewers from the season one finale. Based on the first few episodes of season two, *Entertainment Weekly* noted that "when it premiered a year ago, *The Big Bang Theory* just felt like a dumb show about smart guys." But now? "As the new season proves, [it's] evolved into something better. Penny is now smarter; she's the person we identify with, who's watching the geeks with amused skepticism," and "Parsons has become the show's quivering, riveting center."

While there were still growing pains behind the scenes, the show was beginning to find its footing. Co-creator Bill Prady appointed Steve Molaro as his second-in-command, while Chuck Lorre continued pulling double duty between *Big Bang* and *Two and a Half Men*.

Bill Prady: There's a quest for what's called "the Number Two." Ultimately I championed Steve. He was getting the show on a level that other people weren't. So I said to Chuck, "This guy should come to editing, this guy should come to casting," and so on, in an effort to get him the battlefield promotion that I was hoping he would have.

Without a writers' strike to contend with, season two would be the ultimate test of whether viewers would stick around for an entire season. More specifically, the big question was what would happen for Penny and Leonard following their first date.

Bill Prady: After an exhausting first season, we came back in June and started up the writers room; just having conversations about where the season could go. I think one of the things that I ultimately came to embrace about Leonard and Penny as a couple is that they had a rough go of it, they broke up and got back together, and there were periods where they saw other people. It didn't feel the same as Ross and Rachel's relationship on *Friends*; I always believed their relationship was written as, "These people are inevitable partners." And I don't think we ever wrote Penny and Leonard that way. We said they legitimately *could* be the person for each other and we were rooting for it, but they had a lot of obstacles. So when they'd break up, it wasn't false jeopardy for the audience. Them not winding up together was an absolute legitimate path forward for the series, and it could've been. They could have easily been that couple who once went out and now are friends.

Steve Molaro: My relationship with my first girlfriend ever was very close to the dynamics between Leonard and Penny. I was an overweight, lonely outcast–late bloomer who didn't really start dating anyone until I was maybe eighteen or nineteen. The woman who ended up being my first girlfriend was very much like Penny, so it was easy for me to channel her energy into the character as the series went along. I understood Penny and Leonard's dynamic and how they impacted each other's personal growth. That first girlfriend of mine was wild and fun and had so much more experience, whereas I had zero. So it was just something that I got on a cellular level.

Unfortunately for Penny and Leonard fans, their potential coupling quickly dissolved in the season two premiere. Penny lied to Leonard about graduating from community college, but when Leonard found out, he insulted Penny by saying he was "absolutely" OK with dating someone that wasn't smart. She slammed the door in his face, and by the next episode she was already going out with someone else. (Though to be fair, that only lasted one episode as well.)

Meanwhile, if Penny was becoming a more three-dimensional character, the same couldn't be said of Howard Wolowitz, who continued to objectify women and make gross comments, such as how he was looking forward to the winter months because that's when women are vulnerable from putting on weight and would need extra loving.

Simon Helberg: It was challenging to defend him in the way that I feel like actors have a job ultimately to defend the character they're playing. I used to have an acting teacher that would say, "You have to be your character's lawyer," meaning you're trying to find their point of view. Howard was a little tricky to make human. There definitely was a layer of sleaze that was oozing off of him, but I also felt like he certainly was the butt of the joke at the same time. I felt like it was actually making fun of him. He was an offensive and inappropriate person, so I was personally pleased that he became more of a respectable human as the series progressed, and he became more three-dimensional. And the fact that you don't have to search too hard to find a handful of qualities and jokes from our show that didn't age well, to me is a good sign that we're growing up as a culture in some ways now.

Bill Prady: Wolowitz was the first one who got married on the show, and I always thought that was a great evolution. But if we were writing that role now, I think very much you'd do it differently. But the psychology underneath it was a man so *desperate* for love who had been damaged; his father abandoned him and his mother, so he had no healthy relationship to model his behavior on. He didn't have a loving mom and dad that he could look at and say, "Well, that's how you love and are loved." When he finally had a girlfriend, and could say "my girlfriend," or "my fiancée" or "my wife," those words were never taken for granted by him. I don't know if that makes up for the way some stuff is depicted, the stuff that's a little rough.

While Howard was on one path, Sheldon was on another. In the sixth episode of season two ("The Cooper-Nowitzski Theorem") the following exchange occurred between Penny, Leonard, and Howard.

PENNY

I know this is none of my business, but I just, I have to ask…what's Sheldon's deal?

LEONARD

What do you mean, "deal"?

PENNY

You know, like, what's his deal? Is it girls...? Guys...? Sock puppets...?

LEONARD

Honestly, we've been operating under the assumption that he has no deal.

PENNY

Come on, everybody has a deal.

HOWARD

Not Sheldon.

Over the course of the first twenty-three episodes of the series, Sheldon never spoke about his sexuality or romantic interests. It was relatively clear that whatever his preferences—or lack thereof—science was his first true love, followed by his love of all things sci-fi and fantasy. But one thing was certain: A character who wasn't actively pursuing a relationship on TV was extremely rare, and a major step forward for those who have always felt unhelpful societal pressure to conform to certain standards.

Chuck Lorre: Sheldon's passion was learning; understanding the secrets of the universe. That made him unlike any character I certainly had ever seen. He wasn't trying to find himself in a relationship; he *was* in a relationship, and it was with science.

But Lorre also wanted to take it a step further. While it was never formally mentioned on the series, Lorre believed Sheldon was asexual, meaning someone who does not experience sexual desire or attraction. According to the Trevor Project, the leading national organization providing crisis intervention and suicide services to LGBTQ+ youth, asexuality is defined as "an umbrella term, and exists on a spectrum. Asexual people...may have little interest in having sex, even though most desire emotionally intimate relationships."

Chuck Lorre: I had, for several years, championed the idea that Sheldon was asexual. He had no interest, which I thought made him remarkable.

Bill Prady: Chuck and I were of the same mind, absolutely.

Maria Ferrari (executive producer, writer): If the show was still in production, I feel like there would be more talk about Sheldon's sexuality—if he was asexual or if he just had a very low libido. I always thought that was an interesting topic—if a person with a really low libido and someone with a really high libido make a relationship work. That's something we talked about a lot once he and Amy had a deeper relationship. It was always a really tough balancing act, because you wanted both characters to be happy.

Steve Holland: Later, we took our time with Sheldon and Amy, but even though Chuck said he perceived Sheldon as asexual, the show never identified him as asexual. That was just our sort of thinking. He's just Sheldon and he's somewhat spectrum-y, although we were careful never to identify him as that, either. I completely understand that people were frustrated when he wasn't referred to as being identified on the spectrum, but Sheldon was never meant to be a spokesman for a group of people, which is why we also tried to keep labels off of him. We did what we thought was best for the character, but at some point, while you have to be aware of what people are saying, you also have to tune it out a little bit.

Chuck Lorre: Early on you'd get those ridiculous notes, such as "Wouldn't it be nice if..." or "When is Sheldon going to get a girl?" I would get those notes early on from well-meaning CBS executives who were wondering why we weren't doing what had been done elsewhere. But Sheldon just didn't care. He was not attracted to anybody. He was attracted to science. There was kind of a sense that we had our own lane; that no one else was doing this. It's a biological imperative to couple up; it's how we're wired. But there are those amongst us who opt out. And they had not been on television. I had certainly never seen it. Television was always *Get the girl, Get the guy, I'm lonely, I need someone, Sex is going to make me feel better, I want to be in love,* et cetera, et cetera. But Sheldon was complete without a relationship. And that broke ground a little bit, along with the fact that he could articulate those wishes. He was not unconsciously avoiding contact with people. He looked at it, he analyzed it, and said, "I want no part of this." [*Laughs*] Science was his mistress.

Jim Parsons: I as easily accepted his *asexuality* as I eventually did his *odd sexuality* once Amy was on.

Chuck Lorre: There was no one on television who said, "I'm in love with science," and that choice, I think, went a long way with making him an iconic character. He wasn't driven by the culture or people's expectations of what he should do or shouldn't do or how he should behave. He made his own choice. In a way, that's heroic without looking heroic. He had transcended the cultural pressure on all of us through advertising and television and film and magazines. He had a lover; it was called physics. And he was fine with that. And obviously, we eventually did enter Sheldon into a relationship, but we did it very slowly, and in a way that made us feel like we hadn't done a ninety-degree turn at all.

> Besides, Sheldon had more important things to focus on, like teaching Rock Paper Scissors Lizard Spock to Raj. The game was originally created by Sam Kass and Karen Bryla, because according to Kass on his website, "it seems like when you know someone well enough, 75–80% of any Rock-Paper-Scissors games you play with that person end up in a tie." It first appeared on *The Big Bang Theory* in the eighth episode of season two—"The Lizard-Spock Expansion"—and again in season five. While it was a fan-favorite moment, the dialogue Parsons had to memorize was as complex as the game itself. ("Scissors cuts paper, paper covers rock, rock crushes lizard, lizard poisons Spock, Spock smashes scissors, scissors decapitates lizard, lizard eats paper, paper disproves Spock, Spock vaporizes rock, and, as it always has, rock crushes scissors.")

Jim Parsons: Having to do that scene was just a good time. The audience reaction was the hard part, as well as having to hold for a laugh in the middle of some of the mechanical-type monologues. But I also seem to remember that was one of the blessed times I actually kept a sense of humor while fucking up. That was not something I always did. I also didn't want to spend all night doing it.

Kaley Cuoco: I did not envy the stuff Jim had to say on the show. I don't think I could have done that. I never wanted to mess with his process, but

I said to him after that scene, "I would have just asked to preshoot that." I can't imagine the thought of having to do that in front of the audience. But within those moments, you'd think, "Who else could do *that*?" It was truly unbelievable.

Adam Nimoy: For what it's worth, Rock Paper Scissors Lizard Spock still makes no sense to me. I still can't follow the logic! But it was always fascinating for me to see how *Star Trek* and Spock kept cropping up in popular culture. I never got tired of it. Leonard Nimoy never got tired of it. It's the otherness of Spock, the outsider that he is, being half Vulcan, half human, that seems to attract so many of us to him. It's Spock's control of his emotions, his role as a science officer, his superior intellect, that makes Spock such a hero to Sheldon.

And boy, was that evident in "The Bath Item Gift Hypothesis," one of the most beloved episodes in the series. When Sheldon received the gift of a lifetime from Penny—an autographed napkin from his hero, Leonard Nimoy— it took the show to new heights.

Chuck Lorre: Spock was such a North Star for Sheldon. The character that had transcended raw emotion and intellect and logic was a character that was kind of worshiped by Sheldon because it's what he wanted to be.

The episode, which aired right before Christmas 2008, centered on Sheldon's annoyance at having to buy Penny a gift once he discovered she bought something for him. As a result, he spent the rest of the afternoon searching for the perfect gift(s)—which turned out to be several professionally wrapped gift baskets filled with bath products. He would give Penny the gift basket that he deemed of equal value to what she got him.

Later that evening, Penny gives Sheldon his gift—a napkin. She smiles and says, "Turn it over." He does, and in mere seconds, it's clear Sheldon's world has been rocked forever. He reaches for the support of the chair behind him—his body going weak—when he reads what's written on the napkin: "To Sheldon, live long and prosper, Leonard Nimoy." The live studio audience doesn't merely cheer—they gasp—aware of the magnitude of the moment. And then, Penny remarks, "Yeah, he came into the restaurant.

Sorry the napkin's dirty—he wiped his mouth with it." Sheldon completely loses it, and Parsons gives a performance so well executed, it is the singular moment most referenced among fans and TV critics.

"I possess the DNA of Leonard Nimoy?!" he says, with his mouth quivering and body shaking. "Do you realize what this means?! All I need is a healthy ovum and I can grow my own Leonard Nimoy!" Nimoy himself called it "one of the greatest, funniest" moments. Here's how it happened...

Steve Molaro: It's actually not the best episode, which people tend to forget, but it *is* one of the best moments and scenes of all time. The plan was Penny would give Sheldon an autographed picture of Leonard Nimoy. I changed it to a napkin because I knew we could up the stakes. Bill and Chuck had to attend a runthrough, so [writers] Eric Kaplan, Dave Goetsch, Adam Faberman, and myself stayed in the room to finish the scene. And an autographed picture—something you could get on eBay—kind of bummed me out. I was like, "We have to be able to do better than this." We wound our way to a napkin, and Adam suggested it was smudged because Leonard Nimoy wiped his mouth on it. As soon as I heard that, I knew it was his DNA. Now, with that said, Chuck does not like being handcuffed to an outline or a plan or writing to an ending. He'll say, "It will go where it wants to go." So when he and Bill came back, they read what we wrote, and I could just feel him getting angry. He looked at me and said, "I thought it was supposed to be an autographed picture." I said, "I thought this was better." So Chuck and Bill read the scene, and Bill starts laughing when he was reading the part about "You gave me the DNA of Leonard Nimoy." And I looked at Eric, and Eric goes, "All I need is my own healthy ovum and I can make my own Leonard Nimoy," and Chuck burst into laughter. It was just magic from the first time it happened. And that napkin scene was a turning point for me. I felt like that moment cemented me and Chuck.

Eric Kaplan (executive producer, writer): I can believe that I was the one who used the word *ovum* because my mom is a biology teacher, so maybe the word *ovum* falls from my lips more readily than it does from others on the writing staff.

Jim Parsons: The scenes leading up to it didn't flow as well as the rest did. But once we arrived at the gift exchange, I couldn't believe my good fortune in being given such a scene. It was one of those classics that you almost immediately know when you read it out loud at the table read. It has to do with really crackerjack comedy ideas coming from the most passionate character-based places. One of the things that gives me chills in a good comedy is when a character—in this case, Penny—is the unlikely person to deliver such a meaningful moment to a character like Sheldon. There's nothing on paper that says that should be happening, so when it does, there's something very moving.

Although Leonard Nimoy wasn't even in the episode, the reaction from Sheldon was something that Leonard's son, Adam, had seen play out many times in real life.

Adam Nimoy: It's so great because it's so symbolic of the fan experience. I saw that so many times where people lost it when they came across my dad. I think it's wonderful. So many people want to freak out like Sheldon did, but they would try to hold their stuff together. There was nothing better

The napkin. The autograph. The hug. The gift baskets. Cuoco's and Parsons's reactions. All of it worked perfectly to create one of the most beloved scenes in television history. *Photo™ & © Warner Bros. Entertainment Inc.*

than walking with my dad on a public street and watching people as they recognized him. I loved that.

Steve Molaro: And the napkin was really signed by Leonard. We sent it to him, and got it signed at the last minute before we shot it.

> If viewers thought the scene couldn't get any better, they were underestimating the writers, who managed to up the ante even further. Sheldon runs to the bedroom to retrieve Penny's gift baskets—not one, not two, but *all* of them—which in his mind, still wasn't enough. And so, in a moment that fans thought they'd never see, an affection-averse Sheldon gives Penny an awkward but grateful hug to show her just how much the gift—and her friendship—means to him.

Chuck Lorre: We had created a character who could not tolerate physical proximity with anyone. He didn't want to be touched! Couldn't shake hands! And when he wraps his arms around her and she turns to Leonard and says, "Sheldon's hugging me!" the show went to another place. The joke was *I have his DNA and with a healthy ovum, I can make my own Leonard Nimoy,* but the physical contact took the show to another level. We all understood that immediately. Something was happening that we didn't anticipate having so much emotional impact, and it gave us courage to go further.

Steve Molaro: The hug was Chuck's idea. When we watched that scene in that first runthrough, you could feel the electricity on the stage. It was just one of those times when you can't wait for it to go on TV. That hug was so real. It stopped being a script; we were just in this moment with Leonard and Penny and Sheldon. It was just magic from the first time it happened. And that was a turning point for me because after a lot of internal struggle, I felt like that moment cemented myself as part of the team. Like, we do this together.

Jim Parsons: The construction of the scene was more moving to me than the joyous ecstasy that the character was going through. The emotion I feel even as I talk about it now has to do with the chill it gave me that they put something like that together. This was a character who displayed so few emotions, especially early on, and the writers came up with the most ridiculous trigger for him to finally reveal emotion *and* to such a degree that he was compelled to hug Penny. It was a wonderful moment to get to do it because we had just enough history and information behind us. We were all very aware of the stakes, and they were not cheaply earned. The episode and that moment hit at the right time in the series for the show.

Critics agreed, immediately recognizing the impact of the moment on the series as a whole. IGN's James Chamberlin wrote, "I would consider most of this episode to be good, but the gift exchange at the end was gold…Holy crap. Sheldon's reaction to the gift was quite easily the funniest minute and a half of TV I've seen in years." *TV Guide* magazine named it one of the one hundred best episodes of all time, *TV Line* declared it one of the best episodes of the series, and *Vulture* named it in their list of "9 *Big Bang Theory* Episodes That Will Win Over Skeptics," with writer Kimberly Potts noting, "The most consistent laughs to be found on [*Big Bang*] come from the relationship between Sheldon and Penny…and the comedy chemistry between Parsons and Kaley Cuoco is often at the center of the show's best episodes."

Kaley Cuoco: My scenes with Jim—which we called the Shenny scenes— were so funny and so real and authentic, and we always looked forward to them. And if you notice, I'm always laughing in my scenes with him, and that's because it was real. Penny was literally finding hilarity and joy out of these people—and so was I—because it was funny. What I was saying in a scene was what I would really say and how I really would react.

Kunal Nayyar: Kaley as Penny had this really sweet laugh or even a look that she would do when Sheldon was just being Sheldon. It was so disarming and endearing and nonjudgmental. It's something I had never seen on television—that kind of relationship.

Judy Parsons: It's one of my very, very favorite episodes because it was the first time Sheldon had ever shown any physical emotion.

And here's a fun fact—for as much emphasis that was rightly put on having the napkin signed by Leonard Nimoy, getting the gift baskets in the arms of Sheldon to give to Penny was more of a headache than anything.

Jim Parsons: Sam [Huston Jr.], who worked with Scott on props, had to load me up every time. And I just remember both of us understanding that we needed it to look as awkward as possible to the point you could barely see me because you could only see gift baskets. Mark Cendrowski came out to help rearrange where everything should go, like I was a Christmas tree. But that's the point! It was certainly one of those things as an actor, you know how it feels, but you can't know if it looks funny until you see it on screen.

Scott London (prop master): And anytime you have gift baskets, they are a pain in the butt because they're wrapped in cellophane, and then the director of photography freaks out because of the reflection, and then noise for sound because of the crinkling. It's a nightmare. I've had sound mixers get annoyed by the computer fans on laptops. But these microphones are so sensitive. In the end, I used tulle instead of cellophane for the gift baskets, and it's great because it comes in all different colors and it's transparent. I still use it to this day, especially on flower bouquets so it won't crunch.

> **But if there was a character who would never be caught dead bringing a gift basket of any kind for any reason, it would be Dr. Beverly Hofstadter, Leonard's mother, who was introduced in the fifteenth episode of the second season. Lorre recruited Emmy winner Christine Baranski—whom he first worked with on *Cybill*—to play the crusty and cynical psychiatrist.**

Lee Aronsohn: Chuck and I had worked with Christine on *Cybill* and loved her. We knew the woman's rhythms. We knew what she could knock out of the park. So we gave her some juicy slowballs right over the plate and she hit them out.

Christine Baranski: My association with Chuck Lorre changed my career. I owe a lot to him, so when he came knocking on my door again for *The Big Bang Theory*, and I read the [script for Beverly] I thought, *Oh, OK, I know how to do this.* Just like Maryann on *Cybill*, she was another really terrific lady with those dripping one-liners. And a very different character, which was great. But what intrigued me about [the show], and still one of the reasons I'm happy I did it, was those young actors. They are super famous now, but they weren't famous back then. Nobody knew those names. They were all just young, and the show was so original. And when I came on the show, *Big Bang* was hot. But then as I continued over the years to come on, it simply became a mega hit, a cult hit. And for me, nothing but joy. Even now, when I'm on vacation in Florence or in Dublin, people will approach me and say, "Are you Leonard's mother?"

Menopause. Penis. Urinate. Masturbate. Orgasm. These were just some of the words that slipped right off the tongue of Dr. Hofstadter without hesitation.

Chuck Lorre: She talked about human anatomy in a clinical sense, which you saw with Leonard. Like, "Is he satisfactory in this regard, biologically?" She was looking at it almost like he's a lab animal in an experiment, so that is what made it worth doing. It was coming from a place of scientific curiosity.

Christine Baranski: All those references to body parts and all of it was just scientific data, you know, like talking about Leonard's sex life, or about anybody's sex life...that was her world. I certainly never played a character like that. The simpler and more direct you were with the character, the better. She spoke in declarative sentences. You didn't have to try to be funny to be Beverly. You just have to be convinced of what you were saying. And say in as matter-of-fact and dry a manner as possible. It would just land, and the audience would explode. [The hard part was] having to hold for a very long laugh and keep a straight face.

Kaley Cuoco: I remember when I heard Christine was coming on the show, and I assumed most of her stuff would be with Johnny. Then I saw that most of her scenes were with me, and I was totally shocked. *And* really excited. She has such an intimidating presence, but she's so the opposite of that. She's so funny and warm. Plus, she's known Chuck forever, so it felt like family when she got there. She cracked me up, and it was such an honor to have so many great scenes with her.

Christine Baranski: Kaley and I had a bar scene in season three where we got drunk. And it was so wonderful. Well, wonderful/terrifying because they rewrote the scene while we were on set. In between takes, Kaley and I just bonded. Because when you're sitting around waiting for your rewrite, you're hanging by a thread. And we were supposed to be playing drunk. Later in the series, there was this girlfriend relationship between Penny and Beverly, and that to me was just so great. There were so many one-liners that

Their characters had a very interesting relationship, but off-screen it was nothing but love and admiration for Christine Baranski and Kaley Cuoco. *Courtesy of Kaley Cuoco personal collection*

I just thought were so pissingly funny. And so many touching moments. To make all of those characters not only highly intelligent and funny, but so human, so lovable. Even Beverly. *Even* Beverly.

But Beverly and Leonard's ice-cold relationship never quite thawed until the second-to-last episode of the entire series, when Leonard's emotions finally bubbled over, and he let his mother see just how scarred he was from her lack of support and affection.

Johnny Galecki: We had that big, heavy, dramatic scene, which was great. Christine couldn't fly in for that episode until the Monday before the Tuesday tape night, so we only rehearsed it once together. [Co–executive producer] Anthony Del Broccolo texted me after the runthrough and said that was some of the best acting he had ever seen. And then after we did the scene in front of the audience, he said, "I take that back. *That* was the best acting I've ever seen." That's just not me tooting my own horn! [*Laughs*] He was including Baranski in that, of course! And to be able to create that kind of a mood shift on that stage after so much laughter for so long was really stilling. It's much harder to make people laugh than it is to make people cry.

But both Baranski and I felt the writers were trusting us with something special, so we wanted to meet that trust tenfold.

Christine Baranski: It's really a great payoff to play characters like that—ones that are emotionally very closed, because when they do open up, the audience is just like, *Oh God, I knew there was a person there, I knew there was this other side of her.* When that scene finally came, it was really poignant. One of the proudest things I've ever done is be part of that show. Chuck is a huge linchpin in my career and my success. I would do anything for him.

Johnny Galecki: And I actually didn't understand that last scene with me and Christine at first. It was one of the few scenes in a multicamera sitcom that didn't end on a joke. I kept thinking, *Where's the punchline?* And I realized there wasn't one. I realized the tone that they were giving us. And I mean "giving us" because I really feel like that episode was the writers' gifts to me at the end of the show. To do something really dramatic like that... I'm going to cry. My sister always says, "It's not a party until Johnny starts crying." I'm a sentimental, emotional hamster. [*Laughs*]

Eric Kaplan: That was an opportunity where we were like, *This is the last season, so we can depart from the sitcom rule that nothing ever changes, and he can actually make some psychological growth with his mother.* We were able to do something risky in their relationship and I thought it was lovely.

Baranski's first *Big Bang* episode—"The Maternal Capacitance"—also featured one of the most beloved Penny and Leonard scenes, when Leonard—who feels defeated from dealing with his mother—gets drunk with Penny, and she instructs him to erotically kiss her neck while sucking a lime.

Kaley Cuoco: We preshot it, but we also did it in front of the audience. We were the last ones to shoot that day, and once we wrapped, Johnny said to me, "Hey! That was really fun!" and I said, "That *was* really fun! I had a blast with you." We had genuine, childlike fun doing some of those scenes, especially early on, when it was a lot more of those storylines. And we were dating then in real life, so I think it came a little easier to us than it needed to. [*Laughs*] There wasn't a lot of rehearsal, and I think we nailed it pretty quickly! But it was visually so funny with the lime sticking out, and then swapping the lime, and then laughing as our characters were drunk.

This scene was further proof of Cuoco's and Galecki's impeccable physical comedy skills, and their magnetic chemistry. *Photo™ & © Warner Bros. Entertainment Inc.*

Johnny Galecki: The physical comedy of the scene was so fun. It was also great to play Leonard in a position like that, which was probably the most pornographic thing he had ever experienced outside of maybe reading Sigmund Freud. [*Laughs*] And acting drunk is actually hard to play, so I would ask Scott London, our prop master, to cut up a dish sponge into pieces, soak it in whiskey, and put it in a disposable coffee cup with a lid on it and give it to me. I would just smell that to bring some sense memory in, and kind of stumble around a little bit and loosen up, which helped me a great deal. And Kaley, of course, thought I was crazy. But that's what Scott London and I did for every drunk scene from then on. He'd be like, "Don't tell them I'm doing this for you!" And I'd say, "Scott, it's shards of dish sponge! It's not like I'm sucking a few drops of whiskey out of these things!"

The "lime scene" as it's called, took place on Penny's teal-colored couch, a piece of furniture which Cuoco had some seriously strong feelings about.

Kaley Cuoco: I hated the couch in Penny's apartment. I remember thinking, *Can't she get a new couch?* But the apartment was so her when we started. It was like a twenty-one-year-old's total Limited Too / IKEA, just-starting-out apartment. It was messy, but it was really Penny. I think that's why I wanted my dressing room to be so out there, like I would never have a pink room in my house, so it was just an expression of the show and of her.

Season two was on a roll, though, ironically, the episode that most fans don't often talk about ("The Work Song Nanocluster," aka the Penny Blossoms episode) just happened to "reveal" one of the best-kept secrets of the show. Well...kind of. You see, throughout the series, Penny's last name (until she married Leonard and it became Hofstadter) was never revealed. It was never even a story or plot point, but die-hard fans always wondered. The producers said they just never gave Penny a last name, and then after a while, it became superstitious to come up with one. But in the second season's eighteenth episode, Penny receives a delivery of her Penny Blossom accessory creations. The props department, led by Scott London, weren't about to put a shipping label that just said "Penny." And so, years later, eagle-eyed fans zoomed in on that label and found a very hard-to-make-out surname: Teller.

Steve Molaro: Props had to put a label on it and it happened to be caught on camera. We didn't sanction it, we didn't write it, and we didn't intentionally put it there. It's fun to think about, sure, but we certainly never talked about it.

Scott London: It's amazing these producers don't communicate better. [*Laughs*] I think it was Bill Prady, because he's friends with Penn and Teller...but I was told, "make it Teller," because I always say, "What do you want for a last name?" For a while, I used my last name, London, as her last name just so there was something. But the only name I know that was given to me was Teller because I had to put a last name on the label or on the driver's license. I mean, you can't just tell me to ship to Penny with no last name!

Bill Prady: Scott said, "I have to have a last name," and I said, "Will we ever be able to read it?" and he said, "No." And I said, "All right, well, make sure it's Greeked enough that you can't make it out." And he said, "What should I put there?" And I think I might have said "Teller" because of Penn and Teller, Penny Teller. I think it might have amused me in the moment. But I had assurances it wasn't going to be seen, that Scott just needed it for the visual shape of the block of type. But, *emphatically*, Penny's last name is *not* Teller. I don't know how that image of the shipping label exists and fans were able to see it or make it out. It's like the roommate agreement—they had to fill pages with words. Prop people have to make things that will look real, but the intent is that you will not see them.

Kaley Cuoco: I do remember that shipping label! Scott London was so brilliant. He really took it so seriously, and had no idea that this last name would be such a thing!

Jim Parsons: I mean, she's not Prince or Madonna! She's a normal girl in Pasadena named Penny something. But yes, very early on, I remember looking at the mail in a scene and it said Penny London. We all found it amusing in a charming way that the prop master had given her his last name. It was just perfect Scott. And I'm such a curmudgeon, it's the kind of thing where I look back now and think, *This really is so funny this went on.* I remember the time this was a whole topic of conversation and I was like, "As if we don't have enough to think about, we gotta talk about superstition about giving her a goddamn last name!" But now I think it's fun.

Steve Molaro: Her last name being Teller is absolutely not canon. The canon is that she does not have a last name that we ever assigned to her, including us saying, "I don't know, put Teller on the label." Even though that happened, that does not mean it's her last name. We never decided to know what it is, and we're never going to make one. Even when she and Leonard got married, we made sure to edit around even hearing what her name would be. And the driver's license that says her last name…it's not even the right address or the right height, either.

Kaley Cuoco: There were times I maybe had an idea what her last name actually was, but then it was almost weird for me to think she had a last name. She was just *Penny*. I think it was a fan who once said to me, "Wouldn't it be funny if your name was Penny Penny Penny, and Sheldon knew the whole time and then everyone just started doing the knock, and then later he was like, 'I knew that was your last name!'" But no, I kind of love that it was just Penny, and then Penny Hofstadter, which I thought was so cute.

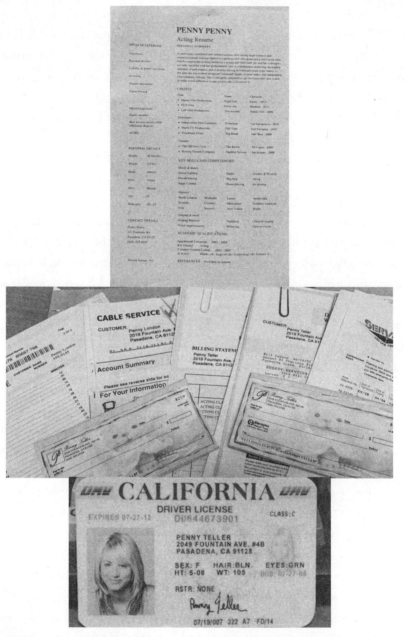

Proof that Penny never had an official last name before she became Mrs. Hofstadter. Over the years, prop master Scott London, who wanted every prop on the show to be authentic, sometimes gave her his last name, or Teller (for Penn & Teller), or even her first name, Penny. *Courtesy of Scott London*

As it turns out, the character of Barry Kripke—played by actor John Ross Bowie—has its own fascinating naming story.

John Ross Bowie ("Barry Kripke"): I had auditioned for Leonard twice [originally], and I read for another role I can't quite remember in season one before I got the Kripke audition at the last minute in season two. And full disclosure, [the producers] went out first to Kevin Sussman for the role of Kripke—who was actually named Stewart Kripke in the audition sides. But Sussman had a movie and couldn't do it. I came in to audition and saw Bill and Chuck and Ken Miller and Nikki Valko all in the room. I was interested in the role because I had never seen this kind of alpha nerd bully. There was something so aggressive about Kripke, and I played him very sure of himself. I straightened my back…and kind of led with my crotch in a way that I don't usually in real life. I got some laughs and then Chuck said, "He should have some sort of a vulnerability, maybe a speech thing." And Prady chimed in with, "Yeah, maybe sort of a Tom Brokaw liquid *L*. Can you do something like that?" I claimed that I could do a very subtle, understated Tom Brokaw liquid *L,* and instead I did this horrific Elmer Fudd thing, which is technically not a lisp. I was corrected very early on in the show's run by a speech pathologist I'd gone to college with. It's called a rhotacism. I just turned the *Rs* and the *Ls* into *Ws*. Chuck has this throw-his-head-back cackle that I became very familiar with over the next few years, and he did that and Prady laughed, and I was feeling great. Then there was a knock on the door and someone sticks their head in and goes, "Chuck, there's a phone call from Leonard Nimoy." Normally if I get my fucking audition interrupted I'm livid. This time I was like, "Listen, we just met but you should probably go take that." I think it was Leonard Nimoy signing off on the use of his name in the Saturnalia episode. And like half an hour later I'm driving home and I get the call that I'm supposed to show up at Warner Bros. the next day and they want to keep the speech impediment. They've also changed the character's name to Barry because it sounds funnier with the speech impediment. And the next morning I went to work on [season two, episode twelve's] "The Killer Robot Instability."

As the season came to a close, Kevin Sussman made his first appearance as Stuart, nearly two years after first getting—and then not getting—the role of Howard Wolowitz. But Sussman thought he screwed up and wouldn't be invited back.

Kevin Sussman: My agent had said, "Chuck has a guest star thing for you on that show—*The Big Bang Theory*." It started off as one episode, but there was a possibility that it would recur. The comic book store wasn't even a permanent set yet. And I was convinced that the first episode would be my last because I had a speech that they rewrote while we were acting it out in front of an audience. I tend to overprepare, and those lines were in my bones, so I was not used to working on a TV show where in the middle of shooting they'll just change up the lines. We had to do take after take of me trying to get those new lines, and I was convinced I had just destroyed any relationship I had with Chuck Lorre. To my amazement he kept having me come back.

Eric Kaplan: Kevin Sussman is deeply thoughtful about the craft of acting, and brought such honesty to every scene, which meant it would be different in every take. And the writers were losing their minds because you kind of want to hit a take and know that that take will be there for show night and not feel like you're strapping into a rocket ship. [*Laughs*] There was this one scene at the comic book store when a woman walked in, and Stuart had to say, "Don't all look at the same time." And Kevin basically sang it, like, "Don't all look! At the same time!" He *sang* it—which is bananas *and* so refreshing. Unless the script says, "sing the line," you don't expect one of the actors to suddenly sing it. But it was exhilarating! So what I'm trying to say is, Kevin Sussman is fantastic!

Bill Prady: I've never seen a performer more capable of getting in his own head when he works as Kevin. If someone would say, "Can I give Kevin a note?" we'd say, "Don't give Kevin a note. Just have him do it again. Do it again and see what you get." [*Laughs*] It's a wonderful energy he brings; even if the character is being down, there's a manic quality to what Kevin does. He's just brilliant. And what a sweet guy.

Steve Molaro: Kevin's self-professed anxiety just made us like him more.

He was struggling with a line once and he jokingly yelled at himself, "Come on, Sussman, pull it together!" The phrase, "Come on, Sussman, pull it together!" is something Steve Holland and I still say to this day. [*Laughs*]

Kevin Sussman: There was one scene in the comic book store that I'll always remember when a hot girl walks in, and I tell the guys something like, "Watch and learn." But I was having such difficulty with the line that right before we shot it, I was still pacing around in my dressing room, worried I didn't know how to do it. I just couldn't get my hooks into this line and screwed it up every time in rehearsal. So when they called me to come do that scene, and I say, "Watch and learn," all that came out was, "It, it, I, ooh, ooh, eh…" and then I just turned and walked away. I wound up not saying it at all except some kind of half sounds. And I heard Chuck laughing from the side, and he was like, "That's it! Moving on." I never had to do the line I was having such difficulty with. He recognized that we weren't going to top my stammering. In the end, I was especially proud of that moment.

Johnny Galecki: I always thought Sussman would intentionally throw himself off and that's what gave him that unpredictable timing and cadence. No two takes were the same and I loved working with him because it kept me on my toes. I complimented him on this once and said, "I see what you're doing and I think it's great and it makes me better." He said, "No man, I'm just terrified and feel like I have no fucking clue what I'm doing." Granted, he may have taken a few more takes than others, but it was always worth it.

Sussman had nothing to worry about, and was brought back for the penultimate episode of season two. In the season finale, Sheldon, Leonard, Wolowitz, and Koothrappali head off to the North Pole to find magnetic monopoles (as one does), and Penny realizes just how much she'll miss Leonard. The series still wasn't a bona fide hit, but it finished fortieth in the ratings at the end of the season—a significant improvement over sixty-eighth from the season before. And, as a sign of immense confidence, in the spring of 2009, CBS renewed *Big Bang* for a third—and fourth—season.

The show's popularity also translated to critical acclaim as well. The Television Critics Association awarded *Big Bang* their prestigious Outstanding

Achievement in Comedy honor at the 2009 ceremony that summer, and the American Film Institute named the show an official selection on its list of Television Programs of the Year. And although they didn't win, both Parsons and Christine Baranski were nominated for Primetime Emmy Awards for Best Actor in a Comedy Series and Best Guest Actress in a Comedy Series, respectively.

TIME FOR A HOT BEVERAGE...

Atom Breaks

> Every episode of *The Big Bang Theory* featured numerous breaks in the action by way of revolving atoms to separate scenes. Most viewers didn't give it a second thought, but for Emmy Award–winning editor and co-executive producer Peter Chakos, it was an opportunity to insert a bit of a hidden message within each scene.

Peter Chakos: Interstitials or bumpers, as we call them, propel the viewer into the next scene. It started out with all kinds of ideas to find something we could drop in that said, *Science.* I was searching the internet, pulling GIFs, which weren't even called that at the time, but it's what we call them now. They were short animation pieces, but they were all chemistry graphics. Chuck kept calling them "old science," so we started thinking about something inside the atomic world. We reached out to the guy who animated planets on *3rd Rock from the Sun.* They started out a little bit different than they ended up. We even thought about putting the image of the next scene in the atom. But what we did do is get interstitials with different colors and movement that reflected the scene that just happened or previewed the one to come. I started to match what my comedic take on the end of a scene was with what the interstitial was doing. I gave them names. One was called "Up Yours," so if somebody slams somebody [or has a comeback to what they say], the atom would swoop up like an arm coming up at you. If it was a goofy ending, I had one that would swirl through called "Oogle Google." If the scene was a hard-hitting, funny moment, it would come straight at the camera, which I called "Coming at Ya." And then if the scene was with Penny, Amy, and Bernadette, I had one with three atoms called "Triple Threat." If the four guys were in the scene, it would be atoms from the four corners that would come straight at you. I also started to match the colors to the scene. I would use the aquamarine color if we were coming out of or going to Penny's apartment because it matched her couch or what they were wearing. My assistant and I knew, and that was it. I never told anybody.

Chapter 8

NOTE CARDS, A SPECIAL COLOGNE, AND AN EIDETIC MEMORY

If you ask actors what's the secret sauce to a sitcom's success, they'll often point to the writing. Ask the writers, and they'll point to the actors. The truth, though, is somewhere in the middle. You must have fantastic writers who know how to craft dynamic, interesting characters, but you also need brilliant actors to bring those characters to life. When the two come together—as they've done on so many iconic sitcoms over the years—it's magic. *The Big Bang Theory* cast was no different. From the original five to the final seven, they didn't just read the words off the page. They made Sheldon, Leonard, Penny, Raj, and Howard real people with whom we identified, laughed, and cried. And now, Parsons, Galecki, Cuoco, Nayyar, and Helberg reveal the lengths—from meerkats to thousands of index cards—to which they went to fully realize their characters.

Jim Parsons as "Sheldon Cooper"

Chuck Lorre: Jim's process was to be wildly prepared. He made all his decisions the night before the table read as to how he was going to read his script.

Jim Parsons: I really did love putting in the time, staying home on the weekends and repeating these words. It brought me a lot of joy and pride to be able to use these multisyllabic words they were giving me and still ferret out the comedy rhythms they put in there. I loved the chance to solve that puzzle. I'm not saying it didn't get a little tiresome and old at some point, but overall, I really did love it. And it was just such a joy to be able to go into a pretape day and a show night with that level of confidence behind me that I knew what I was doing. That's where it would remind me as much of an athletic event as anything. I wanted to be ready to nail my triple axel when it was time to skate for the gold. [*Laughs*]

Kevin Sussman: When people talk about what Jim was like on set… while he had a lot of fun, he was the one that had the most work. Every episode he had these frickin' monologues with all this jargon, and so much of what I remember about hanging out on the set—which was mostly like hanging out with your friends at summer camp—was Jim constantly walking around with a big stack of index cards going over his lines. I used to think to myself, *Holy cow, he's doing this* every *episode*.

Kaley Cuoco: Jim always wrote *every single line* of his down on note cards, which blew my mind. You'd open a drawer on the set and there would be note cards.

Jim Parsons: There wasn't a set piece that didn't have my scripts or note

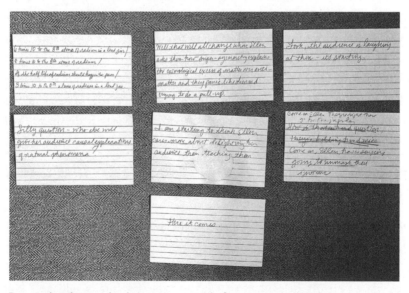

Jim Parsons hand wrote his lines on note cards for every episode. These in particular are from season 12, episode 18, "The Laureate Accumulation," in which Drs. Pemberton (guest star Sean Astin) and Campbell (guest star Kal Penn) appear on *Ellen* as part of their fictional Super-Asymmetry press tour. *Courtesy of Steve Molaro*

cards in it. Now, it was rare that I was able to use them during a scene; it was always just a reference between takes. But, oh, how I loved a notepad! It was so rare that I had a scene where it made sense for me to be with a notepad, but to know you're walking into a scene where you could see your lines the whole time...what a luxury! That is a whole other style of acting! It may not even be called acting, I'm not sure. But I loved it; it was such a treat.

On rare occasions, the writers would rewrite a monologue during tape night and Parsons would have to relearn a mouthful of dialogue on the spot.

Jim Parsons: There were a couple of times it irritated me because it was irritating to have worked on something so long and then it would change. It sounds so childish in retrospect, but it was my honest reaction. There was one instance specifically where they changed my stuff before we even did a take. I came down, and I lost my shit. I really did. Now what does that mean, exactly? I don't know, we did the show. [*Laughs*] But for me, I really got mad. It just made me angry and kind of close to tears in a weird way, because I had been drilling these lines and they had the director say, "OK, we're going to cut this, we're going to change that." I was like, "Wait, we're not even going to hear it first?!" But that was rare to get changes... and most of the time, it was really thrilling because their changes would be really good, and you had something fresh to give the studio audience who had already seen the scene a few times. And so that was really fun...when it wasn't frustrating.

Throughout the years, Parsons was always asked if he learned anything about physics, or if he felt smarter as a result of playing Sheldon.

Jim Parsons: I've always had a respect for science and a fascination with certain aspects of it, but I didn't learn a goddamn thing, I'll tell you that. Nothing stuck. [*Laughs*] [Professor] David [Saltzberg] definitely made it easier. He was really helpful in that he was able to usually tell me, "Here's all you need to know." For instance, "You're going to point at this when you say that; you're going to point at that when you say this." He was the perfect combination of being scientifically brilliant *and* being able to talk to a science dodo bird like me. He understood the kind of paint-by-numbers aspect that was necessary for the acting to get to the comedy.

Professor David Saltzberg: Jim would really research all these words on the page. And it was remarkable how I never had to tell him how to pronounce something because he did the work. In fact, once, he even found a little mistake. We had the words "electrical dipoles," when in fact somebody would say "*electric* dipoles." And he figured that out from his research, and we fixed it. I said to him after that, "You know a lot more than you're letting on."

Jim Parsons: It would have been something as simple as trying to Google it, but anytime I typed it in, nothing came up for "electrical dipoles," but it did for "electric dipoles." [*Laughs*] That would have been as "smart" as I got about it. Doctor Google, you know!

> But not everything about Sheldon required taxing preparation. For example, his hyperventilating-like laugh came about organically.

Jim Parsons: They must have written something that triggered it for me. I think it was more driven by the necessity to figure out how to set this character apart who doesn't understand humor. So when he finds something funny, or when he says something funny, it can't be a normal reaction. I don't know why that was what came out of me, but I felt intuitively that I couldn't have anything that looked like the kind of honest reaction you would expect.

Johnny Galecki as "Leonard Hofstadter"

Johnny Galecki: I still have my first few scripts and all the backstory of notes in a binder that I wrote, which to anyone else would look like hieroglyphics. It was a very Leonard-like binder with a Chewbacca sticker on it. I showed it to Steve Molaro, and it was really creepy how accurate things turned out to be. I wrote about Leonard's relationship with his mother even though she wasn't introduced until season two. Some things I got right, and other things were just funny. Kaley always used to make fun of my binder. Those were my secrets, my private foundation for the character. Half of those backstory notes were love letters to Penny. I think that's what Kaley got a kick out of…the obsession, the loving obsession that Leonard had. [*Laughs*]

Kaley Cuoco: Oh my gosh, the backstory and the research! He probably made fun of me because I had done zero research to play Penny. I'd give him a hard time and be like, "Got your binder?! It's season ten, hope you know what your backstory is now!" I gave him so much shit. I was like, "What was Leonard doing before this last scene? Where was Leonard? Tell us!" I was so bad! I remember when we were dating and I'd go to his place and see *Big Bang Theory* scripts lying around, and I'd go through them just to see what he did. And they were marked and circled and had notes. That's when I realized, *Oh, so you're really working on this.* But even so, I'd tell him, "Dude, no one else could be Leonard! It's you! Believe in yourself. Every word that comes out, every expression, every sweet look on your face…you *are* Leonard, you're not going to fuck this up."

Since 2007, Johnny Galecki kept a binder with notes he had written hypothesizing about Leonard's backstory. During the last season, he sat down with co-creator Chuck Lorre (and the binder!) to reminisce over what he got right—and what might have totally missed the mark. *Courtesy of Steve Molaro*

Galecki actually based many of Leonard's characteristics on a dear childhood friend from Chicago, Tommy Loeper.

Johnny Galecki: I grew up with Tommy from the age of seven. He had a specific way about him that never left me. I still remember his posture. Leonard was really Tommy Loeper, but I also based the posture and physicality on a meerkat. That's where the clasped hands came from. With almost every character I play, I try to base them on people I admire. And I often go through books of animal photos because an animal is never putting on a persona or falseness. You look at a photo of a panther, for example, and the photos are pure, and that's an ingredient I try to choose for each character. So when I saw this photo of three meerkats looking up with their paws clasped, I thought it made sense. I also based the character on Judd Hirsch's character in *Taxi*. Not in terms of mannerism or performance, but as far as the purpose that the character would serve. And that's why I asked Judd if he'd be willing to play my dad in the season nine finale.

Steve Molaro: I mean, the fact that he looked to a meerkat for some of Leonard's mannerisms with the hands together and the head up, is one of the many reasons why Johnny is awesome. If you really look, Leonard carries his body differently than Johnny. It was fascinating to watch.

Kaley Cuoco: Johnny also had a very specific smell that was just for Leonard. I don't think he'll ever spray that cologne again, but because I was around him so much, I knew that smell. He was very superstitious about that.

Johnny Galecki: I read an article in *Esquire* many, many years ago about how your scent is your essence, and I thought, *That's really interesting*. So I'd pick a specific scent for each character I'd play. As a kid, when I would walk up to Tommy's apartment in Chicago, there was all the ventilation from the dry cleaning, which had this very clean, fresh smell. So I found this cologne, called Clean, that reminded me of that smell, and reminded me of Tommy. Over the years, I went through like two bottles of it. One day I forgot to spray it on and didn't realize it until I was in the middle of a scene, so I asked our second AD [assistant director] to grab my cologne from the bathroom. I *had* to have it. And I know that makes me sound like a crazy person, which is somewhat true, but everyone's process is what it is. And then you become kind of superstitious. Oh, and by the way, I think I gave the last little bit of cologne I had to Chuck Lorre.

Chuck Lorre: That cologne might be sitting in a medicine cabinet somewhere. I stopped using cologne a long time ago, so it's either in a cardboard box or has found its way into a medicine cabinet.

Johnny Galecki: There was also a vase in my room I had to touch and say an internal monologue before I went on set. It's a confidence game. And if you don't have that confidence you're not gonna serve the writing or your castmates. Some nights I would really get in my own way with a long speech or something, and Kaley would come over and whisper in my ear, "You got this." Next take I'd nail it. You need to have that.

Kaley Cuoco: He would get so in his head about everything, especially if he had a big scene. I'd say, "Who cares if you fuck up? I hope you mess up because it's funny! It's OK! But you got this, you do." He would get really flustered, but it would be perfect nearly every time.

Johnny Galecki: It's not manual labor, so I don't want to paint it that way, but even ten years in, I would wake up at 3 a.m. to work on my script and make notes. You want to show up for the writers, the cast, the audience, and not let anybody down.

Kaley Cuoco as "Penny"

Chuck Lorre: Kaley would do a cold read and knock it out of the park. She was flying by the seat of her pants, but she never rested on her laurels. She was always working. She made it look easy, which is part of the genius. That's when you know there's a lot of work going on.

Peter Roth: At every table read I sat across from Jim and Kaley. I remember going up to Kaley and saying, "When you get the scripts, you must spend a good deal of time rereading them and highlighting them," and she said, "No, I never read them." I said, "Wait a second, are you telling me these are cold reads?!" and she said, "Yeah, it's just something I do." I swear, if you saw Kaley Cuoco at those table reads, it was perfection. Her timing was so impeccable.

Johnny Galecki: Oh fuck, it was so annoying. I remember there was a speech the writers wrote as a dare for her that was at least a full page, if not more, and it was all physics jargon and she just nailed it. As Simon said once, she doesn't even open a script, she just puts her hand on top of it and by osmosis absorbs it, and it's amazing. I would go over to her house and walk through the gate, and there would be three feet of scripts piled so high from production assistants that had thrown them over the gate. And she never opened them! I mean, *months'* worth of scripts laying in her yard. And yet she always knew her lines. I would study those lines so much. Whatever Kaley's process is, or sometimes lack thereof, she knows exactly what will make things shine and pop, just by her own instincts. She's an anomaly.

Kaley Cuoco: Chuck still doesn't believe me when I told him I didn't prepare for our table reads. I even said to him once, "I'm sorry, you think after I shoot on Tuesday nights I go home and rehearse Wednesday's script?" He's like, "Yes, I do think that!" I said, "Well, that's not the case, I hate to tell you!"

> **Even though Cuoco has an eidetic (photographic) memory and the material did come relatively easy to her, she most certainly did have a "process."**

Kaley Cuoco: The detailed version is that our scripts wouldn't change a ton from the time we got them to when we shot the episode, so we would rehearse as the week went on, and then block on Monday, and it would just seep into my memory from all of that. Also, I knew Penny so well, I knew what she was going to say before I read it. I just was myself in Penny, and she was a piece of me. And I may have copied Jennifer Aniston on a few things. [*Laughs*] I might have watched *Friends* a few times and thought, *Oh, I gotta give that look or that thing with the hair that she does.* There were definitely Rachel Green / Jennifer Aniston vibes. She had the iconic hair, so I wanted Penny to have iconic hair. And the outfits! To this day you can name a scene that Jen was in as Rachel Green and I know exactly what she was wearing. I know every single facial expression she made on that show. I idolized it, so a lot of my choices probably did actually come from her. It was never meant to be imitation, because I don't believe you can teach those instincts. It's part of your soul. And Jen gave so many unbelievable reactions on that show. Her eyes and the way she conveyed something, there really is no class for that.

Peter Chakos: There were actually a handful of lines that I would turn to my assistant and say, 'Jennifer Aniston,' because she was right on and reminded me of her.

Kaley Cuoco: Mark Cendrowski and I would laugh because there would be so many reactions that Penny would have, that he'd go, "OK, for this one, why don't you do number forty-two? Or, let's try number 202 for this one." He'd make it seem like I had a thousand ways to do it. To this day, he'll text me after watching *The Flight Attendant*, and say, "I loved that moment where you gave us eye roll number forty-three." [*Laughs*]

Chuck Lorre: Kaley is so special. Some people are lucky, but she's the real deal, and that speaks to everybody in this cast. Everybody had done the work and they were just locked and loaded. It goes back to Nikki and Ken for bringing in such remarkable actors.

Simon Helberg as "Howard Wolowitz"

Kaley Cuoco: Before we would do our cast curtain call at the start of the Tuesday night taping, Simon had to run down the apartment staircase and scream like a crazy person. We all had our thing. I had a camera and was always taking photos of everything, but Simon would run down the stairs and scream and then come back up. Every show night! And because the audience was already screaming from excitement, you couldn't hear Simon screaming.

Jim Parsons: I don't even think he'd go all the way down the stairs. He'd lean into the stairs, from that fourth-floor platform, and scream down. I guess we could call that tradition or superstition, or we could call it psychotic. I think that's between Simon and his good doctors. I can't speak to that. [*Laughs*] But in all seriousness, one of the things I think Simon and I connect so deeply about is a certain lifelong struggle with anxiety.

Simon Helberg: I generally run in a high octane of nervousness in terms of performing and functioning, so I was always very, very nervous about so much on the show. It got better in time, but I really do idle at an excessive level of anxiety and nerves.

Kunal Nayyar: I would always take a fifteen- or twenty-minute preshow nap and never set an alarm, because Simon's dressing room was next door to mine and even before he ran down the stairs and screamed, he would always do this warm-up where he would grunt and make this primal yell. That would be my cue to wake up. [*Laughs*]

Simon Helberg: I did it every single tape night and also before most pre-shoots as well. I still do. I was always kind of embarrassed about it, but then eventually I was like, "No, it's not *that* crazy." It's also a good litmus test for "Will these people allow me into their lives or will they send me to an asylum?" And they allowed me into their lives. I may have turned the decibel down a little bit as the years went on. But the truth was, I really liked to warm up. And when I learned that my warm-up in my room was something that would wake up Kunal, I will admit I took pride in that. [*Laughs*] But the stairway thing...yeah, I don't know how that really started...it just became a tradition. But I did *not* go all the way down the stairs; Jim is correct.

> **And as heavy as Parsons's physics dialogue was, Helberg was often tasked with speaking different languages, from Russian to French, and even having to learn sign language.**

Simon Helberg: I had to learn them all for the show. I had to speak Klingon at some point as well. Chuck spoke a little Russian, so I remember him helping me with that. I had to speak Mandarin, which was the hardest, but I loved doing it. It's very musical to learn a new language. But it was like they'd wheel in a trunk, open it and say, *Let's see what kind of tricks we can have Howard do...languages, magic, impressions, monkeys, animals?*

Kunal Nayyar as "Rajesh Koothrappali"

Kunal Nayyar: In the beginning of the show, I was super intense about my process. I always had my script with me and it was highlighted with notes. But it was too intense, because in this format, you just have to relax and trust your instincts. The first two or three years, I was really pushing and trying to make a joke. It took a while for me to really let go. If there was anything that helped me relax, I really enjoyed interacting with the live audience, whether it be looking at the crowd or waving and meeting eyes with someone. That really made me present.

Anthony Rich (first assistant director, director): Both Kunal and Kaley had the ability to pick up the script and start doing it. The two of them were almost like "no-process process." They just kind of showed up and did it. Half the time, Kunal was coming from the golf course or going to the golf course. So, they were always making fun of him.

Jim Parsons: Yes, Kunal would sometimes arrive from the golf course, in what I would refer to as a golf costume, but was really just golf pants and a golf shirt. There was nothing he couldn't wear. I've said it before and I'll say it again, that when you look like Kunal, at least from my taste level, you can throw on any schmata you want and still look cute. And this was even more so because it had that preppy look to it.

Kevin Sussman: I loved working with Kunal. He's so delighted by everything, he would just start cracking up in a scene. So, for me, one of the true pleasures was cracking up Kunal.

> Nayyar's costars loved cracking him up, but they also loved scaring the daylights out of him, as evidenced by the time Helberg shared a scene with him and a tarantula for "The Alien Parasite Hypothesis" (season four, episode ten). In the episode, Raj and Wolowitz battle it out for who's the hero and who's the sidekick in their friendship.

Simon Helberg: Kunal was very scared when we had a scene with that tarantula. He was so deeply, deeply terrified that it actually comforted me and it made me want to really fuck with him, ultimately, because people were throwing fake spiders at him. So when we shot the thing, I felt like I had so much power being so close to Kunal with this tarantula on me that it made me forget that there really was a four-pound hairy spider leaving a trail of God knows what kind of ooze on my shirt. [*Laughs*] But the natural dynamic that existed between Kunal and I off the set from day one was really inherent in what we were always doing on the show. We ribbed each other, we busted each other's balls, and we loved each other and got really annoyed with each other. We were like brothers.

TIME FOR A HOT BEVERAGE...

Hoodies, Orthopedic Shoes, and Alien Pins:
The Secrets of the Costume Design

As far as we know, Raj is not available for personal styling and makeup tutorials, but we're pretty sure he'd have a future in it if he decides to make a career change. *Courtesy of Kaley Cuoco photo collection*

From Mary Richards to Carrie Bradshaw, television has influenced our style for decades. But perhaps no show's costumes were as easily identifiable on a weekly basis than of those on *The Big Bang Theory*. Tight neon jeans with kitschy belt buckles? You bet. Crimson-purple UGGs? Of course. A long-sleeved T-shirt under a Flash T-shirt? We'd expect nothing less.

While Howard's, Penny's, and Sheldon's wardrobes certainly evolved over the years, it never was about staying on trend for these characters. They were comfortable standing out, even if they didn't see it that way. Their uniforms were their armor, their pride, their happy place. Frankly, we should all feel so confident in orthopedic shoes.

Big Bang costume designer Mary T. Quigley was the first to also have a co-producer credit on a sitcom—something that first happened when she worked on Lorre's other sitcom, *Two and a Half Men*. Her vision was unique and methodical—and certainly unorthodox. But it was that distinctive approach to costume design that inspired the Smithsonian's National Museum of American History to come calling at the end of season twelve, a prestigious honor reserved for only the most accomplished in her field. Warner Bros. Television donated Sheldon's iconic Flash T-shirt; Leonard's recycle T-shirt and hooded cargo jacket; Penny's pink tank top and UGG boots; Howard's plaid shirt, red turtleneck, and neon blue jeans; Raj's sweater vest and jacket; Bernadette's yellow cardigan and floral dress; and Amy's brown wool sweater and green knee-length skirt—all curated by Quigley.

Mary T. Quigley: Sheldon's three-quarter undershirt was almost a second skin, like a superhero. And the T-shirt over it gave him strength. I kept him in the same shoes from ECCO for twelve years, but had like twenty pairs of them. Someone like Sheldon was a creature of habit—once he finds a shoe, that's it. And then I decided Sheldon had to have that two-tone, almost Members Only jacket that he wore since the pilot. Sheldon was all about form and function, but he was protecting himself, too.

Jim Parsons: I was completely comfortable and it was fine, but after twelve years of wearing those T-shirts, I really got so sick of it. I wouldn't wear that now for any amount of money. [*Laughs*] And then after the pilot when we came back to film the second episode of season one, my hairstyle became more of a precise, plastered-down look. I always felt it suited the character and made life easier for everybody when it came to continuity. I did get tired of it, so I have felt very happy to have not had that look for a few years now.

If Sheldon's style changed the least over the years, then Penny's most certainly changed the most.

Kaley Cuoco: Early on, I remember those hot girl jean shorts, the tank top, the colored UGGs—and obviously the blue shirt I wore in the pilot, the one hundredth episode, and in the finale. Penny dressed really sexy early on with spaghetti strap tops and really short shorts that you would never find in my house. And my hairstyle in the pilot—the blunt bob with bangs—was how I wore it for the audition. I can't believe how many hairstyles I had over the course of the show. It started as the blonde short bob, then it grew, and then it was short. I really wanted long hair like Rachel Green, so I had all the extensions, and then wavy hair, and then top knots, curly hair, stick straight hair. And buns! The buns, the buns, the buns!

Mary T. Quigley: Penny was the hot girl from Nebraska who lived next door, wearing her Daisy Dukes and really tight tank tops. Penny was so far away from that style when the show ended, but we had to give a nod to it, which is why I put her back in the blue shirt with the purple pattern in the last scene. When the show first started, I wanted her shirts to be slightly lower cut, so I'd pinch it in the middle and do a quick stitch, and we'd call it the Quigley Scrunch. It changed the look of it. I wanted Penny to have that innocent sexy look...she was used to being the hot girl, but she wasn't dressing that way to turn heads; it was just normal for her. And the UGGs were the style in the mid/late 2000s, and Kaley loved that. The first UGGs we saw Penny in were tan and shorter, but then I switched her to the crimson-purple ones. Then to complete the look, I put her in a lot of different floral sweats from Lucky. It was a cute style, and Kaley felt like she was in pajamas all the time, which she liked.

Meanwhile, Johnny Galecki wanted Leonard to have a completely different look than what audiences came to associate with the character.

Johnny Galecki: I initially imagined Leonard as a curly redhead with freckles and glasses, but I couldn't do that because I had to go back to do the play in New York and had already established a certain aesthetic. I do wonder how that would have changed the show or especially the dynamic between Leonard and Penny. Maybe it wouldn't have at all. But my idea was much more a Kevin Sussman / Stuart aesthetic. And when Kevin came on the show, I thought he would have been a really interesting Leonard, which I learned much later that he did audition for Leonard early on. It explained all the death threats that he sent my way. [*Laughs*]

Mary T. Quigley: Leonard had such a softness to him, especially at the beginning. I dressed him layered like that on purpose because he was hiding. He was more comfortable the more layers he had on. His mother was always staring at him and psychoanalyzing, so his wardrobe had to be something he felt comfortable in, even though the writers mentioned the thermostat as a reason for all the layers in later seasons. But once he was dating Penny and had a little confidence, I stopped putting him in the top jacket over the hoodie. Then you had the T-shirts, which eventually transitioned to open, button-down shirts. He got confidence, for sure, but Penny had something to do with that, whether it was secretly taking him out shopping or just them being a couple. He still had the T-shirts, the cords, and the Chuck Taylors, but the style was a bit more confident.

As synonymous as hoodies and Chuck Taylors were with Leonard's style, his crimson-patterned robe was just as memorable.

Mary T. Quigley: I wanted Leonard to have something that was retro and lent itself to a different time period. Beacon robes are made from beacon blankets, and their slogan is "beacon blankets make warm friends." And since he didn't have many friends and was so bullied, it attracted him. He liked the geometric designs in the fabric, and I also liked that the belt had tassels, which reminded me of a graduation cap and mortar board and linked to his intellect. Usually I get doubles of everything, but I did not get doubles of that robe. That was one of a kind.

Johnny Galecki: I liked it, but the tie on it on the belt would get stuck on things all the time. That was kind of his comfort uniform. Now, as for his glasses, those were mine initially, but when we shot the pilot, they were a problem because when I would look up, the lights would hit them. Chuck said, "We can't have that," before asking me if I was really going to wear those on the show anyway. And I said, "Yeah, I've been wearing them all week in rehearsal." Apparently he thought they were just my reading glasses. I said, "No, this is a character choice!" So we had to pop the lenses out, because every time I would look up—especially since Jim was so much taller than me—we would get the glare. So for all twelve seasons, Leonard doesn't have lenses in his glasses. But one time I needed to rub my eye and without thinking, put my finger through the frames. They were like, *Cut!*

And then there was Howard Wolowitz. To call his style unique is like saying the *Titanic* was just a boat.

Simon Helberg: Howard's look was so bold that by the time I stepped out onstage wearing that outfit, I knew who this guy was. I think there were a couple pairs of jeans that I needed assistance with because they were so tight, particularly around the calf. There was some buttering up of the thighs to get the pants off. In the pilot, Mary Quigley had to make a unitard turtleneck because the clothes I wore were so small that the turtleneck was probably for a six-year-old, and it didn't stay tucked into my pants, so she had to sew on a diaper with snaps that basically would hold it in place and prevent it from coming undone. I thought if the show got picked up, this is going to be a long go. But eventually we found some turtlenecks from the long and tall kids department and we could tuck them in. And then to get all those sharp belt buckles so close to so many vulnerable parts, plus the tight pants, and the pin on my turtleneck that would jam into my neck…I was always trying to get used to being smothered by my own wardrobe. But it was also negative twenty degrees in the studio when we would shoot, so it kind of went a long way.

Mary T. Quigley: Wolowitz's look was certainly out there at the time. In the way he was written, he *thought* he was the suave one. If anyone had a closet full of different clothes, it was him. The turtleneck he wore was his interpretation of how Clark Gable used to dress on hiatus between films because Gable used to wear white turtlenecks with a white sweater over his shoulders with white pleated pants. So that was the turtleneck part. And then the colorful skinny jeans were sort of Beatles and Monkees to me, so that's how I came up with the haircut. He thinks he's kind of a rock star. Sometimes I'd get the jeans at Urban Outfitters, but I also dyed a lot of white jeans because I really wanted a saturated color.

However, there's one secret that only Helberg and Quigley know, and she says it will never be revealed.

Mary T. Quigley: The reason why Howard wore the alien pin is between Simon and I, and never to be told. [*Laughs*] Simon and I swore we would never tell anyone why we did it. But there were lots of different alien pins because I had multiple colors depending on what he was wearing. And then the belt buckles were an example of his flashiness.

Helberg won't reveal the reason behind the alien pin, either, but when asked if it's a fascinating reason or just silly, he says this:

Simon Helberg: It may be a little bit of both. That's all I'll say.

But as Wolowitz matured, got married, and became a father, his clothes—while still quite fitted—weren't as loud as they once were, which was a deliberate choice by the writers.

Steve Holland: Howard basically wore the same thing, but we tried to pull away from the bright, bright colors. It was almost subtle enough that when we were doing an episode in season eleven, if we showed a flashback, you could see him in those bright lime green pants, which we had kind of gotten away from...just small changes to let the character grow up a little bit.

Mary T. Quigley: He also began to wear slightly more muted plaid shirts instead of tight T-shirts over the turtlenecks.

But one thing that stayed constant was Wolowitz's bowl cut hairdo, which (thank goodness) never really took off in the real world.

Simon Helberg: It was kind of unspoken that I would never do anything drastic to my hair, so it was always possible to achieve Howard's look. There was that time that Kaley cut her hair and everyone was like, *Whaaaat?* But they never did tell us that we couldn't do anything; it was just sort of expected that when we came back from summer hiatus, we had the same look. I'm sure I could have lobbied to change it, but I felt like it was very specific to him and he would never see any reason to upgrade that style. They flat-ironed it and sprayed it to keep it in place. It had a little movement, but I just wanted it to look like a solid block of hair that you'd find on an action figure or something. I also figured out that if I cut my hair the second we wrapped for the summer and didn't cut it over the next three months, then it was the perfect Howard length by the time we returned.

We'll get to Kaley's pixie cut later in the book. But speaking of hair, Raj's style changed more than audiences might have realized. There was the baseball cap, followed by the mullet, followed by sideburns nearly as long as the mullet, followed by the wavy-looking perm. Then there was the flat-ironed look that lasted most of the series...

Kunal Nayyar: Curly hair is a pain in the ass, because in every scene it might look different, so for continuity's sake, I think they were like, "Let's just iron his damn hair down." And then, ugh, it just became this thing.

Until season eleven, episode ten ("The Confidence Erosion") when Raj revealed that when he first moved to the United States, he wanted to fit in, and since Howard's hair was straight and he was the coolest person Raj knew, he tried to adopt a similar look.

Kunal Nayyar: It was so nice when [we stopped straightening it] because it was almost as if he was regaining his identity that he had lost. It happened in such a beautiful way. He had a fight with his best friend, and said to Howard, "You've bullied me my whole life." Even though he really hadn't, he's like, "You've just put me in this box and I want to be free of it." It was so well done.

But one thing Nayyar never minded over the years was the ridiculous costumes Raj wore for costume parties, or just, uh, parties.

Kunal Nayyar: Fuck. [*Laughs*] But I actually enjoyed dressing up as Catwoman! All that leather spandex was empowering...brought out my inner sex goddess, and I loved it! I loved it a little too much. It may have gone missing on a couple of weekends. But I really enjoyed wearing that costume. The most uncomfortable was the Aquaman costume because of the horse. I couldn't sit down or go to the bathroom because then you'd have to take off the horse and it would be this whole thing. So I had to hold it all night, and it was a long Halloween shoot. The most humbling thing that I probably ever had to wear was when I broke up with Lucy (season six, episode seventeen) and I'm eating lobster half naked. I was wearing three or four pairs of underwear to really push up the gut, because we had to make him look like he had completely let go. So that was very humbling to watch with lobster on my chest hair. And look, I wore cargo pants for twelve years. I'm never wearing cargo pants again. [*Laughs*] Or a checkered sweater. I can't.

(left to right) Helberg, Parsons, director Mark Cendrowski, Galecki, and Nayyar (sorry, Catwoman) embraced their inner superhero personas, no matter how, um, interesting the costume. *Courtesy of Kaley Cuoco photo collection*

Mary T. Quigley: From the track jackets to the cargo pants, every element he wore could have been hip alone in a different outfit. He just put it all together at the same time. And God bless Kunal because there was one purple jacket that was dear to my heart in the early years, and I said, we gotta bring it back for the last show, so he flung it over a chair in the final episode.

Except for Penny, you'd never know the show took place in the very mild climate of Southern California. Amy Farrah Fowler dressed for a cold climate 24/7.

Mayim Bialik: I was definitely well layered. I was always sweating because Amy had so many layers on and didn't really have a sense of different seasons. It was always sweater weather for her, even when everybody else was in short sleeves or tank tops. But I specifically chose not to wear Spanx or any shapewear on the show, so in that sense I got to be comfortable. Many times

I would think I looked much bigger than I actually was because of all the layers, but not enough to wear Spanx. I just didn't want to do it. Plus, the tights Amy wore were exhausting to get on and I had to change tights for every outfit because they were very particular in the wardrobe department, which I understood.

The purple jacket and orthopedic shoes were a staple of Amy's wardrobe, as seen in episode 278: "The Change Constant." *Courtesy of Jessica Radloff*

Bernadette Rostenkowski had a very specific look early on—knee-length dresses with tights and a cardigan—but that eventually changed.

Melissa Rauch: The first time we saw Bernadette, she talked about how her mother picks out her clothes, so that really set the tone for her style. Then Mary Quigley and I figured out what worked best for my body type, and there was one sweater—a cropped cardigan—from the Bloomingdale's line, Aqua, that we thought looked awesome and really fit well. Mary tried to see if they could make any more sweaters like that because they only had them in a couple colors, but then she was like, "Fuck it, we're going to make 'em!" She found someone who hand-knit all of those sweaters and got them in about twenty different colors. Meanwhile, I didn't mind the tights because my legs are basically translucent. Anytime I was on camera on any show without tights, or my arms exposed, they'd break out the body makeup, which would be another twenty minutes applying it and another twenty minutes getting it off. That's why I think The Cheesecake Factory outfits were the only dislike I had, and there was nothing I could do about it because those outfits were already established.

Off duty, the actors were all about comfort—and video games—in their dressing rooms. *Courtesy of Kaley Cuoco photo collection*

Chapter 9

THE UNIVERSE EXPANDS

On September 21, 2009, *Big Bang* returned with an additional three million viewers from the second season finale. Traditionally, ratings fall after the premiere episode, but *Big Bang* was different, growing in overall numbers and the coveted 18–49 demographic each week to become CBS's number one scripted series, as well as television's number one comedy among women and men 18–49. Per *Forbes*, "After two solid but unimpressive years on air, *Big Bang* sky-rocketed up the Nielsen charts" in season three. More so, "in addition to charming 14.3 million overall (putting it at no. 8 among scripted shows),…even in repeats the show cracks the top 3 among all network sitcoms behind its originals." The *Forbes* article concluded that "for a network [CBS] that makes up in viewers what it lacks in buzz, *Big Bang* is something of a rarity."

So why was season three so pivotal? Aside from sharp writing, strong characters, and a desire to see what would become of Penny and Leonard (the season three premiere also marked the first time the characters had sex), the producers decided to shake things up behind the scenes and on camera.

First, there was the addition of writers Maria Ferrari, Steve Holland, and Jim Reynolds—who would all go on to earn executive producer credits—and with the exception of Reynolds (who would go on to create the CBS comedy *The Neighborhood* in 2018)—stay with the series through the finale episode. Even though all three talents didn't have much clout early on, the *Big Bang* writers room was so male-heavy, it made Ferrari's presence in particular all the more critical.

Maria Ferrari: I didn't know anything about the show beforehand. I had to download like twelve episodes on BitTorrent the night before my interview. But it was just a very unusually smooth interview. *Caprica*, the spin-off prequel for *Battlestar Galactica*, was premiering at the time, and I was very excited. It just so happened it was a show Chuck was watching, too. I ended up being what they were looking for, which was a girl who was also interested in topics that the boys were interested in, and I think that was an element they hadn't had in previous iterations of the staff. In fact, there were not any other female writers heading into that season. There had been two, but they weren't there by the time I got there. At that time in my career it was normal to be the only female in a room. I was lucky to have worked with any women at all. There were a lot fewer women in writers rooms back then, and there certainly was not the same sort of scrutiny of writers rooms that there are today.

Steve Molaro: It was always great to have Maria in the room. We didn't have a lot of female writers, so she brought a specific perspective to the characters. Those are the voices you want. She helped round out Penny as a character. But gender aside, she was really good at gang-writing and picking up on how to do that because it's a skill that not everybody has or not everybody's used to.

Like Ferrari, Steve Holland hadn't really watched *Big Bang* before his initial meeting.

Steve Holland: When I took the meeting, you couldn't find the show anywhere. It wasn't on iTunes. I had seen a handful of episodes, but not all of them. The best I could do was read recaps of every episode online, but I wasn't going to go in and pretend I'm a scientist. I did understand the obsessive nature of these characters, and I was always a comic book collector, a pop-culture junkie, and a *Star Wars* fan, so I understood that culture.

On *Big Bang*, and even now on *Young Sheldon*, Holland and Molaro are known as "the Steves." Jim Parsons jokes that they're practically married, even though they both have their own spouses and families.

Steve Holland: We were friendly acquaintances for years at Nickelodeon when I was working on *All That* and Steve was working at Nick online in New York, but it was when we were both on the first season of *iCarly* that we became close. For those first six or seven episodes, Steve and I were basically the whole writing staff, and it was really fun and we just clicked. We also worked on *Zoey 101*. Eventually I was also writing on the first season of *Rules of Engagement* and was waiting to hear if it was picked up again, and Steve got an offer for two shows—a show called *Aliens in America* and *The Big Bang Theory*. I remember watching both of the pilots with him in the writers room at Nickelodeon. He took the job at *Big Bang*, and I went back to *Rules of Engagement*, which did get picked up. It was a great place to work, but it was always on the bubble, so eventually Steve was like, "I think you'd be a good fit over here." But I was hesitant because I knew that almost the entire writing staff had quit or been fired in the first two seasons. I thought, *Well, I'm on this show*—Rules of Engagement—*that's really lovely, but not a lot of people watch it and I don't know if it's coming back. Or, I can go to this place*—The Big Bang Theory—*that seems like it's been famously rough, but is starting to do really well*. I obviously took the job at *Big Bang* and it changed my life. It was an amazing decision, but it was a scary decision to make.

Speaking of Steve—Molaro, that is—the Rubik's Cube tissue box holder next to Sheldon's spot on the couch belongs to him, and first appeared in the beginning of season three.

Steve Molaro: The Rubik's Cube tissue box holder was mine, so it's back at my house now. My friend, Nicole Gastonguay, made that for me to put on the set. Now they're all over Etsy, but she thought of and made the first one.

Now, with a solid writing team in place, the writers and producers started thinking about expanding the cast.

Steve Holland: There was always a desire to have more female scientist representation because it was a very male-heavy show. It wasn't a thing where we were like, *We're going to write this character and have her be part of* *the show*, but it was a thought that this was important for us to do. Bill and Chuck wanted to highlight women in science as well, but it had to be the right role. You don't just write a new character, and say, "This is our new female scientist." You have to find the right roles for people. Sara Gilbert kind of filled that role early on, but she wasn't part of the show as much by season three. I think Amy only turned out to be a neuroscientist because we cast Mayim and she was a neuroscientist in real life. In fact, in the episode where we first meet her, I don't think we ever say what she does. It just became a matter of writing to those character's strengths. As Chuck has always said, we have to treat these characters like human beings first and foremost. The jokes will come later.

> In the fifth episode of season three—"The Creepy Candy Coating Corollary"— the show introduced a new character in what was maybe going to be only a very minor role. A young actress with only a few credits to her name—who was also at the unemployment office just months earlier—got called in to audition. Enter Melissa Rauch for the role of Bernadette.

Melissa Rauch: I still have the email for the audition that read, Enclosed please find the material for the above appointment…Bernadette, guest star. She's a cute, sweet Catholic girl; a super smart biochemist who starts dating Wolowitz, played by Simon Helberg. Shoot date: 9/23-9/29. I auditioned on September 15, 2009, but prior to that audition, I hadn't had one in so long that I called my agency and said, "I'm sorry, but is there anything out there you think I'd be right for?" I needed to work and hated having to make that call, but I just decided to do it. My agent said, "It's very slow," and then two days later I had an audition for *Big Bang*. Needless to say, I was thrilled I got the courage to make that phone call.

Steve Molaro: Her reading was so different from everybody else's. She was funny and cute, and as she walked out, I remember we were all like, *Whoa, she was great. Let's use her!* It was that simple.

Nikki Valko: Melissa Rauch equals comedy gold, and we don't say that easily. We see a lot of actors. She walked into that room and it was like, *Wow.* We had never met her before. She knew where every beat was, every moment. It was a flawless audition, and that's the gold. And the role was only for one, maybe two episodes. Certainly it wasn't what it became.

Ken Miller: You just want to hug her all the time because she's so darn nice. But that sass coming out of that tiny little person...she was a force. That's a lot of presence for someone itty-bitty! It was just a funny visual, and it was just so funny to later see her put the pit bull attitude next to Wolowitz, who was such a mama's boy.

Melissa Rauch: I saved the dress I wore for the audition, which was super close to what ended up being Bernadette's look, and a green cardigan. I wore glasses, even though it didn't say Bernadette wore glasses. There were so many girls auditioning, so I thought, *I need to do something a little different.* I had crappy $10 prop glasses in the glove compartment of my car for auditions, so I decided to throw 'em in my bag just in case. And when I got there, there were so many women auditioning that I thought, *I don't have a shot in hell.* But I put on the glasses as a last-minute decision, and it wasn't until I got the role and was about to do the table read a few weeks later when Nikki Valko and Ken Miller sent a note to my agent saying, "The glasses were really great in the audition; she should wear them in the table read." One of the things I got to keep after *Big Bang* was over was the actual glasses I wore to play Bernadette. I keep those in a special drawer for my kids to have as a special memento years from now, just like how I also saved my parents' voice mail message from the first time they saw my name in the opening credits when I became a series regular.

> The character breakdown called Bernadette a "sweet Catholic girl," but Rauch is Jewish in real life. However, the writers felt that part of the comedy in a character like Bernadette was that Howard's mother really was hoping her son would marry a Jewish girl.

Melissa Rauch: Bernadette originally had the cross necklace and these little cross earrings. They really went for it with her being a devoted Catholic. When you think about who Wolowitz could date that would potentially be someone that would bother his mom or create storylines there, it was genius of them to go in that direction. And the level of how religious she was sort of faded over the years as that character evolved.

Steve Molaro: We always liked that Howard's mother would be unhappy that she wasn't Jewish.

Melissa Rauch: Other than me being Jewish and Bernadette being Catholic, there is so much crossover between Bernadette and myself as far as big moments in our lives. She had her babies before me. I got married a little before, but otherwise, I felt like I was able to work out a lot of things that I was yet to discover in my own life in Bernadette's shoes beforehand. Much like Bernadette fell in love with this group of friends, I did as well.

Kaley Cuoco: Melissa is just the sweetest human being, and so funny. And she was someone that appreciated my nonstop photo taking on set. She was my ally. I love her.

Cuoco and Rauch in costume as Penny and Bernadette during a break in filming the season ten premiere, "The Conjugal Conjecture," in which Penny and Leonad get married again, this time in front of family and friends. *Courtesy of Kaley Cuoco photo collection*

Melissa Rauch: I tend to be a pretty anxious person going into new situations, so I was just very, very worried, but everyone couldn't have been nicer. I remember Kunal standing up as soon as I walked over for the table read. He shook my hand and said, "So nice to meet you." Kaley invited me to join her at spin class, which was really cool. And Simon heard I was a writer as well, so he had done some research and had a bit of info on me to start a conversation, which was really sweet.

Simon Helberg: Who was she? Which character did she play? I have a slight memory. We never did solve that murder that happened on set, so it has to be the little squeaky-clean one, the one you least expect. It was Mrs. Rauch. [*Laughs*] No, I was like, *Where did she come from?* I just hadn't really seen her work before. But when you're at the table read and everyone looks up from their script to see who this person is...it's that moment of *Holy shit, there is someone spectacular here.*

Johnny Galecki: Melissa is one of the most talented people I've ever met. Her presence was so refreshing. She's such an amazing writer, too.

Melissa Rauch: I had done just a few episodes when I saw Johnny at a restaurant. I wasn't a series regular yet, and I was unsure of whether I should go over and say hello. Before I knew it, he was over at my table asking my husband and I to join him. It was such a kind gesture and made me feel so welcome. But I'll never forget on tape nights when I first started, you'd get a meal ticket to go to the commissary and get your dinner. However, during my first week, I accidentally tossed a bag in the trash and threw my meal ticket out. Because I'm such a follow-the-rules person, I didn't know if I'd get in trouble for losing it and I didn't know who to ask, so I was looking to see if I could spot my bag with the ticket in the garbage can. Johnny passed by me—and I had very little interaction with him up until this point—and said, "You all right there? Just picking through our garbage?" He was really funny about it, but I was *mortified*.

Johnny Galecki: Melissa and I just really hit it off. She's so quick and so funny that I just immediately took to her, you know, outside of the trash can incident. [*Laughs*] I saw her working so hard, and I think it probably reminded me to continue doing the same. The most frightening and exciting part of any job is day one, and she handled it beautifully.

Jim Parsons: Melissa was the first person that was becoming a regular presence outside of the original five, which must have been a weird feeling for her. And in the first six months that we worked together, I started getting really irritated that she and I didn't do more together. I wanted to see our characters interact more because I just really liked her. She was not only fresh meat, but a pleasure to be around. [*Laughs*]

Melissa Rauch: Jim and I bonded over New York City and what we were missing about it. We had both unknowingly lived blocks from each other before moving out to LA and discovered we loved the same diner. We didn't really get the chance to work together much when I first joined the cast, but I loved talking to him so much.

Rauch's portrayal of Bernadette also helped begin the slow and necessary transformation of Howard Wolowitz from an inappropriate, sexist man-child to an upstanding, reformed husband and eventual father.

Simon Helberg: Howard was such a sleazy, philandering, lothario for so long, I didn't know if that was just his fate to continue that sad cycle, so when Melissa came on, I thought, *Oh, this is going to be really fun.* She was written differently from the other women Howard had gone out with or gone for. And when I met Melissa, I was immediately and completely won over. Her charm is irresistible, and as well as her signature voice, which got higher as the episodes went on. Initially I don't think dogs in St. Louis were rolling on the ground covering their heads with their paws. But it was there. And I thought, *Oh my God, finally, someone who is smaller than me!* She really is the kindest, gentlest person. I don't know how to say it in a way that rings of clichés, but I really do mean it. I might have exploited her as some kind of makeshift therapist throughout the years because her eyes are just enveloping so you let go completely. I have a really strong memory of her first episode—that scene in the restaurant where the date happened. I remember the feeling and the exchanges and the looks and saying something about a crucifix, and then the scene in the car doing magic for her. It was like having the best partner you could have. You're really only as good as your partner, so I was happy to be doing the show in tandem with her forever from then on out.

But if you go back and watch those early episodes, Bernadette is a much more mousy, one-dimensional character. Thanks to Rauch's talent, and the writers getting to observe her chemistry with Helberg and the rest of the cast, she became so much more interesting, and really went toe-to-toe with Wolowitz.

Chuck Lorre: Over time we made Bernadette somewhat nefarious. She was a cutthroat corporate character. You didn't mess with her. Part of the joy of that was her voice is a wonderful instrument. It's like a piccolo on acid. And then, she's tiny. So those two things juxtaposed with this balls-to-the-wall killer woman who doesn't even think twice about cutting some moral corners to get things done...it was joyful to watch. The character became so much more than what was originally created.

Steve Holland: We hadn't quite figured out that character in those early episodes. Melissa worked more than the character worked early on, so we had to figure out how to make the character work. Bernadette didn't really understand jokes at first, but that's definitely not who she became. Melissa just popped.

Melissa Rauch: There was a lot of joking from fans, like, "Are you going to yell at me?" [*Laughs*] Or "You seem so nice, but we know how Bernadette is." I was so excited to play that edge with Bernadette because it wasn't there in her first couple of episodes. The layers they gave to her, in the same way that they gave layers to all the characters, was so rewarding to play. I loved that they had female scientists. On another show, you might have writers say, "We already have a female scientist that's one of the girlfriends, we don't need another one," but that wasn't the case here. It's a credit to our writers that they developed such rich, complex women in the same profession who were wildly different. That's how it should be, but it doesn't always happen. Here, it did.

Bernadette's demeanor wasn't the only thing that changed as the season progressed. Her voice got higher.

Melissa Rauch: It always shocks people when they hear me speak in real life, since I don't sound like Bernadette. Her voice is way easier on my vocal cords than my own voice. It's crazy. I think there's something about the higher register for Bernadette's voice that doesn't rub up against the vocal cords in the same way. Whenever I would imitate Mrs. Wolowitz, Carol Ann [Susi, who played Mrs. Wolowitz] would coach me on proper vocal care, whether it was a specific kind of lozenge to take or drinking enough tea. That was her natural voice, but she did so much to take care of it. So for the weeks I knew I'd have to do Mrs. Wolowitz's voice, I used the Bee-keeper's Propolis spray, plus some other pastilles that she recommended. She was a big Ricola lady, so I had those, too. Fans will often ask me to do the voice, and I am more than happy to oblige. I've been asked in doctor's office waiting rooms to do it. [*Laughs*] But this was my dream job, and I had that job because of the people that watched the show, so I find it flattering.

> **Rauch's first episode also marked Wil Wheaton's first guest appearance. But getting Wheaton—best known for playing Wesley Crusher from *Star Trek: The Next Generation*—to play a version of himself that was Sheldon's archnemesis almost didn't happen.**

Wil Wheaton ("Wil Wheaton"): I was actually really against the show when I first heard about it. I thought it was going to be making fun of people like me—lifelong nerds. Whenever somebody in entertainment wants to do something about our culture, odds are the nerds are going to be the butt of the joke. So I was super not into it. But at some point I gave it a chance, and then I was disappointed in myself for judging it that way. It was really unfair to the creators. I became a massive fan and tweeted about how much I loved it, when Steve Molaro saw that tweet and invited me to set.

> **That was it—a set visit, not a role. That invitation was quickly amended into something better, but even still, Wheaton wasn't immediately on board.**

Wil Wheaton: I got an email from Bill Prady's assistant saying he'd love to have a conversation with me. And bless Bill forever, he talked to me like I was a person he deeply cared about who knew nothing about his show. He was so kind. I have lived my life in the entertainment industry, and my experience up to this point was, by and large, producers are dicks. And my experience on *Big Bang* fundamentally changed that. Turns out that it's not that producers are dicks, it's just that I had the unfortunate experience of working with two really awful ones in my life and assumed all were like that. Bill and I are extraordinarily good friends now. But I got on the phone with Bill, and he said he wanted me to come on the show and play a version of myself.

Bill Prady: He was unsure about playing himself in the show...which is not unusual. You become an actor so you don't have to play yourself. You become an actor so you can be other people. Molaro was the one that pointed out that Wil lived around Pasadena at the time and he certainly would hang out in the comic book store where the guys went because Wil did in real life. So, they said, "Let's get Wil." And at the time, I was the one who would wind up making that call to potential guest stars to try and get them on the show.

Wil Wheaton: I felt playing myself was cheating…that it's not something I've earned. Or it was going to be a one-off where someone would say, "Hey, look, it's the kid from *Star Trek*," and then it's over. And I didn't want that. I loved the show. I wanted to be part of the show. So, I said, "Bill, I love that you're asking me to do this, but would you be willing to see me for a character?" He said, "I understand 100 percent where you're coming from. No actor likes to play themselves. But you are the only actor who can play Wil Wheaton." He still promised to bring me in when they were in the process of casting someone that fit my general description, but he really wanted me to play myself. He told me to take some time to think about it, so afterwards I called my friend John Rogers, who was the co-creator of *Leverage* on TNT. He was quiet for a minute until he said, "Are you fucking serious right now? You have been given an opportunity to be on one of the most popular television series in the English-speaking world, and you're asking fucking questions about it? What the fuck is wrong with you? Get on the phone to Bill Prady and tell him you will do whatever he wants you to do or we're not friends." So, I called Bill back and said yes.

Bill Prady: [*Laughs*] Yes, he did, and thank goodness. I remember being terrified to also call him and say, "We made your character evil," but man, he was happy about it! He went, "Oh, my God, this is the greatest thing ever!" It gave him a character to play—"Evil Wil Wheaton." [*Laughs*] And then the character evolved over time and ultimately became a friend of the guys, but I loved that he was okay with that.

Wil Wheaton: The man who was my father was a really awful person and made me feel small and unworthy and like an imposter every single day of my life until I ended contact with both of my parents a number of years ago. I never had the unconditional love and support that I think you need to feel really comfortable taking creative risks and just existing. I was just constantly afraid somebody was going to realize that I was a fraud. That's how I felt going into *Big Bang*, especially playing myself. Because what am I going to do if they hate me *as me*? I think a big part of me being reluctant to play myself was like, "If I can't play myself, what can I do?" Thank goodness it all worked out well. God bless Mark Cendrowski for getting a subtle, hilarious, nuanced, un-self-conscious performance out of me. Because my anxiety could really have messed all of that up. And it didn't. I've been incredibly blessed in my life to be in two casts that became family: *Star Trek* and *Big Bang Theory*. These two shows gave me the family that I didn't have.

Melissa Rauch: I adore Wil Wheaton. Everyone adores Wil Wheaton. He's such a genuine soul who you can't help but smile around him. It's one of the many reasons I think his work as the asshole version of Wil Wheaton on *Big Bang* is so damn funny and perfectly done. He is so *not* that guy. The polar opposite, in fact, and he just nailed it every time.

Wheaton, Rauch, and Sussman during a rehearsal day. Rauch and Wheaton both made their *Big Bang* debut in the season three episode, titled "The Creepy Candy Coating Corollary." *Courtesy of Melissa Rauch*

And as worried as Wheaton was that he would be playing himself, turns out he didn't have much to worry about.

Wil Wheaton: My wife and I were in San Francisco when a jogger came by and said, "I'm so sorry to bother you, but I think I've seen you on *The Big Bang Theory*." I said, "You have." And he said, "This is really embarrassing for me. I know that you play Wil Wheaton, but I don't know what *your* name is." And I was thrilled. I was beside myself. I was like, "Thank *you*." I go all the way back to not wanting to play myself because I didn't think it would count. Turns out that it did.

The good fortune continued for the show. On November 16, 2009, "The Adhesive Duck Deficiency" aired, and instantly became a fan-favorite episode. Leonard, Raj, and Wolowitz were off on a camping trip in the desert to catch the Leonid meteor shower, while Sheldon remained at home. Penny slipped in the shower and dislocated her shoulder, leaving Sheldon as her only hope to get her to the hospital.

Steve Molaro: One of the driving forces behind that story is we wanted to find a way that Sheldon had to drive. We knew he couldn't drive, and we thought it would be funny to find circumstances in which he had to get behind the wheel. So that was part of the genesis...and then you're asking yourself, "How would she get hurt? Well, she slips in the shower and has to go to the hospital." We were pushing the boundaries of Sheldon and Penny in that episode. He accidentally touches her chest, so we were exploring what we could do with that relationship and what might feel too much and what would just be really funny.

Jim Parsons: I remember trying to stage the scene where it looks like Sheldon might have just touched her breast. That whole episode was the kind of magic that I grew up watching on TV and wanting to be part of.

Maria Ferrari: I helped Molaro with an early draft of that episode, which was a really special experience. I went home and was like, "Oh yeah, I did it! That's going to buy me at least a week!" [*Laughs*]

Jim Parsons: I also remember sitting next to Kaley as Penny in the hospital waiting room, filling out the medical forms for her and asking, "When was your last menstrual period?" and she glares at me, and I say, "I'll put 'in progress.'" [*Laughs*] It was just one thing after another of them butting styles. She needed help and comfort, and he just couldn't give it to her. I don't watch reruns, but that episode occurs to me on my own, because it's particularly special to me. I think I'll go to my grave particularly happy to have done that one, particularly happy to have done that scene in the waiting room and that scene in her bedroom, trying to get that shirt on her, and that scene in the car when I'm driving her. It was just so much goddamn fun. There is an ease to what Kaley does that I'm always amazed by.

Maria Ferrari: The Sheldon-Penny dynamic was the heart of the show. In junior high–high school, I didn't get to participate in dating, but I had so many friends that were boys... kind of that brother-friend zone you get in. Those were really, really valuable to me, because that was as close as I was getting to this feeling of having a boyfriend. I kind of saw that in Sheldon and Penny, and I think I described it to Chuck as being emotionally sexy. Those are the moments that are the most exciting to me. In the two hundredth episode, when Penny was talking to Sheldon about how she probably wouldn't have liked him in high school, but she's so glad she's his friend now, it's kind of like grown-ups healing from that original hurt.

Steve Holland: A lot of times, especially in season three as a new writer, I wasn't really in the room for a lot of the writing. If you weren't in the room, you just worked regular hours. You'd come up with stories, hang out with some of the other writers, bang story ideas around, and then at six or six thirty, go home. But for whatever reason, I was there late-ish that night in my office when they were doing the rewrite. They had gotten to the tag—the last scene of the episode—and didn't have anything. They were like, "Who is still around who can help?" I came in and pitched the tag that was Leonard, Koothrappali, and Wolowitz sitting around and telling ghost stories around the campfire, and it was Koothrappali who said, "*...and he looked over and saw...she was his cousin!*" It was the callback to Wolowitz who earlier in the episode admitted he had slept with his second cousin. That got a good laugh, and it got a good laugh at the runthrough the next day, which was the crack in the door that got me in the room more and more.

Kunal Nayyar: And when we were filming that scene that takes place in the desert, Raj, Leonard, and Howard got high, and I took my shirt off. And Chuck Lorre said, "Put the shirts back on," because [we] have gym bodies and these characters should not have gym bodies. I was in very good shape around seasons two and three and was working out a lot. And then after that I took my shirt off like twenty times on the show, and no one said anything!

Simon Helberg: Yeah. [*Imitating Kunal*] "Standards and practices came up and said, 'All of the women in America are going to get too hot and bothered if you take your shirt off. They are going to start ripping their clothes off.'" [*Laughs*] That's hilarious.

Galecki, Nayyar, and Helberg during filming of "The Adhesive Duck Deficiency" in season three, which marked a turning point for new writer (at the time) Steve Holland. *Courtesy of Kaley Cuoco photo collection*

At this point in the series, the phrase "Bazinga!" had been introduced and mentioned in four episodes (Sheldon first said it in the season two finale, "The Monopolar Expedition"), but it had yet to take off as a quantifiable catchphrase. That all changed in the fourteenth episode of season three—"The Einstein Approximation," otherwise known as the ball pit episode.

And whether the cast and writers liked the term or not (and eventually they didn't), a new expression was born.

Steve Molaro: It's a complicated story. In the episode, nobody really wanted to hang out with Sheldon, so he goes from one friend's place to another, until Leonard 'rescues' Sheldon in the middle of the night in a ball pit at House O' Fun, a children's play center. And also, Sheldon made a joke for the first time in the ball pit, so we thought it would be funny if he said something, but then he was just kidding. Chuck felt it was important to shine a light on the fact that Sheldon was making his own joke at that moment, so that request came for him to say "Gotcha" or some sort of *I'm making an attempt at humor*. When we were looking for a way to do that, Lee Aronsohn said, "What's that other word we heard?" which was writer Stephen Engel's use of *bazinga*. Stephen would intentionally play terrible practical jokes in the writers room to be funny, like a room bit. He would have a grapefruit, and when he finished his grapefruit, he would put the two halves back together with scotch tape and say, "Hey, would somebody like a grapefruit?" You'd say, "Sure, Stephen, thank you. This grapefruit looks amazing." And we'd pull the two halves apart knowing that they were taped together, and he would say, "Haha, bazinga, gotcha!" And that's where it came from. It's kind of a boring story, actually. [*Laughs*]

"Bazinga" is used sparingly throughout the rest of season three. But viewers loved the word immediately, and it became a staple of Warner Bros. and *Big Bang Theory* merchandise. The writers still find it rather amusing.

Steve Holland: We had a complicated relationship with *bazinga* because it felt like it was becoming a catchphrase in a sort of not-great way, so we retired it almost entirely. After season four or five, we almost never said it, but it was always the thing that was associated with *Big Bang*. And sometimes in a detrimental way, because people would use it to mock the show sometimes. We maybe said it thirty times—if that—over the course of 279 episodes. But we couldn't escape it. And yet, people loved it and latched on to it and it was part of the show's identifying features.

Chuck Lorre: We said, "Oh no, we do not want a funny catchphrase. We do not want to go down that road; it's a cheap road." But no one agreed with us. [*Laughs*] They all kept writing about it as if it were a part of the show. And we dropped it immediately when it became a T-shirt. We still can't get away from it, but no harm, no foul. At the time, we were trying to grow the show, and a show with catchphrases is not the show we wanted to do.

Steve Molaro: I was afraid that it was just going to wear out its welcome. Those catchphrases are a double-edged sword. If we were going to mention the word, there had to be a really good reason or joke.

Jim Parsons: I fell into the trap of people who thought I said that all the time on the show, but the truth is, I didn't. What I did was sign T-shirts with my face and that word on it time and time again, so in that way, I have kind of an "eh" relationship with the word. It doesn't mean anything emotionally to me. But everybody felt so deeply in their own ways about it.

While no one was keen on the word *bazinga*, there was even more animosity toward the actual ball pit scene, which was built on *Big Bang*'s stage and featured Sheldon popping up and down like a human whack-a-mole.

Jim Parsons: I hated that. Hated it. [*Laughs*] It was a lot more effortful than one would imagine it to be, or I would have imagined it to be. And the balls were so dirty. I had to go to the bathroom during a break while we were shooting that scene, and I wiped my hands on these paper towels, and I realized I was covered in a light gray ash from these balls. I was like, *I'm so fucking disgusted!* But there's nothing I won't do for a scene, as it turns out, between snakes, monkeys, and God knows what else. Jim as a human, would never, ever, ever, be in this position. But I dove right back in and just kept going. I mean, I was being paid, so there was that. Maybe it's just that I'll chase a paycheck. I have no idea. But I did it. And while I did not like being in the ball pit specifically, I did like being part of the scene because I just thought it was a wonderful comedy device.

Johnny Galecki: Oh yeah, the ball pit was disgusting. We were literally covered in dirt during the pretape because they had rented like two thousand balls and they were filthy from prior use. We didn't make a lot of requests over the years, but when we did that scene for the live taping, we asked them to please hose the balls down with some Clorox or something before we got back into the pit.

Judy Parsons: I actually liked when Sheldon was in the ball pit. A lot of Jim's real personality kind of came through in that, but also, I thought, *What a beautiful show about friendship*. Leonard knows Sheldon's wacky, and all these crazy things are going on in his head, but he's his friend, and he very patiently tries to work him out of the ball pit to the point where he actually gets in the ball pit.

> As season three drew to a close, the writers came up with an idea to have Koothrappali and Wolowitz put Sheldon on a dating website. The payoff was that he would meet a girl who was basically Sheldon in female form, and leave Koothrappali and Wolowitz wondering what kind of Pandora's box they just opened. There was no grand plan for what followed next, or even if the woman the producers cast would be back in season four. But what transpired would change everything for the series, from ratings highs to critical acclaim.

Steve Molaro: I pitched the idea of Raj and Howard putting Sheldon on a dating website and they find a match. I don't even think I finished the sentence when Chuck said, "Well, go write that!" So we did. But at the time, there were no plans for anything beyond that episode, which was the finale that season.

> Unbeknownst to the producers, Mayim Bialik—best known for the NBC '90s sitcom *Blossom*—was getting back into acting after a decade-long break. The reason? Her health insurance from being a grad student at UCLA— where she got her PhD in neuroscience—was expiring.

Mayim Bialik: My then husband was a grad student also, and we had an infant and a toddler, so I figured if I could get a couple guest spots I would get enough to get my Screen Actors Guild health insurance. But I wasn't planning on being a regular actor; I didn't think anybody would want me on a TV show again. I did an episode of *Bones* and an episode of *Saving Grace*, but for the most part, casting directors didn't know who I was. They were all too young, and anyone worth their weight as a casting director wouldn't just hire someone who was a teen actor and left the industry at nineteen. So I had no qualms about auditioning for *The Big Bang Theory*.

And not that it was a requirement, but Bialik had never watched *The Big Bang Theory* prior to her audition.

Mayim Bialik: Someone told me I was mentioned on *Big Bang* in an earlier season (season one, episode thirteen, "The Bat Jar Conjecture"), so I thought it was a game show, like, I must have been on *Jeopardy!* as an answer. I literally Googled Jim Parsons the day of the audition 'cause they were like, "We want a female Jim Parsons." That's how I prepared for the audition— watching Jim Parsons on YouTube for thirty seconds.

At that point, Bialik realized that no, this was not a game show, and more important, there was something very unique about the character of Sheldon Cooper.

Mayim Bialik: After I watched a clip of Jim Parsons, I realized Sheldon is a very special character. As a grad student in the sciences, I know a lot of special people, and I think in academia, especially, you run into a lot of unusual people who have a lot of Sheldon qualities. So when I auditioned, I believe I didn't make eye contact. It was a choice that I made as the character, and even when I got the part, we rehearsed it both ways. We rehearsed it with Amy making eye contact and one without. And I think someone said it was a good sign they wanted me to make eye contact because they said, "Maybe that means they'll bring you back!" Whereas if you look down, it's hard to imagine them keeping a character going who never makes eye contact. [*Laughs*] So I definitely felt like I understood who that character was, and that personality. But you never know what they're going to go for. No idea.

Steve Molaro: Kate Micucci, who would eventually play Raj's love interest, Lucy, auditioned before Mayim, and we thought she was terrific and really funny. And then Mayim came in, and aside from being awesome as well, Chuck loved that she actually had a PhD in neuroscience. It could have gone either way between Mayim or Kate, but because Mayim could bring an authenticity to the science and to the intelligence of the character, Chuck was like, "I think that's so cool. Let's go with her."

Ken Miller: When Mayim came in for the audition, Chuck said, "You know, we're looking for a female version of Sheldon," and Mayim goes, "I got it." She knew exactly what she was going to do with the character. But the role could have been one-and-done if it didn't click. And it was anything but. They kept writing for her.

Mayim Bialik: I'm not a comfortable auditioner, and I was auditioning along with a group of women who I assumed were more talented and competent than I was, because that's just the kind of female I am. [*Laughs*] I'm nervous for every audition, but I had a nursing infant that I had left at the park with their dad. I also barely had clothes that fit me. I had a girlfriend who took me to J.Crew just to get me some clothes that looked safe for auditions. So I was in some sort of J.Crew pencil skirt and a little cardigan set that I got on sale.

Nikki Valko: I think Mayim would admit this herself—at least she did to us—that she's a little awkward socially with people who she doesn't know, so it was perfect. It really was. Again, we got really lucky, because it was a tough role.

Mayim Bialik: The original way I presented Amy was much more consistent with certain spectrum-y features. The character definitely grew and changed, and they had her come out of her shell more, but I took a more clinical approach with Amy, without wanting to label her. There was a professor who I was very close to at UCLA who I actually based Amy on. I haven't reached out to tell her, but maybe it would be safe to do so now. There was a lot about her personality and the way she spoke that kind of skimmed the surface of not quite friendly, but also wasn't not friendly, so that was some of my basis for Amy early on.

Peter Chakos: I directed the episode when we first meet Amy. During the runthrough Mayim was doing this thing where she wasn't looking at people, and in my opinion, I didn't think that she was as different as Sheldon, so to speak, so I said, "Maybe don't do that." But then Chuck said, "Maybe you should kind of look away from them," and she said, "I specifically was told not to do that." [*Laughs*] So she did it that way, but then Chuck said, "No, go back to what you were doing." I exhaled. But I get why it was something that was discussed. When we did the flashback episode where Sheldon meets Leonard for the first time, he wasn't looking at him; he was looking away or looking down. But to me, I never saw Amy Farrah Fowler doing that when she first met Sheldon.

Lee Aronsohn: By the way, when we were writing the role, we were talking about how this woman should have a middle name. We figured her parents were from the late '70s, early '80s, so they would name her after Farrah Fawcett. And we liked the alliteration of Amy Farrah Fowler.

Based on that one scene, there was a certain spark between Parsons and Bialik as Sheldon and Amy that led the producers to think maybe this wasn't such a one-off role after all.

Jim Parsons: My sister was a big fan of *Blossom*, but I probably saw Mayim more on *Beaches* than on *Blossom*. Shortly before *Big Bang*, Todd and I were fans of TLC's *What Not to Wear*, and we just happened to watch the episode that featured Mayim, so that's one of the first things I said to her when we first met. Anyway, when she came on the show, I didn't know what the plan was because it was for one scene in the finale and we went on hiatus after that. But I quickly started counting Mayim as a major gift they had given me. I didn't realize how meaningful it would be to be paired with somebody like that, as an actor. It's not unlike how it feels in real life when you're single and all your friends are paired off. It can feel very lonely, so I felt this immense sense of gratitude that I had that kind of partner.

Mayim Bialik: I was walking on to a show where he was the standout star; his character was so special to people, and everyone on that cast was so talented, so it was very intimidating. Thankfully Jim and I have a very similar work ethic, although I'm much more chatty, I think, than he would like me to be most of the time. [*Laughs*] He tended to be much more focused, in general.

And even to this day, Bialik hasn't seen every episode of *The Big Bang Theory*.

Mayim Bialik: I've really seen only a handful of episodes; it's kind of embarrassing. When I came on, I didn't even know that Raj's character couldn't talk to women unless he was drunk. I didn't know Sheldon had a spot and I felt like a real dodo when I tried to sit there when we were blocking one of my first scenes in the living room. Our director, Mark Cendrowski, was like, "You can't sit there. That's Sheldon's spot." I was like, "Oh yeah, of course!" but I literally had no idea what he was talking about. So embarrassing.

Chapter 10

THE LOVE STORY OF LEONARD & PENNY *AND* JOHNNY & KALEY

The love story of Penny and Leonard is not an easy one to tell. Sure, they had more starts and stops than most—eventually resulting in marriage, and at least one child that we know of—but so much of the authenticity of that relationship you saw on-screen was because of the true love and respect that Kaley Cuoco and Johnny Galecki had off-screen. Scenes that they shared early on as their characters were the catalyst for the eventual romance that developed between them in real life. And when that romantic relationship ended, their professional commitments and on-screen dialogue helped Cuoco and Galecki heal in a way that might otherwise not have happened. They developed a friendship that runs deep—and is in many ways the true love story of the show. Three plus years after *Big Bang* wrapped production, the duo are as tight as ever, which was made evident by the countless Zooms that they did together for this book in order to pay homage to Penny and Leonard—and each other. At times, it's hard to know where Penny and Leonard end and Kaley and Johnny begin. Or vice versa. As Galecki says now, "To this day, she and I are so dearly close. We are family."

Kaley Cuoco: I think a lot of what made Leonard and Penny work so well was my relationship with Johnny off camera, which turned into such sarcastic banter that bled into Penny and Leonard. Johnny and I's relationship, in a way, was mimicking Penny and Leonard. They were always giving each other shit, and Johnny and I have a similar relationship—which you do after years of being together. We've always had each other's backs, and you can't lose that. And I do think it happened on-screen. It made our relationship funny and endearing.

Cuoco and Galecki had sizzling chemistry from the start. *Courtesy of Johnny Galecki*

Although Cuoco and Galecki were the most well-known stars thanks to 8 Simple Rules and Roseanne, respectively, when Big Bang launched, the two didn't know each other. But when they met, there was an immediate connection—and for Cuoco, a desire for something more.

Kaley Cuoco: I had a very big crush on Johnny early on. I was so not even hiding it. He has such swagger. We were both dating people at the time, but I only had eyes for Johnny. Then, when I found out he had eyes for me too, I was like, *Uh-oh, this is going to be trouble.*

Johnny Galecki: I have a healthy ego, but you really have to kind of club me over the head to let me know you're flirting with me. I had zero idea of any sort of crush before Kaley and I began dating.

From the start, the script called for Leonard to have a crush on Penny, declaring that their "babies [would] be smart and beautiful." On paper, it

never should have worked—she was a gorgeous, naive, aspiring actress from Nebraska; he was a brilliant experimental physicist with no swagger, mommy issues, and a lack of confidence. But that was also the draw—two people from different worlds with an intrigue for each other (in all fairness, more so from Leonard than Penny, at least initially). It's a classic formula that, when done right, can work so well. From Ross and Rachel to Sam and Diane to Tony and Angela, Penny and Leonard had that same potential, which became apparent in the sixth episode of the series—"The Middle Earth Paradigm"—when a drunk Penny, dressed as a sexy kitty cat, kisses Leonard at her Halloween party after her ex-boyfriend shows up. It was technically the first kiss for Cuoco and Galecki as well.

Kaley Cuoco: I knew I looked *real* cute in that outfit, so I was feeling really good about myself. [*Laughs*] And I knew he thought I looked cute because he commented on how cute I looked in that outfit earlier. But I was definitely nervous before that kiss.

Johnny Galecki: I mean, Kaley Cuoco as a kitty cat? Come on!

Kaley Cuoco: All the scenes up until we actually got together in real life, it was obvious there was always something there. There was chemistry and we were crushing on each other. That was the whole first season until we actually got together for real.

Johnny Galecki: But let's go back to how it was kissing me for the first time. I want to hear more about that. Do I kiss differently in character?

Kaley Cuoco: I was very nervous with both [the on-screen and real-life first kisses]. I mean, I was kissing him as Penny before we ever dated, and it's weird when you have a crush on someone and you're kissing them as actors.

The crush continued to grow stronger for Cuoco, which made filming "The Nerdvana Annihilation" later that season somewhat of a turning point. In the episode, Leonard has a dream and saves Penny in the elevator shaft. The two are literally nose-to-nose, their bodies intertwined; it would seem like a dream scenario, but the reality of the situation was that it was getting harder and harder for Cuoco to hold back her feelings.

Kaley Cuoco: It was not an enjoyable experience for me.

Johnny Galecki: First of all, print that. [*Laughs*] We had to be in each other's arms—and for quite some time, because it was a bit of a stunt that we were doing. It was a whole thing, and it was a pretape since it took a little while. Kaley didn't look freaked out at all. In fact, she looked extremely happy in those arms. That was certainly one of the moments that I think—

Kaley Cuoco: I think we fell a little in love in that elevator shaft.

Johnny Galecki: We felt something, yeah. I think that was a massive turning point [in our relationship]. At that point, both she and I knew that something mutual was felt, and that it was going to be more of a distraction from the work to try and continue to ignore it than to actually recognize it and surrender to it.

Kaley Cuoco: I was like, *Uh-oh.* I was crushing so hard on him. So much so that I was like, *Get me out of here*, because he had to hold me up and we had to do this really close thing. Even my cheeks were really red. I was super nervous and kept thinking, *Oh my God, oh my God, oh my God.* I was just a nervous wreck being that close to him in the moment.

You'll have a greater appreciation next time you watch this scene in season one, episode fourteen ("The Nerdvana Annihilation") on HBO Max since it's where Cuoco and Galecki realized there was no turning back from their real-life romantic feelings. *Photo™ & © Warner Bros. Entertainment Inc.*

The dream sequence where Leonard was holding Penny in the elevator shaft is captured in a photograph of the pair on Penny's refrigerator. But as executive producer Steve Molaro points out, that picture could technically never exist.

Steve Molaro: It makes me crazy because technically that photo was from the fantasy sequence, so it shouldn't be a real photo on her refrigerator. Unless Leonard said, "Hey, we should go re-create this image I have from a dream of mine and get in the elevator shaft and have somebody take a picture of us," it doesn't belong there.

Kaley Cuoco: And Leonard doesn't have his glasses on, either! All these things are wrong with the photo, but you couldn't really tell where we were, so it worked.

As season one was coming to an end, Cuoco's crush on Galecki remained just that—a crush. While the four guys often hung out outside of the show, she did not. As the youngest in the group, she was off doing her own thing— or at least the guys thought she was. It wasn't long before that all changed during one of the guys's getaway trips to the picturesque, ritzy seaside town of Montecito, California.

Johnny Galecki: We would finish rehearsal and Kaley would just take off. She was the youngest—and beautiful, of course—and would just get into her cool car and peel out. And we'd still be standing in the parking lot talking about rehearsal. We just thought she was too cool to hang out with us. But I guess she didn't know we were hanging out all the time. So, obviously when the guys and I went up to Montecito, she wasn't there because we had given up on inviting her places. But we were talking about her, so I called her and left a voice mail saying, "Hey, we're all here playing board games, drinking wine, hanging out, and Montecito is only a two-hour drive from LA." As soon as I left that message, she called right back. She was like, "I just broke up with my boyfriend!" And she was upset.

Cuoco wanted to know where in Montecito they were—the San Ysidro Ranch, Galecki told her—so without hesitation she told him, "I'm coming! I'll be right there."

Kaley Cuoco: When he called me, I was at home, and I packed a bag and hopped in my car and just drove.

Johnny Galecki: I went down to the front desk and got her a cabin, which ended up being the cabin next to mine. By the time she showed up it was pretty late, and I had gone to bed. And then I got a call. It was Kaley. She said, "There's a bug in my room." I was like, "Yeah, probably. You're in a cabin." She said, "You have to come and kill it." I said, "I'm not doing that." Now, still to this day, I don't know if this story is bullshit or not, and if she was flirting with me because she had just broken up with her boyfriend, but I did *not* go over to her cabin. I knew I would be contributing to a stinkerbell actress if I did that. And the whole point of the trip was for all of us to be equals and get to know one another better. So I declined the demand to go kill a bug in her room. But apart from the bug, I smelled a rat and was thinking, *Is this your way of inviting me into your hotel room basically?* Which she later admitted it was. That was her way of flirting that night. And poor thing, she had just broken up with her boyfriend and we all know what that feels like. But it's such a funny story to me now and shows how clever and adorable Kaley is. You see it in her work now as a producer; she has a way of making what she wants to happen, *happen*. And then at a certain point, it was also what *I* wanted to happen. But at that point it felt a little bit premature, especially from someone who was literally jilted from a relationship four hours earlier.

Kaley Cuoco: There was *definitely* a bug in my room and *I was* flirting with him! So both were true! I was like, *Ooh, this could be a good way to get him in there!* But that didn't work. [*Laughs*] I couldn't believe he turned me down. I still think he turned me down because he knew what I was doing. I used the bug as an excuse, and he *still* did not come over.

Johnny Galecki: Well, I'm not that easy, Kaley. I'm not just a piece of meat. There's a heart in here. There's real blood that pumps through my veins, believe it or not. I have feelings. At least take me to dinner and a show first! Bug in her room. Jeez.

Kaley Cuoco: But we still had a really fun weekend! I miss those days of being able to do that. We did a lot of those little weekend trips together as a cast, and it was so great.

When asked if each cast member had their own captain's hat, Galecki jokes, "I think we just shared Simon's. That was before [contract] negotiations." *Courtesy of Johnny Galecki*

While Cuoco and Galecki didn't act on their feelings during that particular trip to Montecito, once the dust settled from her breakup, Galecki took it upon himself to make the first move.

Johnny Galecki: I had gone over to the Smoke House Restaurant in Burbank after rehearsal. I was there for a bit when I texted Kaley because I knew she lived in the valley. I said, "Hey, I'm just having a glass of white wine. Are you nearby?" And she texted back *yes* and was there in like twenty minutes or something. She later told me she was like forty-five minutes away when she got that text.

Kaley Cuoco: That's really pathetic that I just didn't even make him wait for like ten minutes.

Johnny Galecki: Oh yeah, she just hauled ass there. It's not pathetic; it's really cute. And that's when I was like, *Oh, okay, there's some mutual sharing of feelings here.* And honestly, for me, those feelings just got to a point where even though I didn't know if it was professional, I felt like not exploring those feelings was going to be more distracting professionally than not.

Kaley Cuoco: I was so excited when he texted me. I was like, *Oh my God*. And I knew that was going to be trouble—getting a glass of wine with him. I *knew*. And we kissed at the bar! It's so dark in there that you almost feel like you can do anything, but then it was like, *Uh-oh, I think this is really going to be bad.* [*Laughs*] We started kissing in the bar area, and then we were kissing in the parking lot. Johnny can get really in his head and want to hide, whereas I'm the direct opposite. I would have told everybody the next day at the table read. I would have announced it and said, *We're together!* But he was like, "We can't tell anyone!" So we kept it quiet. And don't forget, it was different then. Social media was nowhere what it is now, so it was easier to keep it hidden. You didn't know as much about people as you do now. It's a different world.

Johnny Galecki: After that kiss at the Smoke House, she said, "You gotta come over to my house," so I did. And then she disappeared. She came back having showered, wearing nothing but a towel, and sat on my lap. I was like, "Okay, I guess we're dating!"

Kaley Cuoco: [*Laughs*] I remember being in a robe and fully clothed underneath! We obviously remember things quite differently, but I love this story.

Johnny Galecki: I promise that my version is correct. I'm only kissing and telling because Kaley loves this story.

The two "jumped right in," Galecki says, but agreed they wouldn't tell anyone. And they swear they never hooked up at work in their dressing rooms.

Kaley Cuoco: It's not like we could make the excuse we were going to one of our rooms to rehearse because everyone knew I didn't rehearse. They wouldn't believe that. They'd be like, "That doesn't sound like Cuoco!"

Johnny Galecki: But there was one time Chuck busted us hiding behind a car in the parking lot. It was after a show when we went outside, and we saw Chuck walk solo out of the stage. We were by some cars, and we ducked down, like kids hiding from their parents! And he totally busted us, but he was classy about it and didn't say anything. We just didn't want anybody to worry.

Chuck Lorre: I can't remember that. That might be one of those things I compartmentalized like, *I can't deal with this, I don't have the mental, emotional bandwidth to deal with an on-set romance.*

Kaley Cuoco: [*Laughs*] That is such a Chuck answer! But yeah, we never even had [sex] in our dressing rooms. Absolutely fucking not. Not a chance in hell. I wouldn't do that. I'm not in the mile-high club. None of that. And Johnny would say that as well; when we were at work, he was very serious. He was also so prepared. I mean, he's spraying Leonard cologne on and touching plants! I'm like, *We're on a sitcom!* He was way more serious than I was. I think I would actually do that before him, if that makes sense.

Johnny Galecki: I don't think there was even a kiss in our dressing rooms because when we were at work, we were at work. And it was nice to have

Cuoco and Galecki goofing off in the hair and makeup room. *Courtesy of Johnny Galecki*

a separation between work and romance. But when we did *The Late Show with Stephen Colbert* the night the series finale aired, he asked if anyone had sex in their dressing room, and I was the only one that confessed. *[Laughs]* It was with a girlfriend years later, but I wasn't working with her! That's the difference! Very succinct difference there. That was not a line crossed.

Kaley Cuoco: Anyway, when we were dating, Johnny was very worried about ruining the fans' outlook on Leonard and Penny, because they weren't even dating yet at that point in the series. He was so cerebral, and I'm like, "What?! Who fuckin' cares?! They're gonna be fine!" He was really worried about that. And I guess I got that.

Johnny Galecki: *Ruining* is a strong word. I think *complicated* is a better word.

Kaley Cuoco: Yeah, maybe. I was so infatuated with Johnny at that time; definitely not anymore. *[Smirks]*

Johnny Galecki: Wow.

Kaley Cuoco: I was just *so* crazy about him, I wasn't thinking that way. But I guess in hindsight, I kind of understood. He was very protective of what the fans would think, because we wanted them to want Leonard and Penny together so badly, that if they saw us together in real life, it could ruin the fantasy.

Johnny Galecki: And if we broke up, how would that affect their acceptance of the characters? I didn't like the idea of people feeling like, *Oh, Joanie and Chachi really do love each other!* At that point in my life, that felt embarrassing. I would feel differently about it today. Love is love, and you risk anything and everything for that. But at that time, it was complicated for me, and we didn't talk about it. And Kaley was really respectful of the parameters that I had about it.

Although Cuoco and Galecki went to great lengths to keep their newfound romance a secret, several key people started to figure out something was going on.

Bill Prady: They were talking about having gone to a theater to see a documentary about *water*. Johnny's taste was very eclectic, [but] at that point I was like, *There's no way that any woman on the planet goes to see a documentary*

about water unless she's passionate about water, or she's sleeping with the guy.
[*Laughs*]

Johnny Galecki: And it was a Russian documentary on water! Not really Kaley's jam. There were subtitles, though. Maybe I was doing it as a character thing for Leonard, I have no idea.

Nikki Lorre (second assistant director, director): Anthony Rich [first assistant director] and all of us who were part of the weekly rehearsal team figured it out, but here's how I knew: Johnny can sleep through *anything*. If I had to get him for a scene, I would knock on his dressing room door and say, "Johnny? *Johnny?!* JOHNNY!" He sleeps like a dead person. Well, he was late one day, and we're calling his cell phone, calling his house phone, and he's not picking up. We started to get worried. I think I must have still been the production assistant at the time, because they sent me to his house to make sure he was okay and wake him up. But when I got there, there was this whole gate situation, and his bedroom was in the back. I call Anthony

Before smartphones and social media became as common as they are now, Cuoco and Galecki were able to go out in public—whether on vacation or at home in LA—without anyone catching on to the fact that they were an item. *Courtesy of Johnny Galecki*

back at the studio, who hands the phone over to Kaley, and *she* tells me what the code is and how to get in. I remember thinking, *How do you know all this, Kaley?* [*Laughs*] But I had to bite my tongue.

Johnny Galecki: I remember that day. I forgot to set my alarm. And Nikki is banging on the sliding glass doors of my bedroom and I was like, "Oh shit!" That's hilarious.

Kaley Cuoco: Yeah, we didn't tell anyone for a long time. I don't even know how many months later, but we were in New York, and I said to Johnny, "I think we should tell the cast. It's starting to feel like we're lying to them." Johnny said, "I'm going to call Jim right now. I want to tell him." We call Jim on speaker, and Johnny says, "I'm in love with Kaley," or "I really want to be with Kaley," and Jim goes, "Ah! Does she know?!" I started laughing and yelled, "Yes, I know! I'm here!" Jim thought Johnny was telling him that he liked me and was going to tell me that. It was the cutest reaction, like, *Does she know?!*

Johnny Galecki: I know, I was like, "Yeah, dude, we've been seeing... never mind."

Jim Parsons: I remember getting the call and I was somewhere in LA... no, I think I was in Florida. Well, it doesn't really matter, probably, but I was outdoors when I took the phone call. The biggest thing I remember was Johnny saying it won't get in the way of work, which was nice to say. And honestly, it really didn't.

Simon Helberg: First off, I find it hilarious that we are talking about the location of Jim at the moment he found out. It's like when Kennedy was assassinated—you don't forget where you were. But no, that is amazing. Johnny came over to our house to tell me and my wife. The way I feel about it now is how I felt about it then, which was I found it somewhat hilarious, the amount of gravity that was given to it, because it was *not* surprising. I understand things can get complicated when business relationships get personal, but it was like, "Yeah, you guys were flirting," and then, *Wait a minute; two actors in a cast? Dating?! Like, hold the front door! I'm outta here! Get Kevin Sussman!* No. [*Laughs*] I remember being like, "...And?!" And then, "Is she pregnant?" No. [*Laughs*] But, it was not a big surprise. I think it's funny. And I am happy that it all worked out in the sense that it didn't throw a huge wrench into the dynamic on set after they broke up, because things can get complicated.

Johnny Galecki: Kaley was in New York, but I went over to Simon and Jocelyn's because I said I needed to talk to them. We went out on their back porch and sat on the steps and as I took a deep breath, Joss gasped and yelled, "No! Kaley?!" I was shocked and kinda hurt, honestly. You would have thought I'd run over Jocelyn's dog or something. She seemed so offended and concerned. I was like, "Jesus, I'm not that much of a nightmare to be with, Joss." [*Laughs*] Now, I know she presumed I was going to tell them Kaley was pregnant. Jocelyn was many, many, many steps ahead of any scenario Kaley and I would have considered. She had taken it to a whole different, soap opera level. And I, not knowing that she'd made that presumption, took it quite personally that she'd have that reaction to our simply dating. I think my ego is still a little bruised. [*Laughs*]

Kaley Cuoco: Johnny and I did a lot of things together with Simon and his wife, Jocelyn, and I think once they saw how much we liked each other and loved each other, everyone was into it. I'm sure they were probably more worried when we broke up, which was hard, yes, but it wasn't some traumatic thing that we brought everyone into.

Johnny Galecki: It was hard, but Kaley's right. We never let it affect anybody, I don't think.

Anthony Rich: If anything, they were just adorable together and so lovely to be with, both together and separately.

In season three, Penny spends the night at Leonard's, and the next morning she's wearing his button-down shirt, dancing to Shania Twain's "Man I Feel Like a Woman" while making French toast. It's such a sexy, carefree moment that it is a favorite of the fans, as well as of Cuoco and Galecki.

Johnny Galecki: That was hot. Kaley, that was really, really cute.

Kaley Cuoco: That's a GIF, by the way.

Johnny Galecki: Still to me? Thank you.

Kaley Cuoco: No, it's a GIF, old man. It's a GIF. Not a *gift*. A GIF. Do you know what I'm saying?

Johnny Galecki: I know what you're saying. [*Laughs*] There's really nothing more hot than a beautiful woman in your dress shirt. Put that on the record.

Kaley Cuoco: That was really so fun, dancing. And Sheldon comes in and I offer French toast. I remember the whole thing.

Cuoco texted Galecki a GIF of this moment—from season three, episode three, titled "The Gothowitz Deviation"—while they were reminiscing about the scene. *Photo™ & © Warner Bros. Entertainment Inc.*

But after nearly two years of dating—in which they even considered getting married at one point—Cuoco and Galecki decided they were better off as friends. While the cast and crew knew they were an item, they decided not to tell them when they broke up…at least not right away. All the while, the public was none the wiser that they had even been a couple.

Johnny Galecki: We're from very different worlds, but we also seem to melt into each other's worlds in certain ways. It was a lot of fun to teach one another different things, but then when I came to wanting different things, that made things more complicated. Obviously I was interested in Russian water documentaries and she was not. No. [*Laughs*] I think one of the things that created a chasm between us was my strict policies of privacy, and Kaley being very, very open about her life. I was very uncomfortable with being public about it, and I think that hurt Kaley's feelings a little bit, and I can understand that. It certainly wasn't because I was embarrassed of her or our relationship, but I wanted to be protective of the audience's acceptance of Penny and Leonard, and without distraction from the tabloids. I'm private in general, but it made me especially uneasy because we were working together, and the show was kind of snowballing at the time as far as viewership. And at a certain point it felt like we were living this lie because we were going to award shows and functions and pretending like we're not a couple, when in fact we were a very loving couple.

Disagreements over how public or private to be about their relationship aside, there were other factors that contributed to their decision to break up.

Johnny Galecki: For instance, I might be a bit more scrappy than Kaley. [*Laughs*] She's a very elegant and fashion-minded person, and I learn a lot from her to this day. She'll tell me where to go for a drink in New York, and it's this gorgeous, incredible place with these incredible mixologists and things like that, as opposed to my interests, which run along the lines of going out, intentionally getting lost and talking to a stranger at a bar and getting some dirt under my fingernails. We just had very different interests in what I think we wanted from our experience of life. It's not to say that I don't like very nice things, but we just had different interests. But I adore the friends that we are. I think I might value my relationship with her more than any other previous relationship or relationship afterwards. Even for her to say, "A lot of these stories for this book have to do with Johnny, so let's get him on our Zoom"...I mean, that's awesome. We just have such a bond that I appreciate so much. And I think that's part of our great friendship.

Kaley Cuoco: Johnny and I also ran out of things to talk about, because we'd be at work all day, and then we'd go back to one of our places together, and say, "So how was your day? Simon was funny today, right?" And we'd laugh because we had no mystery. But we were together for a long time. We really adored each other, and we were lucky because as our breakup was happening, there was no foul play, there was nothing bad about our relationship...it just ended. Yes, there was some hurt there for a bit, but it didn't take us that long to go back to what we were before we were dating and be friends. He was front row at both of my weddings, and we've been so supportive of each other ever since. We adore each other.

Johnny Galecki: We continue to love one another, just in other ways. And here's the other thing, but when people know that you're in a relationship, they also know when and if that relationship ends whether you're in the public eye or not. I think this is one of the reasons people keep romantic relationships under wraps for some time. I mean, yes, it's fun to share a dirty little secret with your new partner, but also, if the relationship ends, it can cause a lot of embarrassment and distraction during a time that's already emotionally difficult. To be honest, maybe a love like that should be beyond the abilities to deny it. Though my intentions were always caring and protective, I certainly see in hindsight the damage that my stubborn stance might have caused. But that said, I can't say I regret anything. I was working with the tools I had at the time.

Shortly after Cuoco and Galecki broke up in the spring of 2010, the writers were also writing toward a Penny and Leonard breakup. It was just a coincidence.

Bill Prady: I remember being worried because we were on a trajectory towards a Leonard and Penny breakup, and being concerned that I didn't want to hurt somebody who had been through that recently. But they were amazing. I remember Kaley mentioning something we had written, and her telling us it was surprisingly accurate to something they'd gone through.

Kaley Cuoco: Too many things felt oddly similar! I used to think there were cameras in our houses since things felt eerily close to home.

Nikki Lorre: It was obviously very hard when it ended for them, but I was just amazed by how professional they always were, and even though it was hard and raw at times, there was always a love for each other. They obviously made a pact that no matter what happens, they weren't letting the end of the relationship affect what was going on in the show.

For as well as Cuoco and Galecki handled their breakup, it took time. Ironically, it was a work commitment that helped speed up the healing process.

Johnny Galecki: I remember so vividly sitting in my dressing room reading a book when I was told Kaley and I would be interviewing each other for a special feature on the season three DVDs. I don't think it had even been a week since we had broken up, and I was like, *Oh fuck, are you kidding me?* Nobody knew we had broken up. So we went downstairs and cracked each other up so much to the point she nearly peed her pants, she laughed so hard. I walked out of the interview, and thought, *OK, we're going to be all right.* It was a really beautiful moment, a definite turning point.

Kaley Cuoco: I do remember that. We very seamlessly made our way through that time.

But unlike their characters, at no point did they try to get back together after they broke up.

Kaley Cuoco: No.

Johnny Galecki: I changed my number immediately.

Kaley Cuoco: [*Laughs*] Amazing.

A few weeks after Cuoco and Galecki broke up, they were filming an after-sex scene in bed when Penny quotes Yoda, and Leonard becomes emotional at his girlfriend's knowledge of one of his lifelong passions. He says, "I love you" for the first time; Penny does not reciprocate.

Kaley Cuoco: I did something very funny in that bed scene that got left in. When Leonard says "I love you," I look at my watch as a way to find a distraction from what he's just said but I didn't have one on. I was like, *Uh, nope,* as if there's nowhere for Penny to go. Chuck goes, "That's so funny! Leave it in!" Chuck and I laughed about that so hard.

Johnny Galecki: We had just recently broken up in real life, so that wasn't a great day for me. [*Laughs*]

The cracks in their characters' relationship are evident in that moment, but it wouldn't be until the next episode—season three, episode twenty, "The Spaghetti Catalyst"—that it would become official.

Nikki Lorre: In one of the first episodes that Anthony Rich directed, they wrote a scene of Penny and Leonard breaking up, and the scene was in the laundry room, and it was really hard for Johnny and Kaley because they felt like they [the writers] were reading too much into their own relationship and the words weren't crediting Leonard and Penny's relationship as much. It went all the way up to the writers room, I believe, and the writers had to explain this wasn't a comment on Kaley and Johnny's relationship. They said to trust them because they were honoring Leonard and Penny. Johnny and Kaley took it very, very seriously, but even with that, they never blew up or got defensive or dramatic. They persevered in what I can only imagine was a really hard, awkward situation to work through. And I think having gone through a relationship and a breakup just freed them to be the most intimate with each other in a way where they could call each other out on their shit whenever they wanted with such love that it was hilarious. It was almost like a brother-sister dynamic because they had gone through that together. They just knew each other's buttons and could tease each other. It was pretty funny.

Anthony Rich: In that episode, Sheldon says a line like, "I don't know what the paradigm is; I don't know what I'm supposed to do!" because Penny and Leonard hadn't really officially broken up, since she had just run off from the bowling alley in the last episode. In regards to the script, Kaley said, "Wait, have [Penny and Leonard] broken up? They allude to it, but there's no real answer." Now, she and Johnny were totally good and everything [stemming from their breakup], but they were very protective of the characters [so] it turned into this huge thing. They were like, "How do we just dismiss Leonard and Penny's relationship and move on?" But we made some tweaks and it ended up being a really lovely episode.

Kaley Cuoco: I remember being very, very emotional during that episode, and especially during those specific scenes. I think I needed to cry.

Penny and Leonard's relationship might have been over, but then again, it never really was. As with many modern couples, they frequently hooked up or got back together. But when they did wind up in bed again, Cuoco and Galecki were convinced it was Chuck Lorre's doing as a way to mess with them.

Kaley Cuoco: All of a sudden, we started noticing there were extra make-out scenes for our characters, and/or sex scenes. I was like, "I think Chuck is fucking with us!" We were *convinced.* Convinced! Like, *Yeah, they want to date and break up on my show, well, here you go!* and he was writing all the little doodads in there.

Johnny Galecki: Even though it was organic for the characters, I think he would fuck with us. [*Laughs*] If it was an accident, it was a very timely accident.

> This isn't the first time Cuoco has mentioned her theory—she recalled it on actor Dax Shepard's *Armchair Expert* podcast in the fall of 2020—where it was picked up by nearly every entertainment news site. But no one ever checked with Lorre to see if it was true. Now, he's opened up for the first time to set the record straight, explaining that not only did he not do it to mess with them, but it would have been incredibly wrong and insensitive if he had.

Chuck Lorre: No. Not at all. Making a good show has no room for fucking with anybody. There's no *Let's mess with Kaley and Johnny.* The goal was to make a great show and make every minute of every episode count. And that was the *only* goal. We don't have that kind of freedom to risk a TV series that you put your heart and soul into to mess with somebody's head. No. But I think that's charming that they think we had the mental capacity to mess with them. [*Laughs*] Penny and Leonard having difficulty sustaining a relationship was one of the reasons to keep watching—to see if they could make it. You were rooting for them to find happiness.

> When Lorre's response was relayed to Cuoco and Galecki, they conceded perhaps they took their theory too far.

Johnny Galecki: I guess that was pretty egotistical of us to think that. [*Laughs*] We were reading into things a little too much. I'm going to sleep a little easier tonight.

Kaley Cuoco: You are right, that's so self-involved of us. But I am glad we know now because Johnny and I have joked about that for a long time. He's right, though—he *was* too busy to fuck with us! I'm glad we don't have to bring that up anymore.

> But around six months after Cuoco and Galecki broke up in real life, Cuoco decided to open up about their relationship for the first time in an interview with CBS's *Watch* magazine in September 2010. The story went viral, with fans stunned that the two were a real-life item. Now, Cuoco looks back on how she didn't plan on admitting something so personal, and Galecki's reaction to the story.

Kaley Cuoco: It wasn't like I decided, *Hey, this will be the magazine that I tell!* It was so not that way. I mean, why would I choose *Watch* magazine? I'm sorry. It was just an interview, and then the writer started asking me, and I was like, "Yeah [we were in a relationship]."

Johnny Galecki: I was outside having my coffee and my cigarette when she shoved the magazine in my face. [*Laughs*] And all I could say was—and I *am* proud of this moment—"The photos of you are beautiful." And then I gave it back to her.

Kaley Cuoco: Johnny was like, "Why didn't you tell me?" I said, "I didn't even think it was a big deal." And then when I saw the way it was written, it wasn't what I expected. I really didn't think of it that way, so I guess that's why I didn't say anything for a while.

Johnny Galecki: It truly didn't bother me. And this is such a testament to my relationship with Kaley . . . we really handled that time very, *very* well.

> And they did. The characters would go on to have two weddings on the show, which for any other former real-life couple could be weird, but was the complete opposite for Cuoco and Galecki.

Johnny Galecki: It wasn't weird. A wonderful thing about walking onto the stage, much of the time, was that I got to leave all my personal drama behind. I had to. But you would think it might have been weird given there was a time Kaley and I did consider marrying, so those scenes would have been complicated at the very least. But she and I are seasoned professionals, and we've been doing this since we were kids, so we used it as a bit of therapy.

Kaley Cuoco: Johnny and I got so close through the show and our experiences. There was such a comfort level, and he always was so supportive of me. We had a lot of talks where I'd be like, "I don't know about this," and then we'd go outside and have a chat. Whatever I needed. We would almost finish each other's sentences. We knew each other's characters so well, but he was just constantly a steadfast person in my life, on that show, on that set. I also knew if things weren't going well on set and if someone didn't like something, he and I were always 99.99 percent on the same page. Except for the one fight we got into. Do you remember?

Johnny Galecki: I'm crying right now.

Kaley Cuoco: Oh my God. He is.

Johnny Galecki: A little bit. I miss you.

At this moment—perhaps as a way to take the focus off Galecki's emotions— Cuoco throws out a memory of a ridiculous fight they got into over—of all things—tuna fish.

Kaley Cuoco: We got into a fight because he was eating tuna during the scene and I got pissed. It was a day Johnny was late, so I was already annoyed. And he decides during the scene, which did not contain food, that he was going to rehearse and eat tuna.

Johnny Galecki: I was trying to lose weight for a play I was doing at the time. Which I dedicated to Kaley, by the way. [*Laughs*] I even said to Jim, "Does this tuna bother you?" And he said, "No, I don't give a shit." And then Kaley walked in and said, "Oh my God! What is that fucking smell?!" I was like, "It's my fucking tuna, man."

Kaley Cuoco: [*Rolls her eyes*] It smelled so horrendous, and finally I was like, "I can't do this scene with you. This is *disgusting*. Go eat somewhere else and then come back and do it." So Johnny walked off and threw his tuna in the trash. He was like, "Fine!" We both stormed off. I was like, "I'm not working with tuna-head today. I just can't." I mean, I was *livid*. And Johnny was like, "Is that how you talk to me? I needed my food!" It was so dumb, but we were pissed at each other. He called it Tuna-Gate. But here's the thing...after twelve years together, we were practically married. We spent so much time together. I always knew Johnny and I were good. He was always going to have my back and vice versa. No matter what. That's what made him a good scene partner and friend. And during all the other stuff, like the negotiations, Johnny and I were very tight through that. We said, "We are all one team, and there's nothing I don't know that Johnny knows and vice versa." We told them very early on to just consider us one. And that's what we did.

Johnny Galecki: I think it came from our mutual experience, having been doing this for a very long time, and knowing how important it is if you can find that. I would never fear that Kaley was throwing me under the bus for any reason, even if it meant a million more dollars in her pocket.

Cheers to 15-plus years of friendship. *Courtesy of Kaley Cuoco photo collection*

Chapter 11

WITH GREAT RISK COMES EVEN GREATER REWARD

After three seasons following CBS hits *How I Met Your Mother* and *Two and a Half Men* on Monday nights, *The Big Bang Theory* was ready to strike out on its own heading into the 2010 season. The network announced that the series would move to Thursday nights at 8 p.m., which is typically seen as one of the most lucrative for ad buyers ahead of the weekend. At the time, *Forbes* noted that "CBS is so enamored with the show's ratings growth it's now betting it can jump-start an entirely new night of comedy."

It was a tremendous endorsement, but one that came with a lot of risk if *Big Bang*'s ratings declined. Kelly Kahl, CBS's chief scheduler, told reporters, "If you are going to walk into a new night with comedy, you better come in with big guns—and that's what we've done." The move even came as a surprise to Warner Bros. Television president Peter Roth, who told the *New York Times* that he was "amazed at the aggressiveness of the CBS schedule," but added that while it is "a risky move…it's an intelligent move. Obviously, our hope is that the audiences will migrate."

Lee Aronsohn: We were all worried. You never know. But it was a gamble worth taking, because if it does succeed on its own, then it becomes the anchor of an entire night, and that makes the show much more valuable to the network. So it was kind of thrilling that they were taking that chance and giving us that shot at that time slot, but it's also nerve-wracking.

Bill Prady: All you can ever do is try to make the best show you can. It's not like, "The show has moved to Monday, so we have to make the show more Monday." What can you do?

Chuck Lorre: It was really clear into year two that the show wasn't going anywhere. We were succeeding and had caught *Two and a Half Men* in the ratings, and were actually beating it. When CBS moved *Big Bang* to another night in season four, I was terrified to go away from our little comfortable nest, but in the end it didn't matter; the audience came with us.

After moving to Thursday nights, *Deadline* noted that *Big Bang* "quickly [became] the top-rated series on the most lucrative night of television," and added more than a million-plus viewers to its premiere ratings from the previous season premiere.

Lee Aronsohn: The fact that we succeeded made us *very* valuable to the network. And what's valuable to the network is job security.

Johnny Galecki: People forget that the show wasn't a hit right out of the gate, and it took some word of mouth and some growing, but when we hit the top ten in the ratings, I was at the Warner Bros. gym one morning when Kaley came running over and jumped on top of me as I was doing sit-ups and started yelling, "We're in the top ten! We're in the top ten!" It was very, very exciting. My trainer looked at me and said, "We're not working out any more today, are we? You guys need to go celebrate." It was still early in the morning, but it didn't matter. That was a really, really special moment.

Cuoco and Galecki would soon have even more to celebrate. Weeks later, they—as well as Jim Parsons—negotiated their salaries from $60,000 an episode to $200,000 an episode. *Deadline* reported that the number would rise to $250,000 in season five, $300,000 in season six, and $350,000 in season seven, in addition to other incentives.

But as far as the fans were concerned, the only thing they cared about was what would happen for Sheldon now that Mayim Bialik would be returning as Amy. Season three ended with Howard and Raj wondering what the hell they had done by introducing Sheldon to his "perfect" match on a dating website, so now it was time to see how the writers would organically weave

her into the canvas. As it turned out, Sheldon's life wasn't the only one about to change—Penny's was, too.

Ken Miller: The show really took off in the third and fourth seasons. In my opinion what really cemented it is when it was pretty much equal men and women. Now Penny had a posse, too, and it really worked.

Mayim Bialik: They decided after that summer break that I would be brought back, but they book you one episode at a time, which is not stressful at all! After my episode in the season three finale, I literally thought my character might never come back. I had been out of the industry for so long...it really could have gone either way.

Steve Molaro: I didn't know how important it was going to be at the time when I came up with the idea of Sheldon being matched with Amy on a dating site. I thought it would be funny that Koothrappali and Wolowitz would fill out a dating profile and be shocked that a match was found for Sheldon. That's how it started; what it would grow into would reveal itself later. But Chuck was the biggest early adopter and proponent of Mayim. Even when we felt that the character may be polarizing—because some viewers weren't comfortable with the idea of Sheldon being involved with a female—Chuck was like, "I don't care, you put that face on TV!" We, in the writers room, were into it, but we didn't know where it was going to go. We didn't know they were to have a second date, or how that was going to play out and keep evolving through the years. But we went into it like we do with all additions to the show and all the characters: We're hopeful and trying to do our best to make it grow into something better and interesting; that was one of those that obviously did. But it took a little while to shake off the "female Sheldon" description and let her become her own person.

Mayim Bialik: There was some negative attention when I joined the cast because some people held Sheldon very near and dear to them and didn't want him to change or become a cheesy boyfriend. To me, there was never a chance of that, and I think our writers actually handled that arc of him becoming more interested in romance very, very well.

Jim Parsons: I know at the audition they said they needed a female version of Sheldon, basically, but that's untenable long-term. There was no choice but to evolve the character. And at some point in season four—I don't know if something caused it or not—I remember saying to Todd, "I will not let this character go without a fight." That was notable for me, only in that I almost never disagreed with the writers. But at some point I felt a certain way about working with Mayim that I was like, *If for whatever reason we seemed to be weaning her off of this show as a character, I would go and talk to them*. I said this years ago, but I believe it even more now that one of the smartest things that the writers room ever did was introduce Bernadette and Amy at a point where, as far as interests and storylines go, we did not need them yet. The writers did not let the well run dry before they were like, *Oh God, should we adopt a kid? Should we bring in a monkey?* You know what I mean? They plugged these people in to see what was going to work and how it would work, and I thought it was genius.

This was news to Bialik, who actually thought she was going to be written off the show early in season four.

Mayim Bialik: The week that I was offered a regular contract, I had told my manager, "I think this is my last episode; I think they're done with me and have done all they want to do with my character." And that made me really sad. I told my manager, and she called me back later that day and said, "You're not going to believe what call I just got. They'd like to offer you a full position as a regular!" [*Laughs*] Like, no one was sending me covert messages; it was a completely self-generated fear that I wasn't fitting in or whatever it was. It was completely my own craziness. But once I was made a regular, I was still teaching neuroscience and tutoring piano. Then all that stuff kind of petered out because I had a full-time job. But I was not used to that! I had gotten my PhD about five years before. I was living my best hippie, science, mom life pretty much out of the industry. So it completely changed everything.

Melissa Rauch also got similar news, but even then she wasn't convinced it would be a permanent thing.

Melissa Rauch: I remember being in my dressing room, hearing that the show was interested in making me a series regular, but because it wasn't a full series regular, they didn't want a big announcement. It was almost like it was a trial run, meaning I wouldn't know week to week if I was going to be on. And then at one point, it just became all episodes, which was a huge shift because I had a little more stability. Both Mayim and I were eased in, so I credit the producers with making the transition seamless in that it wasn't forced down people's throats. As a fan of the show, if they had been like, *Here's your new cast members!*, I think there would have been something very jarring about that. And if I knew then what I know now—in terms of what the job turned into—my nerves would have been off the charts. I would have *imploded*. It was just supposed to be a onetime job. The fact that it was so gradual was such a lesson in life: One step at a time, one day at a time, and don't always look at the endgame, which is something I tend to do so much. It was such a gift and lesson that's a great reminder even now.

> **That same advice could be credited for how the writers approached Amy early on. Granted, she was there as a possible love interest for Sheldon, but the real relationship was the one that would unfold between Amy and Penny. Those who never had a close friend growing up—or felt part of a group—would relate to the excitement Amy felt when she was finally able to have that as an adult. And not just with any female, but with Penny—someone whom she admired and adored.**

Steve Molaro: Amy had a desperate craving for a social life that she never had, and I understand that. It was nice to be able to take some of those feelings and experiences from high school and have a place to put them with Amy. The desperation of wanting someone to think you were their best friend. And not only someone, but someone as cool and popular as Penny. I know that feeling. I've said those words that Amy said. So to have that kind of outlet was extremely cathartic.

Chuck Lorre: Initially, Amy was just an offshoot of Sheldon. But that didn't work at all. So all right, it was a baby step. And then when she became enamored with Penny—to have a friendship with a woman like that—meant so much to her. The show evolved because it was seen through different eyes. Molaro took the show to another level of personal, and that very much made it a better show, a richer show, and it opened the door to stories that wouldn't have been told otherwise.

Mayim Bialik: Amy kind of falling for Penny was such a sweet sister romance. And also, really ahead of its time in terms of gender fluidity and sexuality. It was Amy saying, *I appreciate that this woman is beautiful!* It's so sweet! The girl crush was some of my favorite stuff that I got to do. And because I knew Amy had to often be all over Penny, I would often hold back in rehearsal just so Kaley didn't have to rehearse the intensity with me, like me being up in her business all week. [*Laughs*]

Chuck Lorre: It was a very one-sided infatuation. Amy was desperate for a friend. Forget about a lover! She wanted a friend. And the fact that she focused on becoming friends with Penny and Bernadette enlarged the character in a wonderful, wonderful way. It also allowed us to go really slowly with the relationship with Sheldon. There's a magic trick in getting a show to continue and to stay relevant; it *has* to evolve, but it *can't* evolve. It's sort of a paradox. Archie Bunker can't become a fuzzy-feeling, tree-hugging liberal, but he can't stay as one-dimensional as he is. He has to grow, but it has to be incremental.

Kaley Cuoco: The beauty of having more seasons is bringing new people in, so bringing the girls on was a total natural progression. I loved how it started with them dating the guys, and you just saw this whole show turn into something else, but very organically.

While the ratio of women to men was certainly now more balanced on-screen, it was still disproportionately male in the writers room. In 2010, writers rooms weren't under the necessary scrutiny that they are today, but even back then, Lorre, Prady, and Molaro were aware that they needed more female voices in addition to Maria Ferrari. That started with the addition of Tara Hernandez in season four.

Tara Hernandez: One of my first pitches was about Penny and Bernadette going bridesmaid dress shopping without Amy, and just a classic feeling-left-out story, especially in a trio of friendship. Those friendships can be harder to maintain. Steve Molaro took that and ran with it, and they wrote an amazing episode that involved their first hug. And at that point, Maria

Ferrari was going to take maternity leave, so there were actually no other women in the writers room. Being in a gender minority in a space is always extra complicated in an already complicated job, but what I appreciated early on, especially from Steve Molaro's leadership, is he never pigeonholed us into like, you can only tell the female stories. But I know it was important for me and Maria, as well as all the writers, to explore what our female characters were passionate about. We knew what the guys were interested in, but what about the women? So anytime we got to tap into what excites them, like Amy with her Victorian Christmas, were my favorite stories to tell.

Maria Ferrari: If the premise of the show at the beginning was these guys want to meet women…it really treats women not as people, as if there is an exotic prize-like characteristic to them. One of the things I loved about Amy was it showed that women also have trouble getting the things that they want. And then when the guys did get girlfriends, they realized that it was the beginning and not the end of their journey.

Nikki Lorre: Seeing women in those roles—both an awkward, painful introvert like Amy, or even someone that's kind of in between the pretty girl next door and her in Bernadette—that gave more of a breadth of the kind of characters you want to see represented on TV. It's not just the all-American guy and the girl next door, it's like, *No, no, there's a lot of diversity in that cast and those characters.* There was something for everyone.

Steve Molaro: And obviously Maria and Tara were important in helping flesh out the female characters and stories, but they were a crucial ingredient in that writers room across the board.

While season four still leaned into a lot of sexual humor, Lorre says looking back, he wishes he took a different approach.

Chuck Lorre: There were never any notes [from CBS Standards and Practices] in the last four or five years of the show because the show didn't really go there. There was never a storyline where Wolowitz built a robotic hand (as he did in season four, episode one, "The Robotic Manipulation") to pleasure himself with and the hand locking up and having to take him to the emergency room to free him from the grip of this hand; that would never have been a conceivable story later on. It was only early on when we were

Rauch, Bialik, and Cuoco in one of their characters' many car scenes. The friendship between Bernadette, Amy, and Penny was an important social commentary on career, romance, and being female. *Courtesy of Melissa Rauch*

still finding our way. At the time it felt like a good thing to do because it was making us laugh. But it was a dirty story about masturbation on a family show. The same thing with the kissing device and Raj and Howard making out with each other. It was hilarious, but those stories faded as Wolowitz became a husband and a father, which took precedence over anything of a sexual nature. They were no longer characters flailing about trying to resolve their issues with sex and loneliness. They were people in relationships, and their stories got more sophisticated. I hope. The same can be said of Penny and Sheldon's friendship. She understood his frailties and strengths and loved him for both. And to me, that was a good example of how the show grew up. Intelligence is a spectrum. I wish we could go back in time and wish we were better, but I'm grateful over time we did grow up and the show grew up with us. Perhaps a more sophisticated and wiser executive producer-writer would have seen what was missing sooner, but I didn't. I didn't understand what we had immediately. But I learned.

Speaking of learning, while Lorre has always been known as one of the most successful, prolific figures in the industry, there's also been a lot reported about his temperament over the years: from "Why Is Chuck Lorre So Angry?" a 2007 *Entertainment Weekly* article that shed light on his frustration with TV critics and industry peers who didn't give his shows the respect he felt they deserved, to "Success Softens the Show Runner," a 2009 *New York Times* feature that said even though he'd mellowed, he still fought with the CBS Standards and Practices team, who wanted to rein in some of the edgier humor. He will be the first to admit that he hasn't always been easy, but in large part due to the success of *Big Bang*, he learned being angry wasn't the only way to be successful.

Some of that was due to his daughter Nikki Lorre's presence on set (she rose from a production assistant in season one, to second assistant director, and then to director), but it was also due to being around actors who were by and large drama free. There was no Roseanne Barr, no Charlie Sheen, no Brett Butler, to raise his blood pressure. And he learned there was power in asking for help, which he did frequently. After years of turmoil, it was *Big Bang* that essentially gave him the space to breathe.

Nikki Lorre: I didn't really see what he went through earlier in his career. I was going to school and living with my mom in San Diego, so I didn't have a front-row seat to some of the more traumatic experiences he was going through on shows like *Roseanne* or *Two and a Half Men*. It wasn't really until working on *Big Bang* a couple years in that I became aware of how hard it was for him. That's why being able to be part of a show that didn't have such darkness around it, whether it was from a particular actor or actress or other complications, was really important. And also, being part of a show that really mattered to a lot of people, and being able to create a foundation and scholarship to help kids go into the sciences as a result of this show…that all helped begin a shift.

Even so, Cuoco says she never felt intimidated by her boss, mainly because she met him at a young enough age that it didn't even dawn on her to feel that way.

Kaley Cuoco: Chuck is like a father-figure to me. We have a really sweet relationship and we have a little bit of a hidden language, a little bit of a side wink, a little bit of a side laugh. I love to make him proud to this day. I still need and want that from him. He's been a huge part of my career. And if you look at his shows both behind the camera and in front, it's the same people. He is *so* loyal. He remembers. When he believes in you, you're in the circle. There are not enough loyal people in the business, and it's one of the traits I learned from him.

That didn't mean Lorre was a softie—hardly—but he was also in a place where he could shift his attention to the work, and the greater impact of what his team was producing.

Nikki Lorre: One of my dad's biggest fears and anxieties comes from not being understood. So if he hears a song in his head, or has a joke in his head and he wants to see it come to life...when people don't do that, automatically, I think he freaks out that people aren't understanding what he wants. And so people definitely tiptoe around him...but it's him being frustrated that what's happening in his head isn't happening here. And the best way to solve that is to try your best to do that calmly and efficiently. I'm not ignorant to the reality of who he is and the pressure people feel from working for someone like him. I think the reason my dad comes off as scary and angry is because he spent a good period of his life both poor, to put it simply, and not healthy. He had some medical issues that were scary. He had moments when he wasn't sure if he was going to be able to provide for his family. So I think it seemed impossible for me for there not to be some sort of connection to that in his career, because his career was kind of born out of the need to make a living, to provide for himself and his family. With that being said, I think he realizes now that he's made it, and his family is financially safe; when he's not overwhelmed by that impulse, he's really good at taking a step back and thinking, *How can I give back to the same people who have made this life possible by enjoying the shows that I've made?*

Chuck Lorre: Nikki was such a wonderful person to have around. The joy of walking around the stage and seeing my daughter was something I really

Chuck Lorre and daughter, Nikki Lorre, backstage during a tape night. Nikki rose through the ranks on *Big Bang*, and made her directorial debut with season nine's "The Spock Resonance." *Courtesy of Nikki Lorre*

loved. But she was in a tricky situation. She was my daughter and everybody knew she was my daughter. This was not a secret situation, but she had been there since the second pilot as a PA and had literally done every job on the ladder. It was into the eighth season when I encouraged her to take a chance and consider directing. She didn't want to feel like she was jumping the line because of being my daughter. I said, "You've been here eight years. You could have been a doctor by now!" And she had a wonderful relationship with the cast, which was entirely her doing. The greatest joy was the moment she first directed ("The Spock Resonance," in season nine). It was so clear that she was ready. So yeah, it was always special to be able to spend twelve years with my daughter and watch her grow into a professional.

Nikki Lorre: I wanted to make sure, before I took on that leadership role, that everyone knew me and trusted me and supported me. And not because of what my last name is, but because of the relationship that we cultivated over the years. Eight years is technically enough, but I wanted to make sure it was emotionally enough for actors that had dealt with me as a PA and then as a second AD that's knocking on their door to bring them down to stage and putting them in hair and makeup, is now giving them a note for a character that they've played for nine years! It's a very delicate thing. I was happy to wait for it to be the right time, whereas my dad was like, "Go! Do it!" [*Laughs*]

Johnny Galecki: I think he really enjoyed being there as much as we did, and he saw how much we cared and how much we put into it. And he also got to see his daughter, Nikki, every day, too, who worked her way up and directed a few episodes. So I think for him, that stage felt more like family than maybe some other projects.

It's one of the reasons Lorre now says if he were to walk back onto stage 25 again for the first time, he wouldn't panic quite so much.

Chuck Lorre: I'd tell myself to stay calm, it's gonna be okay. Don't panic. There were a lot of choices that were made over the course of all those years, some of them good, some of them not so good. The choices that you make at any given moment, because you're trying to make a great show. That's all I was trying to do. I wanted to make every episode a great episode, which you know, creates some pressure. [*Laughs*] But the stress and pressure and anxiety over the potential of failing, or of a scene not being funny, doesn't help the process. You have to stay calm.

That mantra came in handy more often than not, but perhaps none more important than in September 2010, when Lorre experienced one of the scariest days in the entire run of the series. Kaley Cuoco, an avid horse jumper and competitor, was riding at a ranch north of Los Angeles when her horse spooked and she fell off. She felt fine and even laughed at the mishap, until seconds later when then the horse tried to leap over her, only to land on her left leg. "I didn't feel anything, but then I looked and I'm like, 'Wow, my foot's facing me...that's not normal,'" she told Ellen DeGeneres on her talk show a few weeks later. When the paramedics cut off Cuoco's boot, she got the first glimpse of the extent of the damage and was rushed to a nearby hospital.

Chuck Lorre: That was the darkest, most frightening time in all twelve years. Kaley could have lost her leg. It was a series of miracles that allowed us to get through that and for her to come out the other end of that healthy. I was at a golf course that weekend about to play golf when my assistant tracked me down to tell me what had happened. Kaley was out in Camarillo, about fifty miles north of Los Angeles. I didn't know the severity of the injury at that point, except it was bad. They had rushed her to a facility nearby where the accident happened, when all of a sudden I turned and saw a man named Dr. Stephen Lombardo on the golf course. He's part of the Kerlan Jobe Orthopedic Clinic for Sports Medicine at Cedars-Sinai. They're an extraordinary medical group that works with a lot of athletes and sports teams, and Dr. Steve just happened to walk by as I was on the phone. It was heaven-sent. I said, "Steve, here's what's happening. I don't know what to do. Can you help me?" He got on the phone and arranged for an ambulance to take Kaley immediately to Cedars-Sinai in Los Angeles. Within an hour or two of that phone call, she was at Cedars in surgery with the best surgeons available to stop an infection because her leg was wide open.

Johnny Galecki: They were talking about amputating her leg, which was devastating to hear.

Kaley Cuoco: Before I went into surgery, they made me sign something that said, "We don't know until we get in there and see this leg, and it could come out that you don't have it anymore." That wasn't the case, obviously, but I had to sign something that said, "OK, you can." Everything ended up fine, and I was up and working a week later, but the doctors acted like I was never going to walk again. It's still too much for me to go into, and it sounded way worse than it was. And of course it was spiraling and everyone was freaking out, which I get. It scared people.

Johnny Galecki: But I think it scared people in a good way, myself included. The first day I saw you in that state, I just shed tears in my garage.

Chuck Lorre: But it was an absolutely miraculous intervention that I ran into Dr. Steve on that golf course. Every time I see him, I say, "Thank you! You saved Kaley! On a lesser level, you saved *The Big Bang Theory*!"

Kaley Cuoco: Chuck came multiple nights to the hospital, as well as

Johnny. And several nights, Chuck played his guitar and sang for me. He'd just show up and play.

Johnny Galecki: I didn't know that. [*Johnny starts choking up*] That's beautiful.

Nikki Lorre: My dad's a human being that cares deeply about people. It's not just the lead actress that broke her leg; it's a human being that needs his help. Of course that would be his first instinct, because why wouldn't you use everything in your ability to save someone you care about?

Kaley Cuoco: Once I was out of the hospital and everything was okay, Chuck sent me a huge rocking horse for my birthday, which was a couple months later. The card said, "This is the only horse you're allowed to ride." [*Laughs*] And it had ribbons and bows all over it!

Chuck Lorre: It was a really cool rocking horse—a beauty! A grown-up could sit on this thing!

Scott London: I offered to bring her dumplings to the hospital when she was there, but she didn't want them because she was on so much medication. [*Laughs*]

Various members of the cast and crew visited Cuoco as she recovered from major surgery following her horse-riding accident in 2010. *Courtesy of Kaley Cuoco photo collection*

Kaley Cuoco: My accident also happened when we were in the middle of one of our biggest contract negotiations. I don't know what possessed me to say this—and it is so fucked up given how serious the injury was—but the minute I came out of recovery from surgery, I said to Johnny, "Did the deal close?" And he said, "Yeah, we got it." It had closed while I was in surgery, and of all things, that's what was on my mind. [*Laughs*] So terrible.

Cuoco wasn't supposed to be able to walk for months (her response was a very appropriate "You're fucking kidding me!"), but once she was fitted in a walking boot, she was on her feet a few weeks later.

Johnny Galecki: She only missed one episode of the show. She was a trooper. They put Kaley behind a lot of things on the set, like the couch or the bar, so you couldn't see the boot.

Chuck Lorre: We made her a bartender at The Cheesecake Factory to hide her injury! And she was a terrible bartender! We just wanted to keep her off her feet as much as possible. She's a terrific actress, but she also trains like a world-class athlete. She played competitive tennis early in her life, and she's ruthless about physical conditioning, which I think had a lot to do with her fast recovery.

Kaley Cuoco: Also, Easter egg, but when Keith Carradine guest-starred as my dad ("Wyatt") around that time, there's a scene where I storm off from the living room to my bedroom because I get frustrated with him. Except that is not me walking to my bedroom. That was the one instance where we used a body double for me because I had my boot on from the accident, so if you look closely, you can tell. They wanted me to storm out, but I wasn't able to walk that fast yet. And in all the scenes in that episode, if you pay close attention, I'm not moving. It's so brilliant. So the one time I had to really move, it was a body double. And a couple episodes later, in "The Justice League Recombination," where I was dressed as Wonder Woman, you'll see one leg looks bigger than the other because I have my boot on. But Mary Quigley was amazing and covered the boot to look like it was part of the costume.

And then in Chuck Lorre's vanity card following the November 4, 2010, episode ("The Apology Insufficiency"), he wrote the following...

CHUCK LORRE PRODUCTIONS, # 309

Following Kaley Cuoco's horseback riding injury, I've instituted new rules governing acceptable leisure activities for the cast of The Big Bang Theory.

1. No friggin' horses. This includes those found on merry-go-rounds and in front of supermarkets.

2. The only motorcycle you can get on is the one you're accidentally crushing in your big-ass, air-bagged SUV.

3. All cast member motor vehicles must adhere to U.S. Army guidelines for attacking Kandahar. (Galecki's Tesla is a terrifically fuel efficient vehicle but is essentially a hundred thousand dollar go-cart. From now on it is only to be used for backing down his driveway and retrieving mail.)

4. The only permissible boating activity at Comic-Con is in your hotel room bathtub.

5. Alcohol should only be ingested at home, and while seated in a big comfy chair. Wild and carefree dancing that celebrates your incredible and well-deserved success is only allowed on New Year's Eve, and only with a sober celebrity parasitic flunky to lean on.

6. And finally, sexual acts must be performed while horizontal. Certain high-risk Kama Sutra positions might be allowed, but only after consultation with Chuck Lorre. Like with dancing, a spotter might be required.

Johnny Galecki: Chuck said I'm only allowed to drive my Tesla Roadster up and down my driveway and to retrieve mail. There were all-new rules.

Kaley Cuoco: Thanks to me. [*Laughs*]

Johnny Galecki: The Charlie Sheen debacle was also happening, so between seeing how that affected the crew, and seeing Kaley's accident—as much as she was an absolute fucking trooper—it taught the entire cast, myself included, a lesson of how these things affect two hundred people. I sent all my motorcycles up north. And Kaley and I had a talk with Kunal, like, "You can't do that shit in Las Vegas." We all represent one another.

Kunal Nayyar: I don't remember this conversation at all, but it's funny. I was the most innocent of all those guys! I know I got all the crap because I would go out and enjoy and I was young, but no way. Johnny Galecki was way wilder than I was!

In January 2011, after the holiday break, *The Big Bang Theory* was renewed for an additional three years, extending it through to May 2014. In a press release, CBS's Nina Tassler said, "It doesn't take a theoretical physicist to see why this show is a BIG part of our comedy future. From ratings to critical acclaim to pop culture buzz, it's struck a chord on all levels." But other changes were afoot, mainly the dismissal of executive producer and *Two and a Half Men* co-creator Lee Aronsohn, who Lorre originally brought on to help *Big Bang* get off the ground in the early days.

Lee Aronsohn: There were a couple of reasons. One was that they didn't need me anymore. Once I was gone, the show went on for another eight years, so obviously they didn't need me. [*Laughs*] But by that time, the voice of the show had been established, and Steve Molaro had risen to the point where he could take a lot of responsibility on the show. Bill also had gotten a lot of experience under his belt and could take over. And I think my presence became equal parts hindrance and help, because I'm very opinionated, and probably once they could do it on their own, they didn't need me being quite as much a control freak as I was. And at the same time, Charlie Sheen was going off the rails, so it just seemed like a much better idea for me to step back from *Big Bang* and concentrate on *Two and a Half Men*.

When I left, I got some very, very nice emails from cast members like Johnny and Simon that made me feel good about what I contributed to the show. I carried that with me. In retrospect, I can't believe how lucky I was, how blessed I was to be part of two shows—*Two and a Half Men* and *The*

Big Bang Theory—that really were, probably, besides *Modern Family*, the last huge [broadcast network] sitcoms. They are certainly the last two huge multicamera sitcoms that will ever be. I've traveled around the world, and there's never been a country that I've been in where somebody doesn't say to me *The Big Bang Theory* was important to them. They shared it with their parents, it got them through something, it always made them laugh. That's something you can't buy, and you can't plan on it, either. I was just trying to keep my health insurance when I teamed up with Chuck early on, so I considered myself blessed and lucky that I met Chuck and could make a little bit of a difference.

> **The producers took some big swings for the remainder of season four, starting with a Bollywood-style song-and-dance number between Raj and Bernadette. Raj had a rather intense crush on his BFF's girlfriend and eventual fianceé—which came to a head in this intimately choreographed routine.**

Melissa Rauch: That was very much like rehearsing a micro-mini-musical. They brought in a wonderful choreographer and it was really one of the first times Kunal and I had the opportunity to spend a lot of time together. He has the purest heart, and even when I was just getting to know him, there was this sense from him that he is always rooting for others. They gave us a recording of the music to practice at home, and I remember obsessively drilling it every second I got on the drive to and from work or getting ready for work or doing the dishes. "You are my heart... My universe!"

Kunal Nayyar: That was a lot of rehearsal with a full-on choreographer, but Melissa and I had a great time. She's the easiest person in the world to get along with. Anyway, because it was Raj's dream, we could make it really funny, but it was a fine line for me between making fun of my culture—which is a fine line I straddled the entire show—and just allowing it to be as silly and ridiculous as it is. How much can I get away saying without insulting, you know? I still get emails from people saying, "You really insulted your culture by saying this and that," but that's the nature of comedy. You're never going to make everyone laugh, and someone's going to be offended by all the colloquiums that you bring to light about your own cultures. So the dance sequence was one of those moments where I was like, *Oh, this could go really badly*, but it ended up being really fun.

And there were certain things that I said on the show that I wish I could unsay now, given the current political climate, but it's nothing so life-changing. It was a different time where people were not so sensitive to the divisiveness around us...and there was a lot more tolerance between people. We were not so offended by making fun of each other. Everything we said was not the end of the world.

There's only one line—and I don't even remember it [entirely], but it was something about a prostitute—I wish I could take back. [*Ed. note:* It is "Madhuri Dixit is a l-leperous prostitute!" in an exchange with Sheldon from season two, episode one, "The Bad Fish Paradigm."]

But even though Raj made fun of India, he was very [proud to be] Indian. He wore his culture on his sleeve. There's a scene that rarely ever gets brought up, but it's a very beautiful scene where Howard and Raj are sitting in a car together in front of a Hindu temple and talking about religion and science. Raj wants to show Howard how he can make an amalgamation between spirituality and science and what that means to him. I thought, *Why don't more people talk about that instead of him insulting his culture?* But that's just the nature of things.

Season four came to a close with some not-so-welcome romantic pairings. Leonard was now dating Raj's sister, Priya (played by Aarti Mann), a respected lawyer who was also jealous of Leonard's friendship with Penny. It is an outdated trope, which fans weren't shy about letting the producers know.

Steve Molaro: Uh, talk about a polarizing character. I wish I could tell you we thought about these things in advance like that; we didn't. It seemed like a fun storyline that Leonard's been dating Koothrappali's sister. That was as much as that moment had. It was never, "Ooh, if Leonard was dating Koothrappali's sister, then we'll do X episode and Y episode!" That's not how we did it. We were just desperate to find the next episode and that was it. And if something grew out of that, great.

Much to the eventual relief of Penny and Leonard fans, it didn't. But there
was another close call in the season four finale when Raj and Penny ended
up in bed together.

Peter Chakos: As the editor, I am protective of the cast and the characters, and didn't like that Penny even came close to sleeping with Koothrappali. It was such a creepy moment.

Bill Prady: Chuck proposed that Raj and Penny sleep together accidentally
at the end of the season, and Steve Molaro just hated that. Their drunken
night together—where they technically hadn't slept together—I'm *sure* that
Steve spent weeks just driven by fury, to find a solution! One of the things I
always love about Molaro is that his approach to the show is first as a fan. I
think the best job Steve ever had was probably when he was at Nick at Nite,
because it was all about old TV shows, which was his childhood. So, his
approach to *Big Bang Theory* was always to honor the fans—which doesn't
mean do what they would want, but it does mean provide them with something they will appreciate. That was always a drive for Steve.

Steve Molaro: I really did not like that season finale ending, and Bill
is right. I spent the entire hiatus being upset about it and grinding on it
to come up with a path that I knew, even if I did, I still had to convince
Chuck that it was a good idea that would be worth doing. I went upstairs
to his office right when we got back to work to start that next season and
said something like, "This is really bothering me. I think I have a way that
we can come close and get out of it and preserve the characters as they are."
He didn't love it, but he knew it was important to me to the point that he
conceded.

Chuck Lorre: Over time I learned to loosen my grip and allow other people to exert their vision and their talents. And the more I did that, the better
the show got. There are elements of this show that simply wouldn't have happened had I kept a stranglehold grip on things. If someone is really excited
and passionate about something, my job is to get out of the way. Or help
them execute that passion.

Steve Molaro: He was just looking to just shake up the dynamic. But
that was one of the moments I was probably the most passionate about not

doing. Once Chuck gave in to me having them not sleep together, he came up with the specific detail that she was trying to help him with the condom. He was like, "If you really want to find a way for them to not have been together, I think you should do it like this," and that's what we did. It was brilliant.

Chapter 12

JIM PARSONS AND THE ROLE THAT CHANGED EVERYTHING

Two months after *The Big Bang Theory* was picked up by CBS, and a month before production would begin on season one, Simon Helberg and his wife, Jocelyn, decided to grab some frozen yogurt one afternoon. The cast hadn't really hung out much yet, for no other reason than personal schedules and because work hadn't started.

Simon Helberg: It was July 2007, and Pinkberry was becoming this phenomenon; people were literally getting $100 parking tickets just to get a scoop of sour frozen yogurt. My wife and I were in line, when I looked at the guy in front of us and said to Jocelyn, "I think that's Jim [Parsons]!" But I wasn't even 100 percent sure because I had only spent a few days with him, and that was months ago. I was like, "I'm pretty sure that that *is* him," but I kept looking at him from the side just to make certain. And sure enough, it was. He had just moved around the corner from us, and I had just gotten back from my honeymoon. We were about to start the second episode... but I kind of knew right away that he was a special kind of guy, and that I wanted to be friends with him. Which we did. We became really close really fast.

Jim Parsons: I remember that moment at Pinkberry so well. And it must have been three or four months after that when we were hanging out and something came up about Simon and Jocelyn's wedding, and they said, "It's insane that you were not at the wedding!" Because it had just happened five or six months earlier, and now we were so entwined in each other's lives.

At that point, we were seeing them much more than anybody else that was their friends or family that had been at that wedding. We brought it up again when Todd and I got married many years later, which was, there will be people that years from now you'll be like, *I can't believe you weren't at our wedding*, and there will be plenty of people you look at pictures of at the wedding and go, "Who the hell invited them?!" [*Laughs*] That's just the way life is.

In many ways, standing in line at Pinkberry—where paparazzi were always staked outside hoping to grab pictures of the latest celebrity—was significant for another reason: it would be Parsons's last few weeks of total anonymity. While it took time for *Big Bang* to capture the zeitgeist, there was no overlooking Parsons in person. At six foot one, with boyish good looks and a slim frame, he was easily identifiable "in the wild," and his likeness was about to be seen everywhere, from bus stop billboards to ads in *TV Guide*.

But more than anything, viewers were fascinated by Parsons's portrayal of the neurotic, brilliant physicist. Sheldon Lee Cooper was a different kind of leading man—a socially awkward, perhaps even spectrum-y individual who owned his quirks and complexities. In his mind, there was simply no other way to be. And why would he want to? This was a character who believed he was always right, so pity on everyone else who orbited the world around him. He was a genius. And it took a one-in-a-billion actor to bring him to life. It took James Joseph Parsons.

Judy Parsons: I don't think anyone really imagines this kind of success. Jim always wanted to be a movie or TV star when he was little, except around fifth grade when he had a science teacher who greatly influenced him and got him into meteorology. So for a brief period of time he wanted to be a meteorologist when he grew up. He later said to me, "I think I really only wanted to be a meteorologist because I could be on TV giving the weather reports." [*Laughs*] Now I look back on that and think, *Why didn't I encourage more of an acting career?* but we just didn't come from a family that took kids to acting lessons or anything like that. I should have, but I didn't. There were a few small things that he did as a kid, but when he hit high school, that's when he really got serious, and that was his whole life.

He loved it. But when he went to college—as much as I hate to say it—I did not want him to major in theater. We were a middle-class, working family, and we lived very nicely, but I thought, *Oh, Jim, you just can't do that! Look at the low percentage of people who actually make it.*

It was Jim's dad—and Judy's late husband, Milton "Mickey" Joseph Parsons Jr. —who convinced her this wasn't just a hobby; the performing arts was really where Jim saw himself succeeding.

Judy Parsons: Jim started out as a communications major and I was fine with that. But then all he talked about was wanting to be in plays, and at the college level, unless you're in the theater department, you really don't get much of an opportunity. But after a while it was his dad who said, "You know what? We're going to have to stop this. *This* is what he's really good at. *This* is what he really wants. And if he really wants it, he needs to do it." So I gave in and gave up my thoughts of a lawyer or doctor for a son—you know, the stable, high-paying job—and said, "Okay." And Jim went into it full blast. He got his undergraduate degree in theater at the University of Houston, as well as a scholarship to get his masters degree from the University of San Diego. And then from there, he went to New York. He survived and got some early roles, but still, I would always think, *Oh gosh, what if this doesn't work out for him?* Well, six years later, *Big Bang* came along.

Jim Parsons: Even with the amount of auditions that I did, success happened for me in a relatively short time, all things considered. I was only in New York six years total before *Big Bang* went to series. Along the way, I started getting little things (roles in *Garden State* with Zach Braff, and CBS's *Judging Amy*, opposite Amy Brenneman) that made me feel that I was part of the community. I owe a debt of gratitude and a huge thanks to anyone who ever cast me in anything, even a student play, only because that's the thing that lets you know you're probably on the right path.

As the story goes, Parsons's audition for *Big Bang* was so surreal for Lorre and Prady that they had him come back and do it again to make sure this multilayered, fully realized performance wasn't just a fluke. As difficult as it was to cast the rest of the characters—in both pilots—Parsons's casting was

by and large the easiest. He was the unanimous choice, and *The Big Bang Theory* had the potential to be the breakthrough role he had been working toward all his life. But when the first *Big Bang* pilot wasn't picked up and Bill Prady called to tell him the news that it was being reconceived, Parsons made a life-changing decision, aware of the stakes at play.

Jim Parsons: Bill Prady called to tell me that there's winners and there's losers and there's somewhere in between. [*Laughs*] And we were in between. That was a weird time, but also a very fortuitous purgatory, because the months between hearing the first pilot wasn't being picked up and then waiting to shoot the second pilot is what led me to give up drinking for nine years. I was like, *OK, I need to focus, I need to get healthier,* so as the date approached that we were going to do the second pilot, I said, "Well, I'm going to clean up my act." When I knew that we were going to do it again, it slowly began to dawn on me that this is such a unique and special opportunity. I wasn't so much preparing for success as I was preparing to be able to live with myself if the second pilot didn't work. Whatever happened, I wanted to know I did everything that I could. I just didn't want to live with regret.

Judy Parsons: It surprised me because Jim was never that big of a drinker. But I think that was part of his inner dedication, like, *I'm gonna give that up, and focus completely on this part.* And he did! I was a little shocked the first time he didn't get a margarita when he came home 'cause in Texas we drink a lot of margaritas. But he stuck to that.

Jim Parsons: I wasn't being so good at focusing myself during that time. I didn't have any schedule I had to keep. It's not that anything got out of hand, but I knew that there was work ahead, and I wanted to be ready for it. I wanted to get out of this limbo-ish haze that was going on, but I still didn't have anything to work on since we were waiting on a new date to shoot the pilot. So it was kind of my own project I could give myself. My thinking was, *I'll still go out and see people, but I'm now going to do it completely sober.* I started moving my schedule into more of a "Be up in time for the first hour of the *Today* show" type of thing as opposed to getting up at the end of *Regis and Kelly*. And I really liked how I felt once I stopped drinking and started setting a schedule. I kept moving the goalpost, so to speak. I had no intention of going nine years. Instead, I was like, *I'm going to wait and see if we get picked up. If we get picked up, then I'll have a drink!* And then from there it was *Wait and see if we got picked up for the back nine episodes.* And then from there it was *Do we get a second season?* And then, *Can we get Emmy nominations?* It was always something to the point it became a little bit of a superstition.

Kaley Cuoco: I had met Jim as a sober person. He had never gone for a drink with me. So nine years later, there was a moment when we were backstage before a curtain call, and he showed me a picture of a cocktail on his phone, and said, "This is what I'm having tonight." And I looked at him and said, "Can we have a drink together?!" And he said, "Oh yeah." Then we would talk about what our dream drink would be whenever we wrapped tape nights. Everyone knows I love to drink, so it was fun to see that side of him. It was like a different person coming out and letting loose a little bit. I can't imagine the stress I'm sure the show put on him, because there was so much riding on his shoulders and so much to memorize. It was such a specific character that I can kind of see why he needed to put drinking aside. The show was twelve years of intense focus for him. That's a lot to take on.

Jim Parsons: The last couple of years I wasn't drinking I was constantly out to dinner with friends going, "Oh, I want a glass of wine or a cocktail before dinner," and they were like, "Do it! Why not?" And I was like, who am I if I'm going to have a drink again? I know that sounds ridiculous, but like so many aspects of life once you get on a successful show, your identity becomes so wrapped up in the routine, if nothing else, that to step outside [it] is always a little jarring. What will the ground feel like, you know? So, if there was a "problem," it was figuring out how to allow myself to be myself again, meaning when I did allow myself to start enjoying alcohol again, I was in such a different life position than I'd been. It was nine years, and the person I was who had stopped . . . well, it was a completely different existence. It took me a minute to understand that I could reintroduce things like enjoying wine at dinner again without being in an unstable life. As exciting as that time was for me, it was very, very unstable. I wouldn't trade a second of it, and I don't need to go back, either.

That discipline—especially in those first few years—was essential, but as a self-proclaimed "anxious" person who was balancing a tremendously difficult, verbose role, it was also all-consuming for Parsons.

Jim Parsons: Early on in the series, I came home from work on a Friday after rehearsal and there was a suitcase packed. I said to Todd, "What's happening?" And he said, "We're going away for the weekend," and I said, "No, absolutely not. I *can't*. I have lines to learn." And this was around season one, so I was especially panicked about giving up *any* time to go anywhere. Todd eventually had to tell me, "Look, we've already booked it. It's not just me. The cast is going to surprise you—Simon and Jocelyn, Johnny, Kunal, etc." I remember saying again and again, "I am not going. I don't care that they're all doing that." I don't even know if I said that was sweet. I was just like, "You people have lost your fucking minds! I have to stay here and practice. I have to be ready whenever I feel the moment comes to be able to go through these lines again." In the end, I took all the stuff with me to Montecito, and that was the first time I didn't spend as many hours as I normally forced myself to be comfortable with the material. And it went just fine. But I would take the note cards with me that I used to write all my lines on, and just constantly go over them, whether it was a weekend trip or to a dinner. I was just so grateful to have a focal point like this, because after spending so many years at a little job here and a little job there and unemployment here, it wasn't just that I was grateful for a specific acting job, but I loved having something that I was expected to do. I can overdo it as well, but over time I found I could do the role without doing all that insane prep.

Simon Helberg: We actually rehearsed together on that Montecito trip because we had a scene in that episode. It was kind of rare that Jim and I had a scene alone together, so we were like, "Let's run it!" We prepared a lot. I remember Jim saying without the weekends, there would be speeches he just wouldn't have been able to learn. I probably overprepared as well for so many years, just panicking, and working on weekends. You eventually teach your nervous system that you're going to be OK, but it might take twelve years! You're like, *Maybe I don't have to murder myself every episode.* The great struggle for me was always to delineate where my preparation started to bleed into unproductive or unhealthy panic. Plus, when you're a performer, you want to leave quite a bit of mystery in your performance to discover things. So it was a fine line, and I still grapple with that.

> But none of the work came easy for Parsons. That's not to say he isn't naturally gifted—quite the opposite—but it involved an extraordinary amount of preparation. But you couldn't tell from his performance, and that was one of the reasons why audiences were so drawn to the character of Sheldon. There was an outward effortlessness to it that made the character—who in anyone else's hands could seem too far-fetched and unbelievable—believable. But for Parsons, it was like running a marathon: rewarding, but exceptionally grueling.

Ken Miller: At the last table read of the season, Jim burst into tears because he was just so grateful to be a part of a show that had made it a full season. He just broke down and cried right at the table read. It was really beautiful. There was just an innate sweetness to him, which lent itself perfectly to this character, because it's hard to pull off being that socially inept and offensive and not have people hate you. That's a special skill that Jim possesses, because you cared about Sheldon. And it was because Jim brought that to it.

Jim Parsons: I know exactly what triggered that reaction. It was a scene that they'd written where Leonard and Penny were going to go to dinner on a date, and they had Sheldon be the one that she came to to ask about [whether she should go out with Leonard], which, of course, because what worse person could you ask, and he explained Schrödinger's Cat to her. I was *so* moved. We had been through the writers' strike that year and we'd come back, and I was so grateful for the work and I loved playing the part, but part of that, too, was it had been a season of line after line and story after story where they were so artistically weaving so much science stuff in. You felt the inspiration when you read it, and it just was too much for me at that moment. I remember Chuck calling me on the phone later that day to make sure I was okay. He was like, "What's wrong?!" [*Laughs*] But there was nothing wrong. I was just so grateful.

Kunal Nayyar: I remember it specifically as if it was yesterday. And I remember not at all being uncomfortable with the emotion of the moment.

It wasn't like, *Oh, my God, there's someone crying.* Instead, it was like, *I feel you. I feel everything you've been through. I get it.*

And in many ways, it was only the beginning. Critics took note of just how complex and difficult Parsons's role was; meanwhile, audiences became obsessed with the character, which translated to his likeness on T-shirts and memorabilia.

Jim Parsons: Steve Silver, our cinematographer, said, "I have watched so many people sabotage things for themselves," and I don't think he was saying I was doing that, but it's a conversation I never forgot. You do understand how people could do that. I kept myself on a pretty tight leash for a majority of my time, and I still do. I was pretty early to bed, and I always had a book. The first few years of the show, I was slowly working my way through almost all the Agatha Christie novels, and they were just very comforting to me. The books were something that was so out of my reality that it was a wonderful place to go. But it did get old.

Johnny Galecki: Early on, when marketing and publicity would send us on press tours, it was just me and Kaley. She had worked on *8 Simple Rules*, I had worked on *Roseanne*, so the two of us were the most recognizable in the cast at the time. But Jim deserved to be there as one of the faces of the show. And later it became a five-fingered fist with all of us. We were all contributing equally, and everyone was just as talented as the next person. And Jim, because he's brilliant in that role, was just shot out of a cannon.

Jim Parsons: I remember a New York trip that was planned for the two of them. We had done so many episodes by then in the first season, that it was the first time I realized I needed a personal publicist and why I got one. Because I couldn't fathom that I had done as much work as I had done and that I wouldn't be included on a planned trip. I don't mean it negatively-sounding at all, but it was one of those career–life lesson moments where you realize, oh, *This is the industry.* Which is a costly game, because publicists aren't cheap. It's just a tough world to navigate, and you want to stay true to who you are without allowing yourself to get run over. And the irony is at some point you're like, *Oh gosh, would anybody else go, please? Please!* [*Laughs*] It was a curious thing to journey along with one show and a role for twelve years, because there are some new things to talk about sometimes, but overall, you're like, *I don't know what else to say in these interviews or on these press trips.* There was never enough time to expand upon things when you're doing two-minute or five-minute segments of press interviews.

Johnny Galecki: I recall walking into the gift shop on the Warner Bros. lot, which is really for tourists more than anything, and there were T-shirts with Jim's face on it as Sheldon. And I got so excited for him...but I think that attention became more complicated, as it would anyone. Because when you find someone like Jim, and people are reacting the way that they did to that character, you take it and run with it. You build a bonfire out of it.

Jim Parsons: It was a fifty-fifty combination of cool and really odd. It's one of those things that you're like, it all makes sense in theory until it's actually happening to you and then suddenly you have nowhere to place it. But also, it's a wonderful thing and it speaks to a successful project and a devotion and love from viewers that is very meaningful. I didn't buy anything, but my mother—for years—would buy tons of it and I would arrive home for the holidays to sign it for whoever this was being sent to. Sweet, but odd. My mother also has this enormous entertainment center in one of her guest rooms that is filled to the gills with *Big Bang* paraphernalia and photos. I was in that room one morning doing some journaling and I looked up and was like, *This is probably mentally weird for me, to be sitting here trying to journal thoughtfully with this kind of shrine.* [*Laughs*] I was like, *I need to get away from this. I don't want to look at this while I'm trying to think.* And I don't mean to sound as disassociated from my life as I probably do at times. I don't feel that way. But it does take some getting used to.

Judy Parsons: There's pictures, mugs, *Big Bang* glasses, the *Big Bang Theory* Lego set that my grandsons put together. I also have the programs from the Broadway shows he's done. It's definitely a Jim Parsons room when you walk in there, but I love it! And I have a pillow that says, "This Is My Spot." We bought a little brown couch to go in there and I've got the little pillow right where he would sit, so it's just a fun place.

Jim Parsons: She ordered most of it. And I probably could have gotten her more things but I would never think to ask for a bag of swag with my face on it. [*Laughs*] Warner Bros. was very sweet to my mother, and several times

Whether you want to call it a "shrine" (as Jim Parsons does) or a *Big Bang*–themed entertainment center, there's no denying that Judy Parsons is very proud of her son's success, and the impact the show has had on fans around the world. *Courtesy of Judy Parsons*

during the run of the show she would get a box of swag or merchandise. She has a director's chair with her name on it, and it's one of the perks I didn't expect to see, but it was neat for the other people in my life when they got stuff like that. I was just doing my job and happy I could work.

Judy Parsons: Jim's experience has completely opened our eyes to the fact that actors and actresses are just regular people. Yes, he's this big star, yes, he's been on Broadway and in movies, but he's still just Jim. He's still just our family member.

Jim Parsons: I can't put myself in her shoes of watching her son as a character on TV every week for twelve years. She was asked if she sang "Soft Kitty" to me. She was always very good at being empathetic to people asking that, whereas me being closer to it, I'd be like, *Oh, come on!* But seeing her experience with it and with her friends and coworkers gave me a really nice perspective. It wasn't that I needed anything to add to my own personal gratitude and knowledge of good fortune, but it gave me a place to put it. Just like the Emmys never felt real for me because the real Emmys I would watch on TV, not be there in person! So it was helpful to have her perspective, because going through an experience like this made me realize how fortunate I was to be raised the way I was with the people I was. I was very grateful that none of this happened to me until I was into my thirties. Because it's a lot. And I can't even fathom being any younger than that.

Judy Parsons: When the show became successful, it changed *his* life forever, but it also changed our lives, too. All of a sudden he was a name that everybody knew. I remember we visited New York City after *Big Bang* became popular, and I looked up and saw a T-shirt in a gift shop in Times Square with Jim's face on it. It's a very unreal feeling. People always ask me "What does it feel like to see your son's face on TV?" And the first few times it was really just an unreal experience, like, I can't believe it's my son that's

Judy Parsons encountered her son's face on T-shirts while on a trip to New York City. Surreal, to say the least. *Courtesy of Judy Parsons*

doing that. And then we started getting recognized at different places when we'd go out. Sometimes Jim would say, "Oh, I'm sorry they bothered you about that," and I'll say, "Bothered me? Oh, no. I am *thrilled*!" When people walk up and say, "Excuse me, but are you Jim Parsons's mom?" And I can go, "Yes, I am!" . . . I mean, it's wonderful. Jim has been so generous to us.

But it can also be a bit startling, as Parsons experienced early on while out with first AD and occasional *Big Bang* director Anthony Rich and their spouses.

Anthony Rich: My husband, Joey, and I used to run into Jim and Todd at the Grove (an outdoor shopping center in Los Angeles) all the time when they lived nearby, and after about the second or third season, when it got to be really popular, he kind of had to stop going outside. Or, he would go, but with a hat or glasses on. The four of us went on a double date around that time, and we bought tickets for Cirque du Soleil right at the beach in Santa Monica. Joey and Todd went off to the gift shop, and Jim and I went to get popcorn and drinks for everybody. There was this young woman working the concessions, and she literally gasped and said, "You're the guy! You're *him!* Oh, my God, you're *him!*" And then it was like out of one of those movies where all the sudden we were surrounded by people wanting to take photos with him and meet him. It was scary, actually. And he was good about it, but to go from, like, nothing, to suddenly you're in a swarm . . . it's just a lot. And yet, through it all, he's one of the most humble people I've ever met.

Jim Parsons: I was in my thirties already when this happened and in a long-term relationship with Todd, so I've always sympathized with people who want to find a partner in life and are doing it when the whole world knows who they are already. I was so lucky I was able to meet somebody, before anybody—besides my own family—gave a shit who I was. [*Laughs*] Todd and I were set up on a blind date when I was twenty-nine. I was really at the lowest point as far as that went. But when we met, it happened so quickly, and we've been together for eighteen-plus years now. Looking back, you're like, *Oh my God, I forgot how really depressed and frustrated I felt about love at the time.* Things were picking up in my career, and I remember saying to a friend, "If I could approach my dating life like I do my career, I'd be in great shape." That being said, with the advent of smartphones with cameras on them, at times you feel like another piece of architecture that someone is passing by that they want a picture of. People are really, really nice overall, even though I know some of them are only seeing me through the lens of Sheldon, so it really isn't bothersome because it comes from such a sweet place. But there are those circumstances when it feels very disconnected in a world that I don't think anyone gets used to. But that's rare, and I've gotten better at claiming my own time and space. When I'm out with Todd and running around, it is not unknown for me to say no when someone asks for a picture. I know other actors would never say no, but for my own sanity sometimes, I have to set up some boundaries for myself. It's just the way technology and social media have turned things. It's a piece of collateral to post or whatever. And again, at a certain level I get it, but I don't necessarily have to take part in that.

Melissa Rauch: One of the many things I love about Jim is his authenticity. What you see is what you get in the best possible way. There's no BS and he's going to be real with you at all times, which is everything in a friendship. He is a very present person, so when you're talking to him, he gives you his undivided attention. It is also what makes him such a remarkable actor. I remember going to see him in *An Act of God* on Broadway and because of my schedule that summer I could only come to the first preview. You would've thought watching it that he was deep into the run and had done a zillion performances because he was so flawless. It wasn't until we went to see him backstage afterward that I learned he had lost his voice leading into that night and had been on vocal rest. It was miraculous that he was able to do that without anyone being any wiser. That show was entirely him the whole time, being a one-person show, so for anyone to do what under normal, healthy circumstances takes unbelievable stamina, precision, and immense talent... but for him to do that under those circumstances and just crush every moment honestly blew my mind. He is a true master at his craft.

Nikki Lorre: I always felt this kinship with Jim because he's just a very kind, hilarious, brilliant performer and person. But in spite of all the attention that the show was getting and all the nuance that comes with the politics of what happens when a show becomes successful, I understood early on that these are all just human beings trying to live their lives and do their jobs in a very stressful situation. I tried to never put too much unnecessary emphasis on any of it…not that these people aren't amazing, but at the end of the day, we're just people doing a job. I always felt like Jim and I particularly bonded over that. People can change a lot when they have success—and that's not always a bad thing—but it's impossible not to be an 'it' person in this industry and not have that affect who you are, whether it's more important or more special. I think Jim went into this profession knowing he has a talent and knowing that he is passionate about what he does, but always knowing he is who he is, and it doesn't matter how many awards he wins or how famous he becomes, he's still this guy with a dark, sarcastic sense of humor that is passionate and committed. And I always loved that about him.

Pictured in a quiet moment backstage, Jim Parsons watched his life change overnight when he became the breakout character of *The Big Bang Theory*, winning four Emmys for his performance. *Courtesy of Nikki Lorre*

That perspective came in handy when the acting nominations started rolling in, beginning in 2009 with the Television Critics Association Individual Achievement in Comedy award, and a Primetime Emmy nomination for Outstanding Lead Actor in a Comedy Series. (Parsons submitted his performance in "The Bath Item Gift Hypothesis"; Alec Baldwin won that year for his portrayal of Jack Donaghy in *30 Rock*). But a year later, in 2010, Parsons's second nomination was the charm. He took home the gold for the season three episode, "The Pants Alternative," where, ironically, Sheldon attends an awards ceremony and gets drunk before he accepts the Chancellor's Award for Science.

Jim Parsons: Once you're nominated, you have to face the possibility that you might have to get up onstage, and I had a dual feeling that was both exciting and terrifying. When they called my name, there was a certain breathless, weak-in-the-knees feeling that happened even though I obviously knew I *could* win the Emmy, but when it does happen, it's really hard to actually accept. I mean, I did! Obviously! But you're like, *Oh my God, this really happened!* And that never went away. I'm a normal human being, and what I mean by that is there's always a million reasons why the good things shouldn't happen. I don't think I have a low self-esteem or anything; it's just knowing the company you're in (in this case, Baldwin, Steve Carell, Larry David, Matthew Morrison, and Tony Shalhoub) and actually taking that trophy home. That's a different reality. And of all the times I won, it certainly surprised me in the moment. Maybe that's why it wasn't until the fourth time that I finally thanked my dad up there.

Judy Parsons: That was such an unreal moment hearing that my son was nominated for an Emmy, and then when he actually won. On the night of the Emmys, the whole family would get together to watch here in Texas. The very first time we ordered Chinese food in recognition of how they're always eating Chinese food on *Big Bang*. And then he called me and I was just bawling! We did that every time he won, and then the year he didn't, we said, "Well, the heck with Chinese food! We'll try something else!"

Jim Parsons: I got my mother on the phone as I walked to the Governor's Ball, and I very distinctly remember that feeling of *I wish I could have* *watched it with you because that would have made it more real than the actual Emmy that I was carrying in my hand on the way to the Governor's Ball.* That was how I felt. And I still feel that way. She was crying, and it was just such an otherworldly feeling and moment between the two of us. Maybe even perhaps the only really important thing about that, if you have a loved one you can connect with through it.

> While it was a true moment of happiness, fans started to notice that at the Emmys—which coincided with the start of *Big Bang*'s fourth season, as well as the cast's first big contract negotiations—Parsons was looking physically different than in previous seasons. He was always slim, but his face had a hollowed, gaunt look, which drew concern from fans, as well as coworkers.

Nikki Lorre: There were certain years we were worried about Jim because he started getting really skinny and was just clearly stressed out because the role itself, not just the fame, became very, very challenging. They would write these scientific, jargon-y monologues for him, sometimes on the spot, and sometimes the pressure just got to him. And he got through it, but it was a lot. It goes back to the fear that especially actors deal with in this industry. Even if you're on a hit show and nominated for Emmys, there's always a fear.

Jim Parsons: The weight loss bothered me, too, when I saw playbacks or photos. There are photos of me from the first Emmy win in 2010 that I don't like because of that. It wasn't accidental, and it wasn't just wear and tear from stress, but I do think it was another level of me exerting control where I could. I was on a very restrictive diet of low sugar and carbs, and not because I had any weight to lose—that wasn't it. It was about health, but also, I enjoy a schedule and having a purpose and a project that I really can devote myself to. It is only me looking back on it that I can see it like that. Once the results of that started to bother me, whether it was photos or whatever, I swung the pendulum in the complete other direction. I was so prepared not to let myself get that kind of skinny again. You have no idea the things I'd eat with abandon, because I was like, "I have got to keep the weight on!" [*Laughs*] That didn't last either because that was a ridiculous thing to do, but oh my God, it was so fun eating all these things again!

I think I'm one of those people that I sometimes go overboard in a lot of areas—in a lot of different ways—and it relates to trying to do something to alleviate anxiety. I recently said to a friend, "I realize what I have is an anxiety problem. And I'm using this or that to alleviate that." But you live and learn. I still don't have enough perspective to say for sure that the contract negotiations are what triggered it . . . but that's kind of what it was for me.

Parsons lost weight on his already slim frame because of the stress of the first major contract negotiations. His gaunt appearance was evident as he returned to work at the start of season four (pictured here with Mayim Bialik in the third episode of season four titled "The Zazzy Substitution"). *Photo™ & © Warner Bros. Entertainment Inc.*

That same year also saw the introduction of Amy Farrah Fowler, which would help mark a shift away from the constant scientific dialogue.

Jim Parsons: I became more relaxed with the process and more willing to go into certain scenes on a tape night not having quite the at-home rehearsal time behind me that I spent the first many years going through. I mean, there were a couple of weekends where I was going around my house ranting and spouting out these lines and trying to say them, and sometimes they did make me a little crazy. So I kind of eased up on myself a little bit, but at some point I didn't say quite as much anymore in the science vein. A lot had to do with the relationship between Amy and Sheldon. I had relationship stuff to talk about, and while Sheldon might do it awkwardly, it wasn't always a science hoop to jump through verbally.

> Amy Farrah Fowler's arrival was monumental for many reasons, but on a more subtle note, it gave Parsons a chance to be even more playful with both the movement and musicality of a scene. Take, for instance, season four, episode five, "The Desperation Emanation," when Amy tells Sheldon she'd like for him to meet her mother. He freaks out, sends Amy a relationship termination letter, changes his email address, phone number, and apartment address, only to have Amy show up at his door anyway. In an effort to evade her, he gracefully glides his body against the hallway wall just as Leonard opens the door, and later, does what can only be described as an insanely complex stairway song and dance to "The Stars Nearest to Me." But to hear Parsons describe it, he's still surprised when he's called a gifted physical comedy actor.

Jim Parsons: It's only been in the past five to ten years that I have come to understand I am a very physical person. Growing up and into adulthood, to call someone physical would mean that they played sports, or they were athletic, which would probably mean that they were straight. I thought for all those reasons, not playing sports, not being athletic in any sense I had seen before, and not being straight, I thought, well, I can't be a physical actor because that's just not who I am. I never want to say I never consciously used my body in the comedy or any other comedy I had been in, but that was just kind of how it needed to happen.

Mayim Bialik: I *love* his physical comedy. There's such a playfulness. And there's something about someone who's that tall having such flexibility with their body that's really special. I could see him from two hundred yards away and be like, *That's Jim walking.* There's a real specificity to his body and such presence.

Bill Prady: He created what will be an iconic television performance. Jim is part of a select group of actors who create characters who become part of the cultural landmark. That he was acknowledged at the Golden Globes and

Emmys...my reaction was, *That's right. That's correct.* Because you're seeing a kind of once-in-an-era performance. The fact that Jim Parsons could take a basket of Sheldon's prickly qualities and turn that into a character you loved, is a credit to him as a performer and a person.

Wil Wheaton: I was *really* intimidated by Jim when I first met him. He has a million things going. He doesn't have time for me and my bullshit. But he was amazing. I am a better actor for having worked with Jim. I learned to look at the entirety of the piece, to look at the whole script as a piece of music. There are harmonies, a chorus, a bridge...and when it works, when you're doing it right, you're feeling that rhythm and everybody's writing that rhythm.

> That genius resulted in another three Emmys for Parsons's portrayal of Sheldon Cooper. After his first win in 2010, he won again in 2011, when he was also nominated alongside costar Johnny Galecki. But there was plenty of riveting drama behind the scenes. Only six months earlier, Charlie Sheen—Chuck Lorre and Lee Aronsohn's leading man in *Two and a Half Men*—was fired from the show for his erratic and tumultuous behavior, and was now expected to present at the Emmys.

Jim Parsons: I remember finding out that Charlie was going to present at the Emmys, and it was my category. I found it oddly nerve-wracking, not that anything was going to happen, but it had been very, very weird to be working daily with Chuck on such a positive creative experience while such an incredible amount of shit was hitting the fan, literally, next door on *Two and a Half Men*. I was really nervous that I'd have to get up there if I won, and sure as shit, I got up there.

Johnny Galecki: I even told Warner Bros. I was going to boycott the Emmys that year because of Charlie. He was putting hundreds of people's jobs in peril, so I told Warner Bros., "sorry." But then I realized, if I were to have won, Charlie would have accepted the award on my behalf. So I went. But I thought Jim handled a very charged situation very, very well. I wouldn't have handled that as classily.

> When it came time to present the category, Sheen actually surprised the audience by having kind words to say about his experience on *Two and a*

Half Men, and wishing his former cast and crew nothing but the best in the upcoming season. He then read the winner's name—Jim Parsons, who came up onstage, and the two exchanged pleasantries, including a hug. Sheen handed Parsons his award, who then quipped, "This is so odd for so many reasons."

Jim Parsons: I don't know exactly what Chuck was thinking at that moment, I really don't. And it ended up being fine, but later at the Governor's Ball, Simon said to me, "I really wanted you to get up there, take the award and say, 'Winning!'" which had become Charlie's go-to phrase. [*Laughs*] I could kick myself that I wasn't wittier or quick enough to have thought of that on my own because God damn it, I think that would have been showstopping. That would have played on every reel of the Emmys from here to eternity at that point! But no, I didn't think of that. Winning. Ha!

Simon Helberg: I remember Jim's face when I told him that. He was like, "Oh my gosh..." He's right, that probably would've been one of the most iconic moments. I'm not trying to pat myself on the back. If I had thought of it earlier, I would've whispered to Jim to say that if he won. Because it was *so* in the zeitgeist at that moment. It was so ubiquitous and everywhere you went was Charlie's meltdown. I don't know how he got a catchphrase so quickly. But maybe now, with the help of this book, the world will know what could've been.

Jim Parsons: That may be one of the biggest regrets I have of the entire twelve-year experience of *Big Bang* is that I wasn't smart enough to think of that myself and do it.

Chuck Lorre: [*Laughs*] Wow. That's pretty good. Twelve years and Jim's main regret was he didn't have a snappy rejoinder at an odd Emmy moment... that's very cool.

Jon Cryer (*Two and a Half Men*) would win the Emmy for Outstanding Lead Actor in a Comedy Series in 2012, but Parsons would end up collecting his third and fourth Emmy in 2013 and 2014 for playing Sheldon Cooper. In the Lead Actor category, he is tied for the most Emmy wins ever along with Michael J. Fox, Kelsey Grammer, and Carroll O'Connor.

Jim Parsons: I have lovingly referred to my Emmys as the four sisters at some point or another. [*Laughs*] I remember each experience very distinctly, and they were all an unexpected delight. I would think, *Surely they're not going to give it to me! I mean, look at him over there! He's wonderful! Look at him, he's so handsome!* [*Laughs*] I don't know if I thought about it that much, but that's the feeling.

Parsons with husband, Todd Spiewak, at the Primetime Emmy Awards in 2011, the year that Charlie Sheen presented him with his second Emmy for the role of "Sheldon Cooper." *Courtesy of Jim Parsons*

Though he'd won Emmys before, Parsons's acceptance speech for his fourth Emmy in 2014 was the most personal. In it, he thanked his father, Mickey, who had passed away thirteen years earlier in a tragic car accident. "He encouraged me to be an actor, and in a career that hinges so much on confidence, that was a really great gift," Parsons said. Now, eight years after the win, Parsons has had more time to reflect on the moment.

Jim Parsons: It was much more true in retrospect than I realized. It wasn't just that I was allowed to pursue acting, but what was perhaps more meaningful was that he never gave a hint that it could be a bad idea. That led me to believe that it wasn't a bad idea, which built confidence. So much has happened in my life in the twenty-plus years since he's been gone. I know how fortunate I am as a human in general, never mind the career. It's hard as someone raised in the South to say there's any sense of gratitude from experiencing a traumatic event like that, but everything that has happened that I love does in some way or another relate back to that event, and the choices I make and the things that happened. If one wanted to get really deep about it, especially with the homosexuality of it all, I don't know how my dad would have reacted to [my coming out]. But I do feel at peace with it. I feel that I've even had some sort of emotional, spiritual contact with him. I feel very certain that he knows of this and is obviously very happy about it and helps me in his own way. I came out to my mom a couple years after my dad passed away, but it was really because of Todd. Until I had somebody that I was like, *Oh, I have to share this person with my family*, that was really the trigger for me.

As more opportunities presented themselves to Parsons in the wake of his meteoric rise in Hollywood, it was more important than ever to keep those loved ones close to share in the experiences. That same year, Parsons was asked to host *Saturday Night Live* with musical guest Beck.

Jim Parsons: *SNL* was the best, most fun, specific entertainment industry event tied to the perks of the job that I've ever had. There's nothing that I've done that was more fun and more exciting. And this is fully admitting that I was just as nervous, because it *is* terrifying. Still, I would recommend it to anybody. They are so good to the guests there. But the schedule for the writers is brutal, and I don't know how anyone outside of the third year of college can keep those hours. And the other thing I would add, is that not only was I scared, but I wasn't even that good. I was fine. This was the first *SNL* after Seth Meyers had left to do his own late-night talk show. I couldn't tell the difference, although it came up a couple times from several people that they were going through a transition. But I wouldn't have had any idea. The whole experience was just a blast.

Judy Parsons flew out from Texas to see her son make his *SNL* debut, as well as *Big Bang* executive producers Steve Molaro and Steve Holland, who took the red-eye from Los Angeles to New York.

Judy Parsons: Oh, that was a strange night! I was totally out of my element for that. It wasn't *his* show—it was *SNL*. I'd seen so many people host it, so then seeing him up there hosting was another one of those times that just left you with kind of an unreal feeling. I thought he did a great job. I'm always amazed at how well he seems to be composed and handles it all while seeming so at home and relaxed.

Steve Holland: We were like, *This will be fun, we'll see Jim host, and catch up with our friends*, since we knew Taran Killam and Kenan Thompson from our Nickelodeon days. I had never seen *SNL* live before, and it's a fascinating thing to watch. I got to hang out with Judy at the after-party, which was adorable.

Steve Molaro: I remember for some reason we had a tough time getting past the guards downstairs and into the actual studio, that was stressful. And I had never been to *SNL* before, so I was overwhelmed by the surreal experience of it and was punchy from the red-eye flight, so I honestly don't remember a lot about Jim's actual performance other than it was probably great. He definitely looked really snappy in his suit. Beck was the musical guest. And like the *SNL* studio, Beck is also smaller in person than you'd think.

Steve Holland: And since we were also in the middle of production on *Big Bang*, we actually wrote the Xbox One-or-PS4 episode (season seven's "The Indecision Amalgamation," which aired April 3, 2014).

Jim Parsons: They were so sweet to come, and I loved when I learned they broke a story together on the airplane. I see them all the time because they're working so closely together on *Young Sheldon*. I don't think they bill themselves as a writing team that I know of, but they're basically married. [*Laughs*]

In the years since *SNL*—and those four Emmy wins—Parsons has continued to rack up the award nominations for acting, as well as producing, on various projects. But it's Sheldon Cooper who will always be the character that fans reference, and Parsons is just fine with that.

Jim Parsons: I am really honored to be the actor who is tasked with playing Sheldon who has connected in that way. The reaction people have to him and so many other things about this life in Hollywood, they never seem exactly the same to me, meaning it doesn't feel like the same thing as when I was watching shows and beginning to be attached to characters. There's a certain feeling of, *It's not that this isn't real, but it can't be exactly the same 'cause I'm doing it.* I'm also not completely displeased that I have trouble comprehending all of that because this industry can be so divorced from reality at times. But logically, it's been nothing but a blessing in my life.

Judy Parsons: It's so rewarding when people come up and tell me what joy watching those reruns brings to them. A former neighbor told me that the only time they saw their daughter, who has many health issues, laugh and smile is when she watches the show. She said, "As long as she's concentrating on that, you can tell that her body just relaxes and she enjoys it." I even had a doctor tell me that he recommends *The Big Bang Theory* to his patients who are suffering from depression because "everybody needs laughter." I mean, what a joy to hear that. I have gotten Christmas cards from people in Germany just thanking me for being his mom.

Jim Parsons: A few months after *Big Bang* ended, my mother texted me to see what was going on since I had just moved back to New York and said, "Are you happy to be there?" I said, "I really am." I was telling her some of the things I was doing and people I was seeing, and she was like, "Well, that's great!" followed by, "I'm in a real depression." And I was like, "Oh, God! Why?" And she said, "Because the show is over." I literally almost didn't know what to write back! Like, should I ask if she wants to talk to someone? I mean, I was the one in the transition period of life, but the point is, it can affect a parent's life in a very profound way that you just don't get. And maybe I don't want to, frankly. There's no rulebook to being a parent of someone who suddenly everybody knows. It really is trial by fire for the family members as much as it is for the actor themselves, if not worse, because there's not that focus of the job to keep coming back to for them. With us, if you choose to not get lost in all that hubbub, there's something to hold on to.

Chapter 13

THE SYNDICATION EXPLOSION

Nothing was more vital to the long-term success of *Big Bang* than when Warner Bros. Domestic Television Distribution started airing it in syndication on Turner Broadcasting's TBS and Fox television stations at the start of season five. Thanks to the leasing agreement, *Big Bang*—which was also about to celebrate its one hundredth episode—became the United States' top-rated sitcom and the eighth most-watched program on TV. New audiences discovered it on cable, and then started watching new episodes air each week on CBS. *Big Bang* was not just a niche Comic-Con success story—it was now a bona fide mainstream hit. The Television Academy also took note, and in 2011, nominated the series for the first time for Outstanding Comedy Series.

Nina Tassler: It happened pretty quickly, where people discovered the show for the first time in syndication, got excited about it, and then began watching first-run episodes on CBS. It's like a halo effect. Chuck knew that this show was affecting people's lives in a way beyond just your traditional entertainment value. His shows have social relevance, and *Big Bang* had a sociocultural relevance. We saw deeply personal, emotional experiences, and I think that really typified how unique the show was. You could be hysterically laughing one minute and you would finish the show and go, *This stays with me, this lingers. It matters.*

Jim Parsons: It was a really wonderful, fun feeling to suddenly have those ratings. It was pure gravy. Success is so elusive in this industry, but in this instance it was so obvious what had happened—the show had been released in syndication, it was being seen by more people, and it was generating more audience for the new episodes. Even talking about it now, there's a certain thrill in it.

Steve Holland: I remember when the show beat *American Idol*—when it was still on Fox—for the first time at the end of season five, and we were like "Oh, my God."

And for the record, when *Big Bang* did beat *Idol*, it was truly an out-of-this-world moment, with *Entertainment Weekly* noting that "the margin wasn't small in the adult demo: *Big Bang* had 16.1 million viewers and a 5.2 rating… while *Idol* had 15.4 million and a 4.4 rating."

Nina Tassler: Beating *American Idol* was insane. Just insane. I remember being gobsmacked. There was a lot of dancing around the office that day.

Season five brought more than just outstanding ratings; it also introduced some of the series' most beloved episodes and moments, starting with the kissing robot machine in "The Infestation Hypothesis," which was invented to help Leonard and Priya once she moved back to India. In the episode, Raj and Howard demonstrate what it's like to kiss with the device, which then turns into a sight gag that makes it appear like the two of them are making out. And while Lorre acknowledged that he wouldn't have done a scene like this in later years, it still stands as one of the funniest moments between Raj and Howard.

Simon Helberg: The first image that pops into my head when you mention the robot kissing machine is Scott London, our prop master, who's just a beefcake of a man, with a spiky '90s haircut, who looks like he should be on a yacht grilling shrimp. He was such a friendly giant with the huskiest voice, who was incapable of whispering. He was tasked with building an anatomically correct tongue sticking out of a box. And he had to operate it! He was under that table that we were leaning on because it was operated by a quick rig puppet, basically. It wasn't like we had Jim Henson's company there. There are gifts sometimes that are given to you, and those scenes where you just know it's going to kill.

Kunal Nayyar: We just had to go for it, and trust that any insecurity you feel in that moment you will be able to overcome. We were doing take after take and it was getting more slobbery and guys were coming in and wiping it down with antibacterial wipes. Meanwhile, I was trying to control my laughter while shoving my mouth into it more and more. And Simon was *really* getting into it, putting his hand behind it, etc. I kept saying, "Oh my God, it's so weird, it's so weird!" Not the weirdness of kissing a guy, but the weirdness of kissing someone in the machine. That was definitely one of my favorite moments on the show, though, both as a fan and as an actor.

Chuck Lorre: I was so delighted, but it was such a misguided attempt at innovation, and the two of them making out basically, via this mechanism. [*Laughs*] I don't think that's been done on television before. A great deal of the comedy is on Leonard's face trying to wrap his head around what they're doing. The comedy is very much played on the observer, who makes it ten times funnier.

Scott London: That machine was a nightmare. Usually I make multiples of everything in case it breaks or something happens to it. But there's only one of those for each guy. The arm that went up was the center of a curling iron; the box was part of an electrical box, and the head was a soft, spongy, painted softball. It was just a pain from day one, but it was never supposed to move. The tongue was never supposed to go in and out. They did a producers' runthrough right before they broke for lunch, and said, "Scott, can you make the tongue go in and out?" and I went, "Uh, sure, no problem." You never say no. It has to come together or I lose my job. [*Laughs*] So I literally went over to my storage unit at the Warner Ranch to find electronic gadgets in boxes. I had to mold the lips and hot-glue those on. I then had like ninety minutes to get a tongue, bore a piece of wire through the back of that, and then get the right length on it to go in and out, because there's only so much room on the ball. Then I bent the wire just right and drilled a hole in the table top so I was able to be underneath the table with a rod. I'll never forget when we did the scene and they said, "Moving on." I've never been so grateful to have something work the way they wanted it to. And then, in between all that, I'm shopping for all that Chinese food.

Season five also saw the introduction of a female black-throated magpie-jay named Lovey Dovey in episode nine, "The Ornithophobia Diffusion." Sheldon is initially terrified by the bird, which has taken up residence in his and Leonard's apartment, but she wins him over and he decides to adopt her. It's one of Jim Parsons's favorite episodes, but Melissa Rauch is still scarred by filming with her feathered castmate.

Melissa Rauch: That bird went off the rails in one of the scenes. It started losing its mind and flew up into the rafters. And hit a light. And then came back down fine, but for a second the bird was like, *I'm outta here!* And while we were doing that episode, I held the bird at one point, and it put big claw marks in my skin that didn't go away for like a couple weeks.

Jim Parsons: Well, Melissa's very delicate. I don't believe I came away with any scarring, other than emotional. I loved when I had to yell, "Lovey Dovey! Come back, Lovey Dovey!" Oh, I just thought that was hysterical. Sheldon just couldn't live without it! I had grown up with two parakeets. They were so sweet and they loved to talk to me. This was a different situation on the show, because it was a very large bird compared to a parakeet. You don't realize how big those damn birds are until they're sitting on your arm, but I was intrigued by it and excited because I love working with animals on set. That was also one of the few times I had a full story with just Melissa and Mayim. I really enjoyed being a part of that trio.

Steve Molaro: And several seasons before that episode, there was this crazy bird we would occasionally see in the tree outside the writers room window. It was definitely not the kind of bird you'd normally see in Burbank. We really wanted to identify what this weird bird was, so fast-forward a few years later, and we needed to pick a bird for the episode. A professional bird wrangler brought in some choices for us to see—and one of them was a big blue bird that looked exactly like the mystery bird we had been spotting outside. We were so excited to finally identify it, so that's who we brought in to be Lovey Dovey. And after we did that episode, the mystery bird outside the writers room just started hanging out nearby all the time.

But birds and kissing devices aside, there was no prop that was more beloved by fans than Amy Farrah Fowler's tiara, first introduced in episode twelve, which, ironically, aired on the twelfth of January, 2012. In "The Shiny Trinket Maneuver," Amy tells Sheldon that a paper she's written has been given the cover story treatment in a reputable science journal. She explains how she's been dreaming of this day for a long time, but Sheldon being

Sheldon, he's only focused on what's happening in his life. She storms out and he realizes he must apologize. With a little help from Penny, he buys Amy a tiara. When he gives her the bag, however, she's insulted that Sheldon thinks a piece of jewelry will rectify his behavior. However, when she sees what it is, any irritation immediately melts away, and Amy is beside herself with happiness. To this day, it remains the scene that Mayim Bialik is most asked about. Here's how it came together:

Steve Molaro: We had decided that Sheldon and Amy were fighting, and Chuck thought it was funny that even though it's not something to be proud of, Sheldon tries to smooth things over by buying her an item. And as much as she wants that not to work, it actually works. I don't remember how we arrived at a tiara, but I remember writing "It's a tiara, I'm a pretty princess, and this is my tiara!" That all just flew out of me in one stream when we hit that part of the script. Maybe I always wanted a tiara. [*Laughs*]

Chuck Lorre: It is one of my favorite highlights in the series and a genuinely wonderful, hilarious moment. I just heard joy coming out of Mayim's mouth.

Mayim Bialik: "It's a *tiara*!" That's the only way I rehearsed it, it's the only way I was asked to do it. I had no idea that there was a whole physical, weak-in-the-knees thing until I saw it, but that's absolutely the number one thing people want to talk to me about. There's a tremendous amount of joy in that interaction.

Jim Parsons: I laughed at no one more than I laughed at Mayim, but normally it was in subtler moments. When it was a big thing like the tiara, Mayim was all-out, go for it—what you expected a good performer to do—like she performs this really good stunt coming off the high wire, and now we're going to stand here and let her do her stunt and then we'll all applaud, basically. [*Laughs*] As opposed to subtler moments watching her in character talking and saying ridiculous things and eventually I just couldn't hold it in and would start laughing. But the bigger moments seemed to me more athletic and stunt-like, so [my objective was] just get out of her way and let her do it. I never wanted her to have to redo a scene because *Oh, Jim broke while you did that part!* But I understood what a big moment this was, kind of like the proposal years later. You were watching a whole other side of a character open up, in that kind of nothing would be the same after that because they had a new well to draw creative water from, as it were.

Originally, when Amy saw the tiara, Bialik was supposed to say "Put it on me!" only five times, but the audience reacted so enthusiastically that she said it seven times in order for Penny's "You look beautiful" line not to get drowned out by laughter.

Kaley Cuoco: Everyone comes alive in front of the audience and it's a whole different experience. Obviously, a rehearsal day is going to be quite different than Tuesday night in front of a screaming crowd who's so excited to see you. It's a feeling like none other. And you ride the audience's wave. And sometimes you do get bigger, and wonder, *Did I get crazy?* but they love it and it just works. It was just a totally different experience than the rest of the week.

Amy's tiara had a long shelf life on the show, appearing in the season five finale, "The Countdown Reflection," as part of Amy's bridesmaid look at Bernadette and Howard's wedding, and again in season seven, episode fourteen, "The Convention Conundrum." Amy also wore it on her wedding day to Sheldon in the season eleven finale, "The Bow Tie Asymmetry," as well as at the Nobel ceremony in the series finale, "The Stockholm Syndrome."

Mary T. Quigley: I looked at six tiaras for a long time. I ended up going with the first one I looked at, because you always come back to the first one, right? But I spent so long staring at them because it's so important to her. It had to be over the top, but not; it couldn't be the typical little princess and it couldn't be the queen. You have to talk it through. [*Laughs*]

Two episodes later, *Big Bang* introduced another iconic recurring bit that would remain throughout the run of the show: *Fun with Flags*. A video podcast featuring Sheldon—and then Sheldon and Amy—the show within the show was another one of those playful, childlike ideas that brought such delight to Sheldon, and subsequently, viewers.

Lee Aronsohn: Bill Prady is really into flags. He'll tell you anything about the conventions of flags, and so from that comes designing the apartment flag. I come from a family of attorneys, and from that comes the room-mate agreement. Everybody brought something to the table that was just really arcane and nerd-like and which fit right into one of these character's mouths.

Bill Prady: It was Chuck, though, who caused *Fun with Flags* to exist, because the first time it was mentioned in a script, Sheldon was talking about how he had to go do his *Fun with Flags* show. And Chuck said, "Well, if you're gonna mention it, I want to see it." So yes, I love flags. I have an obsession with insignia, so anything like coats of arms, which people erroneously call crests, but coats of arms is correct. Coats of arms and flags and symbols…it's just a thing that tickles some part of my brain that I can't explain.

Mayim Bialik: I loved *Fun with Flags* so much, especially the one we did with Wil Wheaton. I loved the awkwardness that Jim and I got to play for those characters. I would have done *Fun with Flags* every week if they would have let me.

Bill Prady: There were many *Fun with Flags* episodes that never got written…so many ideas I had for the show within the show because there were many, many good things about flags I always wanted to explore.

Jim Parsons: I don't remember ever not liking *Fun with Flags*, in costume or regular clothes. That was always fun. The time she was a pretzel and I was in lederhosen…I enjoyed that very much. It was just fucking ridiculous. [*Laughs*]

Mayim Bialik: I remember there was a notion that we don't want the pretzel salt to look like a nipple because of the placement.

Mary T. Quigley: Yes, I struggled with salt placement on Amy's costume.

That episode led to a hilarious encounter months later when Steve Molaro and Steve Holland were overseas on vacation.

Steve Molaro: Holland and I were in Germany at this little bar, talking about Bavaria and what does that mean, etc., when this couple sitting next to us says, "Well, I don't know if you know the show *The Big Bang Theory* when Amy's dressed as a pretzel on *Fun with Flags*…" Steve and I looked at each other, and then said, "This is gonna sound crazy, but we actually work

"Fun with Flags," the fictional online show originally created by Sheldon, was always a hit with real-life viewers, even if Sheldon and Amy had very limited viewership. *Courtesy of Kaley Cuoco photo collection*

on that show! We wrote that!" It was so wild that here we were halfway across the world and they were trying to explain Bavaria to us through Amy and a pretzel costume.

Steve Holland: The fact that that was their go-to reference for explaining to us what people think of Bavaria. [*Laughs*] It was Und ich bin ein a Pretzel!

The iconic episodes just kept coming in season five, with the larger-than-life Amy and Penny painting that Amy commissioned as a gift to her "bestie" in episode seventeen, "The Rothman Disintegration." Amy's desire for a best friend was just another example of how the women's storylines were crucial to the show's success, and one of the main reasons—if not the main one—for tuning in each week. As the *Hollywood Reporter*'s Lesley Goldberg wrote at the time, "the unlikely friendship between Penny, Amy and Bernadette offers the opportunity to tell stories about various forms of the female nerd." But perhaps most important—how the female nerd and the popular girl offer richer storytelling when told as adults and not the typical high school storylines viewers are used to.

Chuck Lorre: One of the best discoveries of the series was when Amy, who is a lonely character, found friendship and camaraderie with Penny, as well as Bernadette. She had women in her life that she loved and could talk to; she had never had that in her life prior. Her falling in love with Penny and Bernadette may have been more important than falling in love with Sheldon because of how it deepened her character.

The Amy and Penny painting currently hangs in the hallway of the Chuck Lorre Productions office building on the Warner Bros. lot, which might catch some visitors off guard, but for the most part brings total delight.

Steve Molaro: Ha ha, that thing! I see it every morning, framed in all its glory and it makes me happy. I remember at the time, Robin [Green] and Kristy [Cecil], the line producers, called me and said it was getting made, and wanted to know if Penny should not look entirely happy in the picture. I don't think we had even figured that out, but since it was getting made, I was like, "Sure, that seems funny." And to me, the best part of the picture is this frozen, not-entirely-real half smile on Penny's face while Amy has this real smile. And Chuck knew that if we hung it on the fourth wall that the audience doesn't see, that it could be there but you'd never have to actually see it, which is where it ends up.

Chuck Lorre: I was very proud of that because I realized there's a wall in that apartment we never see that it could be hanging on forever. The actual painting couldn't have made me happier because it showed you Penny's discomfort and Amy's absolute joy of being with her friend. She worshiped Penny. You can't look at it and not smile or laugh. And having Amy's hand on Penny's shoulder made it even more wonderful, because then it becomes, *Is it my friend or is it my hostage?* [*Laughs*]

Mayim Bialik: The size of it was definitely shocking the first time I saw it because it really is enormous. Kaley and I posed for some photos that the painter based it on, but my hand was not over her shoulder originally, so that was added in. But for whatever reason, if you look super close, it definitely doesn't look like a woman's hand. It's certainly not my hand. And so every time I look at it, all I can see is this giant hand!

Kaley Cuoco: It was so horrible, it was great! The whole episode was so

exceptionally written. I remember Melissa and I staring at it in a scene, and
the audience was screaming. It was so outrageous that in one take, I cried.
I was cry-laughing which was a different emotion than I expected. I didn't
rehearse that. It was just a priceless moment when Amy gives it to Penny,
and then Penny is so devastated that it ends up making her cry. I really feel
like that's the audience holding us and taking us to another level, and I don't
know if I'll have that experience again.

The Amy/Penny painting made its debut in "The Rothman Disintegration" in season five,
and then reappeared in "The Property Division Collection" in season ten when Penny officially moved out of her apartment and in with Leonard. *Courtesy of Alex Ayers*

**Amy's girl crush on Penny was delightful to watch, but the writers eventually
toned down Amy's adoration the more comfortable she became with her
active social life.**

Steve Molaro: It just faded away organically as things became more serious with Sheldon. There wasn't a choice to stop. It just didn't feel like it was
a part of who she was, eventually, as she got more confident and grew as a
person.

A moment of downtime on the set for a napping Johnny Galecki and Kaley Cuoco early in season one. Cuoco admits she was crushing on her costar from the beginning, but he didn't become aware until months later. *(Courtesy of Kaley Cuoco photo collection)*

The everyday style of Kunal Nayyar and Simon Helberg couldn't have been more different from that of Raj and Howard (pictured here in 2007 while filming the second episode, "The Big Bran Hypothesis"), but they certainly made it work. *(Courtesy of Kaley Cuoco photo collection)*

Cuoco (pictured here with Jim Parsons and Helberg in the early days of *Big Bang*) says, "There was no one that would make us laugh harder than Simon. In some of those living room scenes…the tears would be flowing because of how fucking funny he would make things." *(Courtesy of Kaley Cuoco photo collection)*

SEXY !!

In 2008's "The Codpiece Topology," Howard, Raj, Sheldon, and Leonard went to the Renaissance Fair. Whether or not you found their look "sexy" is a matter of personal opinion, but the *Big Bang* production crew certainly got a kick out of labeling it as such. *(Courtesy of Kaley Cuoco photo collection)*

Apple co-founder Steve "Woz" Wozniak guest-starred in season four's "The Cruciferous Vegetable Amplification" (pictured left to right: Chuck Lorre, Jim Parsons, Wozniak, and Bill Prady). Wozniak was one of many real-life figures integral to the field of STEM (science, technology, engineering, mathematics) to appear as themselves on the show. *(Courtesy of Kaley Cuoco photo collection)*

In the early years of the show, before some of the cast got married and had kids, Helberg, Nayyar, Parsons, Galecki, and Cuoco were inseparable on and off the set, eating meals together before tape nights and vacationing on weekends. *(Courtesy of Kaley Cuoco photo collection)*

Perhaps the most iconic prop ever featured on *The Big Bang Theory*: Kunal Nayyar made sure to capture a photo of Jim Parsons holding the Leonard Nimoy–signed napkin ("To Sheldon, Live long and prosper! Leonard Nimoy") that Penny gifted Sheldon in "The Bath Item Gift Hypothesis." *(Courtesy of Anthony Rich)*

"The Einstein Approximation" was the official title for episode fourteen of season three, but it's best known to fans as "The Ball Pit" or "Bazinga" episode. In this candid moment, Parsons and Galecki look like they were having a ball of fun, but in reality they were disgusted by how filthy those plastic balls were. *(Courtesy of Kaley Cuoco photo collection)*

In episode sixteen of season three ("The Excelsior Acquisition"), Spider-Man co-creator Stan Lee (pictured here in between takes with Cuoco and Parsons) guest-starred as himself. *(Courtesy of Kaley Cuoco photo collection)*

Contrary to what their expressions might be saying, Galecki, Parsons, Helberg, and Nayyar didn't quite realize the show's level of popularity until their first appearance at Comic-Con. *(Courtesy of Kaley Cuoco photo collection)*

Season four introduced Mayim Bialik (pictured here with Cuoco, Parsons, Helberg, Galecki, and Nayyar) and Melissa Rauch (not pictured) as series regulars, although Bialik didn't think she'd be sticking around for long. She was shocked when the producers wanted to make her a series regular. *(Courtesy of Kaley Cuoco photo collection)*

Three Santas, a reindeer, and a guy with a Menorah on his head walk into a bar...kidding. Galecki, Helberg, Parsons, Nayyar, and Cuoco got into the holiday spirit before the show went on break in this undated early-season photo. *(Courtesy of Kaley Cuoco photo collection)*

An up-close look at what the characters ate anytime they ordered Chinese food. Prop master Scott London made most of the food you saw on-screen, and he tailored each dish to the actor's preferences. *(Courtesy of Steve Molaro)*

Melissa Rauch and Kaley Cuoco have a snack on the Warner Bros. private jet while flying with the rest of the cast, along with co-creators Chuck Lorre and Bill Prady and executive producer Steve Molaro, to San Diego for Comic-Con in July 2011. *(Courtesy of Melissa Rauch)*

Perhaps this was Stuart's doing? Either way, it made for a cute moment between takes for Helberg, Nayyar, and Rauch. *(Courtesy of Melissa Rauch)*

In April 2015, for episode twenty-three of season eight, "The Maternal Combustion," Christine Baranski (second from left) and Laurie Metcalf guest-starred together for the first time as Leonard's and Sheldon's mothers, respectively. *(Courtesy of Kaley Cuoco photo collection)*

Jim Parsons (in the background) looks on as Mayim Bialik (in Amy's tiara) and Kaley Cuoco play bridesmaid for Melissa Rauch's Bernadette on her wedding day in the season five finale. *(Courtesy of Melissa Rauch)*

Bob Newhart (pictured here with Jim Parsons) won his very first Emmy for portraying Professor Proton/Arthur Jeffries on *Big Bang*. The inspiration for the character came from Steve Molaro, who watched *The Uncle Floyd Show* as a kid and wondered as an adult if he could hire him so they could hang out. *(Courtesy of Kaley Cuoco photo collection)*

In episode seventeen of season eight, "The Colonization Application," Penny and Leonard get busy with body paint, which wasn't even the most interesting "costume" Galecki and Cuoco have worn on the show. (Cupid costumes and sex-dungeon attire, anyone?) *(Courtesy of Kaley Cuoco photo collection)*

"Before" and "After" caption these two polaroids of Penny and Leonard's Las Vegas wedding, which spanned the season eight finale to the season nine premiere. But for Cuoco, the premiere will be remembered as the episode in which she reluctantly had to wear a wig to match the length of her hair from three months earlier. *(Courtesy of Kaley Cuoco photo collection)*

BEFORE

SEASON 9 FIRST EP! '15

AFTER '15

Fort Cozy McBlanket deserved more than a one-episode appearance on *The Big Bang Theory*, but there's always this photo to commemorate the occasion. Parsons and Bialik are pictured with executive producer Steve Molaro. *(Courtesy of Steve Molaro)*

Shamy forever. That's it. That's the caption. *(Courtesy of Kaley Cuoco photo collection)*

During a rare moment of downtime on the stage, Jim Parsons relaxes on the stairs. *Big Bang* is one of five stages on the Warner Bros. lot to have a formal dedication and is forever known as *The Big Bang Theory* Stage. While other shows now film there, you can still visit the set as part of the Warner Bros. Studio Tour. *(Courtesy of Nikki Lorre)*

"I had the dressing room of all dressing rooms. I went nuts decorating!" Cuoco says. Customized pink carpeting, a bar, a custom-made pink plush couch, and even a pink door to match, Cuoco's "Penny princess" dressing room was a relaxing oasis/gathering spot for all who visited. *(Courtesy of Kaley Cuoco)*

The crew put together a yearbook for the final season and hired a photographer to re-create old-school class/prom photos. Director Mark Cendrowski joined Bialik and Parsons for theirs, and one can only hope this is now a life-size portrait in his home. *(Courtesy of Alex Ayers)*

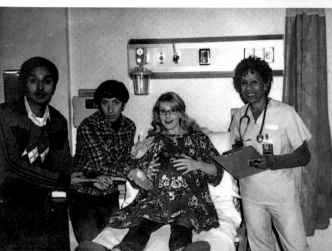

Vernee Watson (who now stars on *Bob Hearts Abishola*) made five appearances as nurse Althea Davis during *Big Bang*'s run, including the pilot episode. Here she is with Nayyar, Helberg, and Rauch when Bernadette went into labor. *(Courtesy of Kaley Cuoco photo collection)*

Parsons (with the notecards he used to memorize all of Sheldon's dialogue) poses for a photo in the hair and makeup room with Rauch and costar Laura Spencer (who played Emily Sweeney). *(Courtesy of Melissa Rauch/Kunal Nayyar)*

Thanksgiving in March. Shortly after Mrs. Wolowitz passed away, the power in the neighborhood went out, and the food she had stored in the freezer—including her famed brisket—started to defrost. The gang gathered for one last meal to pay tribute to Howard's mother. *(Courtesy of Melissa Rauch)*

It's always time for a calming, hot beverage, and chamomile tea usually did the trick (for Sheldon at least). *(Courtesy of Nikki Lorre)*

Rauch, Cuoco, and Bialik together at the 2014 Screen Actors Guild Awards, where the show was nominated for Outstanding Ensemble in a Comedy Series. The show received six SAG Award nominations over its twelve-year run but never won. *(Courtesy of Melissa Rauch)*

Rauch (wearing a baseball cap to pay homage to twelve seasons) embraces Bialik during the cast and crew's final flash mob, along with co-creator Bill Prady. *(Courtesy of Alex Ayers)*

Costume designer Mary T. Quigley was responsible for the characters' final Halloween-themed episode, and it didn't disappoint. Sheldon and Amy dressed up as Howard and Bernadette, while the Wolowitzes went as Mary Poppins and Bert. *(Courtesy of Melissa Rauch)*

Executive producer and showrunner Steve Holland runs through scenes from the series finale with co-executive producer Andy Gordon, co-creator/executive producer Chuck Lorre, and script coordinator Alex Ayers in the writers room. On the board, "L" stands for Leonard, "S" for Sheldon, "P" for Penny, and so on. *(Courtesy of Steve Holland)*

Helberg, Bialik, Nayyar, and Parsons rehearse the Sweden hotel scenes (for the Nobel ceremony trip) for the final episode, with Galecki and Cuoco in the connecting room. *(Courtesy of Andy Gordon)*

The gang's all here! Rauch, director Mark Cendrowski, script supervisor Julie Fleischer, Parsons, Helberg, Brian Posehn ("Bert"), Galecki, Cuoco, Kevin Sussman ("Stuart"), Bialik, and Nayyar gather in the hair and makeup room before filming the final episode in front of a studio audience. *Courtesy of Melissa Rauch*

The last group hug before the cast greets the studio audience for the finale taping on April 30, 2019. *(Courtesy of Nikki Lorre)*

The final moment (a.k.a. the tag) in episode 279 of *The Big Bang Theory* featured the cast gathered around the table eating Chinese food as the show's theme song (performed acoustically by the Barenaked Ladies) is played one last time. Notice that Cuoco is wearing the same shirt Penny wore in the pilot and 100th episode, and Helberg is wearing Howard's Nintendo belt buckle from the pilot. *(Courtesy of Steve Molaro)*

Galecki and Cuoco share a sweet moment before filming the long-awaited scene where the elevator doors open for the first time. *(Courtesy of Alex Ayers)*

The final curtain call. An emotional Galecki, Parsons, Cuoco, Helberg, Nayyar, Rauch, Bialik, and Sussman hold hands backstage before taking their last bow for the studio audience. *(Courtesy of Nikki Lorre)*

One last memory of Apartment 4A: Jim Parsons captures a photo of Sheldon and Leonard's apartment door before saying farewell to stage 25. *(Courtesy of Alex Ayers)*

In 2016, pop icon and actor Selena Gomez posted a photo on Instagram of herself in a dressing room watching The Big Bang Theory *on her computer with the caption that read "The one thing that gets me going before anything...Sheldon Cooper—Big Bang Theory." Molaro saw the post, which sparked an idea.*

Steve Molaro: After I had heard she liked the show, we approached Selena's team a couple of times to have her on, but it never worked out due to scheduling reasons, etc. I'm a fan of hers and would have loved to have had her on. I never even got to pitch it to them, but I had kicked around an idea that Amy had been complaining about her awful stepsister and what a bitch she was. Which would be news because we didn't even know she had one. This, of course, was before we established Amy's dad and mom were still together. When we meet this stepsister, played by Selena, she's beautiful and great and everyone loves her and Amy was just being jealous. It never got further than that. It would have been fun if it could have worked out.

But just like Amy wasn't shy about her passions—be it a tiara, a painting, or orthopedic shoes—Sheldon was the same, especially when it came to his love of Mr. Spock and Leonard Nimoy. It had been three years since Nimoy first left his imprint by signing a fictional Cheesecake Factory napkin for "The Bath Item Gift Hypothesis," and now the producers had an idea to bring the icon on the show for a guest appearance. They devised a storyline where Penny gives Sheldon and Leonard vintage, mint-in-a-box 1975 Mego *Star Trek* Transporters, which has a Spock figure that comes to life in Sheldon's dream after he breaks his and switches it with Leonard's. It was a lofty idea, but one that would come with a great payoff if they could get Nimoy to voice the figurine.

Steve Molaro: I had that transporter and doll as a kid, but Scott London tracked down the ones we used on the show. He still has them in his prop room. While we were coming up with a story we thought how cool would it be if we could use Leonard Nimoy's voice as part of it.

Bill Prady: The origin of the episode—which was very much a Molaro execution—was my People's Choice Award, which is a Waterford crystal. But I scratched it. I scratched the crystal and it upset me. I was in Lee Aronsohn's office, and I saw his People's Choice Award just standing there, and it occurred to me that I could swap 'em and Lee would never notice. But I never did! [*Laughs*] And if Lee's concerned about this, I'll show him my award which has got a nice scratch on it. So that became a story of two identical toys, and Sheldon considers swapping it with Leonard's.

Anyway, Molaro came up with the notion of seeing if Nimoy would do the voice because I think we had reached out to him earlier and were told he wasn't really acting much. But I remember being in my office and the phone call coming in and being told Leonard Nimoy was on the phone. It's hard to explain how important *Star Trek* is to me. I think I went to my first *Star Trek* convention when I was fifteen. So to hear that Leonard Nimoy—Mr. Spock—was on the phone, I was not processing what he was saying. I could only focus on his amazing voice. I thought this was a phone call to see if he'd agree to do the part, but in his mind, he had already agreed to do it! He had one specific note on the script, which is that Mr. Spock doesn't use contractions when he speaks. He says "cannot;" he doesn't say "can't." And I remember just being chagrined that I hadn't intervened and had allowed this to go on. I loved Spock so much, I used to sneak lines of Mr. Spock dialogue from the movies and TV shows into *Big Bang Theory* and give them to Sheldon. There's an episode early on where Sheldon and Leonard are having a fight, and Penny asks, "Well, how do you feel?" And Sheldon replies, "I don't understand the question." That's from the beginning of *Star Trek IV* where Spock has reunited with his mind and his body, and is being quizzed by a computer about his status. So Leonard Nimoy was just one of many fanboy moments. I once said to LeVar Burton, "If I could go back in time and tell my teenage self there would be a day where I would eventually talk to three crew members of the USS *Enterprise*, I'd fall over and die."

Adam Nimoy: My dad didn't usually do that kind of stuff, and said no to guest spots like that all the time, but I'm so glad it appealed to him, and he wanted to do it. He loved community, and he had that on *Big Bang*. And his episode was just so fantastic. I loved it, especially when they kept re-posing the Spock doll as they cut to it. When Sheldon wakes up on the planet with the two suns and no sunscreen...the jokes are just so funny.

Steve Holland: The cool thing was that Leonard actually came to do his voice-over in person. He could have easily done it in a booth, but he came in person to do it onstage just to see the cast and wave to the audience, which was really exciting.

Steve Molaro, Chuck Lorre, Mark Cendrowski, and Bill Prady talk to Leonard Nimoy on set when he came to film his voice-over in the twentieth episode of season five, titled "The Transporter Malfunction." *Courtesy of Nikki Lorre*

Exciting, yes, but for Melissa Rauch, also a little awkward...

Melissa Rauch: When Mayim and I first became regulars, we didn't have bathrooms in our dressing rooms, so all the guest stars would share one. Eventually they built us our own, but in the interim, Leonard Nimoy was one of those guest stars that shared with us. I remember knocking on the door and hearing, "One moment, please!" and thinking, *OK, that's not Mayim, that's Leonard Nimoy!* And I didn't want to have that awkward moment of waiting outside the door, so I ran away. Playing it cool with these people was not my strong suit.

Rauch needn't have worried. Nimoy would later say he had a great time and "was among a great cast and wonderfully talented writers and producers. It's a very smart show, very funny show, and I really enjoyed myself."

Meanwhile, in the same episode, Raj says he wants to tell his parents something, and they ask if he's coming out of the closet. His response: "I'm not gay, I'm metrosexual. It means I like women and their skin care products." In the episode, unbeknownst to Raj, the woman his parents have set him up with is secretly gay, and she assumes Raj is, too. When he says that's not the case, she doesn't believe him. For years, viewers wondered if the show was hinting at an eventual reveal of Raj's sexuality, especially since *Big Bang* never featured a main—or even recurring—character who identified as part of the LGTBQ+ community. At the time, *The A.V. Club*'s Oliver Sava wrote in a column (March 29, 2012), "The highlight of this week's episode is the Raj subplot I've been waiting all season for, dealing with his stereotypically gay portrayal…It's refreshing to see the writers address his behavior with a surprisingly clever story." Sava also wrote, "Raj would be a perfect gay man, if only he was attracted to men. And I still think that he very well might be. It's not like we've ever gotten an intense look into Raj's psyche, he could very well be a deeply in denial closeted gay man."

Steve Molaro: Raj certainly could have been gay, and that was definitely a viable way to go. And he certainly wouldn't be the first gay character on TV. But maybe it was a little more interesting to have a guy so comfortable in his feminine side who's not gay, and explore that.

Kunal Nayyar: I never considered Raj's sexuality to be in question. I always thought he had effeminate qualities—both masculine and feminine. And because of that, he was in touch with his sexuality. He was very comfortable with his feminine side. And if he was gay, it wouldn't have mattered. It wouldn't have been a big deal. But, it wasn't that I considered him bisexual or gay or anything. He was just in touch with his feminine side, which we all should be.

Simon Helberg: I never thought that that was what they were going to do. I think they were playing with that dynamic, and poking fun at masculinity.

At the end of the episode, Bernadette and Howard decide to buy Raj a Yorkie named Cinnamon in hopes that a furry companion will help him get over so much heartbreak. It's love at first sight.

Steve Molaro: Steve Holland's son's favorite character on a show? Cinnamon.

Steve Holland: My son is just an animal lover by nature, but the actual Cinnamon—there were a few of them—was always so shaky and nervous. So we didn't use Cinnamon a ton. But my son always loved it when she was on the show.

Kunal Nayyar: One was called Endeavor and the other one . . . I forget. But they looked exactly the same and were very adorable. I love dogs. I mean, it was a bit overkill when I had to kiss Cinnamon on the mouth and feel tongue on tongue. But, no, I loved it. And then unfortunately, one of them passed away, so there was only one left for the last season. But the dog was just so cute. It's not always easy working with animals because they can be

There's nothing like the love of a furry friend, and Raj and Cinnamon had a bond like no other. *Courtesy of Kaley Cuoco photo collection*

unpredictable, but Cinnamon just sat there and looked cute. I understood Raj's attachment to Cinnamon, because my dog is like my son, basically. When I eat lunch, I sit on the floor and I eat one bite and he eats one bite. So, it wasn't really acting if that makes sense!

Of all the memorable guest stars in *Big Bang*'s run—and there are plenty of them—hands down the most impressive and prominent was Professor Stephen Hawking. The English theoretical physicist, cosmologist, and best-selling author whose book, *A Brief History of Time*, spent a record-breaking 237 weeks on the London *Sunday Times* best-seller list, was also a recipient of the Presidential Medal of Freedom, the highest civilian honor in the United States. He was confined to a wheelchair due to ALS and on round-the-clock care, so his desire to appear on *The Big Bang Theory* was all the more impressive, given the logistics that needed to be worked out ahead of time for season five's twenty-first episode, "The Hawking Excitation."

Professor David Saltzberg: We needed to get a hold of Stephen Hawking, so I asked around to my colleagues and was told that he's good friends with Kip Thorne, who is a professor at Caltech, and subsequently won a Nobel. He said to us, "Yes, I can get a letter to Stephen Hawking." We asked him in that letter if he would be willing to be on the show. And to our great delight he said yes! And that's how it happened. I [later] met Stephen Hawking and we had a dinner at Caltech in honor of his birthday and I sat next to him. It was really nice. You couldn't ask a lot of questions, you know, but you could have a communication with him.

Chuck Lorre: We were in this little library area at Caltech filming his scene where he shoots down Sheldon's math. Sheldon faints in front of him when he realizes the mistake he's made. Sheldon thought when he gave his research to Hawking, he would get an attaboy and the two great minds would connect, and history would record this moment, but it doesn't work out that way. Hawking's dialogue is computer generated, and so we said to him early on, "If you want, we can generate that dialogue, and you don't have to really do anything," but he was adamant about programming the dialogue himself. He had one muscle on his face—there was a camera on his glasses that could read this muscle—and he could move a cursor around and type. He wrote books this way. Forget dialogue on *The Big Bang Theory*; he wrote *books*. So he wrote out his dialogue, and while we were shooting the scene, he generated the on switch that caused the dialogue to be generated from his equipment.

Anthony Rich: Chuck actually directed the scene because the week Hawking was coming into town for a conference was one of our preplanned hiatus weeks, and Cendrowski would always go back to Michigan to teach a class. But Cendrowski had gone and scouted the Caltech location ahead of time and basically laid everything out and set it up. We filmed it on the weekend. But when Hawking recorded his dialogue in the scene, it's not the way it was on the show. So, Jim would say a line but it might be a minute before you hear a response. Now, imagine saying, "Well, what do you think, Dr. Hawking?" and then having silence for sixty seconds until you hear an answer. But in that particular scene, the silence went on longer than expected until we found out it was actually because Professor Hawking was nervous. He had a little bit of stage fright, which delayed the delay even further.

Chuck Lorre: I hope this doesn't sound callous, but there was a moment when everybody was ready, Professor Hawking was ready, Jim was ready, the lights were ready, everybody was ready to shoot the scene, and I realized I was going to look at Stephen Hawking, who is completely trapped inside a body that has no motion, and I'm going to say the word, "Action." And just before I was supposed to say, "Action," it occurred to me, *Oh my God, I'm supposed to say* action. *I don't want to say* action. Action *is not the word that should be used here, but I don't know another word to start the scene, so I think what I said was,* "Everybody ready? OK!" *and then in a very soft voice,* "Action." [*Laughs*] I swallowed it. I'm probably the only one who was concerned with that. He didn't seem to be concerned with it one way or another.

Jim Parsons: Even though I knew that obviously he was game for everything, some part of me felt so inappropriate about putting possibly the most intelligent human being on the planet at that time into a scene in our sitcom. I was really uncomfortable. I thought, "This is *not* right!" I had been faking how smart I was to play Sheldon by saying the lines other people wrote, but I didn't know what the fuck I was talking about, and now I'm face-to-face with possibly the smartest person on the planet! And even though I knew it wasn't inappropriate that this was even happening, there was a part of me that felt it somehow was. Also, his eyes were the definition of piercing. [*Laughs*] There was so much life and information coming through them, and that was amazing and slightly disconcerting. And yet I kept avoiding his eyes because every time I looked I thought, *Oh, my God, he knows things about me that I'll never know because he's that smart.* It was one of the most amazing days I'll probably ever have that I couldn't wait for it to end. I just wanted it to be over, if that makes sense. It was nice when he visited the set, because I could kind of split the focus, whereas I was the only actor on the set when we went to the university to shoot. I was like, *Oh, God. Oh, my God. Quit looking at me. People, quit looking at me.* And I had to fall down and faint as Sheldon next to his wheelchair and, I was thinking, *Oh God, I won't know when to get up, and I'll kind of just lay there on the floor, and ask somebody to save me.* I'm very grateful it happened, but I was just scared to death. And of what? I really don't know, looking back. That's the dumb thing about this. [*Laughs*]

Chuck Lorre: We were honestly so grateful that he did that for us. And he had such a good time, that on Monday, we got a call, saying, "Professor

Professor Stephen Hawking with his fans (er, costars), pictured here with (from bottom counterclockwise) Johnny Galecki, Chuck Lorre, Steve Molaro, Carol Ann Susi, Melissa Rauch, Kunal Nayyar, Mark Cendrowski, Jim Parsons, Simon Helberg, Mayim Bialik, and Bill Prady. *Courtesy of Nikki Lorre*

Hawking is coming to the set to hang out!" He just came to hang out! He wanted to come watch us rehearse. And he spent the whole afternoon with us.

Mark Cendrowski: We had to have an ambulance standing by, because his health was not that good. We didn't even know if he was going to be able to make the trip from England originally. We had to be ready not to do it, but thankfully it all worked out. And when he came to our runthrough on the stage, it just so happened that Simon had to be doing an impression of him. Simon was like, "Oh my God." He did the scene and then immediately turned to Professor Hawking and said, "I'm so sorry! They made me do it!" And everyone cracked up. But then a buzzer on his wheelchair went off, and we saw his handlers come in to move and check things, and we were so concerned. My first thought was, *Oh my God, Simon, you killed Stephen Hawking!* But his handler assured us, "No, he was laughing!" The only way he could communicate was off of his glasses with a sensor on his cheek, so the buzzer would go off when he laughed. We were like, "Thank God!" He just had the best time seeing behind the scenes of our world and how it was done. I still can't believe it.

> Professor Hawking was never shy about expressing his love for the cast and the series. He once wrote on his official Facebook page, "If there is any group of people that I'd say have a good shot at cracking my Theory of Everything, it is certainly *The Big Bang Theory.*"

Simon Helberg: Even when I think about it, I can't believe that happened. I really can't. It makes sense given that our show featured characters who worshiped him or did impressions of him, so I understand it from that perspective, but just the fact that you'd be in a room with him is hard to wrap your head around. It's like if you see a picture of Albert Einstein teaching, and you're like, *that's* the real Albert Einstein teaching students in a classroom?! It's hard to imagine certain people doing anything except existing in pictures or documentaries, and there he was on the soundstage of our show and watching our runthrough and posing for pictures. That was a dream. It really was.

Steve Molaro: He was only in person with us once because he wasn't flying to LA every time he was on. That wouldn't have been feasible. When he was on FaceTime, we would recycle that footage and change what he was wearing, but we would send him the scripts in London, and he would generate his voice saying it and send it to us.

Showcasing incredible figures in the scientific community like Professor Hawking had an unexpected but rewarding side effect.

Chuck Lorre: It's incalculable. It is. Two, three years into the show, we discovered *Big Bang* was changing the life direction of kids; going into STEM (science, technology, engineering, and mathematics) fields was cool because it looked cool on television.

And as if a guest spot by one of the most celebrated theoretical physicists of all time wasn't enough, when this already incredible season came to a close, the producers decided to up the stakes by sending Howard to space. They worked with NASA and real-life astronaut Mike Massimino to make it as real as possible, especially as season six got underway. But first, there was a wedding to plan: the nuptials of Bernadette and Howard.

Steve Holland: Their wedding in "The Countdown Reflection" really came out of the idea of sending Howard to space. It was Chuck's idea to start in the rocket waiting for liftoff and structure the episode in flashback form. I remember when he pitched it I was thinking, *How is that going to work? That seems like a really bad idea.* Of course, it turned out to be a great idea. Part of what made it work is that we really worked hard to make it accurate. We had Mike Massimino, who is an actual astronaut, consult with us and ended up putting him in the show as one of the other astronauts. So knowing that Howard was going to space meant that Howard and Bernadette's wedding plans got thrown out the window and they had to do something last-minute. And then Molaro had seen people who set up photo ops when they knew the Google Earth satellite was going to be passing by and that seemed like a really fun thing to make their wedding special. Once we had that piece then the rooftop seemed like the perfect location. That gave us a good out to not see Mrs. Wolowitz; we could just hear her shouting from the other side of the roof and the chance to finally see her when we did the pull out to the Google Earth photo.

The actual wedding ceremony aside, the sweetest moment of the episode actually came in the tag, when the gang gathers around the television in Sheldon and Leonard's apartment to watch the space capsule blast off. As Howard screams bloody murder inside the spacecraft, his new wife watches in amazement—with the support of their friends—as they hold their breath for a safe journey. The moment was so poignant that Lorre took a break from his typical sarcastic weekly vanity card to strike a more reflective and emotional tone.

CHUCK LORRE PRODUCTIONS, #389

This may sound silly, but I had to stifle tears when we wrote the last scene of tonight's episode. The same thing happened when we rehearsed it. And then again when it was performed in front of a studio audience. And yet again when we watched the final version in an editing bay. I don't know what it is, but there's something primal, something deeply human being expressed when these characters unconsciously hold hands while watching their friend embark on a monumental journey. Speaking of which, I want to take this opportunity to thank you for watching The Big Bang Theory, for being part of our journey. I hope you've laughed a lot and stifled a little. I hope you're holding someone's hand. See you next year.

Chapter 14

THE SENSATIONAL SEASON SIX

A year into syndication, the ratings for new episodes of *Big Bang* were truly out of this world. In season six's "The Bakersfield Expedition," also known as the episode where the guys are stranded in the desert in their *Star Trek* uniforms, the show exceeded 20 million viewers for the first of many episodes to come. As Warner Bros. Television president Peter Roth remembers, "The statistics were extraordinary. It was the number one series in every demographic and every platform, and the number one show on broadcast, on cable in syndication, and internationally."

Syndication was a huge part of that, of course, but the leadership of Steve Molaro—who officially took over as the sole showrunner in season six—cannot be understated. The heart and emotional gravitas he brought to each character and storyline helped turn *Big Bang* into a culturally relevant series with staying power.

Steve Molaro: I happen to be extremely fond of season six. The characters became more human and got into more relationship-y type stories, which was a big shift for us. Holland and I talk about it in terms of a rock band, and somewhere around six and seven is when the show became a stadium band.

Steve Holland: We were given some freedom with that passing of the torch. The show was a hit, and Chuck trusted Steve to try out ideas that we wouldn't have been able to try before. It gave us this added enthusiasm.

Chuck Lorre: If I kept running the show, we probably would have run out of gas. I know that. Because Molaro, Holland, the writers, took the show in directions I was terrified of and probably would not have had the courage to do so myself. The relationship between Amy and Sheldon was beyond anything I could have dreamt up.

Bill Prady: I give Molaro credit for creating and managing Sheldon and Amy's relationship. And I give myself credit for being the loyal opposition to that. For saying that this can't happen. And I don't know if Steve will agree. But my strenuous objection to it caused him to do it even better. Not that he wouldn't have done it great, but I think on some level, his goal was to show me that I was wrong, and what a glorious thing. What a glorious thing to be shown that you're wrong. And in that, that's Sheldon winning the battle over his nature, because there's something finally, *finally* more important and that's this woman that he's fallen in love with. I think that's one of the reasons that the later seasons—each of the seasons has a reason for being neat, but the later seasons you start to see real growth in Sheldon and it's cool to watch.

> Molaro also had an insight into these characters that was unique to him. Success happened for him a bit later in life, which was also part of the appeal of the characters he was writing for. They too were finding confidence, love, and success in their thirties and forties.

Steve Molaro: I never thought about working in TV as a kid even though I loved it. That was never a thing that was even on my radar. I was working as a graphic designer at Publishers Clearing House through most of my twenties, so I was not even remotely in that world. And I was almost forty when I started *Big Bang*. And in many ways, the emotions and feelings I had growing up and feeling like an outcast lent itself to a deeper understanding of these characters. Young Steve would never even believe what was in store. I grew up an overweight, lonely, only child, sitting in front of a television set. Shows like *Happy Days*, *Laverne & Shirley*, and *Mork & Mindy* were just oxygen for me.

Jim Parsons: He would be hard to compete with anybody for who was more excited by and invested in the show in general. And one of the reasons he was such a good fit to run *Young Sheldon* is because it allows Steve to put as much heart as he wanted to always put in. There were certain constraints about the constructs of *Big Bang* that wouldn't allow quite as much, or it had to be balanced in a different way. He knew more about what these characters wanted than we did, and he had theories about their lives that we would never even dream of.

Mayim Bialik: It really was when he became more active as showrunner that we started seeing this development of the complexity of these characters. It was almost like a new show to explore all these different personalities in relation to each other and also in relation to yourself.

But Molaro and the entire crew had their work cut out for them, especially since season six started with Wolowitz in a Soyuz space capsule headed toward the International Space Station and separated from the rest of the gang for the next four episodes.

Bill Prady: There was some hesitation because multicam television is not visually the best for certain things, but Chuck really wanted to do it. I had just so happened to have recently met the deputy administrator of NASA. I called up Lori Garver at NASA and asked if she could help us discuss the possibility of the story. She put me in touch with the wonderful Mike Massimino, who helped fix the Hubble telescope. We eventually gave him a little part on the show playing himself that turned into something bigger because he kept doing such a great job. My feeling was that if you were a scientist or astronaut, the standard I wanted is that they shouldn't want to throw their shoes at the TV. I think we got there because people were very happy about it.

Chuck Lorre: By the time we were doing those stories, the show was successful enough to where we had the time and money to build sets and take our time and get it right.

Mark Cendrowski: We had to make Howard look like he was in zero gravity. I asked to put the cameras on a gyroscope so they floated and you had a constant feel of motion. Then, with a greenscreen we sent one of the other astronauts floating through the background. One problem was that we had the Russian astronaut (played by Pasha Lychnikoff) hanging upside down talking to Simon, who's right side up. But with zero gravity you can't have hair falling down, so we shot him right side up, on the floating chair and flipped the image on the greenscreen. It was a great puzzle to figure out, and once we did, it looked great. People thought we used the plane from *Apollo 13* to film it. We were like, "Oh, we fooled 'em."

Simon Helberg: The show worked to always be 100 percent authentic and accurate, and the space storyline was a very important piece to that. The only CGI stuff they really did was with a pen that floats away, but everything else was just practical effects.

> While the story arc was an impressive technical achievement, it was a more subtle character-driven moment in the premiere episode that spoke volumes about how the show was changing. In "The Date Night Variable," Penny is seen helping Amy bleach her upper lip hair before her anniversary date with Sheldon. Typically, those getting-ready moments on TV and film include a makeover or a montage of various date-night ensembles, but the act of bleaching one's "mustache" is the stuff most women don't want someone to see, even though it's extremely common. And here the number one show on television was saying, *Not only are we going to show it, but we're going to make it as normal as it should be.*

Maria Ferrari: I've certainly bleached the hair on my upper lip, and I've talked to Tara [Hernandez] about it as well. I think Tara and I especially were exorcising a lot of junior high demons with Amy because there's something about being in your thirties and finally being comfortable in your vulnerability that makes it easier for us to talk about. I remember getting teased for the hair on my lip, so it was important that scene could help normalize something so many of us do.

Tara Hernandez: I am all about females talking about body hair, because guess what? We have it. I think we had a joke once about Bernadette lamenting that she shaved her legs for a very tortuous night with Sheldon, and she makes a joke, like I can't believe I shaved my legs for this, and Chuck said, "When do women not shave their legs?" And we were like, *OK, sir!* [*Laughs*] It was one of those *Really?* moments. I loved that Amy talked about her body hair and was finally experiencing things that women do for each other, including bleaching your lip, waxing, getting your ears pierced...all that stuff. It really resonated. Jumping ahead to my time on *Young Sheldon*, it's why it was important to me that we showed the episode where Missy got her period. You can't get away from it—it's part of growing up. It's too important not to show. And yes, you're a comedy, so you want to show it through a bit of humor and joy, but also, as a writer, you want to use the opportunity to say, *What do I wish I saw in these situations? What do I wish was there?* I didn't know until I started getting dark upper lip hair that no one was talking about it.

Eddie Gorodetsky: It's identification. It's "I see myself on television. I haven't seen myself before." The worst thing that *Friends* did was find six people who are really good-looking *and* funny. So you went through this period of time on television where we kind of went backwards, and they just wanted to find good-looking people, and they didn't care if they were funny for a while. Thank God we're coming out of that again. The idea of seeing people you can identify with and going "I'm not a freak. I'm not the only one who has to bleach my mustache" is really important.

Mayim Bialik: The upper-lip bleaching was but one example of many ways that the Amy and Penny dynamic in particular fleshed out a lot of complexity of female identity. I credit Maria and Tara with that, and many of our wonderful feminist, assigned-male-at-birth writers.

> The writers' deep understanding of the characters and their commitment to making each storyline feel true to them was another reason why the show was firing on all cylinders. Take, for example, Penny and Leonard's yo-yo romance. Their first official breakup happened when Leonard told Penny he loved her, but she wasn't on the same page. A few years later they cautiously decided to try again, but Leonard was always hesitant to push Penny too much. The unpredictability and authenticity of their relationship in turn made the first time Penny said, "I love you" that much more surprising and real.

LEONARD

> It's hard sometimes. Everywhere you go, guys hit on you, even if I'm standing right there. And they're all taller than me. Why is everyone taller than me?! You know what? This is all in my head. It's my problem, not yours.

PENNY

Leonard, why do you always do this? Listen to me, you are the one I'm with! You know I love you, so will you please relax because you're driving me crazy!

LEONARD

You know that's the first time you ever said that you love me.

PENNY

Yeah.

LEONARD

We're just supposed to pretend it's not a big deal?

PENNY

That's exactly what we're gonna do...because you're about to make me cry...and we both know if I start crying, you're gonna start crying.

LEONARD

[*Starting to cry*] You're right. You should go!
And then, moments later, when Leonard is in his apartment alone...

LEONARD

She loves me.

Tara Hernandez: That ignited fire in the room, because the episode wasn't built around an "I love you" the way the prom episode was built around it for Sheldon and Amy in season eight. The Leonard-Penny "I love you" came up really organically when they were having a moment of insecurity of Penny working with this classmate who Leonard was threatened by. I just said it in the writers room, like, "Leonard, I don't know why you're so jealous, you know I love you, so relax." It got pitched that easy, and everyone was like, "No, no, no, she hasn't said it before! But you're newer to the room, you might not know." And it was like, "I know, but it feels like that's how it's going to happen for them, especially. The reason Leonard's feeling insecure in that moment is because he hasn't gotten that validation that he needs. Leonard needs to hear that vocalized or else he won't be able to relax about this new partnership that she has." I remember everyone really jumping down my throat about it, like, *No, we're not there yet!* And to his credit, Steve Molaro just sat with it, and was like, "Yeah. I think it's time. I think it's the time for 'I love yous.'" Sheldon and Amy were much more premeditated; Leonard and Penny were not.

For Cuoco and Galecki, the moment is still so special...though for slightly different reasons.

Kaley Cuoco: We did that in one take. Johnny gets nostalgic about that moment.

Johnny Galecki: I do. I think we knew at the time. I mean, you play these characters...but that was an incredibly honest moment between Kaley and I. We didn't need more than one take.

Kaley Cuoco: Steve Molaro or Mark Cendrowski came over and said, "We don't need another take unless you want one," and we said, "We don't either." But that was also the night before our first flash mob, and sorry, Johnny, but that's all I could think about.

Johnny Galecki: Oh fuck.

By the way...those flash mobs? I'll be getting to that later...

Kaley Cuoco: I was like, "We don't need to do it again! I'm ready to daaaaaance!" [*Laughs*] Those were terrific memories for the cast and crew... and the fans, thank you very much!

Johnny Galecki: They were, but *that's* what you were thinking of when we had that special moment? The flash mob?

Kaley Cuoco: No! When we did the moment, it was perfect! It was literally a perfect scene, and I was like, *That's it! Let's go dance!* But even when we do a scene that's great, we usually always do it one more time so they have an option. But they said, "We don't even want an option." It was pretty cool.

The Penny-Leonard "I love you" scene was also interesting based on the fact that the audience didn't really react at first. That would be in deep contrast to the moment that happened a few episodes later in "The Fish Guts

Displacement," when Amy played up a cold to get Sheldon to take care of her. When he discovered she wasn't as sick as she pretended to be, and she urged him to spank her as punishment, the audience reacted so wildly that Bialik and Parsons could barely get through it.

Jim Parsons: First I had to rub her chest with Vicks VapoRub, but I'll never forget the spanking because I couldn't do it without laughing. I couldn't do it! And they said, "Don't worry, we're not going to have your face on camera. It will be on Mayim and her enjoying getting spanked." But then on tape night—and talk about emotions—they told me I was suddenly going to be on camera for that moment. And I was *furious*. I mean, I was spitting nails, I was so mad at these people for putting me on camera. And, I couldn't quit laughing, which was only making me more mad because I suddenly couldn't do my job. It was really weird. I can't even get through telling this story without laughing now. [*Laughs*] Mayim would just go, "Oh! Oh!" making these sexual, sort of awkward, genius-sounding noises. So between her doing that and the audience reacting, I couldn't hold it together. I felt like the moment could never be as good as it could have been in some ways because I never thought I'd have to do it on camera. It's just stupid looking back, what a weird job.

Mayim Bialik: It was a completely off-camera thing when we rehearsed it all week. And I was very relieved because doing that in front of people is *so* awkward. I think my mom might have been there, as well as my dad. All I know is we did it off camera through rehearsal, producer's runthrough, and then at the taping, Chuck said, "Let's do it on camera."

Chuck Lorre: I probably figured there was no harm in shooting it so that we could have a choice in the editing room. Or I might have been thinking, *This is hilarious! Why wouldn't we want to see this?!* But I do remember thinking, *How far can we go with this? At what point do we run from this or embrace it?* I couldn't tell you anything else that happened in that episode other than that scene and trying to be very careful about making sure that we weren't being offensive or crossing a line with these characters.

Mark Cendrowski: It was kind of written as Sheldon saying he's going to spank Amy and then we cut to her face, and you would just see his hand coming through the background, and her reactions. But when we put it on camera in the runthrough, the anticipation of Sheldon saying "Well, I'm just going to have to spank you" was just too funny. Just seeing it on camera, Chuck and Steve and everybody were like, "No, you gotta do it. It's too funny not to." Jim and Mayim could not believe they were doing this, but they were so funny together. And the audience went nuts.

Mayim Bialik: I don't think about the faces I am making in such moments, but people always ask me about my reactions. I'm like, *It's just my face! That's just what my face does when I'm acting! I don't know!* When I've seen clips of that scene, I criticize myself and think, *Oh my gosh, I look so stupid, or my hair looks bad.* And I *was* supposed to look bad because Amy was sick, but there's still a vanity to me as an actor even though my character is so unadorned. And then it became a meme, and it's something people talk about! And when I think about my kids and how they might see that? Oh my gosh, the worst!

The physicality of the moment also harkens back to the first time Sheldon and Amy cuddled—a season earlier in "The Isolation Permutation"—when Amy literally swings her legs onto the couch, and Bialik and Parsons do this genius "dance" of awkwardly trying to be intimate in the most G-rated way.

Mayim Bialik: I'm laughing at the thought of Sheldon and Amy cuddling for the first time. We did that scene a couple different ways. Mark Cendrowski really had a gift for the physicality of my character in particular. I picture him a lot, actually, doing things kind of as Amy would when he would show me things.

Jim Parsons: Amy and Sheldon were characters who were unsure how to act socially, physically, in their own different way. She doesn't know what to do and so she swings for a home run to try and get it done, whereas Sheldon is more the monkey, if you will. He slowly reaches in this way and that way, and one of the reasons they were such a good pair as characters is because mine and Mayim's approaches to how to deal with the exact same issue at the heart of it were so completely different. Her legs going up on the couch...it's just this blunt force, and mine is much more this nervous ballerina dancing around her.

Eddie Gorodetsky: Everyone has difficulty with intimacy, so you want to feel that you're not alone. And these characters had difficulties, too. They had problems communicating, getting dates, keeping it together. The more you can relate or you know someone who's like that, it humanizes it. *Big Bang* seemed big because of the bold colors and the science and comic books, but then you make it small in the storytelling. Other shows often make their storytelling bigger, but it's important to find those smaller moments, too.

Although season six was delving into more "relationship-y" moments, the show didn't forget its DNA, either, which was indulging the guys in their love of all things sci-fi, cosplay, and nerd culture. In "The Bakersfield Expedition," the guys dress up as their favorite *Star Trek: The Next Generation* characters for the Bakersfield Comic-Con.

Jim Parsons: It was fun to be transformed. The only hard part was we shot on an entirely different soundstage, which most people would be like, *So what?* But we were always in our one bubble, so leaving that bubble was always weird. Anytime we shot outside, it was like, *Ugh, what's happening?* Our assistant director, Anthony Rich, used to always say, "We're an indoor cat." And it's true! We work best on *our* soundstage. But I enjoyed playing Brent Spiner's Data. That whole thing was very fun to play with all three of the guys.

Kunal Nayyar: We had a special unit makeup team that would come and do our makeup for that, and it was brilliant. It's not fun wearing all the prosthetics and stuff, but I had a lot of fun shooting those scenes. My favorite line in the episode is toward the end when everyone is eating in the diner and we're dejected and everyone is making fun of us, and I say, "Did we at least rent the car from Enterprise?" They look at me like, *Not, now, dude,* and I say, "Screw you, that's funny!" And then the sexy photo shoot that we did in the desert scene where I'm like, "And now let's do some sexy glamour shots! I'll set the mood! Oontz, oontz, oontz…yeah, I like it, I like it!" I remember doing it like it was yesterday.

Johnny Galecki: It was very, very hot that day—too hot to be wearing a bald cap. I was not comfortable. And I know nothing about *Star Trek*, only *Star Wars*, so I felt very uncomfortable in any sort of *Star Trek* scene or episode. I just felt very uneducated on the matter. But I do remember showing off some *Charlie's Angels* and *Pulp Fiction* dance moves while we were all dressed up. It's not like we had a choreographer for that episode. [*Laughs*] That was all our moves.

At least in "The Bakersfield Expedition," things didn't go according to plan for fictional characters. In "The Tangible Affection Proof," which aired timed to Valentine's Day, 2013, Cuoco and Galecki planned a prank during a dinner scene that went so badly off the rails it landed Cuoco in a plastic surgeon's office, and left Lorre horrified.

Kaley Cuoco: We were doing this scene where Leonard and Penny get in an argument at the table, and we told first AD Anthony Rich we had a prank, and we were going to do it. This would not be funny today, but it was really funny at the time—or at least we thought so—where our argument would get really heated, and Johnny would fake-punch me, and I was going to fall off camera off the chair. So we do it and it gets really heightened, and Johnny comes at me, and . . .

Johnny Galecki: And she landed under the table. And then I started to pretend to stomp on her face.

Melissa Rauch: Simon and I were in the scene as well, and so I was aware that they were planning it, but when Kaley came up from the table with blood on her head, I thought that it was fake blood for a second.

Kaley Cuoco: Everyone was laughing but I did not realize the chair had hit me in the head. Nothing hurt. So then we cut and I came up from the table saying, "How funny was that?" only to realize I had blood coming down my face as if I was in a boxing match. Anthony ran over and was like, "Get a napkin!" I thought it was fine, but no, this thing was spurting.

Johnny Galecki: That's a little dramatic. There was blood involved, yes.

Chuck Lorre: It was horrifying!

Mark Cendrowski: Any cuts on the head bleed a lot worse, but she was cut right under the eyebrow. Immediately it started swelling, so we got pressure and ice on it; the makeup team even tried to cover it up, but it kept bleeding. We were just trying to joke around, but boy, we went too far with that one.

Kaley Cuoco: It wouldn't stop bleeding! At 7 p.m., I had to go to a plastic surgeon so they could stitch it up. The next day on the set there were all these signs saying things like, "No more jokes! No more rough-housing!" I mean, we thought it was so funny, but no one else did. [*Laughs*] And then we had to reblock the scene on the couch after me and Leonard were at dinner, and I'm sitting facing him. Originally I was on the other side, so we had my bangs come down to cover the stitches so you couldn't see what had happened. It was so embarrassing, and the whole thing was a total nightmare.

Mark Cendrowski: Yeah, I tried to avoid shooting her straight on when we were able to film again the next day because you could see the swelling. And our visual effects supervisor, Rick Redick, I believe fixed some of the swelling in postproduction.

While it wasn't Cuoco and Galecki's finest moment, thankfully it was a minor blip overall. The episode as a whole is quite sweet, with Sheldon telling Amy that she's his emergency contact (hey, it's the little things), Kate Micucci making her first appearance as Raj's love interest, Lucy, and Penny assuring Leonard that she loves him and sees marriage in the cards.

A few episodes later, Bernadette—and specifically, Howard—got their moment to shine in one of the series most emotionally charged episodes, "The Closet Reconfiguration." While cleaning/organizing/sanitizing the Wolowitz closet, Sheldon happens upon an unopened letter from Howard's estranged father. Sheldon takes it upon himself to read the contents of the letter, which was sent to Howard on his eighteenth birthday. Rightfully, Howard is upset with Sheldon for invading his privacy and tells him under no circumstance does he want to know what it says. "He abandoned me and my mother," Howard tells Sheldon. "Why does he deserve a chance to explain anything?" Howard eventually burns the letter, but it doesn't matter—Sheldon has told everyone what it said. Howard's angry and hurt, but then, in a show of solidarity—and hopefully closure—everyone comes up with a plausible story for what the letter said (except Sheldon, who literally steals the plotline from *The Goonies*) that might bring Howard comfort. Only one of them is the actual message, but the point is to bring Howard comfort in knowing none of the options were negative; in fact, all of them were extremely poignant.

Anthony Rich: It was kind of an atypical episode, which I hand to Molaro because he started really bringing soul and drama to it. I told the actors,

"Don't worry if you're not hearing the same kinds of laughs that you would've before." There was some heavy stuff in there, and the fact that Sheldon opens the letter and *reads* the letter...that's something that Wolowitz had not wanted to do for all these years on purpose. I was so proud of how it turned out. It's one of the many reasons why I think season six is one of the best.

Simon Helberg: I got very excited, and I felt a bit of pressure. It was also one of the first storyline that had that underpinning of emotion, certainly for Howard. I think it's when the show really came into its own, when you could be in a scene and be moved by something, and then find yourself really laughing, which is not something you see a lot in sitcoms. I really do attribute that shift to Molaro, as well as Melissa...you get some gravity in there, and that's a really beautiful thing.

"The Closet Reconfiguration" saw Howard at his most vulnerable as he grappled with the reality of what his estranged father might or might not have written him in a letter years earlier. *Photo™ & © Warner Bros. Entertainment Inc.*

Before episodes aired each week, episode screeners were always sent out to CBS and Warner Bros. Television executives to watch ahead of time. Nina

Tassler, who was president of CBS entertainment throughout much of *Big Bang*'s run, never called to relay any thoughts or notes. This time, however, she did.

Steve Molaro: We were in the writers room, and I got a call telling me that Nina Tassler was on the line for me. It's one of those things where it's like the principal calls and you think, *Am I in trouble?!* And then, *All right, I guess I should go talk to her.* So I went to my office and picked up the phone and she said, "I had to call you, because I was going to watch an episode at my desk while eating lunch and now I'm sitting here eating my sandwich and crying! What are you doing to me?" She was really touched by the episode and said some really nice things.

Given that the episode was so well-received, and how Howard's absent father was often mentioned throughout the series, one would have expected that viewers would actually meet Mr. Wolowitz. It wasn't to be.

Steve Molaro: There were a number of times we talked about it in the room or came up with stories that would involve that, but it got to the point where Chuck just didn't want to do it.

Simon Helberg: If I'm going to be brutally honest, I was disappointed that we didn't meet Howard's dad. I felt like in some ways it was a missed opportunity to not have him only because they had painted this really intricate picture of that relationship, and sort of forged this road that was either going to lead to it or just be a dead end, I guess. I wanted to know, and since the writers came up with some of the most brilliant and clever ways to tell these stories, I felt creatively it would have been earned because when the writers really did go for those nuanced, layered storylines, they knocked it out of the park. And whenever I got a piece of physical comedy or anything that was totally wild and over the top, I voraciously devoured that, too. But sometimes I wanted more of that meatiness that we would get in some of the storylines we've talked about.

Various possibilities for who could play Howard's father floated around on the web for years—with Rick Moranis gaining the most traction—but it just so happened that the producers did reach out to someone. When that didn't

happen, the idea was basically dropped. So who was it? None other than one of the most famous musicians on the planet: Ringo Starr.

Chuck Lorre: Well, it was a fun conversation based on Simon's haircut and physical appearance that you could buy the genetic link to Richard Starkey. [*Laughs*] I think the idea started with Simon, and it was a good idea. I think we pursued it to the point where we got a solid no [from Starr's team]. But if not Ringo, then I wanted his impact to be such that we didn't actually see him, but we saw the fact that he's missing from this character's life. His absence was more important than casting the character.

Simon Helberg: That would have been the most absurd twist to find out Howard is actually the son of a Beatle from a wild night in the '70s where Mrs. Wolowitz and Ringo had blacked out at the Rainbow Room or something, but it was never to be. Basically I'll be working on my own *Big Bang* fan fiction in twenty years and selling it at Comic-Con. But yeah, we never did get to meet him.

> However, the show did get one of the most amazing comedic legends of all time, when Emmy winner Bob Newhart joined the show in season six, episode twenty-two, titled "The Proton Resurgence." What Stephen Hawking's first appearance did for *Big Bang* in regards to an endorsement of the scientific community, Newhart did for the show's comedy cred. But it was a role that was years in the making, thanks to Lorre's determination to work with the icon.

Chuck Lorre: When I was first getting started in the business in the '80s, I was at the CBS Radford lot—which is where *Newhart* was filmed—and I would sneak onto that set when no one was there. I would just sit there, taking it in because it was iconic to me.

Bob Newhart ("Arthur Jeffries / Professor Proton"): And then over the years, he and I became friends. He would come to me about appearing on his shows, but it never quite fit. In 2013, he called me up and said, "Well, I'm here for my annual turndown!" And I said, "You know Chuck, I really am enjoying *The Big Bang Theory*. I think it's very well written, and you have a great cast. I still have my fastball. It's more like forty-two miles an hour instead of ninety-eight," which it never was ninety-eight. [*Laughs*] I said, "I'd like to do that."

Chuck Lorre: I was over the moon, ecstatic. To be able to know him and call him a friend is quite an honor. He is one of the inventors of modern American stand-up and comedy. He didn't tell jokes, he told *stories*. So when he said he would consider *The Big Bang Theory*, I was all over it. I was like, *We have to make this happen.*

> **But even though Newhart was interested in appearing on *Big Bang*, it didn't mean it was a sure thing. There were a few conditions Newhart had, and it was up to Lorre, Molaro, and the writers to come up with the right role.**

Bob Newhart: One is it has to be done in front of a live audience. I have on occasion done it without a live audience and hated it because I thought it was very sterile. The audience drives you, so you come up with things maybe you wouldn't have come up otherwise. The other condition was that it wasn't a one-shot, meaning that it would be a recurring character. Chuck agreed and said, "OK, let me write something, and I'll give you a call and see if you agree with it."

> **Molaro came up with the idea of Arthur Jeffries, who hosted a children's science show as "Professor Proton." The character was based on a childhood hero of Molaro's that he would watch regularly as a kid.**

Steve Molaro: Professor Proton is from my years watching Uncle Floyd on *The Uncle Floyd Show* when I was growing up. It was a huge, cult-y show in the late '70s and '80s in the New York and New Jersey areas. I had heard him on the radio and that he was still around and available for benefits and parties. I said to my wife, "Hey, would it be all right if I hired him so he could come hang out with us?" My wife was like, do whatever you want. [*Laughs*] So then it became, *What if Leonard and Sheldon have something like that with a science show and wanted to hang out with him as grown-ups?*

Bob Newhart: I loved the character, I loved the script, I loved the writing. And what a wonderful ensemble cast. Jim Parsons was so great to work with and so generous.

Even though Newhart was excited to film his first episode, the usually unflappable Lorre felt an enormous amount of anxiety on his first day on set.

Chuck Lorre: I was a nervous wreck. I wanted so much to impress him and show him he was in good hands, that we were capable of guaranteeing his success on the show. I was nervous the whole time. God forbid if a joke didn't work or a moment wasn't landing. But it's a process. And Bob knows the process. Still, that didn't change my response at all; I had a legend of television on the set, and I wanted to make damn sure that he was enjoying himself.

Mark Cendrowski: We covered the elevator area outside the apartments so when he did appear, it would be a surprise for the audience. But earlier in the day when we told him what we were doing, he was kind of concerned. He said, "Do you want to go to all that trouble? Do you think people are going to remember me?" We were taken aback, but in his mind it was like, *I'm older, and this is a younger audience.* And then when we did reveal him, the audience went nuts. It was like a two-minute standing ovation, and he got misty-eyed. I don't know how many times we had to do that scene because it was just hard to continue after that.

Jim Parsons: It literally stopped the show. We sat there while the audience applauded and applauded and couldn't believe they were seeing him. And honestly, I couldn't believe he was in the flesh-and-blood in front of me and we were in the same room together. And he was doing a scene with me! Bob and Mary Tyler Moore are the two actors I feel like I learned as much from as anybody—and from their shows, especially. Bob's timing is so impeccable. And without naming names, we've all met or worked with people who are there as much for their past glories as they are for what they are actually still capable of delivering. But Bob was quicker than a good deal of our own cast, frankly, and I don't just mean with comedy, but he's so quick. And that's all still there.

Johnny Galecki: He's always been a hero of mine, and a fellow Chicago boy. That's who I wanted to be as an actor, and so to work with him was just a dream. We even became friends. He wrote me a scathing email because I had posted on Instagram for his ninety-first birthday about what a nice guy he is, and he asked me to please stop telling people that he's a nice guy. [*Laughs*] There were many expletives in the email that I won't share, but it was just brilliant.

Simon Helberg: I still want to know why he refuses to go to hot yoga with me. I love him. I didn't get to do a whole lot with him, but I filled in for him at the table read when he couldn't be there. To actually try and replicate his timing was one of the most challenging and incredible experiences that I had had. But with him, the trick is just to pause for an hour and a half between words.

During the live taping, Newhart did something that Lorre has never experienced in his entire decades-long career.

Chuck Lorre: There was a moment with Kaley in the living room and Bob had this joke that wasn't working in front of the audience. It was a line that should have been getting a laugh, but it was just disappearing. I was standing with the writers and they were saying, "We need to talk to Bob about that joke," but nobody wanted to go over and talk to him. We were all too nervous and intimidated. Then it became clear I was elected to go talk to him. [*Laughs*] I walked over to the couch, but before I could get a word out, he looked up at me and said, "Give Kaley that joke and I'll react to it. That's how this is going to work. It's a good joke, but she should say it. And then I'll react." A great deal of his comedy was he would be talking to somebody who was out of their mind, and the comedy was on him reacting. And he knew that. But *we* didn't quite know that yet. And in my entire career, I've never walked up to an actor where the actor says, "Give that joke to the other actor." Never happened! But Bob Newhart understood that that comedy plays better on his reaction to it than on him actually saying it. I don't remember what the words were, but I turned to Kaley and said, "All right, you'll take that line?" and she said, "Sure!" And she takes the line and in the next take the look on his face when he's trying to comprehend what she just said brought the house down. It was one of those great moments where his instincts were impeccable, and he completely understood the moment had to play opposite of what we thought it should play. It was a great lesson.

Newhart was nominated by the Television Academy that year for Outstanding Guest Actor in a Comedy Series. Leading up to the Creative Arts Emmys ceremony, Newhart had previously been nominated for seven Emmys but had astonishingly never won. It all changed the evening of September 15, 2013, when Newhart's name was called as the winner, and he received a standing ovation. Backstage, he said, "I was totally unprepared for that."

Bob Newhart: Everybody loves a standing ovation. I looked out when it was starting to happen, and I was seeing stars—people—that I had never met. And they were standing up for *me*. I couldn't believe it. Stand-up comedians have not really been recognized as actors, you know, because the conceit was *Well, that's just Bob doing Bob*, and *That's just Jerry Seinfeld doing Jerry Seinfeld*. I always said, "Well, if they're not your words and you have to hit marks on the floor, then it's acting!" But anyway, I kiddingly said to Chuck, "Can you send me an audio of, of the two standing ovations because I'd like to play that in the morning when I get up." And my wife and I have been married, uh, fifty-eight years, and she thinks it's kind of ostentatious to put any awards in plain view, but I said to her, "The Emmy goes in a very prominent place in our house. You can't move it to the attic." She said okay.

Chuck Lorre: Nothing makes me happier than knowing Bob Newhart's Emmy says *The Big Bang Theory* on it. When we discussed working on *The Big Bang Theory* he said, "I want to do an arc, and I want to do something that has a chance at an Emmy." So when that Emmy happened for Professor Proton, I felt like I had delivered on a promise. He very much wanted to do something that had enough substance that he would be considered for an Emmy, and he wanted a character arc with several episodes to play out for the story. And it happened just that way.

A week after Newhart won his first-ever Emmy at the Creative Arts ceremony, he and Parsons presented together at the Primetime Emmys telecast. He was given his second standing ovation when he walked out onstage.

Jim Parsons: As they were applauding him and we were standing up there, I literally said to myself, *This is Bob's moment. Do not cry! In any way shape or form, do not lose control!* So getting to walk out there with him on the Emmy stage, where I didn't really have anything to do other than walk out there and to just soak it in, you could feel that emotion taking hold.

Johnny Galecki: I hope the Emmy was an appreciation of how underrated he had been for so long. He told me that when he was on his first series, somebody came over and said, "The show is running long because you keep stuttering all your lines. So, can you not do that?" And he said, "That stuttering bought me a house in Bel-Air!"

Newhart would go on to make six appearances as Arthur Jeffries / Professor Proton on the show, but for his third appearance in season seven's "The Proton Transmogrification," Sheldon would get the heartbreaking news that Arthur had passed away.

Bob Newhart: Chuck told my wife, Ginny, that he was gonna kill me off, so when she asked him why, Chuck said, "Well, I can have him back more often." [*Laughs*]

Steve Molaro: We came up with the whole episode of Professor Proton dying and Sheldon not wanting to go to the funeral because it was *Star Wars* Day. Really, it was just an excuse because Sheldon didn't want to deal with the loss. We thought it would be super cool if Arthur came back to him as a Jedi in a dream and talks to him, so Chuck and I had to call Bob and explain all of that to a man who knew nothing about *Star Wars*. We basically said, "Listen, the bad news is your character is going to die, the good news is he's going to come back as a Jedi ghost in Sheldon's dreams for as many times as we want." I think I said, "Do you know what a Jedi is?" and he said "No," and I said, "All right, this is going to take some explaining." [*Laughs*] So I tried to give Bob the most boiled-down explanation of Obi-Wan to Luke. And then of course, he didn't feel comfortable in that costume. No one said being a Jedi is easy.

Bob Newhart: I hated putting that robe on! They wanted to be authentic and make it exactly the way Obi Kenobi would wear it, and uh, I mean, I was happy about the fact that it brought me back as a character, but it was kind of a pain to put on the outfit. [*Laughs*] It was heavy and kind of restrictive as far as moving. It would take maybe ten minutes whenever I'd have to put on the outfit, because they wanted it to exactly mirror the way Obi Kenobi looked.

Jim Parsons: Oh, he hated that outfit! [*Laughs*] It was just such a struggle to wear that thing! He was uncomfortable, and then he couldn't get his line right because he was thinking about being uncomfortable, and then he'd have to wear it even longer. But it was so perfect, because you wanted that character to be uncomfortable. And, the genius of the whole thing was that Sheldon had "dressed" him like that.

Mary T. Quigley: We built it to look exactly like the real one. It was two or three pieces of robing, and he had to be put in it and stand there for a while. He was hilarious and lovely, but yeah, he didn't like it. [*Laughs*] I said, "Complain to the writers! They wrote it! Obi-Wan isn't even my costume design!" He said, "That's a good point!" It was a lot of draping, poor guy. Such a nice man.

Chuck Lorre: Boy, was he adorable in it, though! And he didn't know anything about *Star Wars*, but he was game.

Bob Newhart: I didn't at that time. But I became a fan of *Star Wars* just from being on the show. I had to become familiar with what they were talking about, and their adoration for *Star Wars*.

Mark Hamill (Himself): Well, that doesn't surprise me that Bob didn't exactly know. He's not exactly in the demographic, but I *adore* Bob Newhart. I mean, both *The Bob Newhart Show* and *Newhart*. He's a comedic, national treasure.

Chuck Lorre: It was a great transition, the character becoming Sheldon's unconscious mind / his inner wisdom that he's able to personify as Obi-Wan. And it allowed endless opportunities to keep working with Bob. Arthur Jeffries became part of Sheldon in a way. Because even when you lose someone you love, they're still in your life. There are still conversations that are had, and they're speaking to you if you're willing to listen. So Professor Proton being Sheldon's better self in a way, was wonderful.

There was also the time the writers wrote a scene with Sheldon and Arthur on Dagobah, the swamp-covered planet from *The Empire Strikes Back*. Newhart was still in his Obi-Wan robe, and this time was sitting on a log.

Bob Newhart: It was very damp, as I remember.

Jim Parsons: "It was very damp." [*Laughs*] I'm telling you, not his favorite

Bob Newhart (pictured here, in the infamous robe, with Chuck Lorre) learned all about *Star Wars* thanks to his time on *The Big Bang Theory*. *Courtesy of Kaley Cuoco photo collection*

scene to do on *Big Bang*, without a doubt. But Bob miserable is very fun to watch! It's good TV!

Despite the less than comfortable conditions during shooting, Newhart still watches *Big Bang* in reruns and is recognized all over the world for playing Professor Proton.

Bob Newhart: I was amazed by its popularity. I still get letters from Singapore. I even got a letter from Russia because of *The Big Bang Theory*. Oh, it's huge. It was just, it was a very wonderful time in my life to be back doing what I do, uh, and then to get the Emmy and recognition. That was something very special. Getting to do the show with just wonderful people, you know, was a very important time in my life. It was a magical time in television. To have a show last twelve years—a *comedy* to last twelve years—is so rare.

Season six came to a close that year with one of the most emotional moments in the series run. In "The Bon Voyage Reaction," Lucy broke up with a devastated Raj, who broke down in Penny's arms after she took Leonard to the airport for his North Sea expedition. Any scene where Kunal Nayyar portrays a vulnerable Raj is heartbreaking as it is, but this one was different—it was the first time that Raj, who suffered from selective mutism—also known as pathological shyness—didn't need the aid of alcohol to talk to a woman.

Kunal Nayyar: There was a real innocence to him. He just wanted love so badly. He wanted to find love with every fiber of his being, and he wasn't trying to find love in a possessive sense. He genuinely felt incomplete without love. And you felt for him. I felt for him, especially when that didn't come to fruition. That moment when he begins to talk in front of Penny, and he says, "What is wrong with me? Why can't I find love? Why can't I *have* love?" and his weeping was just so powerful—just to see someone be vulnerable and say that when there's nothing wrong with him. I think all of us have felt that way in our lives where we truly come to a moment where we feel so lost, and the confidence and who we thought we were is just gone. Yes, of course he's got his idiosyncrasies, but who doesn't? He just wanted to find love so badly.

Tara Hernandez: From a performance standpoint, you were watching magic. And I'm so down with men crying, which Kooth did often and unapologetically.

The breakthrough moment was a long time coming, especially for Nayyar, who understandably admits that playing Raj's selective mutism over the years wasn't his favorite.

Kunal Nayyar: It was definitely frustrating because there were episodes where I knew I could contribute in ways that I was handicapped by the character's issue. There were lots of scenes where I would sit and sit and sit and then I would have to whisper something and Simon got to tell the joke. And then, after a while, I would open scripts and see if I was in scenes with a female character and then I knew I wouldn't have much to do. So after a while, the freedom to be able to speak without that was really nice, just from an acting point of view. Because there were moments when it was frustrating.

Steve Molaro: Koothrappali being able to speak to women was a long time coming. We had been wanting to end it for a while and were just looking for the right way to do it. There were times where we had written entire scenes and then remembered, "Wait! There's a girl in the room, Kooth can't talk." And we have to go back and figure out a way through that. It happened more than once. The selective mutism was a fun idea in the beginning, but I'm glad we were able to move on from it and allow Koothrappali to grow and participate more. And Penny was the perfect person for him to cross this milestone with.

Kunal Nayyar: It's why I was most excited to come back from hiatus that year because knowing that that sort of handicap had been taken away was really exciting.

Although Nayyar and the writers welcomed the change, it was bittersweet to say goodbye—for the moment at least—to Kate Micucci, who played Lucy.

Kunal Nayyar: I really adore her. She's a really lovely human and just a really fun personality to be around. But also, it was the first time Raj was taking care of someone who was dealing with neuroses worse than his. As a character, it was a sweet juxtaposition to what you were used to seeing.

Steve Holland: I love Kate Micucci. I liked Laura Spencer's Emily with Raj as well. Kate was so terrific, but those scenes with Raj and Lucy were actually hard to write because they were two very socially awkward people in a room together. It was difficult because as characters, neither one of them would spark conversation or push conversation. There was fun awkwardness to write, but it became really tricky to write some of those scenes. I probably would have said if he would have wound up with anyone, it would have been Laura Spencer's Emily. But I do think it was nice and real how we left Raj in the finale. Because he's such a romantic, we didn't want to push him into a relationship that felt fine but [was] not what he truly wanted. I wanted more for Raj than that. I think someday Raj will find love, but it just hasn't happened yet.

Chapter 15

BEHIND THE SCENES
OF STAGE 25

On February 7, 2019, Warner Bros. Television president Peter Roth renamed stage 25 at Warner Bros. Studios in Burbank, California. "It will forever more now be known as *The Big Bang Theory* Stage," he said at the dedication ceremony (which appropriately took place in Sheldon and Leonard's apartment). It was only the fifth time in the history of Warner Bros.' hundred-plus years that a stage had been named instead of numbered, with the others being "the *Friends* Stage" (stage 24), "the *ER* Stage" (stage 11), "the *Ellen* Stage" (stage 1), and Lorre's other long-running sitcom, "the *Two and a Half Men* Stage" (stage 26).

Prior to *Big Bang* though, stage 25—which was originally built in 1935—was where films like *The Adventures of Robin Hood*, *Casablanca*, *Bonnie and Clyde*, *Batman Returns*, and *Dave* were shot. But it's *Big Bang* that truly left its mark inside those walls. For twelve years, it was where the cast called home, where they shared their deepest struggles, had their biggest laughs, and formed the greatest bonds. "That stage became our refuge," Kunal Nayyar says. "There was no place in the entire world that was as safe as stage 25 for us."

Jim Parsons: It was very collegial. We were all part of an ensemble. I was the oldest one when we started, in my early thirties, but we were all at a place where we were young adults, and young adults getting more attention in what can be a dangerous town. The fact that we didn't [get consumed by that] is slightly remarkable.

Galecki and Cuoco outside stage 25, which is now only one of five soundstages on the Warner Bros. lot to be renamed for a show. *Courtesy of Johnny Galecki*

Johnny Galecki: It was a very long time together and it's just human to have bad days where you wake up on the wrong side of the bed, which we all did at one point or another. And I feel bad about those days, of course. At the same time, I'm so proud that starting at the ages that we did—in our twenties and thirties—and being on a show that lasted twelve years, there were no real scandals, no DUIs, no arrests, no whatever. You really do represent one another.

Kaley Cuoco: We were all the good kids in school. Funny that the show was about nerds, because we technically were as well. It was such a group of fucking pros. If you were ten minutes early, you were the last person to show up. Well, Johnny was late a couple of times, which was super annoying. But other than that, everyone was just on their game.

Mayim Bialik: People would always say, "Are you all super close, the seven of you?" And we were close in different ways. There were things I needed to talk to Simon about, or that I needed to talk to Kunal about, or that I wanted to talk to Melissa about. When I saw Kaley had an awesome photo shoot, I wanted to talk to her about it. Kaley and I also had animal stuff to talk about, and I always had questions about her horses and her dogs! So just like in a family, you find ways to connect.

Johnny Galecki: We were glued at the hip for many years to the point where if a family member of mine was coming out to visit from Chicago, I knew that Jim was going to be there. And Todd, his husband. They were at my house for meals and everything. And when we weren't in the same room, we would talk two to three times a day, for hours. It created a real partnership. We couldn't get enough of each other, and it was just a fringe benefit to the fact that I really loved spending time with these people and their partners.

Simon Helberg: We would go to dinners together, go on vacation together. It was kind of what you would think it might be, which was an incredible moment where we had opportunities that none of us had ever really had before and it was really fun. It was like going to summer camp.

Speaking of summer camp—rather, a very nice summer camp—the guys, and occasionally Cuoco, would escape two hours up north to San Ysidro Ranch, a gorgeous, rustic resort tucked away in the foothills of Montecito (as you may remember from earlier, where Cuoco asked Galecki to kill that bug).

Jim Parsons: It was the most magical place I had ever been to. I couldn't believe places like that existed. That was my first experience anywhere outside of LA and San Diego, really. It was a very interesting time because we were able to do things like that as a group and not cause a lot of attention and just enjoy each other's company. I remember hiking there, and taking pictures with our new iPhones. Those were new then!

Kunal Nayyar: The first time we went to Montecito, my parents were visiting from India, so I took them along because they had already traveled so far to visit me. I didn't want to then go and leave them, but I also really wanted to hang out with the cast. I was afraid everyone would think I was so weird for bringing my parents, but they were so welcomed and had a great time. Johnny and my mother got along really well because they would smoke cigarettes and drink whiskey and talk about life.

Todd Spiewak, Jim Parsons, and Simon Helberg during one of their early trips up the California coast, hiking and trying out their new smartphones. *Courtesy of Johnny Galecki*

Johnny Galecki: She and I got along great. I love Kunal's mama! We bonded over smoking and drinking and a certain similar sense of humor. I was always very excited when she was coming into town to visit.

Kaley Cuoco: Kunal's mother was obsessed with Johnny. She loved him. That's why he was excited.

Johnny Galecki: [*Laughs*] I remember once a pipe burst outside my cabin, and Simon and his wonderful wife, Jocelyn, were taking a hike and saw this happen. I was sound asleep, I didn't care. But Simon was very concerned about me and started screaming, "Johnny! *Johnny!*" He thought my cabin was going to get flooded and I would drown. I was so warmed by his concern, but I'll never forget that banshee wail he was screaming because he saw the pipe burst. It was just spraying everywhere, but I was like, "Eh, somebody will fix that."

Simon Helberg: It really was the biggest, most insane geyser of water shooting up in the air. I had a lot of panic in my voice calling out to him. I think something primal kicked in. It was like Noah's Ark and we had to abort the ship. Those trips were so fun.

In addition to Montecito, when Cuoco and Galecki were dating, they often vacationed with Helberg and his wife, Jocelyn.

Simon Helberg: In 2009, Johnny, Kaley, Jocelyn, and I traveled to Chicago, where Johnny's from, and we ate pierogies and went to food festivals. But we also stayed at Lake Geneva in Wisconsin, and the four of us rented a house over the Fourth of July. We were having a good time, even though we didn't necessarily know how to work fireworks or the grill, but since Johnny was the older guy, you assume he knows how to do these things. Plus, he's from Chicago and he drives a motorcycle. Turns out, he did not.

Johnny Galecki: [*Laughs*] It's probably the case. I remember I rented a boat. Simon and I had this thing where we have rented a lot of boats together, which makes no sense because neither of us are sailors.

Someone should have told Galecki and Helberg they weren't allowed to operate a boat without one of them wearing their captain's hat. *Courtesy of Johnny Galecki*

Simon Helberg: We also bought a $7 sheet cake on that Lake Geneva trip, so when the fireworks failed and the burgers were a bit too charred, we at least had that. However, as we brought it out from the kitchen, it fell off of the cardboard platter and fell facedown on the carpet. So for the next three days, Kaley and Jocelyn ate the top of the cake down to the point right before the rug, which is of course the civilized thing to do. It's a big sheet cake, you're not going to let it go to waste. Plus, I think that happened in some episode of *Friends*, and Kaley loves *Friends*, so maybe it was all by design and she just wanted to dive into that world.

Kaley Cuoco: I remember that like it was yesterday! Johnny and I hung out a lot with Simon and Jocelyn before they had kids. I still can't believe we fucking dropped the sheet cake. I was like, "I am not giving up on this!" Simon is right...I was like, "If Rachel can eat it off the floor on an episode of *Friends*, so can I!"

Over the years, the cast traveled internationally as well, sometimes on personal trips, and other times to help promote the show. South America was

Well, it's no captain's hat, but these suffice. *Courtesy of Johnny Galecki*

an epic press trip, and to this day, it's amazing the good people of Brazil let Galecki, Helberg, and Nayyar return to Los Angeles.

Kunal Nayyar: Me, Simon, and Johnny went to Rio de Janeiro and São Paulo in Brazil. We were like the Beatles. I couldn't believe it! We were walking down the street and had security and were being chased by people. We were going into the mall and they were shutting down stores and running after us. They figured out which hotel we were in, and hundreds of people showed up. We went out on our balcony and waved at everyone and said a few words. It was like being the Queen of England. I couldn't believe it, but I loved it because it was just an outpouring of affection and love these characters evoked in them. I found it very heartwarming.

Simon Helberg: Brazil was so fun and crazy. Anytime we got to travel for the show, it was just absolutely wild, whether it was Mexico City or Rio de Janeiro in 2011 with Johnny and Kunal. But whenever I'm traveling, I have

Let it be known that Simon Helberg is a good sport, for he allowed this photo in the book. *Courtesy of Kunal Nayyar (with permission from Simon "Good Sport" Helberg)*

an ability to fall asleep anywhere. It's like I get overstimulated. It happens in movies, too. People think that's a sign of me getting bored or tuning out, but I just get maxed out on stimuli. And there's something about the airplane and the womb-like quality.

Kunal Nayyar: I have more pictures of Simon sleeping on my phone than anyone else in the world. He's always sleeping in a car, a plane, or a train. I've never seen anything like it.

There was also the time that Galecki tagged along on a trip with executive producers Steve Molaro and Steve Holland.

Steve Holland: About ten years ago, Steve and I were going on one of our trips, and at the last minute, Johnny had no plans and was like, "Can I tag along?" and we said, "Absolutely!" So it was the three of us. And the funny thing about when you travel with Johnny is if you say, "Well, we're definitely *not* going to go down that road because that area looks sketchy," you will look up and Johnny will be halfway up that road.

Johnny Galecki: Somehow, me and the Steves—that's what we called them—ended up in Prague together. On our summer Europe trips, those two would be in the back seat and they wouldn't stop talking about story ideas for the show. I'd be like, "Guys, we have a week to visit two countries! Please relax! Have a mimosa and chill out!" But they just *lived*, ate, drank, slept, breathed *Big Bang* and these characters. I mean, I loved the show, too, but we're in Prague! I'm like, "Guys, look out the window! Look at the cathedrals!" They could not stop. They were just such champions for each character and for the show in general. It was their passion.

Steve Holland: We'd do it on all our trips, because honestly, when you're in production during the season, there's this constant pressure to produce story, so when you weren't in production, it was fun to be able to brainstorm at your own pace without the pressure of this train bearing down upon you. You'd have a thought and be like, "Hey, what about this?" But I mean, we loved the show, so it was fun to talk about, fun to write, and we loved the characters. So, sure, we'd be in a cab or something, and think, "Oh! This would be cool...what if this happened?" And we would just start bouncing off each other in a way that didn't feel like work at all.

Steve Molaro, Johnny Galecki, and Steve Holland take Europe and dress nearly identically in the process. *Courtesy of Johnny Galecki*

Although Mayim Bialik and Melissa Rauch missed out on some of those early cast trips since they didn't come on as series regulars until season four, they found another way to bond, thanks to Bialik's career-defining role as Blossom Russo on NBC's '90s sitcom, *Blossom*.

Melissa Rauch: I was obsessed with *Blossom*. I had a *Blossom* hat collection. My best friend and I even re-created the opening of *Blossom*. I felt very seen by Blossom, that she was this unique, young girl with her own point of view. Mayim often had to snap me out of it because I would be like, "I'm hanging out with Blossom!" She really indulged me. And then when I was promoting *The Bronze*, she re-created the opening of *Blossom* with me as a way to help promote the movie. I'm forever grateful because she made a childhood dream come true.

Mayim Bialik: [*Laughs*] I remember Melissa freaking out because of *Blossom*. It was very sweet. Also it's very sweet to hear from another young, Jewish actress that she saw someone on TV who looked like some people that she knows in her family, which was another great connection. She and I took a lot of pictures back-to-back like Blossom and her best friend, Six, did, and I got a kick out of that.

Dreams really do come true! Bialik channeled the sitcom character that put her on the map as a clever way to help Rauch—a huge *Blossom* fan—promote her 2015 film, *The Bronze. Courtesy of Melissa Rauch*

The cast's relationships were deepening and they started to create a short-hand, which included nicknames. Some are cute, some are sweet, and some are just, well…interesting.

Johnny Galecki: Someone bought me a jersey once even though I'm the least athletic person in the world, but the name on the back was "Mooks." And I just thought, "What a cute name." So I started calling Kaley "Mooks," and she called me "Mooks" back. We would at times call Kaley "Stinkerbell," which she also loved, because she's evolved enough to know she's not one. She would laugh and roll her eyes at herself in a wonderfully self-deprecating way. And I've always referred to Melissa as "soul sister."

Melissa Rauch: Yep, and Johnny's my "soul brother." And Kunal called me "Boingo." One day he said, "You're so smiley and happy, you're like my little Boingo!"

Kunal Nayyar: I made it up! She always had a bounce to her, so that's what a "boingo" is!

Johnny Galecki: Kunal has always been "Koonky." That was a pet name that a girlfriend had for him when we shot the pilot early on. I don't know if he enjoyed it after they broke up.

Kunal Nayyar: He still calls me that, too. And Simon was always "Sy." Kaley was "Kathy," because we were once at a press conference, and the person called her up onstage and couldn't pronounce her name. They said, "And from *The Big Bang Theory*, Kathy Cumoco!" [*Laughs*] From that day onward, we just called her "Kathy." You'd be shocked how many people cannot pronounce "Cuoco." But the "Kathy" name cracked us up.

Speaking of endearing memories, Galecki's mother had the *Big Bang* theme song as her ringtone, which was adorable, unless you're Galecki, who remembers being extremely embarrassed when he was at a restaurant in Chicago when her phone went off.

Johnny Galecki: Everyone thought it was my phone, of course, and I was horrified. The entire restaurant thought that I had the theme song as my ringtone. I was like, "Mom! Mom! Turn it off! Change it! *Seinfeld* was a great one! *Taxi*! *Cheers*! I can't have lunch with you if you have that ringtone!"

Meanwhile, Cuoco's dad, Gary, was at every *Big Bang Theory* taping on Tuesday nights.

Kaley Cuoco: He never missed a single one. And he would stand up in the audience and give me a thumbs-up at every curtain call for twelve years. Now, I'm sure I was horrified during the times I was in lingerie or having a bedroom scene, but my dad lived for Tuesday tape nights. I think he is still recovering from not having that routine each week. In fact, there's a small, family-owned Italian restaurant down the street from Warner Bros. called Angelino's, and most Tuesday nights my dad would host a dinner there for any of our guests coming to the show. He loved every second of all those tapings. He lived for it. *Lived* for it. And afterwards, my dad would always find Chuck or Bill and say, "Great show!" and do a little fist bump. And then he would give Johnny a high five. Our families are such a part of this show. He was even in every cast and crew photo. All twelve photos!

> **When you're in the same "office" for twelve years—as the actors were—their dressing rooms became their private sanctuary, their place to get away, take a nap, breastfeed or pump, or, you know, set up a bar.**

Johnny Galecki: When we got our first three-season pickup in season four, I decided to get rid of the coffee-stained carpeting in my dressing room and remodel it. But I had to ask permission to remodel the room. And Warner Bros. said I was going to need to put the room back to its original state when the show finished, which was the most ridiculous thing. I sent an email back to Warner Bros. telling them otherwise, and it is one of the proudest emails I've ever written. [*Laughs*] But Kaley took that hundredfold, and really made it look like a princess suite at the Ritz in Paris.

Kaley Cuoco: I had the dressing room of all dressing rooms! I went nuts decorating. It was customized with pink carpeting. Everyone kind of did their own thing to their dressing rooms. Mine was obviously the best. [*Laughs*] But no, I just wanted it to be a fairy tale. I wanted it to be a room that I could never have in my house. It was just a pink, Penny princess motif, and I had the door painted pink, a pink shag carpet, and an unbelievable custom couch. I had a dressing area. I had a bar! I got in so much trouble on tape nights—not me, personally—because I'd be downstairs shooting and would hear commotion in my dressing room. My girlfriends, my aunt, my mom! They loved coming because it would be wine-and-girls night, but I'd have to text them from the set and say, "We hear you!" They'd maybe catch a scene, but they were mainly living it up in my dressing room.

Jim Parsons: I mean, she was essentially the cousin of Elle Woods as far as the look and the style and the attitude of the pink in her dressing room.

Johnny Galecki: Kaley's dressing room looked like a stripper convention was bombed.

Jim Parsons: One time Kaley's bathroom toilet in her dressing room got clogged and she needed a plunger, but was too prideful to let anyone else deal with the issue and the toilet, so she did. But we all knew about it because we had to call maintenance. At some point later that day, maintenance stopped by and wanted their plunger back. She was like, "Absolutely not!" She would not give them their plunger! Look, it must have been a $1.25 plunger—it's a wooden stick with a piece of rubber on the end of it, but they had to account for those things. I guess they had to document it as "Lost a plunger" or "Kaley Cuoco wouldn't give us our plunger back." I don't know what happened. [*Laughs*]

Kaley Cuoco: It's true, and I'm coming out with my own line of plungers now. The Cuoco Plunger. I know what the people want.

Kunal Nayyar: My dressing room literally had a rotary dial phone in it. That's how old my room was. For the first three years, I didn't do anything, and then I got some carpet and made it look nice. And then I redid it again and this time I fit in a bar, because I had a lot of people stop by the show, so it became a place where people would congregate. It was kind of a bohemian/party room. I always had my guitar there and played my video games.

Jim Parsons: Two or three seasons in, [my husband] Todd and I just did the full overhaul and got rid of what the carpeting was from God knows when. I just wanted a recliner. That was all I cared about. I got a nice caramel-colored one with some sort of nice, fake leather. I've never been allowed to have one in any home we've lived in because Todd hates recliners, so this was my only chance. [*Laughs*] Although life is long, God willing, so we'll see. But I sat in that chair every day.

Kunal Nayyar: Jim's room was very clean and sanitary. As was Simon's. But Kaley's was like Disneyland. Lots of pink and glitter and crystal! And Mayim's room was exactly what you'd expect Amy Farrah Fowler's room to look like.

Mayim Bialik: I am the only one who never redid their dressing room. I had Warner Bros. furniture from day one until the day we finished. I literally had a nine-inch television that still had a VCR built in. Everyone said my room looked like a bad college dorm! When I was pumping, I had a Mom-at-work pumping sign outside my door. I think Nikki Lorre more than once accidentally walked in on me pumping! And I had a picture of me when I was little on the door. I'm a pretty bare-bones kind of girl.

Melissa Rauch: My dressing room looked like an airport motel lobby for a good part of the show. Being a struggling actor leading up to getting the job, I didn't want to jinx it by making myself too much at home. Then halfway through season four, I got blue slipcovers for the dreary couch that was in there, but they were ill fitting and I was always trying to get them to lay correctly. Jim would come in and every time before he sat down, I'd say, "Let me adjust the cover" and at one point he just said, "I'm going to sit there, but please stop trying to fix those ridiculous covers before I do." The couch was also insanely uncomfortable, so when I got pregnant, I decided to finally treat myself to a new beautiful, comfy couch. Only problem was it took up the whole damn room.

Simon Helberg: My dressing room had a couple phases, starting with the look of a serial killer who stopped in Santa Fe and got a motel room on his way to continue a killing spree. It had a southwestern, kind of horrifying undertone, and the carpet was frightening, just in terms of what it was concealing. It was bad. But I didn't change it because I didn't think you could do that kind of thing. Once we got a three-season pickup, I was like, okay, I'll put a nail in the wall. I wanted it to be cozy so it had kind of a shag rug, a globe that lights up, and a midcentury desk. I had a giant *Annie Hall* poster and pictures of my kids. I also had a picture of the Japanese poster of *Dog Day Afternoon*, which is one of my favorite movies. I just tried to surround myself with things that inspired me.

> Throughout the years, the cast would get all sorts of gifts, some from family and friends, others from agents and managers, and also fans. But most of the time, unless it was a mountain bike, Galecki would just give his stuff to Rauch.

Johnny Galecki: My agents would send me gifts that I didn't want, and I'd just put them in Melissa's dressing room, like a fountain with a troll in it.

Melissa Rauch: I came into my room one day and there was this huge, plastic fountain that you plugged in and it had running water. It was hilarious. I kept it in there for quite a long time but then I had to eventually let it go because I started getting mosquitoes in the standing water. It just turned into a breeding ground for them. But I have to say, when it was plugged in, it was quite soothing.

Johnny Galecki: My agents also bought me a mountain bike for my birthday. Some mornings when I didn't have time to go to the gym, I'd take the bike out on the lot and ride around just to get my blood going. Then I found the lagoon at the Warner Bros. lot, which was empty of water. It looked like a skate park. So I'd take the bike and ride sideways, do these jumps, and fall off the bike, because again, I'm not an athlete. I'd end up in a bush with brambles all over my hair and my wardrobe and shit. And when I got back to the stage, they were kind of upset with me because wardrobe had to change my shirt, and redo my hair and makeup. They're like, "You gotta wear a helmet. You're gonna hurt yourself." And I'm like, "I'm not wearing a helmet. I'm a grown-ass man." This just went on and on. And part of me, in hindsight, sounds like I was being impossible, but I was just amused by this argument between production and me about wearing a helmet. Well, finally they got so worried about me that one of the producers called Chuck. And Chuck said what I did: "He's a thirtysomething man. I can't make him wear a helmet." Chuck then hung up the phone, called Warner Bros., and said, "Fill up the lagoon." The next morning I'm *plowing* towards the lagoon, and thank God the bike had good brakes, because there were like seven fire hoses in it filling it up. And I'm like, "*That's* a good producer. That is the chess master that is Chuck Lorre." So I sent him a Polaroid of me on the bike wearing scuba gear. [*Laughs*]

Chuck Lorre: Dirt bike tricks for one of the stars of your show...that's horrifying!

Ping-Pong tournaments ended up being a more encouraged form of physical activity, thanks to director Mark Cendrowski. (No surprise, it wasn't the same adrenaline rush for Galecki.)

Kaley Cuoco: Mark shared a love of Ping-Pong with me, so I really give him the credit for starting this tradition. Johnny was the only one not into it as much. We would stay after work and play for hours. I had a custom Ping-Pong table made in hot pink that said *The Big Bang Theory* on it. In fact, I would like to know where that is.

Jim Parsons: I do remember that frequent desire to not rush home, and it just spoke to how much we liked being on the set, playing Ping-Pong and enjoying each other's company.

Kunal Nayyar: Cendrowski was very instrumental in bringing us all together. He's just a great director, like a football coach. And Ping-Pong was a great way for us all to bond. Kaley and I are both competitive, so we would have these brother-sister fights during matches.

Mark Cendrowski: By the end of the first year, it was so popular we had a tournament. People got uniforms made and there were team names. We had singles tournaments, different doubles tournaments, mixed doubles tournaments. Everyone's on equal footing when they're playing, and the whole reason I did it was bonding. So when you take a five-minute break or go to lunch the actors don't just run to their room—it goes back to again that you're a family. You have to trust one another. An actor has to rely on the crew, and vice versa.

Yes, that's a corn husk on Parsons's head. No, he does not remember why he was wearing it. However, what happens during the cast's Ping-Pong tournament stays at the cast's Ping-Pong tournament. *Courtesy of Kaley Cuoco photo collection*

That bond was strengthened even more when Cuoco came up with the idea to have the cast and crew surprise the producers and writers with what ended up being the first of several flash mobs—a choreographed dance within a large group—after Tuesday night tapings.

Kaley Cuoco: The first one we did, Jim didn't participate, but we had him come on at the end and he said, "Bazinga!" And the next time, he said he would do it, and he had fun. It was so cute. It's the same with how I took photos constantly on that set. I forced this on everyone but then they're so happy in the end. [*Laughs*]

Jim Parsons: The flash mobs were both terrible and wonderful. It was always like, "Oh my God, we're going to learn another goddamn dance?! OK, fine." And then, the worker bee in me just loves to try and get things right and do them as well as I can, so I'd be home alone practicing and even write out my own language of choreography. I guess it was the whole thing of *Nobody can help and I can only help myself.* Choreographed dancing is not my thing, in case you were wondering. But one day I was in the kitchen practicing, and Todd taped it without my knowledge and sent it to Kaley. I'm very entertaining for him when I'm not irritating.

Mayim Bialik: It was really fun to see the looks on Chuck's face and our writers and producers when we did those flash mobs. I loved that Kaley initiated that as a surprise and a gift to them and to our audience. It was just so much fun. And those songs are forever burned into my head.

Simon Helberg: We were basically obligated; there was a look that Kaley would get in her eye, and we knew that there was no backing out. [*Laughs*] Some people went to more rehearsals than others, and then it became more and more elaborate as the years went on. I was surprised at the fervor that still existed and the fire in Kaley to continue that tradition, but she was all pumped up, and I think by the end, there were more cameras shooting us to do those flash mobs than there were used in the show.

It's a damn shame this book doesn't have a "play video" option because they are truly a sight to behold. However, you can watch rough videos of them in all their glory on YouTube by searching for "*Big Bang Theory* flash mobs." You'll never listen to the Backstreet Boys' "Larger Than Life" the same way again.

Parsons may have been reluctant to commit to Cuoco's flash mobs, but once he did, he was all-in, and it showed. *Courtesy of Andy Gordon*

Nikki Lorre: Kaley's sister, Bri, would choreograph it, and all her cute dancer friends would come in and show us the dance, which by their standards, I'm sure they're like, this is super easy, but I was like, "Do you see your dance squad here? Median age is like fifty-eight! You do not have people with the knees or capabilities to get low!" There was always a moment of them saying, "Let's try this," followed by, "Okay, maybe we simplify it!" And it was the best to watch Jim, hands down, because you could tell how seriously he took it. I wouldn't call him a natural dancer, but he is so committed, so he was accurate. He was so much fun to watch.

Chuck Lorre: The joy in Kaley is palpable. It's infectious and it spread throughout that whole crew and cast. I was completely surprised when it happened, and in a way, it cemented the family element that occurs on a show after many, many years. The fact that everyone committed—from the camera guys to the sound guys—they're out there dancing their hearts out. It was very moving *and* hilarious.

> Not long after, Lorre and the writers decided to stage their own flash mob to surprise Kaley, the cast, and the crew. Tragically, it never saw the light of day.

Tara Hernandez: During Kaley's second flash mob, Chuck turned around and said, "We should do one of those." And because it came from *him*, it was like, *I guess we're doing this!* And we hired an actual choreographer who gave us legitimate choreography.

Chuck Lorre: We rehearsed for several weeks and then we gave up. There simply wasn't enough time to write the show *and* to learn how to do a flash mob dance. We had five or six rehearsals on the stage after everyone had gone home, because we wanted it to be a surprise, and it was just *awful*. It was just a horrible thing to see, and at some point we collectively threw our hands up and went, "Bad idea."

Eric Kaplan: But Chuck showed the most promise because he's a musician. He has the most honest-to-goodness rhythm. And Tara Hernandez. She was a dancer.

Tara Hernandez: [*Laughs*] Yeah, but even for someone who did grow up dancing, I was like, *This is legit hard!* It was fast and it was complicated. There were props. There was a ribbon section. There were formation changes.

"Dancers" in progress, featuring Chuck Lorre, third from right. *Courtesy of Andy Gordon*

We rehearsed this for weeks on the *Young Sheldon* set, on the *Mom* set. But it just got to a point where we needed to schedule another rehearsal, and then we kind of weren't putting the performance date on the calendar... but we were going to come down the stairwell wearing sparkly vests and everything. It *is* atrocious, that is true. I was shocked that people could do any of it, to be honest. I mean, people were having breathing issues.

Holiday gatherings on the set were a little less stressful—and physical. Anytime a Tuesday tape night coincided with one of the eight nights of Hanukkah, Bialik would invite the cast and crew to light the menorah in her dressing room. Bill Prady, Melissa Rauch, Simon Helberg, and more were regulars.

Mayim Bialik: I would host in my dressing room, which is completely illegal [because it's a fire hazard], and the fire department would probably sue us if they knew, but we would extinguish the candles after the legally allowed time to extinguish them. I would basically put out the word—like an underground invite. [*Laughs*] Word would spread, so we had people who loved Jewish culture who weren't Jewish, but really wanted to be part of it. We had people from the painting department, from the art department, people who I didn't even know were Jewish and would show up in my dressing room reciting Hebrew. It was awesome and really sweet to have that connection. A lot of people on our stage ended up learning about the Jewish holidays. And because Jim's husband, Todd, is Jewish, Jim got greeted for every holiday! He's what I considered Jewish-adjacent. [*Laughs*] When I would bake, I would say to Jim, "Here's a honey cake for Todd!"

Jim Parsons: [*Laughs*] It's one of the things about Mayim I personally love and just get such a kick out of, and a lot of it does have to do with the fact that my ear is more attuned to these traditions because of my husband and his family. They're not as religious as Mayim is, but the traditions are very prevalent. I really like that she did that, and I think it's very moving that so many people from so many different areas of the production would respond to those invites.

Simon Helberg: Sometimes Mary Quigley would give us costumes to do a curtain call in, so I remember wearing a menorah on my head once. And it's like, you put on a Hanukkah hat one time and you can never live it down.

And then all of the sudden you're invited to every Hanukkah party because one time you put a menorah on your head.

But they were a family, and family means indulging in unique headwear. Or inviting your colleague's family to your parents' home in India.

Steve Holland: My wife was going to be in New Delhi for a day, but Kunal said, "She should go stay with my family." and I was like, "That's sweet, but she doesn't know them at all, you really don't need to offer that." And he said, "You Americans are so funny! In India, if someone's coming, you go and stay with their family. We open up our house!" She was only there for like six hours, so she didn't, but he really wanted to make sure we knew it was an official invitation. And here's another thing about Kunal, as well as Simon and Johnny—they would take the crew out to this bar called the Red Door after every shoot night. They'd take the sound guys out, the camera guys out, and just open up the tab. Every week.

Kunal also likes to give speeches. So at the People's Choice Awards or if we were having dinner together as a group and people were toasting, Kunal would always do it. He's so lovely and earnest, but Simon would always sit behind Kunal and make fun of him. They had such a funny off-screen relationship and banter that we used a lot as the inspiration for their on-screen relationship. Kunal would be in the middle of this heartfelt speech, and Simon would be behind him, teasing him, and Kunal would be like, "I *know*, Simon! I know you're making fun of me right now, but I don't care, because this is important and I'm gonna give this speech!" [*Laughs*]

There were plenty of light-hearted, sweet, and funny moments on the *Big Bang Theory* Stage throughout its twelve years, but the experience wasn't without its challenges. Whether it was adjusting to fame or feeling like an outsider, the cast has never really opened up about the difficulties they went through on a personal level as the show became more and more popular around the world. And unless you were in their shoes, it's hard to know just what that level of fame feels like when everybody knows your name, but you're still figuring out who you are.

Simon Helberg: I really had to learn how to deal with a lot of that stuff, and that's all happening at the same time as you're becoming famous, which is weird. Your life is changing, your lifestyle is changing, and believe it or not, fame is not the healthiest. It doesn't tend to make the issues that you have lessen. And then after we'd come back from summer hiatus, I'd always have the concern of like, *Oh no, do I remember how to do this thing?* So it's a good thing we had twelve years to practice managing those kinds of thoughts and feelings. But the fetal position does wonders. [*Laughs*] And just wailing and pounding on the floor, also, is a great way to let out some of that emotional baggage. But therapy. And friends. And family. And it's not that the success is a burden— because it's truly a fortunate thing that I feel incredibly grateful for—it's that whatever you're bringing to the party is ultimately distilled and then explodes into something tenfold the size of what it was. It's not really a coincidence that you see people have a challenging time dealing with that. Or people who have anxiety or depression or substance abuse problems—they don't tend to get better with fame, they tend to get worse.

Kunal Nayyar: Just like Simon, I went through my own anxieties. Mine were not related to my performance on the show. The anxiety for me was how to navigate this new world where everywhere I turned, someone wanted something from me. And for the first time in my life I had to build a cage around myself. And in that cage, I was going nuts. I was having panic attacks while driving on the highway. All my worst fears of claustrophobia and heights sort of rose to the surface. And I think it's because I began to believe an identity that didn't really exist. When you begin to play a character on television, people want to meet that character; they don't want to meet *you*. So I'm meeting people with love and adoration and respect, thinking that they want to get to know me and spend time with me. And what broke my heart was the realization that, *No, they want to meet the character, and Kunal is no longer really an identity. Now you're Raj.* I had to be careful about the people I was allowing into my life, and it was difficult for me. My naivete dissipated quickly. It was hard to not be able to say hi to everyone, to hug everyone, hang out with everyone. You have to find your balance. The more comfortable I became with fame and accepting of it, and understanding of it, the more those anxieties calmed themselves. And I was tired of being pushed into a corner by my own mind. I thought to myself, *Why am I attacking myself with my imagination? Because that's all it is. Nothing real is happening. It's just a thought I believed in.* But at the time, I didn't know there was such a thing. So I started meditating, following gurus, reading, and understanding the relationship between me and my mind. That was the journey; that *is* the journey. Everyone dealt with something.

Kaley Cuoco: I remember the day I announced my divorce (in September 2015, from Ryan Sweeting, whom she married in December 2013). *Entertainment Tonight* happened to be on set, and I wasn't going to do an interview, even though they were there to talk about the show. I was in a scene in the comic book store, wearing a purple sweater, and sitting on the couch between Jim and Johnny, while Simon and Kunal were singing this ridiculous song in their little band (season nine, episode four, "The 2003 Approximation"). And I am hysterically laughing. Genuinely. And they used it. And that was the scene we were shooting when *ET* was watching us, and

SEASON 9

Cuoco was all smiles here, but it was the same time as the news of her divorce (to ex Ryan Sweeting) was about to be announced. She credits filming this scene in the comic book store watching Nayyar and Helberg perform (as part of Raj and Howard's fictional band) in helping her get through the day. *Courtesy of Kaley Cuoco photo collection.*

I remember sitting there, thinking, *My divorce is about to be announced right now.* But Simon and Kunal had me laughing so hard that tears were coming down my face as they were performing this song, and I just got to sit there and watch them as Penny, but it was also me. And it just took me totally out of what was going on in my personal life. And everyone [in the cast] knew what was going on with me and they were very protective. I just remember the drama going on behind the scenes, but shooting that scene was a really wonderful escape.

Kevin Sussman was also going through his own difficulties, both with fame and his personal life.

Kevin Sussman: During the middle of the show's run, I was going through a divorce, and living in a little studio apartment. The show was becoming really popular, and I was starting to appear on it more and more, so there'd be this weird duality of having people get so excited when they would recognize me, and then later that day I would go to my crappy little studio apartment with a bed in the middle of it, and just lay there. I was really depressed going through a divorce and then, within a span of ten minutes, feeling like I'm a celebrity to feeling like I'm a total failure and a loser inside his studio apartment. It's something I never got used to. There was one time, I was laying on that bed in the middle of the apartment watching TV and some dude walked in thinking it was a different apartment. It was my fault for leaving the door unlocked. But he walked in, looked at me, I looked at him, and he had this weird look of, *Aren't you . . . ?* and then he just sort of apologized and left. But sometimes it was so weird, like I had one foot in the world of being on this big, hit TV show, and then even when I was a series regular, I would sometimes go long stretches without being in episodes. It was so odd to be like, "I'm *on* that show! I'm actually a part of that show," as I'm sitting there, on my bed, eating cereal and just feeling confused about my place in the world.

And the first time Johnny Galecki was nominated for an Emmy for Outstanding Lead Actor in a Comedy Series in 2011, he also was battling Bell's palsy—unexplained facial paralysis—and thought he was going to have to leave the show if he didn't recover.

Johnny Galecki: I was at my sister's house in Chicago and kept getting teary out of my right eye. I took allergy medicine and when I woke up, I was still teary, but this time I was also drooling and one side of my face was entirely drooping. I thought I had had a mini stroke. My sister burst into tears, and as we were on our way to the hospital, I called Chuck and told him I was paralyzed on my right side. I said, "I'm going to help you recast my role, and I would love if you would also consider me for a staff writing position on the show." And of course Chuck calls all the best doctors in the world and looks into things and says, "It sounds like you have Bell's palsy." But I was really thinking my acting career was done. And later at the hospital after running tests, they confirmed it was Bell's palsy. So, when the Emmy noms came out, I hadn't told my team I had Bell's palsy, but now I had to. I said, "Half my face doesn't work, so if you could put the cameras on the left side of my face, that would be great. And I'll be carrying a bandana to wipe my tears away because my one eye won't blink." But it all worked out fine. Still, to this day, when I get overexhausted, I can feel some weakness on that side.

> That's the thing about fame; for the most part people think actors are living a near-perfect life, hanging out with other famous people, and earning enough money to fix any problem.

Kunal Nayyar: The first few years I was ruled by fear. I was so afraid of doing or saying something wrong. I may have pretended I was happy-go-lucky, but the truth is, I was terrified. That's why I was kind of a lone wolf in the early years on the show. Not on purpose. And to be honest, I really wanted the cast's approval. I wanted to feel like I belonged, and really wanted everyone to like me. But to be honest, I probably didn't bond with them as much because I was intimidated. Deep down, I felt insecure and that I didn't belong, like they didn't like me and I'm just an idiot. It was all me, all my imagination probably. I think as self-preservation, I just hung out with my friends where I felt safe and comfortable. And I did have a very full life. I lived in a house with some of my best friends, and my family was always visiting. This is what Indians do wherever they go. I created New Delhi in Los Angeles. And then once season three came around, I began to feel more comfortable rehearsing, being on set, hanging out with people. I got very close to the crew, many of whom came to my wedding in India in 2011. And I'm still close to them. But as close as I was to the cast, I was very, very close and attached to the crew as well.

And yet, everyone was going through their own doubts and insecurities, even if they didn't vocalize it.

Johnny Galecki: As my publicist will say, doing panels and press is terrible for me because I don't have that mask on that I do when I'm playing a character. I wouldn't sleep for two weeks before I had to do *Letterman*. I always loved it after, because he's such a hero of mine, but that was especially nerve-wracking.

Simon Helberg: I remember when Kaley was getting her star on the Hollywood Walk of Fame and she said, "This is like the second time in my life I've ever been nervous." I thought she was kidding, but no. I say that not in a disparaging way, but I couldn't be more jealous. Everybody has a very different go of it, but it's important to tell yourself that you're going to be OK even with so much changing around you. In the end, I'm happy I was able to find ways of bettering myself and could enjoy the experience more. But I really didn't know how to deal with a lot of that anxiety except by pacing. No joke, I don't think I sat down in my dressing room for the first nine years of the show. Anyone who would ever walk by would say it was like one of those sad little dogs that is just tracking a strange little pattern in the grass where they're pacing and you're like, *Why is there no grass growing there?*

Kaley Cuoco: And yet there was no one that would make us laugh harder than Simon. When we were shooting the opening sequence early on where we were all eating—and remember, those scenes are without audio—Simon would just casually say, "I think my left testicle is hanging out." And he's saying these things because he knows no one can hear what he's saying, but we were all crying from laughing. So every time I watch that opening, I think of the jokes he was saying. And I know he had anxiety, but he was actually the one who brought everyone else's anxieties down because he always had us laughing.

Bialik also experienced her first premenopausal hot flash while in the middle of filming a scene, which was beyond scary.

Mayim Bialik: I had my first hot flash on set and it was during filming. Of course I thought, *Well, it's because I'm layered so much.* I was in Penny's apartment. And I thought it was because of all the heavy clothes, which I had been wearing for years without having a hot flash. In the early years they used to make me wear a tank under every shirt with a sweater or a vest over it, but I finally got them to give that up because it was just too many layers. But yeah, I had my first hot flash on set. I believe I was forty-two years old when it happened, so I hit perimenopause early! I haven't had a lot since then, but my first one was on set. And it was very disturbing because it's a different heat than you've ever felt before. I was like, *Am I sick? I feel like I have a fever but I don't feel sick.* And my hair instantly curled up, because it was straightened all those years. I was like, *What is happening?!* I couldn't remember my lines, my head wasn't working right. I ran up to my dressing room and tore off my layers and stood under the air-conditioning. I didn't put it together until a couple days later.

As the years went on, the close camaraderie that the cast established remained, but the overnight trips and late-night dinners kind of petered out as families grew, and work commitments and opportunities expanded.

Johnny Galecki: When you start a sitcom, you just hope to survive. I think once we ended the show we felt like the last animals on the ark, the fact that that show had that kind of success and gave each of us that kind of success and changed our lives and our families' lives. We would all cry at the last table read of each season, because we weren't going to be in the same room for three months or something. It was really, really special. And then it gets to a point, after a few years, of just being completely together, even on our off hours, where you gotta go see your family. See your old friends. Check in on everybody. So, those times dissolved quite a bit, which I think was completely natural. Things did become more complicated the bigger the show got and the bigger the renegotiations became. We all still carry the same torch for one another, but there were occasional resentments and high emotions. You can't deal with a billion-dollar property for a network and it not be complicated. Also, we were older. Simon had two kids, Kunal got married, as did Jim, and Kaley. I was the only single boy there for a time. And now with my child, I completely understand that type of primal protection that you want to create for the people around you.

Stage 25 was a safe space for the cast, and it remained that way for all twelve seasons. *Courtesy of Kaley Cuoco photo collection*

Chapter 16

THE EMMYS, A SCAVENGER HUNT, AND THE STORYLINE KALEY CUOCO HATED

By all accounts, the start of season seven was pretty mundane as far as behind-the-scenes activity. The five original stars were still a year out from their next big contract negotiations, ratings were still on the rise—and continuing to defy all expectations—and Steve Molaro was comfortably running the show. *Big Bang* also continued to rack up Emmy nominations—with Parsons winning his third Emmy for Outstanding Lead Actor in a Comedy Series in September 2013—but the series lost to *Modern Family* again for the coveted Outstanding Comedy Series award.

To this day it's a bit puzzling why *Big Bang* never won Best Comedy. *Modern Family*—while a groundbreaking and deserving show—lost its luster as the years went on. *Big Bang*, on the other hand, only got better. Depending on who you talk to, it's still a sore spot for many. And while ratings and popularity meant more in the long run (i.e., money), there's something to be said for winning the highest and most prestigious award in television.

Peter Roth: Oh my God, you have no idea how much it bothered me. There was one year in particular…it was the fourth consecutive year in which *Modern Family* won. And we were really hurt. And quite angry. Yes, it's more important to have the ratings than the accolades, but we felt strongly that that particular year, it was a great, great season. And even the people at *Modern Family* didn't think it was their best year. *Big Bang* was on fire. And we really thought we would win. So that was painful. And also, the entire cast deserved Emmys, not just Jim. He certainly deserved it, but they were all so good.

James Burrows: I don't know why *Big Bang* didn't win, but it took *Friends* nine years to earn an Emmy for comedy series, so you never know what the thinking is, or what the competition is. Multicam tends to be a little bit of a stepchild.

Christine Baranski: Honestly, where were the Emmy wins? Jim Parsons won, but Jesus, the writing on that show! I mean, don't get me started, because *The Good Wife* and *The Good Fight* have yet to get Emmys. And I'm like, *Aren't you guys looking at how brilliant these shows are?* It's so unfair. I know how good these shows [are].

Chuck Lorre: We were so grateful to be involved in this unbelievable hit show that millions and millions of people watched and loved and cared about, so to get caught up in being resentful or aggravated about not winning Outstanding Comedy Series would miss the point. We had so much to be grateful for, and not the least of which was that [many people] involved in the making of the show became financially set for life. Sure, it would have been nice, but it wouldn't have changed anything we did. We made the show we wanted to make. We had a tremendous amount of autonomy and freedom. But for some reason, during our run, the Academy had a less than favorable view of shows with a live audience. Multicamera comedy somehow got considered a genre that was less-than. Shows like *Modern Family* were shot like little movies, and I think we were never going to be taken terribly seriously because the culture changed. That's OK. Bill Prady always used to say, "The audience isn't counting how many cameras you use. They're responding to the characters and if they're laughing."

Nina Tassler: It used to bother us at first, but we would always say, "I'll take ratings over awards." It was a very complex, sophisticated comedy with a very loyal fan base, and we were winning in viewership. Periodically I wish we would win Best Comedy, but we were happier with the ratings. And at least it got the nominations. [*Ed. note:* The series earned fifty-five Primetime Emmy nominations in its twelve seasons].

Steve Holland: There were seasons we didn't get nominated that I'm really frustrated by because I think the show deserved it. But the times we did get nominated were incredibly fun, even though I don't think we went into it thinking we were going to win. We described it as grown-up prom. Everyone got dressed up, we rented limos, and we went to the big party. And it was great. We got nominated four years back-to-back, and then that was sort of the end of it. I really thought that season nine, or certainly the episode where Sheldon and Amy slept together ("The Opening Night Excitation"), is the best episode we've ever done, and that didn't get us a nomination. I thought maybe we'd have a shot to get one more nomination for the final season, but it didn't happen. It's hard to have too many sour grapes about a show that was such a gargantuan hit and ran for twelve years. But it's just that there are episodes and seasons I'm so proud of, that I think were just as good or better than the ones we did get nominated for.

Lee Aronsohn: *Big Bang* did not get the respect it deserved, period. I felt like if we did win, people would be so pissed off that we would have wished we hadn't won. [*Laughs*] I don't know. There's always a little voice that says, "Maybe this year!" Even though you know it's not going to happen.

Jim Parsons: The saying that it's an honor just to be nominated is kind of true. After that point, there are so many reasons why shows and people win awards, and others don't. It's all a little ridiculous that we put any sort of art form in competition like this even though it's fun to participate. But with that said, I take full responsibility for having my own completely skewed view of the situation because of my fortuitous experience with my own category. Emmy voters have been really nice to me, beyond my wildest imagination. But there were a couple of seasons where it really was just crackerjack, classic, as good a form of comedy on television as you're going to get. And in that respect, it is a shame, in my opinion, that the show has no Best Comedy Series win to show for that. And when you consider that when we launched in 2007, they were writing articles about the death of the multicam sitcom, and then a few years in we were all attending the Emmys as a nominee for Best Comedy Series...I mean, that in itself is kind of miraculous.

Bill Prady: It would be disingenuous to say when awards season happens that you don't want to be a person who goes up and gets awards. Of course you do. It's frustrating when you're doing what I think was a great version of a multicamera comedy, the great American art form. We didn't win the

Outstanding Comedy Series Emmy, but we won People's Choice Awards, which was always a great evening, because you know ahead of time that you've won. We started a really cool tradition whenever we would win where I would throw a party at a restaurant and it got more elaborate every year. That's not an Emmy, but it was a lovely, lovely night. And one of my favorite possessions is that the Royal Canadian Institute for the Advancement in Science made Chuck and me honorary lifetime members, and the certificate hangs proudly on my wall. Look, I was RadioShack's Salesman of the Month a number of times. Granted, it was a small store, and there was just one salesman and one manager, but still.

Mayim Bialik: And Kunal was always kind of our best cheerleader, even though sometimes we would tell him to shut up, it's too soon to feel good about losing!

Kunal Nayyar: After we lost at the Golden Globes once, I picked up my champagne glass and said, "Hey, at least we'll always have each other!" And oh man, the looks I got, like, *Fuck you.* [*Laughs*]

> **Awards aside, the biggest frustration might be the one *Big Bang Theory* fans had with people who never understood their love of the show in the first place. Sure, it's hard to complain when you're one of the most-watched shows in the history of television, but there were some people that just had a serious disdain for the show.**

Steve Holland: I do think there's a group of people who ignored *Big Bang* because it was a multicam and it looked a little bit cartoon-y sometimes, or for whatever reason people made up their mind without ever seeing an episode and just sort of wrote it off. It seems silly to complain about a show that was a gigantic phenomenon and be like, *Why didn't more people like it?!* [*Laughs*] But similarly, I would get upset not that people didn't like it, but sometimes the reason they'd put forth for not liking it made it clear they really hadn't seen the show. Or they hadn't seen it *in years*. There's a lot of shows that occupied that sort of geek pop-culture space, where if you didn't get certain references, you were excluded from the show, but we always tried to make *Big Bang* an open tent. And sure, that was tricky sometimes… but you didn't need to understand the reference to get the joke. We always tried to be inclusive, so people from all walks of life liked it, or people who weren't really interested in science or pop culture, people who didn't grow up involved in those things, loved these characters, too. And that's a testament to this cast, who were just incredible. There's a small segment of the fandom who felt that the show got away from the pop-culture / sci-fi world, who liked the early seasons before it leaned more into relationships, but the show had to grow. It could have never lasted as long as it did if it was just these four guys nerding out over pop culture. It had to grow and become something else. And it became more universal.

> Plus, the winning formula was the writers and the actors. Anytime Nayyar and Helberg got to riff on each other was worth its weight in comedy gold. Take, for instance, the second episode of season seven—"The Deception Verification"—where Howard accidentally applies his mother's estrogen cream and as a result, becomes bloated and emotional. It was a bit stereotypical, but the innocence in which Howard and Raj freaked out and supported one another was one of the many reasons why their pairing in particular resonated with viewers.

Maria Ferrari: A relative of mine had been inadvertently touching this estrogen product and having this unexpected reaction. I was like, *This is hilarious, I think we can use it in a story.* And Simon and Kunal are great. You could give them anything. They always committed and made everything better than you thought it was going to be.

Simon Helberg: Any opportunity to touch Kunal's nipples...contractually they had to adhere to that. [*Laughs*] So many of those jokes don't age well, and a lot of them are promoting ideas we've grown past, but I also think there are still ways in which these things can be executed or written with a certain level of innocence that is coming from an actual, authentic character-driven place. It's really funny *and* really hard to pull off, but the writers managed to go beyond some of that old-fashioned, familiar territory, and get into a character-driven place. In my memory, just getting to jiggle around with Kunal was a bucket-list item. And I got to be in sweatpants! Although now that I think about it, I did have to be shirtless and jiggle. You can't have everything.

Kunal Nayyar: I remember being like, *Oh my God, I'm going to have to* *show my stomach and my chest*, so I was doing crunches and all that shit, trying to look slightly better. The studio is always freezing, so during rehearsal, right before I had to grab Simon's chest, I blew into my hands because they were cold. And they were like, "Oh, that's brilliant! We have to keep that in there!" And so we practiced that a lot, because otherwise I would just burst out laughing, which I did as well. I remember the scene being not that strange. Is it weird that we were so close it just felt normal? Raj was just always game to help. He was never weirded out by anything. It's such an endearing quality.

Simon Helberg: There's a dance that has to happen with scene partners, and it was always easy with Kunal because you just get the rhythm or you don't. It's chemistry. What Kunal and I had to do—which was slightly different because of Raj's inability to speak in front of women for so long—was like a ventriloquist act.

Kunal Nayyar: I was and am very close to Simon, and a lot of our banter offstage continued onstage. It never felt like work when we were in scenes together. It just felt like we were chilling somewhere. The hardest thing was breaking character, which I did all the time in my scenes with him. He is hilarious—and our friendship, as well as Raj and Howard's—was a real joy for me.

Simon Helberg: We loved each other and we got really annoyed with each other, too. We were kind of like brothers, and in some sense, this great divide between us, too, because we're so different. But there was a real love in the center of it. He and Melissa were really the partners I had on the show for the majority of the run. There was a love affair between Raj and Howard that I always took as seriously as you could take any relationship that's built on love. I know there were a lot of bromance jokes and homoerotic jokes, but Kunal was like my first love.

In all **279** episodes of *Big Bang*, one that consistently pops up on everyone's best-of list, including the actors, happened early on in season seven. It was "The Scavenger Vortex," which saw the characters pair off to find a gold coin that Raj had hid. At the time the episode aired, Oliver Sava wrote in the *A.V. Club* (October 3, 2013): "Over the past seven seasons, *The Big*

Bang Theory has grown to become a nerdy West Coast version of *Friends*, so it's no surprise that this week's competition-centric 'The Scavenger Vortex' is reminiscent of *Friends*' classic 'The One with the Embryos.' Both episodes spotlight the series' tight ensemble casts by putting the characters in increasingly tense circumstances, and while *Big Bang*'s paired scavenger [hunt] doesn't have the high stakes of *Friends*' apartment game show, the mismatched couples bring focus to some of the less defined relationships on the show."

Eric Kaplan: I was pitching this idea for quite some time because my brother, Flippy Kaplan, was involved in a trivia contest at Brown, and if you won, you got to run the trivia contest next year. In the world of nerds, there's a lot of competitive real-life puzzle solving, which has always intrigued me for some reason yet to be determined. So I was always pitching, "Why don't they do some kind of scavenger hunt?" I think it was Molaro who cracked the case when he said that Raj should be the master of ceremonies for it, which I liked. A lot of stuff came together in that episode, and I was quite pleased with the payoff.

Kunal Nayyar: That's the most fun I've ever had shooting because they said, "Just go nuts! Be more and more insane." Anything I got to do with Raj doing showmanship—like when he starts playing music and uses pyrotechnics to kick off the scavenger hunt—was so much fun.

While Raj is being the ultimate showman, no one is impressed with his antics—except for Sheldon—who has the look of sheer childlike delight on his face.

Jim Parsons: The word *gift* is what comes to mind, because I loved that the writers allowed this crotchety, stuck-in-his-way character to have these little moments. For it to be Sheldon who had the attitude of *Oh! This is wonderful!*...that is just the best type of craft work in writing and characters that you can have.

For the scavenger hunt, Sheldon was reluctantly paired with Penny, Amy with Howard, and Bernadette with Leonard.

Kunal Nayyar loved when Raj got to be the ringleader, as he did in "The Scavenger Vortex." It was also one of the more physically demanding episodes, which delighted some (Galecki) and was a bit of a challenge—albeit the best kind—for others (Rauch). *Photo™ & © Warner Bros. Entertainment Inc.*

Steve Molaro: Because of that episode we started crossing the streams in ways we had never crossed them. It was the first time Leonard and Bernadette were ever alone in a scene; same with Howard and Amy. We always felt you could take any two of these characters and put them in a scene and it would probably be good, so that episode is just the shining example of that.

Howard and Amy got off to an awkward start until they discovered a shared love of Neil Diamond while in the car.

Mayim Bialik: I'm obsessed with Simon Helberg. It's as if the teacher paired me up with my favorite person in kindergarten that I got to play with all day. [*Laughs*] He takes his craft so seriously and he's so hilarious, plus an incredibly intelligent comedian.

Simon Helberg: Mayim and I had this unspoken connection, and I know how rare that is. And you better believe I listened to Neil Diamond in the car on the way to work every day that week. Anytime I had anything like that, I just drilled it into my head; sometimes to an unhealthy extent, but I tried to be 100 percent fully immersed.

Mayim Bialik: I knew some of the Neil Diamond songs, but I wasn't as familiar with "Sweet Caroline."

Ironically, while the two loved working together, Helberg didn't think the episode was going to work until he saw the final cut.

Simon Helberg: That was also such a fragmented episode, and we didn't shoot a lot of it in front of the audience. I remember feeling a little disjointed doing it. At the table read I thought it was one of the best episodes ever, but then when we shot it, I just never felt particularly satisfied or comfortable. I was more dissatisfied with myself, but then I remember Peter Roth—who saw a cut of the episode before we did—saying, "Oh my God, this episode had me rolling on the ground!" People still talk about that episode. So it's funny because sometimes there is a bit of a disconnect between your experience and the actual result, which is another huge lesson I learned on the show: Don't trust your feelings. [*Laughs*]

As Molaro pointed out, the episode was also the first time Johnny Galecki and Melissa Rauch had gotten to work one-on-one.

Johnny Galecki: When it came time to do the scene where we ran into the comic book store, Bernadette had to get annoyed with me, and then punch me in the arm. I kept telling Melissa to hit me harder because you couldn't kill a fly with her punches.

Melissa Rauch: Johnny's right—I couldn't even hit him properly. [*Laughs*] Cendrowski was like, "What is with that hit?" I didn't realize what a weakling I was.

Nikki Lorre: I think that was the first time the writers really leaned into Melissa being scary competitive as Bernadette. They maybe danced with it a little bit in previous episodes, but that was the first time she's actually quite frightening. [*Laughs*] I feel like that was the origin story of Bernadette being a boss bitch.

Melissa Rauch: We saw this competitive nature of hers, and then as we got to know her more, it just permeated a lot of different aspects of her life. She had this "take no prisoners" mentality. And then later in the episode, Kaley, Johnny, and I are running up the stairs and diving into the couch and I had to be so competitive again and shove Kaley out of the way. I failed there, too.

Johnny Galecki: I'm just glad Melissa or Kaley didn't get hurt, because I have a tendency to be a little overexcited and reckless when it comes to physical comedy. I've hurt myself a few times, and I've hurt Jim quite a few times. I think he was very tired of my wrestling him. [*Laughs*] I didn't send him to the hospital or anything, but I'm always willing to take a punch, and wrongly assumed that my castmates felt the same.

Kunal Nayyar: I just loved at the end of the game when everyone was really pissed at me! Raj was like, "We're all winners!"

> In an episode that now hits a little too close to home given that the word *quarantine* has become part of our vocabulary over the last few years, Bernadette has an accident at her lab that causes her to be quarantined at the hospital for preventive measures. At first it throws a wrench in Howard's anniversary plans (he wrote his wife a special song that he was going to perform—with the rest of the gang doing backup vocals), but then they move it to the hospital where he sings it for her on the opposite side of the glass partition walls.

Steve Molaro: We knew Simon could play the piano well and sing, so somewhere along the way we came up with the idea that Howard could write a song for Bernadette. We had gotten pretty friendly with Kate Micucci ("Lucy") and Riki Lindhome ("Ramona"), and we knew how talented they are because of their comedy-folk work as Garfunkel and Oates, so we asked them if they would take a whack at writing a song for Wolowitz. They did such an incredible job that we even had 45s of that single made and gave them out as that season's wrap gift, along with little record players.

Simon Helberg: It was just such a great song and had every layer in there that you could want…funny and heartwarming. But the show moves so quickly that when you get something special like that, I needed to drill it into my head. Riki and Kate helped, and allowed me to make certain changes so it was slightly more manageable. But it was all them. I credit Steve Molaro with those kinds of moments, which were so beautifully woven in throughout every episode.

Melissa Rauch: At the time, the idea of being in quarantine seemed so far-fetched. But this was one of those episodes that was sort of out-of-body in the sense of feeling a part of something so special. For so much of my life, a moment like that felt out of reach. It was a dream that I hoped with all my heart would come true, so to be looking at these people who had become like my family—I'm getting choked up talking about it—there was such genuine love there. Those tears you saw from Bernadette while Howard was singing were really mine, recognizing what that moment meant to me. It's so easy to be all-in when you're opposite someone like Simon. He was just so locked in as he was singing that song, and then you look around and see the group as a whole singing with him...it's just more than you can ever imagine.

Speaking of more than you can ever imagine, that's what pretty much every-one on the set felt when James Earl Jones agreed to guest star in "The Convention Conundrum" in January 2014. The episode, which also featured Carrie Fisher, would be the first time that *Star Wars* icons Jones and Fisher had ever met. (I know, crazy). In the episode, Sheldon decides to start his own Comic-Con when he and the guys fail to get tickets to the real one, and obviously, who better than the man behind the voice of Darth Vader to recruit for a start-up convention.

Steve Molaro: Mr. Jones lives in upstate New York, and his personal assistant was the key to making this happen. She was a giant *Big Bang Theory* fan, and said to me, "I really hope he'll do this." I said, "Well, you're with him! Tell him to do it!" So she was really key, and she flew out with him for the episode.

Chuck Lorre: We asked a great deal of him in that episode. He wasn't in great health at the time but he was the epitome of "The show must go on." He was there to work, and he did the whole adventure with Sheldon on the Ferris wheel and the steam room and karaoke...a montage of a wonder-ful day with Sheldon. [*Laughs*] It is crazy. It is absolutely crazy to see those scenes because a lot of people who are part of the *Star Wars* world are very protective of not having that part of their career spoofed or made fun of. They are good actors who wanted to move on, but he had a tremendous sense of humor about it. I think everybody was getting him to do their answering machine.

Mark Hamill: What a great sport he is, because if he wanted, he could preserve that sort of air of gravitas and dignity that he is known for, and yet when he says to Sheldon, "Let me guess: You're a fan of *Star Wars*," you think maybe he's gonna bite Sheldon's head off because he's bothering him in his private moment. For him to then say, "Well, guess what? I'm a fan, too!" and then to be *so* childlike and exuberant about it...again, it's playing against people's expectations.

Jim Parsons: I watched all of the *Star Wars* movies as a child and sure loved them, so I don't think I ever fully accepted or understood what the hell this man was doing on a multicam sitcom set. I grew up with Bob Newhart, like children will, bless their hearts, have to grow up with me in reruns or whatever. There is a certain intimacy toward seeing somebody on your TV screen like that. But that was not how I knew James Earl Jones. I knew him, obviously, as the voice of Darth Vader, and CNN. But more than that, I knew of him from his long legacy of the highest art of acting...this inspirational orb of valiant actors that are floating out there, where you're like, "One day I hope I get to be an orb like that." So there was something unsettling about the fact that he was there on our set in a weird way to me! And he was so kind! And so game to play! But it was that weird feeling of, *Are you sure you want to play with me? I don't know if this is the right fit for you. It's not because you're not doing it well; it's me! I blame myself!* It's really psychotic. I mean, I really should have seen a therapist over an episode like that. It's just crazy. We were in towels in the steam room together! I was shirtless with James Earl Jones!

> **Later in the episode, Sheldon and James Earl Jones stop by Carrie Fisher's house to prank her. Parsons still can't wrap his head around the moment.**

Jim Parsons: That was [*exhales*] *insane.* I really admire her. She was much smaller than I thought she'd be. I was like, "You're so tiny!" She's adorable! She was really adorable.

Nikki Valko: And we would have loved Harrison Ford, but that never got any traction. He just was not open to it.

Ken Miller: Daisy Ridley told Johnny Galecki she was a fan of *Big Bang*, so of course we tried to go after her for a while, but it was before *Star Wars* came out and I don't think Disney or her agents wanted her to do it. It's no fun to deliver the bad news like that, but when you deliver the good news, it's amazing.

> As Valentine's Day, 2014, approached, it had now been three and a half years since Amy Farrah Fowler first appeared as a match for Sheldon on a dating site. As proof of how slow the writers took the "romance," the two characters hadn't even shared a consensual kiss (there was that time that a drunk Amy kissed Sheldon, and then immediately threw up). But the time finally felt right, and in "The Locomotive Manipulation," their first official kiss finally happened. However, behind the scenes it was hardly the romantic moment Parsons or Bialik thought it would be.

Jim Parsons: I was sick with something, like a bad respiratory cold. And it was ironic because I always took care of myself, and here I am sick during one of the very rare times I have to kiss her. *And* kiss her several times because I knew we'd have to do several takes. I was like, *This is unbelievable!* I felt bad about it, I really did. Mayim is always very game and never one to worry about those things too much, although she did have some sort of thing that she was gargling every time we did a take.

Steve Molaro: Yep, Mayim was pounding the Listerine between every kiss. Jim was really sick.

Mayim Bialik: The man was visibly sweating and feverish, so I rinsed with peroxide in between every kiss, every scene, every take, so that I wouldn't get sick. It's such a great scene, and it turned out so great, but it was a really hard night. I also remember having to ask Mark Cendrowski, "Where's the other wall? Where's the camera?" since we were in a train car. To think of all the work that went into it, I'm so glad it was so sweet. I really loved it. Oh, and I did not get sick.

> While fans loved the first kiss, it wasn't even their best one, especially when you consider the lip-lock that happened a couple seasons later in "The Earworm Reverberation," where Sheldon interrupts Amy's date with British Dave (Stephen Merchant) to tell her he wants her back.

Jim Parsons: The first thing I remember—and this is so strange—is Stephen Merchant standing there in the entryway of Amy's apartment. I adored him so much. He's so goddamn funny and smart and very dear, so it was such an odd and wonderful third wheel to have for that moment that we knew was coming. We also knew that kiss and that moment was going to be interesting in front of the live audience because we were fulfilling a moment that we had teased for years. I think this is probably true for all of us, but my heart was racing before they called action on those scenes, especially when the audience hadn't seen it yet. You want to make sure you land all the jokes and big moments that the writers have worked so hard on during that first take. You never get that chance again for their first reaction. You just don't want to fuck it up, whether it's my lines or the camera or whatever. We didn't know how they would react, only that they *would* react. And they sure did. Mayim and I have such a wonderful chemistry on and off camera, and we really understood our character's relationship, which made everything so easy.

Mayim Bialik: It was really a pleasure to work with Stephen Merchant, and I thought it was such an interesting character for Amy to interact with. As for that kiss with Sheldon at the end, that was a very awkward, long kiss, and I had totally forgotten that! As much as you have to be a professional and it's not a big deal, it's always strange to me to kiss someone you're not in a relationship with whether it's on TV or not. The audience loved that, but it's definitely awkward!

In March 2014, *Big Bang* was given another three-season renewal, which would take it at least through its tenth season, tying iconic sitcoms like *Friends*, *Cheers*, and *Frasier*. "The Big Bang Theory is the biggest comedy force on television," CBS Entertainment chair Nina Tassler said in a statement. But it wasn't just a comedy force—it was *the* force—given that during season seven, *Big Bang* also became the top-rated scripted program, overtaking CBS juggernaut *NCIS*.

While Kaley Cuoco and the cast were all but guaranteed lucrative new deals when their contracts were up for renegotiation in season eight, things weren't looking as bright for her character's career. Penny had always been a struggling actress, with her most notable credit coming from the low-budget horror movie, *Serial Apeist*. When the producers of the fictional movie wanted to make a sequel, Penny turned them down, only to reverse course after some advice from Wil Wheaton. She later got fired, which was a relief for Cuoco (and even Galecki), who now admits how much she disliked the storyline.

Johnny Galecki: Kaley did not like that storyline. When I saw that the sequel was in the script I was like, *Oh fuck*. [*Laughs*] But I wanted to support Kaley because she would struggle through those days. She was not happy.

The look on Cuoco's face (with Wil Wheaton) in costume for *Serial Apeist 2: Monkey See, Monkey Kill* says all you need to know about how she felt about the storyline. *Courtesy of Nikki Lorre*

Kaley Cuoco: The worst experience was filming *Serial Apeist* and getting covered in fucking hair from head to toe. I was like, "Really, you guys? This is what's happening?" And Chuck just thought it was so funny. He loved it. I never understood why.

Chuck Lorre: I actually don't recall loving it. We wanted Penny to have some small success in her dream of being a successful actor, but it's not my favorite episode. Doing a show within a show—writing the "bad" scenes that she's in in an otherwise good show—was not our finest moment. The goal was legitimate, which was to put her in a bad movie and see her struggling to make something work. It actually kind of plays into what became part of *The Kominsky Method*, which is I didn't want to make fun of acting. I didn't want to make fun of badly written, badly acted plays or shows. In *Kominsky* the students, for the most part, are good. They have chops. They are not horrible actors who don't know they're horrible. That, to me, has been done. And I didn't want to do it. I find it more interesting to see somebody who is good at what they're doing, struggling.

Kaley Cuoco: I did love when Penny got to show that she was actually a good actress when she performed in *A Streetcar Named Desire*. When we did the table read for that episode, Chuck pulled me aside to say, "You know, I want it to be good. I want Penny to be a good actress." I said, "Really?!"

Johnny Galecki: I loved that direction. And Kaley fucking nailed it. It validated Penny.

Penny's experience on the set of *Serial Apeist 2* was the catalyst for Penny's decision to set her dream aside—which was more of a constant anguish than anything—and focus on what she did have: namely, Leonard, and great friends who would support her in whatever she decided she wanted to pursue next.

Kaley Cuoco: I liked that it was as realistic as it was. So many people are out there who want to be actors, and who are quite good. And that's what is most heartbreaking about it, because she was actually good. And her realization that this is that dream she's had for so long, but she also wants to get married and make real money...a lot of people deal with that. And in many ways, Penny was using her acting skills in those pharmaceutical meetings, along with memorizing all the details of those drugs. It helped make her successful, and I loved that. If Penny had all the sudden gotten a hit movie, it wouldn't have been that realistic. For some people it is, but for the majority, it's not.

Penny's awakening wasn't just the start of a new career, but a commitment to Leonard. The two got engaged in the penultimate episode of the season, which was so low-key, Leonard had to ask if they were even engaged. "Yeah, I think so," she says. But more than anything, it was in line with the roller-coaster odd couple pairing of Penny and Leonard that made them so interesting to watch in the first place.

Johnny Galecki: The engagement was treated in a very low-key manner, because you had seen that kind of typical engagement scene so many times before. I appreciated how the writers approached that, because especially when there's a love like Leonard and Penny had, it's kind of a no-brainer not to [explore what's next]. And I also knew that being engaged, there's still a long road ahead, which could lead to a lot of obstacles, especially if someone is in a transitional period, which Penny was in her life. Molaro and I talked a lot about whether they should end up together because we wanted to keep it realistic, and these are two people with so little in common, so I still knew a lot would go wrong, and honestly should, but that doesn't mean without recovery at some point. There's just very little comedy to mine in everything going right. But I'm so glad they stayed together.

Steve Holland: I'm really proud of how that scene came out, especially where Leonard says that he doesn't want to be her bran muffin—he wants to be her strawberry Pop-Tart. Johnny added a little physical thing to that line where he kind of straightened himself up very proper as he said strawberry Pop-Tart. And I'm also pretty sure that the ring in his wallet wasn't initially in the script originally; we added it in the days leading up to the tape night. Molaro had the idea that he'd been carrying the ring around all these years.

Steve Molaro: Proposals have been done on TV a thousand times, so we were always looking for some kind of new angle on it. The low-key *Is that it?* aspect of their engagement was appealing to us.

Season seven came to a close in an emotionally charged episode ("The Status Quo Combustion"), with Sheldon struggling to accept all the change around him. Penny and Leonard were moving forward in their relationship, which would most likely mean a change in living arrangements. Sheldon was also no longer fulfilled with string theory. For anyone who has ever had

trouble with change, it's a paralyzing place to be when so much is out of your control. So, at the nearby train station, Sheldon took control the only way he knew how and decided to do some major soul-searching by heading off into the unknown, much to Penny and Leonard's worry and concern.

Jim Parsons: I was very curious as to what was going to happen when Sheldon left on a train at the end of season seven. I also enjoyed when Amy tells Sheldon she needed a break and he pulls out the ring from his desk drawer. It may be that I'm selfish and I like when these big moments are all about me. [*Laughs*] When it's a group cliffhanger, that really irritates me. No. Kidding! But the train episode finale interested me because I thought, *We have to get him back.* It intrigued me as to how that was going to happen.

Tara Hernandez: Although Sheldon's reasoning felt very tragic and messy, I love when he romanticizes ideas like, *I'm going to be a vagabond and get on a train.* I like that he did that as a thing to escape to, that he lived out these fantasies of never going anywhere, just moving around from place to place. And then Leonard was always tracking him, like he's his eye in the sky. He wanted to find his buddy, which I thought was very beautiful.

Steve Holland: The story came out of us tearing his world down. We were trying to take away all of his comfort zones and that led us to the thought of the comic book store burning down and him leaving on a train. We actually wrote the second half of that script at Coachella. Steve, Tara, and I had all gone for the weekend, but we hadn't finished the finale script yet, so we wrote the second half of it in my hotel room in the mornings and then would go over to the festival in the afternoons. I also remember what an amazing job our art department did in re-creating Union Station on our set. It was incredible and looked like we had gone on location. And how great was Kaley when she convinced Leonard that they had to let Sheldon go.

Steve Molaro: Over that summer hiatus, Holland and I talked about ways that Sheldon's train trip could come to an end. I knew someone personally who once had a rough night and woke up far from home on a park bench with no phone and no money and had to ask strangers for help, so that seemed plausible to me. We just took away Sheldon's pants on top of it, because why wouldn't you?

Chapter 17

THE TOUGHEST YEAR YET

In the summer of 2014, *Big Bang* was in the news before season eight even got underway. It had nothing to do with Sheldon taking off for the unknown via train, or Kaley Cuoco's decision to chop her hair (though more on that later), but everything to do with contract negotiations for the five original cast members (Melissa Rauch and Mayim Bialik negotiated on a different schedule, since they had joined the series later).

A day before the first table read for the new season, Parsons, Galecki, Cuoco, Nayyar, and Helberg were still without contracts, as talks were pretty much at a standstill between their teams and Warner Bros. Television. Contract negotiations are never easy even though they always get done, but the stakes at play—namely, taking Parsons, Galecki, and Cuoco from $325,000 an episode to a million an episode—were significant enough that production on the new season would not begin as scheduled. The table read was postponed.

At the time, the *Hollywood Reporter* noted, "The move comes as a surprise to the studio [Warner Bros. Television], which previously was not expecting there to be a work stoppage, believing that the cast would arrive back at work Wednesday, with or without a contract."

Melissa Rauch: I was basically in a bubble that summer, filming *The Bronze* in Ohio. I was supposed to be flying back to LA on the red-eye the night before the table read, but then I heard that production may be pushing it because of negotiations. I was selfishly relieved that I didn't have to get on the plane and go straight into work with no sleep. What surprised me was that because the negotiations were so public, people were reaching out to me with condolence-like check-ins, asking if I was doing okay. I think there was this notion that because of the pay discrepancy there was a feeling of being shafted in some way, which wasn't how I was internalizing it at all.

Meanwhile, CBS had already scheduled season eight to premiere with an hourlong episode on September 22. Outward facing, they didn't seem to be worried that they'd have to change the schedule, but obviously the longer the negotiations went on, the more pressure it put on the writers to make sure they had enough time to execute their planned storylines.

Steve Molaro: Heading into season eight was challenging because we didn't 100 percent know if we were going to have access to all the characters. How do you write a season premiere if you don't really know if you have everyone? Or who it was going to be?

Peter Roth: There was no doubt the negotiations that season were going to get done. But I was worried about our ability to deliver enough original consecutive episodes, as well as the impact financially to the studio and certainly to the network. As were the actors. Everybody believes they're on the side of the angels, and it's certainly true when it comes to success or megasuccess. But the definition of a good negotiation is one where all sides have to give up a little bit, and all sides ultimately feel good about it in the end.

And yes, while many could argue that the cast was lucky to be making the money they were—which they rightfully acknowledge—they were also making an exceptional amount of money for the studio and network. Per the *Los Angeles Times* in 2019, "the show brought in $125 million to $150 million in ad revenue per season for CBS," and "its syndication revenue has reportedly generated more than $1 billion for Warner Bros. Television." Not to mention, during season seven the show regularly drew 20 million viewers a week, up 4 percent year over year. It was such a feat—and rarity—that *New York* magazine ran a sprawling feature in May 2014 titled, "Why Are 23.4 Million People Watching *The Big Bang Theory*?" noting, "TV shows are not supposed to be this popular, not in the age of DVRs, Netflix, and cord-cutting. Nevertheless, CBS's *The Big Bang Theory*...is not only television's No. 1 show but also the highest-rated sitcom since *Friends* signed off in 2004."

Nina Tassler: If you have a successful show, you're going to have challenging negotiations. CBS had several really big shows, so it comes with the territory. And Warner Bros. had *ER* and *Friends* previously, so they were used to those kinds of negotiations as well.

Peter Roth: The process can be very, very difficult. And it gets personal. I used to tell actors, "If you live your life comparing yourself to others, you're doomed to be miserable. You're never gonna be satisfied." In the case of the *Big Bang Theory* cast, they were in a place, not dissimilar to the *Friends* cast, where they thought they deserved to be the highest-paid actors in all of television. I mean, when you have a monster hit like that everybody needs to make a lot of money. But defining and coming to terms with what that means and how much that should be, what's fair and what isn't fair, and what's right and what isn't, can get really ugly. And really difficult and taxing.

Nikki Lorre: You start a show and everyone is so happy and so in love with each other, but things get complicated [when you have tremendous success]. There's this cloud that sits over everyone with hurt feelings or strong opinions that, fortunately for us, did not last forever. But it didn't fully go away, either. I think certain camps were formed, alliances. But at the end of the day, they did come full circle to love and respect each other even after that chaotic period of time, which I'm very, very grateful for.

Jim Parsons: Every time I went through a negotiation, my manager would say, "I don't know why it has to be like this." And my lawyer would say, "But that's the way it is." I was the one that would say, "Here's what we should try and do, call me when we have it. Otherwise you go ahead and do your thing." [*Laughs*] It's a wonderful blessing to even be in that situation, but...it's important to have good people around you who can really take stock of the land and advise you, because you're just one person who is living their dream versus a corporation whose business it is to make money, and that's a very different place to come from. And it's not that either one is wrong, which is what I found tricky about it. But if you're lucky enough to get to play in the big leagues at any point in your career, those are the facts that go along with it. It's a weird thing to have your stomach tied in knots, and go, "This is a blessing! This is truly the jackpot! Funny that it feels like I'm going to shit myself!" [*Laughs*] They don't call it show business for nothing.

> As predicted, a week after the first table read was postponed, both sides came to an agreement. On August 5, 2014, the *New York Times* reported that Parsons, Galecki, and Cuoco "got the big payday they were waiting for, agreeing to new three-year contracts with Warner Bros. Television worth about $1 million per episode for each actor." They also noted that "the deal includes other perks like a larger stake in the series and ownership of the show after its original run on network television." *Deadline*, meanwhile, reported that "Helberg and Nayyar will catch up with their counterparts on per-episode fees in Season 10." Nonetheless, all that fans cared about was this statement from Warner Bros. Television: "Production on season 8 of *The Big Bang Theory* will begin Wednesday, August 6, with contract negotiations now having been concluded."

Melissa Rauch: I was happy to get the news we were going back, that [my castmates] would be getting what they deserved. And just so excited to see everybody.

Peter Roth: And whatever tensions there were that first day back, it was over as soon as we did the table read. Everyone moved on, and that is a reflection of the character of the people involved as well as the quality of the show.

> But now the public knew what the cast was making, which brought its own set of challenges.

Johnny Galecki: The fact that those numbers in that renegotiation were made public was *terribly* uncomfortable for me. Where I'm from and where I was brought up...I mean, I don't talk to my brother about our salaries. I felt like it put a certain target on us. It brought the parasites out and had a really negative effect on my personal life. I was happy to be that successful, of course, but I felt like I needed to become much more guarded. I would have been stupid to not be more guarded. I remember Kunal saying to me, "Aw, man, you must be dating every model in the world right now!" And I said, "Dude, I've called off dating for at least six months to a year." Because it really does bring the vampires out at night. I was really uncomfortable with that and still am.

Simon Helberg: There are reporters that like to release the details of an actual negotiation in a deal. You're like, *Wait, how are all the details of this meeting that I just was in already on this website and I just walked out of this meeting?* Who knows? Money is a pretty complicated issue for most people, so it's especially weird to have it so public.

Johnny Galecki: In the same way that I was always reluctant to be public with my personal relationship with Kaley during those two years we were romantic, all it does is distract the audience from the characters. Now they're looking at us differently, as these multimillionaires. That's not relatable, necessarily, to much of the world, to many of our viewers. I don't know who leaked those salaries or those details. I have an idea, but it wasn't anyone in the cast. And I guess it *wasn't* a real hindrance to how the audience accepted us, because they continued to, thank God. Look, these are champagne problems, obviously. But none of us wanted that out there.

> In fact, Kunal Nayyar reached out to *Friends* star Matt LeBlanc for advice. At the time Nayyar told *Glamour*, "[Matt] told me that the journey is crazy, the journey is long, and everybody's going to want something from you, [but] just keep your sanity and stay grounded." Now, eight years later, Nayyar is still grateful for that advice.

Kunal Nayyar: That's what I reached out to him about, really. In relation to that, I would go home to India, and I would have cousins I didn't even know come out of the woodwork. It was a huge deal for India, as a culture, to have an Indian character on America's biggest sitcom. Not an Indian-American, but an Indian, from New Delhi, who sounds and looks like this. It was huge. I understand the cultural responsibility that I held being on this show. So as someone who had been through a similar journey, at least in terms of massive fame, Matt said to stay humble and keep your head down because it's a long haul. That's what Chuck Lorre had said to me, too. It's not that I didn't know that already, but to hear it from people who really have gone through that journey is very powerful, especially when you're young and you're searching.

Three weeks after contract negotiations concluded—Seth Meyers was host-ing the 66th Annual Primetime Emmys when he made a joke referencing Jim Parsons's million-dollars-an-episode payday. The camera zoomed right up to Parsons's face, who laughed and appeared to get a kick out of the moment.

Jim Parsons: Thank God it was that and not something like, *How was it coming back from prison and tax evasion?* It could have been much worse! But listen, it's a shitload of money! I don't think there's any bones about that. I did not feel the need to justify it. Not because I thought I deserved it in some sort of grand, earth-wise sense, while there's starving people? No. It had nothing to do with that, but it was just the facts of the situation. I knew then and I know now that that information doesn't translate to everybody. Here's the other thing: In my own way, it doesn't translate *to me*, either. Do I think that's insane? Of course I do! I'm very surprised at the way at times money goes around the world and where it lands and why. I do think I understood everyone was going to have their own rough estimates of our salaries, and always had. It was just until there was greater success and there-fore money to talk about that it became a hotter topic. We live in a world where you can't type in any celebrity's name on Google without getting "net worth" as a result. I remember my mother getting asked by friends within the first couple of seasons of *Big Bang*, "Does he fly home on a private jet for Christmas?" And we were like, "Wait, *what?!* You have really misunderstood my entering salary for this show! I'm not sure what you think happens as soon as a face is on television!" Money is a really crazy topic, and I was raised very much that it was impolite to talk about and impolite to mention on your own, or certainly ask a question about. To this day, I am very uncertain as to what my parents' financial situation was the entire time I lived with them. I'm very fortunate they taught me to save my money, but I remember when I was younger, asking about their finances, and they said, "It's none of your business!" and I said, "Oh! Okay!" [*Laughs*] And so, it's a good thing they did teach me that, because I don't know that I understand money man-agement skills other than fear-based, *Do we have enough to keep the lights on?*

In fact, Parsons credits his husband, Todd, as the main reason he was able to keep some sort of levelheadedness during the contract negotiations.

Jim Parsons: Todd handled and still handles a lot of those business calls. I won't be on it. He knows what I "need" to know. He filters it. It's one of the reasons I married him and put a ring on it! In fact, on our first New Year's Eve together, we had to take his collected coins to the local Coinstar to go out that night. So we were both very aware what a blessing it was to even be involved in contract negotiations, even though it was trying. Todd knows me better than anyone, and I trust him and his taste explicitly. It's why our production company was one of the major gifts that *Big Bang* brought into my life. It would have never happened, I don't believe, without one of those contract negotiations. And without Todd, there wouldn't be a company, because I'd be like, *I'm not going to do this.* Or it would be a very different company.

> As soon as the eighth season of *The Big Bang Theory* started airing, viewers quickly forgot about who was making what each episode, or that their favorite show was in "danger" of missing its premiere date. Instead, the big news was Penny's new look. Over the summer, Kaley Cuoco decided to cut her hair, first into a chic shoulder-length bob, then a chin-framing cut, and eventually into a pixie. It provoked a lot of feelings from viewers, including *Glamour*'s deputy digital editor at the time, Lindsey Unterberger, who wrote, "The same chic cut I *love* on Kaley, I absolutely *hate* on Penny."

Kaley Cuoco: I just fucking cut my hair off and didn't tell anyone. I did it for an independent film called *Burning Bodhi*, and basically showed up to our *Big Bang* wrap party with short hair. Chuck hugged me and said, "Wow, look at your hair!" and I said, "Do you like it?" I don't know if I was being rebellious. I mean, I did do it for the movie, which was my excuse to cut it. At that point we were heading into our eighth season and something needed to shake up. I was bored and sick of the hair, and what's funny is I thought by cutting my hair, I would spend less time in the hair and makeup chair, even though I loved the hair and makeup team. And then in my attempt to spend less time on my hair, that decision bit me in the ass and it took way longer to do my short hair. I was like, *This is the worst decision! What was I thinking?!* I thought I was cutting off all this time, because I hated going in and getting ready. That's why I was wearing my hair up so much in season six and seven. So then I cut it and it ended up being more work because it wasn't easy to style.

Chuck Lorre: We didn't have a heads-up on the haircut! When you think back on it, it was startling. I wish we had been in the loop. Had she come to me, I would have told her how the ratings dropped on *Dharma & Greg* when Jenna Elfman did the same thing. And they dropped on *Felicity* as well. The audience had become infatuated with the character, and not just the character's behavior and flaws and strengths, but in how the character looked. They became iconic, and to disregard that audience attachment was a mistake. And I witnessed it firsthand. It would have been the same thing if Johnny had come to the wrap party and had shaved his head. We're all in this together! But I love that Kaley recognized it for what it was. She's very self-aware, and we survived it. As bumps in the road go, that was a small one.

Kaley Cuoco: I was justifying it because Penny was starting this new job as a pharmaceutical rep. It was going to have to work because it's what I

Cuoco's pixie cut was actually already growing out here (pictured during the filming of season eight, episode eight's "The Prom Equivalency," with costar Rauch), which speaks to how short it was when the new season began. *Courtesy of Kaley Cuoco photo collection*

was doing. [*Laughs*] I remember the writers figuring out what Sheldon was going to say when he saw her hair and literally would never be able to let it go, which made me laugh. But it's just funny to see how that was such a big deal. I remember actors on other shows who cut their hair and thinking, *Why would they do that?* And then I went and did it! Whatever, there's always going to be haters. Welcome to the business!

Jim Parsons: [*Laughs*] It's one thing to change your hair for a play that's running for six months, it's another thing not to change it for a decade plus. At some point you just go, *I'm going to do it and apologize later rather than ask permission.*

And even though Cuoco had to spend longer in the hair and makeup room on show nights, she still loved the cut, even if others didn't.

Kaley Cuoco: I had fun with it, and I did like it. I'm sure it was being negatively talked about all over the place, but I didn't pay as much attention to what people were saying on social media then. But I do remember we had wrapped an episode, and as I was walking up to my dressing room, an executive said to me, "I just want you to know, who cares what everybody else says? I love your hair!" And I said, "Who said what about my hair?" Her eyes got so big, and I was like, "No, seriously, did someone say something about my hair?" And she was like, "Oh, no, no, I think it looks great." She totally got her foot in her mouth, because obviously it was a topic of conversation! I guarantee that woman probably thinks about that moment a lot. It was not a good night for her!

And yes, while it was jarring to see Penny with an entirely new haircut and wardrobe, it also played into her desire to be taken more seriously, especially as she embarked on a new career in the pharmaceutical sales field.

Mary T. Quigley: When she cut her hair, I wanted her style to be higher end, more mature, with more linear-looking clothes that had an edge. It just signaled a new direction with her new career, and letting go of the Nebraska-farm-girl look. Not that it was that, but it was much more LA-looking now. I put her in a couple of leather jackets. Penny knew to go to Nordstrom

Rack instead of Nordstrom. We also put her in a lot of Theory suits. In fact, her pink suit she wore when the elevator opened in the series finale was from Theory.

Kaley Cuoco: Penny's look was very specific early on, and it did change a lot, which I loved. It got a little more business-y, and then in the later years, I must have worn four hundred shirts from the line Equipment. To this day, I cannot wear another Equipment shirt. I wore every print. I see them, and I am like, "That was Penny!" I cannot wear them anymore. [*Laughs*] But what we love about Penny is her sweats and her T-shirts, and all the comfy scenes. And I would love that, too. I'd read a scene and go, "Oooh! A comfy scene!" But I really liked when she started to get super professional and wasn't a server anymore.

> As the season unfolded, relationships took center stage again, with Penny and Leonard now engaged (though in no rush to walk down the aisle...yet), and Sheldon and Amy making small but significant steps, with their biggest breakthrough coming in episode eight, "The Prom Equivalency." In it, the gang re-creates prom, and Sheldon tells Amy he loves her.

Mayim Bialik: We had so many back-and-forths about how to do that moment. It's a really beautiful episode. I've seen a lot of still photos of the look on my face when he tells her he loves her, and that's a very special moment to have that captured because it was such a long time coming. My job is to make you remember what that feels like. And the writers really nailed that moment. I remember when I chose the outfit that Amy would wear, and I chose very carefully what jewelry she would have on, as well as what lip gloss. I knew that I wanted her to feel special and look special for how special she was going to feel.

Tara Hernandez: We labor over those moments all the time. We knew we didn't want Amy to ask Sheldon to say "I love you," and we didn't want her to set him up for it where he'd feel obligated to say it back. But then someone said we should vocalize that, so then you figure out the moment Sheldon is going to interrupt with "I love you." And it shifts in the script. One line is too early or one line is too late, so finding that moment when a character says, "I love you" are the biggest discussions in the room.

The couple—affectionately known as Shamy—had an unconventional romance built on innocence and friendship. They were two very different but also similar people who most likely wouldn't have been ready for a moment like this to come any sooner than when it did. Most TV characters experience their first *I love you*s as teens or twentysomethings, not as thirtysomethings. What *Big Bang* was showing was that it's perfectly normal to have your firsts—whether it be a kiss, or an "I love you," or sex—come later than the cultural and societal norms we've grown up with. And that mattered.

Mayim Bialik: A lot of people said that seeing someone like Sheldon find and receive love was something they never imagined for their child, or even seeing a couple like that was giving people hope for their kids. I've also heard that from some friends of mine who have kids either on the spectrum or who struggle socially, so it was a really interesting source of comfort without laughing at this character who was the kind of character who would often be teased.

Jim Parsons: I certainly had a fair share of people reach out to me, or that I would come in contact with, because it made a difference to them to have this character out there. Now that we're a few years outside of doing the show, I understand how it could have a positive impact without being a clinical study in what it is to be on the spectrum. You meet someone through a character, and they may be completely fictionalized, as Sheldon is, but they bear similarities to other people in the world who you may not know at all or not be very familiar with, and it changes your view or approach to those other people in real life. And I know this from my own experience of characters and things that I've watched. I'll meet people or I'll rethink somebody I knew who bears similarities to that character, and it will just change [my perception].

Steve Molaro: There are a few young people on the spectrum in my life, so I found myself hoping there might be a significant other out there for them one day who has the kind of patience Amy displayed with Sheldon. Someone out there who would give them time and understanding, just to simply hold their hand. At the same time, I also didn't want to imply that Sheldon needed to be in a relationship to be lovable or complete. People like Sheldon can be difficult to get to know. They can be off-putting or frustrating at times, usually unintentionally, but they also have so much to offer. Sheldon was resistant to a lot with Amy in the first few years, like physical contact or even just the label "boyfriend and girlfriend," and that's where the patience that Amy displayed came in. It was more about showing that the road to love or finding a partner or best friend can manifest in different ways. A lot of things can be scary for someone like Sheldon, and Amy recognized that. And even though they didn't say the words for a long time, I think they loved each other for years before they said it out loud. They just had to take baby steps to get there.

Tara Hernandez: Amy and Sheldon got to have so many moments together that they didn't have growing up. Audiences can look at the show like it's juvenile or wonder why these adults are in a fort, but what was so charming about it was that everyone wants to sit on the floor and eat sometimes. There's a lot of joy in that! And *we* got to sit in forts, jump in ball pits. There was so much joy in the process of making it because the characters were getting to do these things—often for the first time.

Steve Molaro: *Big Bang* celebrated nerds / geek culture, and a big part of that is being able to unabashedly have an interest in something or love something—*anything*—and dig in on a truly deep level without caring how other people judge you. Sheldon and Amy had a sweet innocence to them. Many of us "adults" pretend we've been around the block or know what we're doing. But Sheldon and Amy didn't. They were willing to show that vulnerable side to each other, whether it was awkwardly cuddling for the first time all the way up to them finally having coitus. How nice would life be if we could be as open as they were about everything we don't know?

> Two months into the new season—and almost a week after "The Prom Equivalency" aired—*The Big Bang Theory* family suffered a crushing and immeasurable loss when they received the news that Carol Ann Susi—who played Howard's mother, Mrs. Wolowitz—had passed away from cancer.

Melissa Rauch: I knew she had been in remission, but I had no idea she was as sick as she was. It amped up really quickly because we had heard she was sick a week before she died.

Steve Molaro: As far as significant moments go over the twelve years, losing Carol Ann was so tough. That was such a big blow because she was truly part of our family.

Susi had made her first appearance as Mrs. Wolowitz—Howard's overbearing, loud-mouthed, always-heard but rarely ever seen mother, back in season one.

Bill Prady: Carol Ann came in to read for the role, and afterward, Chuck said, "Could you do it a little quieter?" And she—in a loud voice—says, "Of COURSE!" and read it exactly the same way. [*Laughs*] I loved Carol Ann. My favorite story is when she said to me, "Bill, I've gotta tell you the most amazing story! I'm having lunch with my friend at the Farmer's Market, just having a conversation, when someone comes up and says, 'Are you the mother from *The Big Bang Theory*?' I mean, how did he know?!" She was a lovely lady and I adored her.

Melissa Rauch: She sounded like so many people in my family, because of her authentic East Coast vibe. One of the first things she said to me was something along the lines of "So! You're the new woman in my son's life!" She was so hilarious. There was just never a dull moment with her.

The fact that Rauch could do a nearly identical impersonation of Susi as Mrs. Wolowitz was serendipitous.

Melissa Rauch: I never impersonated her voice on set, so they wouldn't have known. I would have been afraid to insult her. [*Laughs*] But honestly, I didn't know that I could do it until I gave it a try when I saw it in the script. My husband, Winston, heard me practicing in the kitchen and he ran in thinking I hurt myself because I was screaming in that voice. And since we shared a pretty thin wall with our neighbors at the apartment we were living in, I realized I had to practice any Mrs. Wolowitz lines alone in my car so I didn't alarm anyone else going forward!

Steve Molaro: Melissa was amazing at it! It reminds him of his mother, which is weird and funny and understandable. Howard's basically going to marry his mother.

Having a character that was only heard and not seen was not an entirely new concept on sitcoms, but there was something so special about Susi's voice and how she inhabited the character.

Steve Molaro: There came a point, pretty early on, where Carol Ann had such a distinct voice, and it was so much fun to imagine who this woman was. It could never live up to what might have been in your head.

Simon Helberg: She was like this bite-sized person, and you could see the top of her head sometimes over the furniture as she would wrestle around to get backstage. They'd sit her in one of those director chairs behind a wall or something, and there were times we'd go for lunch and say, "Where's Carol Ann? Did anyone break her?' And we'd realize she was sitting back there, waiting to be excused for lunch. What she did was actually very complicated. The nuance she could bring, even with her decibel level always being at the pitch of a screaming eagle hurling from the sky, plus her execution and timing was so spot-on. It's a real challenge to do that without being able to see anybody.

Melissa Rauch: She was always behind the wall with her water, her lozenges, and her bag. She'd be like, "I'm not going to leave my bag in my dressing room! I take it with me, you never know who's gonna rob ya!" [*Laughs*] She thought it was insane of me to leave my bag in my dressing room, so she always had her purse right next to her.

In a very brief moment during "The Spoiler Alert Segmentation," we see Mrs. Wolowitz run past a doorway when she has Raj over for dinner. That was actually Olaf, the show's security guard, dressed as Mrs. Wolowitz.

Steve Molaro: Yep, that was Olaf in a dress. It's almost like seeing Bigfoot go by. And then we augmented him as well with some CGI.

Mark Cendrowski: Any other times you see Mrs. Wolowitz's silhouette was Olaf.

Kunal Nayyar: Olaf is a big guy. In one scene he had to pull me back in through the window. I was like, *How is he going to do that?* I'm like 150 pounds and trying to crawl out the window, but when he did it, I was like a baby. When he actually picked me up as Mrs. Wolowitz, I became limp, like a puppy. And he had to do it in a dress. He was wearing Mrs. Wolowitz's big nightgown.

The cast has endless memories of working with Susi, but some of the most special moments happened off set. Susi didn't drive, so Rauch and Nayyar would take her home after work so she wouldn't have to take the bus.

Melissa Rauch: She never got a driver's license, so she would take the bus all the way to Warner Bros. with all her bags. But she loved it. She was like, "I'm not going to drive in this city with all the crazies!" If we finished work around the same time, I would take her home and we would have all these really great conversations.

Kunal Nayyar: Anytime I'd ever see anyone walking back to their car—whether it was a guest star or the crew—I'd try to give them as many rides into the studio or out because I always felt it was weird not to stop. Carol Ann lived quite close to me, so sometimes I would give her a ride home if she was leaving when I was. I had these fancy sports cars, and I remember she sat in my white Ferrari, and every time I would hit the gas, she'd go "Vroom, vroom! That felt good! Do it again!" She'd make me keep revving up the engine. I was just very drawn to her individuality and her freedom.

Melissa Rauch: She was an incredible woman. In the '80s, she cared for and nursed a good deal of her friends through the AIDS crisis and the end of their lives. She bathed them and everything. At her memorial, a friend of hers said, "There'd be even more people here to talk about her life and how amazing she was, but they're all gone."

Kunal Nayyar: Her wake was held at the Magic Castle in Los Angeles... but maybe six weeks before she passed, every time you asked how she was, she'd say in that iconic voice, "I'm great, darling. I'm lovely! Every day is a blessing."

Melissa Rauch: I had never seen a celebration of someone's life like her memorial. For the one on set, we all gathered on the stage and told our favorite Carol Ann stories through our tears. And Johnny and Molaro put up the little picture of her on the refrigerator in Sheldon and Leonard's apartment, which remained until the very end of the series.

Steve Molaro: We wanted her to be in every episode from then on, so we knew Sheldon and Leonard's refrigerator was the best place to do that.

Simon Helberg: I would look at it often, and it was nice to have a little piece of her there. It was also kind of funny because no one knew what she looked like, and so you could get away with putting that picture of her up there. It felt like a secret nod we had as a group.

Carol Ann Susi (pictured here with frequent guest star John Ross Bowie, who played Barry Kripke) was such a beloved member of *The Big Bang Theory* family that her presence continued to be felt on set following her passing in 2014. *Courtesy of John Ross Bowie*

Melissa Rauch: And, if you look closely, you'll also notice that before Bernadette and Howard remodeled the Wolowitz house, there was a five-by-seven photograph of that same image of Carol Ann on the shelves in the main living room. She was so special, so loving, and funny as hell.

Susi's passing was addressed on-screen a few episodes later when Mrs. Wolowitz died while out of town.

Simon Helberg: The episode aired a few weeks after Carol Ann had passed away, so I felt like it was a tribute to her, and there was some level of catharsis. Of course, it was really painful at the same time. There was the feeling of really just putting a tremendous amount of pressure on getting that scene right. Not by myself, but by the writers and producers. I think that served the scene and in other ways it was unnecessary. We're actors and we know how to do those things in a heavy moment. It's a natural approach when you want everything to go as well as it can or when there's a pressure on a certain kind of scene or story. But ultimately, I think we honored Carol Ann in that episode and after.

Peter Chakos: We were mourning a person, not just a character. So that was really emotional.

Steve Molaro: She was such a beloved part of the family, it was heartbreaking. We knew we had to honor her with the passing of Howard's mom. I think it was emotionally cathartic for us to be able to do that because the sadness of the characters on-screen certainly reflected what we were feeling behind the scenes.

> The writers continued to honor Susi—and Mrs. Wolowitz—by addressing her absence in the episodes that followed, always working to inject humor with an underlying emotional pull. But nothing was as gut-wrenching as episode eighteen—"The Leftover Thermalization"—in which the power goes out, and Howard realizes this is his last chance to eat his mom's home cooking (especially her beloved brisket) before it goes bad. The moment was just as painful for Helberg, who didn't quite let on to how much he was struggling at the time.

Simon Helberg: I remember very vividly, I had flown back and forth to New York because I was getting ready to do *Florence Foster Jenkins*, and had met Meryl [Streep] for the first time. So, between the anxiety of preparing for the film, plus losing Carol Ann and the heavier storylines that were coming up on the show as a result, I ended up with vertigo. I could barely move at some points without having to grab on to something. I was concerned, so I went to get an MRI. Ultimately, it was from making myself crazy, and that was how my body handled that. It was described to me as my brain thought that I was laying down and my eyes thought that I was standing up. So I remember during that episode, specifically, looking into Mrs. Wolowitz's freezer and having a moment of *uh-oh*. It was really hard, and it would come and go. It would kind of take you out for a couple hours, but it lent itself perfectly to the trauma that I'm sure Howard was going through. Heavy stuff is always going to take a toll on your body.

The inspiration for that episode came from a personal place for Steve Molaro.

Steve Molaro: As hard as it was, that was an important episode for us to do because it just felt so real. Mrs. Wolowitz's cooking and her food was such a part of her relationship with Howard. On a personal note, my parents come out to visit my family every year, and I remember looking into my freezer, and my dad had put some stuff that he cooked in there. There was a note on it about what it was. I looked at it and thought, *If he wasn't alive, this would be kind of heartbreaking and touching to see that, this thing that he made, that I would still have.* So we worked our way from that germ of an emotion to an idea of what would happen if the power went out at the Wolowitz house and Howard wanted to save her last meals she prepared. You'd have to honor this thing that she made—her final brisket.

As perhaps the most trying season—both emotionally and physically—was coming to an end, the writers went big with the season finale. Amy, who had started to struggle with the snail's pace of her relationship with Sheldon over the last few years, decided she needed a break. (The straw that broke the camel's back was when Sheldon confided he was thinking about the *Flash* TV show while they were making out). If their breaking up wasn't enough to get fans riled up, then the added reveal that Sheldon had been planning to propose to Amy in the near future was certainly enough to send everyone spiraling, including Parsons and Bialik.

Jim Parsons: I wasn't happy that we were doing that, but not as far as the storyline goes. Whatever the writers wanted to do was fine as far as the trajectory went. I don't like conflict in my relationships, and I didn't like having even fake conflict in that relationship, which makes me realize just how that relationship—both as a character and as an actor—was a very

wonderful thing for me. I loved having Mayim as a partner. I knew Sheldon
and Amy would be fine and the writers would figure out what was best for
the show, but for myself, I knew I wouldn't have fun scenes with her until
they worked this out.

Mayim Bialik: Based on my contractual obligations to Warner Bros., I
knew they'd figure something out for Amy, but the possibility was very open
to me that they might not get back together and just kind of go back to
being a circle of friends. I actually had a very specific notion that that might
happen, so I was really just along for the ride. That was not just something
we said for the press.

Steve Molaro: There were times when we just liked to shake things up
creatively on the show, particularly near the end of a season. It made things
exciting and gave us fun new wrinkles to explore at the beginning of the
next season. This was a chance to see Sheldon and Amy deal with a whole
new range of emotions in their relationship. I always assumed at some point
they would get back together, but that time apart gave us a chance to find
some really fun stories along the way.

**Things looked much more promising for Penny and Leonard, who, after
a year of being engaged, decided to take the next step by eloping in Las
Vegas. However, on the drive there, Leonard confessed that he kissed
another woman during his North Sea expedition a few years prior, which
stunned and devastated Penny.**

Johnny Galecki: I went back and forth a lot about what I wanted to happen. It was kind of mine and Molaro's dream to break them up eventually.
That's just my way. [*Laughs*] And that's what *Entertainment Tonight* will take
out of this book: Johnny Galecki wanted them to break up!

Steve Molaro: We talked about what was going to become of them long-
term in the writers room for a long time. We would talk about what was best
for the show and what was best for stories because there were a lot of moving pieces. We tried to not factor in too much of what the audience wanted
because we knew what they wanted! I think it could've gone either way
for Leonard and Penny in the end, but ultimately it seemed unavoidable.
We liked them together, but we did consider separating them and being

buddies, but still being across the hall from each other. I was familiar with that dynamic, having remained friends with my first girlfriend to this day after we had broken up.

Kaley Cuoco: Sometimes the path to finding the love of your life is just a total mess. I loved their path, the ups and downs, the breakups, and even when they dated other people. You can go back to that early scene in the first episode where Leonard is looking at her and says, "Our babies will be smart and beautiful." He wanted her forever. I couldn't live with them not ending up together after all that time. It was really important to me. But I know that was a hot topic in the writers room of how they were going to do that. No matter what, I found it to be super real and grounded. Shit happens. Fights happen. It was realistic.

> In the end, Penny and Leonard decided to put the incident behind them and go through with their Vegas nuptials, but there's one major reason Cuoco says she'll never forget the episode: her wig. By that point, Cuoco's pixie cut had started to grow out, but in four months' time when season nine would begin filming, she knew it would be a lot longer, and therefore wouldn't match how it looked in the finale.

Kaley Cuoco: I said to the producers, "Please tell me you're not going to write a 'To Be Continued . . .' episode for the season eight finale." And sure enough, they said, "We are." I was so angry I had brought it up because that meant we had to get a fucking wig, and I was livid! [*Laughs*] I didn't want to wear a wig. And bless my hairdresser Faye Woods's heart, because she knows how much I hate wigs, but the wig that was made was exceptional. Still, I was so hateful toward this wig and everyone knew it. I was just being bratty. But I had to wear that wig in the season nine premiere. Then in the next episode we cheated a bit and it was back in a little bun so you couldn't see the length. Then slowly over the next few episodes we started to let it down. Oh, and I still have that fucking wig. Faye gave it to me! It's a joke now, just to sit there and remind me not to make bad choices with hair again. [*Laughs*] There were very few moments of anger for me on *Big Bang*, but that wig, to this day, creams my corn, as Penny would say. I hated it! I was so mad!

Penny's plush pink halter wedding dress that she wore in Vegas had a special meaning for Leonard and Penny fans.

Mary T. Quigley: On the dress tag I wrote, "Pink wedding dress, Penny. Halter with rosette black trim, BCBG, size four." The way I pictured the elopement dress was that it was something that she already had in her closet, so it was perfect for a spur-of-the-moment trip to Vegas. I didn't want her to have to run out to get a dress, but it had to be a believable dress that she had worn before, but at the same time, be special and memorable. The blush color added an innocence to it, and the rosette on the front has a center point and goes around and around, kind of like the universe. It was also representative of how the relationship went round and round. And at the last minute, I decided to put a veil on her, because I figured a Vegas wedding chapel like that would have a few generic veils to pick from. I just think it made the wedding a touch more romantic. More bride-y, if you will.

And then a year later, Penny's white lace, tea-length wedding dress for the more formal, family wedding ceremony had another special meaning...

Mary T. Quigley: I liked that it was floral and lighter; it was more planned out for her because it was the real wedding with the family. At the last minute, I added that little round headpiece, which was soft and pretty, but not typical bridal. And then the flowers, of course, makes me think of Penny and Penny Blossoms.

TIME FOR A HOT BEVERAGE...

Lunch Break

Food was such a big part of *The Big Bang Theory*, from the Caltech cafeteria scenes to Chinese food night at Sheldon and Leonard's apartment. And the cast actually ate it, because each meal was prepared with their personal tastes and preferences in mind, thanks to prop master extraordinaire Scott London.

Scott London: I wanted to be a chef growing up. I could cook a full-blown Thanksgiving dinner at ten years old. But I eventually got up to 333 pounds, and said, "Not the line of work for me."

Johnny Galecki: Scott put his heart and soul into every little takeout box that we had to eat. And he knew exactly what amount of spice that each cast member wanted. I think it was such a wonderful device from the writers because there's something very intimate and relatable to sitting on a couch eating takeout together.

Chuck Lorre: And visually, having Chinese food is more interesting...the boxes, the chopsticks, the dumplings.

Scott London: The Chinese food pretty much got made on the day, so it was always super fresh. I used to make the rice in my prop room. I'd use Minute brown rice, add water, a little bit of sriracha, quite a bit of soy sauce to give it flavor, which would turn it more into fried rice, and then I'd put the vegetable mix with carrots and peas in it after it was cooked. The vegetables were usually frozen when I put them in there, but the heat from the rice alone would heat it up. I had it down to an art. One time we were coming back for a new season, and Johnny was on a soup kick for a long time, because he loved this vegetarian wonton soup, but mostly it was just broth with the sriracha sauce. I'd also chop green onions and scallions in there just to give it a little color and flavor, and we'd keep it in a thermos to stay warm. But on one of our first shows back, I got a little overzealous with the sriracha, and right in the middle of a scene he started gagging. Whoops.

[*Laughs*] Kaley also liked her little wonton noodles so she could scoop the rice up and eat it.

Simon Helberg: Kaley also liked the dumplings. And when this local Chinese restaurant we ordered from went out of business early on, Scott started making the dumplings himself.

Jim Parsons: We would gorge on those dumplings, like bring me another, bring me another. I would eat them between scenes or right after we got done with a scene, because I wasn't eating during it. They were *so* good.

Scott London: For the dumplings, I'd boil instead of fry them for Kaley. And she doesn't like mushrooms, so I'd make sure those weren't in there. And the Chinese food containers had to have sliced cabbage because Kaley liked the crunch of it. Half crunch cabbage, half rice, sprinkle the sauce, shake it up, cover that, and then I'd have two or three of those ready to go for her.

Chinese food became synonymous with *The Big Bang Theory*, and during the show's final season, Warner Bros. Television marketing and publicity had fortune cookies made with cute messages inside, like, "When the elevator is broken, take the stairs," and "If you don't believe in goodbyes, there's always syndication." *Courtesy of Kaley Cuoco photo collection*

Mayim Bialik: Scott knew that I had to have veggie dumplings, or mainly I would pick at the fried rice with no egg. [*Laughs*]

Melissa Rauch: I remember the first time I sat on the couch with the cast eating Chinese food in a scene. Later, I called my mom and said, "I ate Chinese food with them!" I watched them do that for so long and now I was doing it, which felt almost like an out-of-body experience. It felt like, *Wow, I'm a little bit more a part of the gang now.* And I was obsessed with the water chestnuts, and a lot of rice, but I was so worried I'd get caught with a mouthful of food, so I would just focus on eating the peas because those were easier to get down fast.

As complicated as it was to prepare all the Chinese food each week, at least London could use similar ingredients for each meal. The cafeteria scenes were a mix of pasta, salads, and sandwiches, while The Cheesecake Factory was basically every meal under the sun.

Scott London: We had episodes where every scene in the show had food. In the cafeteria scenes, I'd line up ten to fifteen paper plates and make ten

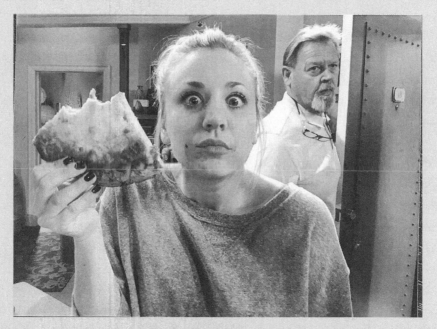

Cuoco eating pizza that Scott London (pictured here) and his team always prepared. On tape nights, the audience was also served pizza, though that was always delivered from a nearby pizza place. *Courtesy of Kaley Cuoco photo collection*

salads, ten desserts, ten entrees, then cover everything in plastic, and cart them out to set. And a lot of times the burgers in The Cheesecake Factory were Morningstar burgers or Beyond Meat. It just depends. Or when they'd eat pizza in scenes, sometimes I made them, other times they were frozen pizzas that I touched up a bit with extra sauce and cheese.

Melissa Rauch: Anytime we'd have salad and pizza, Scott would give me a lot of tomatoes on the salad, which was equivalent to the peas for me in that I knew if I had a line, I could get it down quickly. He would always refresh my tomatoes in between takes. When Bernadette would make dinner, I was always eating cherry tomatoes.

Jim Parsons: I also loved the scene where Penny and I went to an ice cream parlor because I'm a sucker for ice cream. It was so rare to get to do that, so I loved it.

Mayim Bialik: Scott also made the brains that I was dissecting in all of our lab scenes because that fell under props, and because he was such a skilled cook, he used a combination of deli meats and weird meats to mold them into what looked like a brain on camera.

Scott London: Yes, I made good brains for Mayim. [*Laughs*] And my wife, Teri, did a lot of stuff, like when Amy made Meemaw's cookies. She also made the meatloaf that flew out of the toilet. She made all of Mrs. Wolowitz's brisket and lasagna, as well. We had four slow cookers going all day and night in our house. The actors liked all of her stuff.

Simon Helberg: It was such outrageous pampering we had with that. There was so much eating, but that was part of the show. It's about these people that sit around and eat takeout or in the cafeteria and talk about life.

Scott London: Simon wanted pickles always so he could crunch. There was always a brand-new jar of cold Claussen pickles on the cart. In between takes, I'd swap out the pickles because he would eat those things like crazy all the time. Twelve years of pickles!

Simon Helberg: I really enjoyed the fusilli pasta salad and the pickles. That was my cafeteria go-to, and they were both easy to eat and talk at the same time. Funny to eat, too! Nothing like a good pickle punctuation. I was a stickler about eating. If I was eating in the scene, I would eat in the scene.

Scott London: And Jim would move around his black olives because he decided Sheldon wouldn't like those, and that would be a way for him to get around eating in the scenes. He had pasta salad a lot, and in between takes, I would have second and third plates premade for all the actors to swap out if needed, but if they cut in the middle of a take, I'd have to come in with a clean fork and mix the olives back in so he could pick it back out again.

Jim Parsons: I actually like olives in real life, but I needed something to do, so I would spend an entire scene picking olives out of the salad as if Sheldon didn't like olives and therefore, we had to get them out. And so I would talk and move my olives to the side, and then we'd cut and go back, and I'd move them back into the pasta salad and pick them out again. That was my favorite thing to do whenever I had a macaroni salad, like spiral pasta, in front of me.

Simon Helberg: Jim literally never stopped talking for twelve years and you can't really talk with a mouthful of food. At the same time, the way he moved the food around was actually a beautiful color to Sheldon. But I remember being like, "He didn't eat in that scene!" Everybody had their own process.

Kunal Nayyar: I really tried to just not eat anything. If anything, I would eat green beans. I couldn't eat and act at the same time; it really freaked me out. I couldn't do it.

Jim Parsons: The only thing Kunal was fond of doing when we were in lunchroom scenes, or any scene with food, he would always do this thing where he was pretending to just finish a bite of food as he started talking. I noticed this a lot.

Johnny Galecki: I may have eaten the least. Or maybe Jim, too, because he had such a mouthful of dialogue to give, he couldn't fill up his mouth with fried rice. Kaley probably ate the most, but she could afford to, 'cause she works out like a demon. Simon, I don't know *what* his metabolism is, but he could fit into those pants at any point.

Scott London: *Big Bang* burnt me out. I don't want to do food anymore. [*Laughs*] Technically, you have to have a food handler's license, which I have. It has to be someone on the level of prop master or above, or food stylist that can actually cook or handle it. On *Big Bang*, when they yelled cut, the cast ate more, 'cause most actors don't want to eat while they're filming because they have to say their dialogue. There were certain times I had to say, "OK, guys, I have plenty of this, but not enough of this," 'cause they were just going crazy. I used to also do the dishes, but I kind of let the other prop guys handle it now. I did my time. [*Laughs*]

Nayyar with Helberg, the ultimate pickle cruncher, in between filming scenes at the Caltech lunchroom set. *Courtesy of Kunal Nayyar*

Chapter 18

"THE OPENING NIGHT EXCITATION"

In terms of iconic episodes, it doesn't get better than "The Opening Night Excitation" (season nine, episode eleven, December 17, 2015) which drew nearly 25 million viewers. Sheldon decides to skip the long-awaited premiere of *Star Wars: The Force Awakens* to celebrate Amy's birthday. But that doesn't compare to the biggest shocker of all: After five years of dating and a lifetime of celibacy, he's ready to have coitus for the first time.

The episode features the return of Bob Newhart as the late Arthur Jeffries—who acts as Sheldon's own Obi-Wan Kenobi—helping to guide him through this momentous occasion in his life. But the most satisfying part is seeing Amy react to Sheldon's surprise announcement, and what happens when the two finally consummate their relationship. Here the story of how "The Opening Night Excitation," often considered the best in the series' run, came to be:

Peter Roth: I used to hound Steve Molaro about Amy and Sheldon. *Hound* him about whether they would ever have coitus. I really did. And Steve used to take delight in saying, "Peter, you are gonna love this upcoming episode so much!"

Steve Molaro: It was such a delicate thing to have Sheldon and Amy finally have sex. I had been sitting on them sleeping together being an "annual event" for years. It would either be Valentine's Day or her birthday, and obviously we decided on her birthday. We're all so protective of them as a couple and as characters, so there was this immense pressure to get the moment as good as we thought it could be. And then when you actually start putting the plan into motion, it's scary. Especially something like that. Most people have been through that experience for the first time and it's scary. It's intense and surreal and weird, so why pretend it wouldn't be?

Nikki Lorre: There was an energy that everyone wanted to get this right. I think my dad and the rest of the writers never thought they would get to this point, but if the show goes on for so long, and we're exploring this relationship, it's no longer avoidable. For the longest time, they just never wanted to make Sheldon a sexual being, and now that they were crossing that bridge... it was not that it was jumping the shark, but it felt like it had that potential. Like, if we don't do this right and treat it with the utmost respect, then we could really put people off. There was this excited energy, but also wanting to make sure not to taint a very beloved couple. [But] the audience just lost their minds. I was very impressed with how they managed that.

Steve Holland: Their relationship took off on its own from the moment they met, and it was so much fun to write for. But even though you want to show their growth, you're also worried about what part of the show you can't break and have it still feel like *The Big Bang Theory*. We wanted to make sure Sheldon wasn't suddenly going to be a lothario or feel like a different person in a weird way.

Mayim Bialik: I would have been happy for their relationship to never be sexual, and instead just be a romantic, intimate love. I didn't know if we were ready for it. And I think it was really neat to have a nonsexual committed relationship on a sitcom. So Jim and I were both surprised that the writers were ready to take it to this level. But, also in hindsight, I still believe that our writers are correct.

Jim Parsons: The writers have done so many things with these characters that have been seemingly out of line with what was expected, but they always handle it in an organic way that is based on where the show has actually gone to and come from. It's like, *Well, who knew?!*

Since season one, Sheldon always referred to intercourse as "coitus." It's a way for him to talk about sex matter-of-factly and in clinical terms without having an emotional connection.

Chuck Lorre: *Coitus* was a clinical word that seemed appropriate for Sheldon, because he wouldn't use slang. Having Sheldon speak technically about sex felt appropriate. It's a biological expression, as far as he is concerned. But not anymore because he had an emotional experience with Amy. It's a huge growth for the character.

Steve Holland: Which is why before the episode happened, Molaro thought that whenever they do sleep together, Amy should get super nervous beforehand, and Sheldon has to be the calm one who talks her through it.

Steve Molaro: When you have a situation like Sheldon being with a woman for the first time and needing advice in that area, we realized it was the perfect opportunity to bring back Bob Newhart. The pieces started to fall into place, especially with the premiere of *Star Wars* looming.

Jim Parsons: There was no one more inappropriate, and therefore perfect, to be on Sheldon's-losing-his-virginity episode than Bob Newhart. He's just ideal. That's actually the other component of it. No one could be less interested, bordering on *Please don't tell me this*, than Bob Newhart as Arthur Jeffries as Obi-Wan. [*Laughs*]

Steve Holland: I'm a huge *Star Wars* fan, so I had the thought that *The Force Awakens* could be the thing that Sheldon could give up for Amy's birthday. It wasn't even about the coitus. It was just as a gift to Amy, he could skip the *Star Wars* premiere and spend her birthday with her, which seemed like a really sweet thing. And because it was her birthday, that meant we could say it would be an annual event that we could do once a year. That way Sheldon was still pretty much Sheldon.

Mayim Bialik didn't even know that an episode about Sheldon and Amy having coitus was in the works. After all, Amy had just broken up with Dave (played by Stephen Merchant) and reunited with Sheldon after a break that lasted nearly ten episodes.

Mayim Bialik: We found out the big moment was happening the night before we did the table read. I always wait until the next morning right before we sit down at the table to go over the script, but this time I started reading, and I passed Jim in the hallway and said, "Did you read the script yet?!" He said, "No. Do we do it?" and I said, "Yes!" He was like, "*What?!*" He just threw it out there as a joke. We couldn't believe it.

Jim Parsons: It was really insane. One of the great things from my experience at least, was that I never knew what was coming. When Mayim said that we "do it," I went, "Oh! Oh my God." I mean, it was a wild guess! It was absurdist to think that's what would happen.

Tara Hernandez: Because we were working up to all these moments prior to their breakup, we knew they needed to get there, but we also needed to put Sheldon through the paces to really earn this relationship with Amy. The period of their breakup was really to get Sheldon to a place where he wanted these things, which was a hard place for this character. But it felt like once they were back on track, they were really back on track. She wanted to be together in a real way, and we knew that Sheldon had to want it, so he needed to be in a place where he felt compelled to do it. And by losing her [to Dave], he got there.

Melissa Rauch: I heard rumblings there would be an episode coming up where Sheldon and Amy would be getting down to business. The script came in when we were at the taping for the prior episode, so there was buzzing about the fact that this was happening. But I didn't get to read it until I got home late that night. I remember yelling to my husband in the other room because the script was just so good. The next day at the table read, I congratulated Mayim on the upcoming loss of Amy's V-card. We had a good laugh about it.

Mayim Bialik: I didn't even tell my mother about Sheldon and Amy sleeping together! I was so embarrassed! I let her find out through a friend of ours that came to the taping, and he texted her afterwards and wrote, "I can't believe I got to see them have sex!" and my mother goes, "*What?!*" I was so embarrassed to tell my own mother!

From the start, the episode was unlike any other. Instead of the traditional opening scene, the producers went with a text scroll, just like in *Star Wars*. It read: "A short time ago in an apartment in Pasadena…" followed by the iconic Lucasfilm score. It continued, "Episode 194 The Opening Night Excitation: It is a period of great tension. Our heroes, Leonard, Sheldon, Wolowitz and Koothrappali know that tickets to the new *Star Wars* movie are about to be available for pre-sale. If they fail in their mission and can't see it on opening night Sheldon has sworn that they will never hear the end of it for the rest of their lives..." There's a double line break followed by these last words: "They believe him."

Steve Molaro: We knew it was a special episode, so the scroll helped it to feel that way right out of the gate. But we were worried we might not be able to get the score or that it would be crazy expensive. Either it wasn't as bad as we feared, or we paid a lot and I just blocked it out. But I can't think of a more fun, powerful, fitting piece of score to kick off the episode where Sheldon and Amy finally have coitus than the opening fanfare of *Star Wars*. It's perfect.

It was more than fitting, given that the timeline perfectly aligned with *The Force Awakens*'s debut in theaters. And so, in the first scene after the scroll introduction, Sheldon, Leonard, Raj, and Wolowitz are frantically trying to get their tickets for the movie.

Steve Holland: That was exactly what happened to us trying to get tickets. We were all on our phones trying to buy tickets and they were sold out, and everyone was like, "Did you get in? Did you get in?" And then finally someone got in, and was like, "I got in! I got in! How many tickets should I buy?!" That scene was us.

In addition to a guest appearance by Newhart, the writers also brought back Wil Wheaton to take Sheldon's Star Wars *ticket. Wheaton shows up to the theater wearing his Wesley Crusher* Star Trek *uniform, complete with Spock ears.*

Wil Wheaton: "Live long and suck it" is probably my favorite line I've ever gotten to say when I walk into the theater. None of the actors knew I was going to be wearing the Spock ears. When I walked out like that, it was the hardest I have killed in my career, and I didn't even do anything! I just walked through the door. It's like all the years of character building and everything came into that particular moment.

All the guys are wearing *Star Wars*–themed shirts to watch *Star Wars: The Force Awakens*, except for Wheaton, who shows up in his *Star Trek* attire, complete with Spock ears. *Photo™ & © Warner Bros. Entertainment Inc.*

Some of the funniest moments from the episode weren't even the scenes with Sheldon and Amy in bed. Rather, it was how Sheldon decides to tell Penny and Bernadette that he's ready to have coitus, as well as Amy's reaction once she finds out what Sheldon has planned.

Steve Molaro: Around the time we were breaking the script, I was at the wine bar, Augustine, in Sherman Oaks, with a couple of the writers, and we were talking about the moment Penny and Bernadette react to Sheldon's plans. I happened to be holding my wineglass and Holland said, "It would be great if Penny just snapped the top of the glass right off of the stem." We thought that was really funny. It took a couple of tries on set, but a special glass was made that Kaley would be able to pop the top off with enough pressure and without her getting hurt. Eventually we got the perfect take of it after a few tries.

Melissa Rauch: I can picture both Jim's perfect delivery of the coitus line and Kaley's perfect deadpan expression as she breaks that glass. It still cracks me up. I was so worried I was going to laugh during a take when the glass broke correctly and then I'd ruin it. I remember Kaley saying it was really "satisfying" to crush the glass.

Jim Parsons: I was focused on that wineglass and if Kaley would pull it off, only because those props work about 90 percent of the time and the 10 percent it doesn't, it takes forever to get right. It's like, *In this major revealing moment, we're going to depend on a prop gag where we break away a wineglass stem? OK!* But it worked! And it's a good thing too, because there's nothing harder than a well-timed double take from two of your colleagues looking at you, which is exactly what that moment was built to be. And that is hard to sit through, especially with those two sweet faces. [*Laughs*]

Steve Holland: Mayim Bialik is just so good, but I love the scene in the

The moment right before Penny snapped the stem off her wineglass when Sheldon revealed that the third option for Amy's birthday gift would be to have coitus with her. Appropriately, the audience went nuts. *Photo™ & © Warner Bros. Entertainment Inc.*

stairway when Bernadette and Penny tell Amy about Sheldon's plan to have coitus. The way she says, "Shut your damn mouth!" is everything. I think that line was Steve Molaro's. She said it exactly how we wrote it, but she also took it to the next level with her delivery. That delighted screaming gets me every time.

Mayim Bialik: I get asked about "Shut your damn mouth!" a lot. I'm pretty sure that's how I rehearsed it. I always tend to go really broad in my performance and then let them pull me back if they need to. That was one where they didn't pull me back very much. [*Laughs*]

Jim Parsons: I love that line! But I'll let you in on a secret—unless I had guests in my dressing room who were there to watch the taping or hang out, I never kept the live feed on my TV on, so I wouldn't have watched that scene as it was happening. I found it distracting in a weird way. For one thing, I liked to run lines between scenes, and the second thing, I find that watching scenes being taped puts me in a weird headspace, especially if they're having to suddenly do rewrites on a scene. My mind starts thinking, *Oh my gosh, we'll never get to this scene! I hope I'm awake! Should I eat?* I start doing all that and I don't need to do that. [*Laughs*] [But] I would have heard that line from any point at that stage when she shouted it. That's why it echoed in my head—"Shut your damn mouth!" [*Laughs*] I remember it so well!

Tara Hernandez: I think we realized anytime the characters shouted anything, it was hilarious. And Mayim was so good at that. You put the things on the page and hope they're going to work or they are as funny as they were in the room, and eleven times out of ten, the cast is beyond what you wanted, and Mayim's going so extreme in that moment is why we love Amy. She's so authentically explosive in her emotions and says exactly what we're all feeling.

Melissa Rauch: I also remember sharing a look with Kaley when Mayim hit that waxing line—"Let's go get me waxed!"—out of the park. The elated energy coming from the audience was palpable.

Mayim Bialik: Melissa said there was one woman in the audience who was holding her head like she might have a seizure, God forbid! We didn't know! We were afraid we might have to reinforce the railings! I said to Jim, "They might rush the court like after a basketball game!"

Melissa Rauch: Yes, there was that one woman who was holding her head like it was going to explode. I remember the crew joking that the audience was going to go so nuts about coitus happening that they were going to jump onto the stage. I mean, I get it. Not only was a big moment happening for our show, but add in the fact that these audience members were there to witness it being filmed. I locked eyes with a few people, and another lady mouthed to me: *Holy shit* and I mouthed back, *I know, right?!*

Once it came time to show Amy and Sheldon in the bedroom, there was a lot of consideration not just about their dialogue, but what Amy would be wearing.

Steve Molaro: All of us were instinctively on the same page about what Amy should wear for the big moment. Her nightgown shouldn't be overly sexy, but it should be sort of modest so that it would play to the sweetness of what that scene was. When I saw it, I thought, *Wow, they really nailed it. That's exactly what she should wear.*

Mary T. Quigley: I always wanted it to be modest and old-school, and it was. It was a new nightie that she bought and thought was beautiful, and it actually had a matching little robe with the little ruffle trim and tiny rose-buds. It showed that that can be special to a woman, and sexiness isn't just limited to a teddy. That nightgown empowered Amy because it was sexy to *her.*

As soon as Amy and Sheldon got into bed, they discussed the gravity of the moment and whether they were ready. It was a beautiful scene featuring two grown adults talking about consent, and interestingly enough, the episode occurred a year before the #MeToo movement, where the topic of consent on television wasn't as common as it is now.

Nikki Lorre: Especially consent when it comes to a character like Sheldon, where they never deemed him asexual, but he was played that way for the longest time. And then you have a character like Amy, who is a sexual being, or discovering she is. In order to evolve this relationship, compromises need to be made, and you don't want to offend anyone…because there is a community of people who identify as asexual. You don't want to upset anyone by assuming that there's something weird or wrong with them because this doesn't feel normal or right to them. Physicality was always a very uncom-fortable thing for Sheldon, but he was willing to explore it because he loves someone so much, which was a perfect way to talk about consent.

Mayim Bialik: I love this notion of consent, and this was one of the *really* sweet aspects of Amy and Sheldon's relationship. Because they communicated so differently than a lot of other people do, there were aspects of their conversation which intuitively made a tremendous amount of sense, being able to say, "I'm going to do this. Are you OK with this?" It's a really beautiful lesson for all sorts of relationships. I remember hearing from a lot of young people, or parents of young people, about how important it was how Amy and Sheldon dealt with that, and obviously the credit is all to our writers.

> Even earlier in the episode, Penny says to Sheldon, "Sheldon, being physical with Amy is a huge step for you." It was a further example of Penny's growth; years earlier she would have egged Sheldon on. But now she was protective and cautious.

Jim Parsons: Right. Over the years in a lot of scenes—even ones Sheldon wasn't in—she was the one protecting him, or worried for him. In this case, he's matured enough to be ready to be sexually intimate, and yet she is still wondering if this is something he's ready for. She cared about what happened to him, even though he was a pain in the ass.

> Sheldon tells Penny, "Intimacy in any form has been challenging for me, but I'd like to show her how important she is, and it feels like now might be the right time." Penny says, "Sheldon, that's so beautiful." He says, "Then it's settled. Amy's birthday present will be my genitals."

Mayim Bialik: We usually see it the other way around, where the male wants sex all the time and the woman doesn't, and it's a trope we're all kind of bored with, just as a society. Like, we get it. So I thought it was a very sweet way to show some of the creativity of this couple, meaning Amy's patience, in terms of commitment and other forms of intimacy. That was really important, because there were years where they didn't really touch!

> The bedroom scene was filmed without a studio audience, mainly to put Parsons and Bialik at ease. At the episode's taping, those scenes were played back on a monitor.

Jim Parsons: My very favorite thing so far has been the after-sex scene with Amy and Sheldon. I never had the opportunity to relate to anybody in that kind of way on the show, like a pillow-talk scene. I was like, "There's a whole other way to talk on this show that I didn't have access to before!" It was just a more intimate style of acting, meaning not only were you in closer physical proximity to each other, but because of where the bedrooms were on set, we would preshoot those scenes, which was a lovely change of pace. There was just a way of being able to communicate where you were able to take your foot off the gas in a way that you weren't always able to do on the other sets we used. And because of that, I looked forward to doing it again—to being back in bed!

Mark Cendrowski: The script [direction] said: *They wake up. They've just done it for the first time.* And Jim is sitting there very quietly, and you cut over to Mayim. Now, on camera, that's easy to do. But for a runthrough, where everyone's standing there, I can't hide that fact. So during that first runthrough, I had my prop guy get a big piece of show card, and had Mayim mess up her hair. I think we smudged some lipstick on her face. I made her put her glasses askew. And when I called "Action," we see Jim, and then the prop guy pulls the card away, and there's Mayim in all her glory with a crazed look on her face. And it got a huge laugh from the producers. I couldn't wait to shoot it that way for the audience, because the audience wasn't going to see the set-up. And when they did, it worked great.

Steve Holland: I think that was probably the scene we spent the most time going over and tweaking. It's also why we didn't want to put Sheldon and Amy in front of an audience for that particular scene. We didn't want any *ooh*s and *oh*s getting in the way of Jim's and Mayim's performances.

Jim Parsons: And once we had a more physical relationship in the show and more scenes in bed, it was really nice to have a quieter level of scenes with someone, compared to the more robust and energetic situations. I really treasured the more intimate and quiet moments. It's a different way of talking, a different way of listening. She became in a lot of ways, kind of like my partner in crime. And just like so many others on our show, I finally had my person, too. Mayim and I have just had such different lives, and something about that makes our easy connection all the more special to me. Whatever it is, I'm grateful for it.

Melissa Rauch: Watching the postcoitus scene on the monitor onstage while watching the audience watch it…I think everyone had the feeling that TV history was being created.

Steve Molaro: They had the advantage of being much more unique characters, where you've got two people who have never slept together who were almost forty or whatever they were, and experiencing a lot of firsts—for two different reasons—together. That's not a thing we could show with Leonard and Penny, which was a bit more of a traditional relationship, although different in its own way.

In a moment certainly no one could have predicted five years earlier, Sheldon and Amy had coitus. And enjoyed it. *Photo ™ & © Warner Bros. Entertainment Inc.*

Amy and Sheldon basking in the afterglow of coitus was juxtaposed with Leonard, Raj, and Howard sitting in the movie theater feeling the same sense of exhilaration, satisfaction ("I don't think I can walk right now," says a mesmerized Koothrappali) and relief about *The Force Awakens*.

Steve Holland: It was Tara Hernandez's pitch that we could intercut Leonard, Howard, and Raj's nervousness before watching *The Force Awakens* in the theater with Amy's nervousness about coitus, as well as the afterglow for the guys with the movie, and the afterglow for Sheldon and Amy. It was so great.

Mark Hamill: I really relate to what the guys on the show love. And that's why that scene is so funny when the guys look like they just had sex after they finish seeing the new *Star Wars* film.

Steve Holland: But when the guys talked about how great *The Force Awakens* was, that was on good faith that it wasn't going to be another *Phantom Menace*, since we wrote and filmed the episode before we got to see the movie!

Steve Molaro: We heard buzz that it was supposed to be good, so we took a leap on that.

Peter Roth: That was one of my favorite, if not my favorite, episodes of all time. I remember reading the script and thinking, *This is brilliant and so funny*. The execution of it was everything that I had hoped. It was not just simply that they had sex; it was also juxtaposed with the premiere of *Star Wars*, and Leonard, Raj, and Wolowitz's orgasmic experience to seeing the film.

But once the episode was filmed, the biggest question was how to keep it a secret. It would be another three to four weeks until it aired on CBS, and while you wanted to trust the studio audience not to post spoilers online, it's nearly impossible.

Steve Holland: We asked the audience not to say anything, but you can't really enforce it. We just hoped that they would realize that they should let viewers at home experience that moment as they watched it on TV.

As a result—but mainly to increase ratings—the publicity departments at CBS and Warner Bros. decided to get ahead of any spoilers and reveal the big news that same evening. In an email sent to journalists on November 17, 2015, it said: "*The Big Bang Theory* taped an episode tonight which airs Thursday, December 17. The episode features Sheldon and Amy consummating their relationship for the first time after more than five years of dating, although they are currently broken up. (At this time, we are not confirming whether they are back together as a couple.) Further details about the episode are being kept under wraps. Once we have the episode to share, we will be setting up interviews closer to the airdate."

Mayim Bialik: I try not to weigh in too much on marketing stuff, but I think the fact that we did set a TV record for live viewership with that episode shows that the marketing paid off. The interest was less *will they or won't they* at that point, and more *what is it going to be like*, because people had fallen in love with those characters and their journey.

Jim Parsons: In an ideal world, all of that should be only revealed to the viewer who happens to tune in at that moment. But in the business scheme, it makes all the sense in the world. You hear about movie trailers all the time, but it's true of TV shows, too. There are so few things left to reveal once you get there, so you better do it well once people tune in. I wouldn't say there was any disappointment on my end that the studio revealed what was going to happen, but it's just not as fun!

Chapter 19

MISCARRIAGE, PREGNANCY, AND THE VERY REAL TRUTHS ABOUT PARENTHOOD

During *The Big Bang Theory*'s run, no storyline commanded more attention or interest among *Glamour*'s readership than Bernadette's pregnancy and postpartum struggle. While pregnancy stories on TV shows are nothing new, the writers tapped into the emotions that so many women go through and still don't talk about. From the start (season five, to be exact), Bernadette said she wasn't crazy about children, and didn't shy away from letting Howard know. "My mother worked full-time. I had to take care of my brothers and sisters. It was horrible. With their snotty noses...always complaining... I'm sorry, I know it makes me sound like a bad person, but I just don't like children." And she didn't stop there. She spoke of the changes she would experience with her body, with her career, with her social life, and more. It wasn't until years later—and after Howard's mother died—that she began to think about her own legacy and her future with Howard. When she did become pregnant with their first child, the result was richer storytelling that opened up plenty of avenues for a couple who wasn't afraid to dwell in the discomfort of the unknown.

However, in season nine, when the writers first told Simon Helberg and Melissa Rauch that they'd be embarking on a pregnancy storyline for the Wolowitzes (which, interestingly enough, wasn't even in the initial outline for "The Valentino Submergence" and came about only after Molaro half-jokingly mentioned it in the writers room), they both had concerns for two very different reasons.

Simon Helberg: We rarely ever went to producers or writers with any kind of concerns, especially story concerns. That might have been the only time. It wasn't even a deep concern. It was more to hear what Molaro was thinking and to voice what we were slightly wary of, which was potentially upending the dynamic of what existed. How would we sit around and have Chinese food? What happens to our role in the group? Not from an *Oh God, I'm going to be written off the show* vein but from a place of loving what we had created on the show. And was there going to be a real baby on set all the time? I leave my house in real life where there are babies, and this is the one place there aren't babies, and now we're going to have an actor baby? That's a nightmare! [*Laughs*] So there was some of that, too.

Melissa Rauch: For me, it was twofold. It was the interpersonal concern of realizing that things weren't going to line up in my personal life for me to get pregnant at the same time as Bernadette. I was concerned, like, *Oh, if we do it now, that ship has sailed for them to do it again when my timeline does line up.* And then the other concern was how a baby would change the dynamic among all these characters.

Steve Molaro: They came to me and said, "How is this going to change the fabric of the show?" Luckily, the answer was, "It's not going to, because we're never going to see their kid." The baby was just going to be an off-screen presence, like his mom.

Melissa Rauch: He assured us that *Big Bang* wasn't all of a sudden going to become a family sitcom where they're caring for a baby 24/7. He assured us it wasn't going to take us out of the friendship circle with the other characters, which was important for us. Because even in real life, when you have a baby your friendships as you know it shift. You can't do the sort of things you normally do and have the hangouts you normally have.

Simon Helberg: Molaro was like, "We're not bringing babies on the set and it's going to be a gold mine of stories." We weren't going to fight [the decision] anyway; it was really about how do you keep the *Big Bang Theory* vibe going when two of the group now have a baby and most of the show exists with people who sit around playing games, eating food, and being kind of independent. How do we reconcile that? But it was great.

Helberg was already a dad to two young kids when Howard learned he was going to be a first-time father in season nine, episode sixteen ("The Positive Negative Reaction"). Appropriately, even though Howard wanted kids of his own, he freaked out upon learning that his wish was becoming a reality.

Simon Helberg: It's a very humbling moment when you learn you're going to become a parent. For myself, it's a beautiful moment and a profound moment, but simultaneously there are doubts and fears and responsibilities that are going to come up because we all have probably had complicated childhoods and relationships with our parents. And particularly with Howard, who really had no father figure in his life, he didn't have that role model. There was no blueprint for him.

Melissa Rauch: I think the freak-out and the question speaks to all the fear associated with a new parent, and just being a parent in general. You're responsible for this fragile human life, and you really don't have any practical, hands-on experience. Everything is theoretical as far as what you read and classes you take, but it's the greatest responsibility that you could possibly have. You just realize you have to figure it out, day by day, and know that your heart is gonna be walking around outside of your body at some point, and all that you can do is your best on a daily basis. No matter how many questions you ask, or how you try to control it, your job is just to love them and guide them and keep them safe. The fact that those questions were explored was just another layer. And then of all people, to have it be Howard who's going through this, spoke to the beautiful job these writers did with evolving these characters. It's one of the reasons why Howard's journey into fatherhood was beautiful to watch. It was human. You may not have had interest in engineering or a quantum gyroscope, but we all understand what it's like to embark on a huge life change and struggle with the unknown.

Simon Helberg: And that was the same episode we did karaoke at the end, so it was just such fun. Those kinds of stories were the most fun to play.

Melissa Rauch: I remember just loving that scene where I'm sitting on stage in this karaoke bar as everyone starts singing songs with the word "baby" in it to Bernadette. I had to get into a zone of "Do not laugh," because they're working really hard, but I was so afraid I was going to blow a take.

Perhaps one of the greatest karaoke scenes on the show was the montage where everyone ser-enaded a pregnant Bernadette with songs that had the word "baby" in it (except for Sheldon, who sang "America (My Country 'Tis of Thee)"). *Courtesy of Kaley Cuoco photo collection*

Mayim Bialik: I did not know Justin Bieber's song, "Baby," [when Kaley and I] did that karaoke moment, but I loved anytime I got to sing. Mark Cendrowski had a lot of great ideas in terms of our movement onstage. Sometimes Chuck would chime in with things like that that had choreography. I always have ideas, which I think makes a lot of people dislike me, because I'm always like, "I have an idea!" and that can be obnoxious. I'm aware of that. [*Laughs*]

Melissa Rauch: I remember Mayim saying "What is this song?" [*Laughs*] And then Kunal singing [Salt-N-Pepa's "Push It" with the lyrics], "Oooh, baby, baby!" I had a hard time holding it together there. Then you had Johnny almost grunting as he sang, "Push it! Push it real good!" That one I feel like I ruined some takes on. And I was so delighted when Simon sang [The Four Tops'] "Baby, I need your loving! Got...to have all your loving!"

Simon Helberg: I remember really looking into Melissa's eyes as I always was fortunate enough to get to do, and to do that dance together.

Melissa Rauch: I really scored having Simon as my TV husband. Whenever I was out with my own husband, people would shout at him, "Hey! You're not Howard!" And my husband, Winston, who loves Simon as much as I do, would say, "I get it! He's awesome—trust me, I wish he was here, too!"

Bernadette's pregnancy was mentioned in pretty much every episode for the remainder of season nine, but it was really the start of season ten where Bernadette—and Rauch—got to put the spotlight on what mothers actually go through leading up to the birth of a child.

In the second episode of the season—"The Military Miniaturization"— Bernadette hesitates to tell her coworkers that she's pregnant for fear of missing out on a significant research project. "I've worked so hard to get where I am and I don't want to get sent back to square one because I'm pregnant," she says.

Steve Holland: Companies should in no way pass someone over for an opportunity because of an upcoming maternity leave, but it doesn't mean that they don't. That storyline really opened up Bernadette's vulnerability about being pregnant.

Chuck Lorre: Two of our remarkable writers, Maria Ferrari and Tara Hernandez, brought the element of a woman whose passion was work, and the conflict between work, motherhood, and cultural expectations of what [that's like]. Those are stories that we never anticipated in the creation of the show, but they were real. People responded to them because they resonated. Maria was very determined to make the "mom" stories something we hadn't seen before. She was a new mom while we were doing the show, so those things were very much in her purview, and I think helped steer Bernadette into a much richer area, instead of *Oh, here's a funny situation.* She was conflicted over where her priorities should be and what she was supposed to be because of certain cultural expectations, as opposed to *I'm simply who I am*. Somehow we managed to stumble into making much better stories and the supporting cast became lead players, and every bit as critical as the original cast.

> That sentiment was never more apparent than in the following episode—"The Dependence Transcendence"—when Bernadette tells Raj she doesn't feel she has a maternal instinct. She tells him she keeps waiting to feel excited, but it's not happening. It ends up being Raj's father who provides the most sound advice, telling her that "some people are baby people. Some people are not baby people. Doesn't mean you won't love your own baby. Being excited isn't a guarantee of anything."
>
> Digital media brand Refinery29 noted that "the episode touched on the darker and more confusing part of pregnancy," while Allyson Koerner at digital media site SheKnows wrote (December 13, 2016): "[*The Big Bang Theory*] has shown an entirely new perspective of motherhood. It's not for everyone and not every mom feels the same way about pregnancy or raising children…The series has turned a pregnant character into an inspiring woman who is showing a different side to pregnancy, all while giving a voice to women who aren't maternal and showing them and everyone else there is nothing wrong with that."

Melissa Rauch: I remember reading that script and thinking this was not something we've seen before. They really shined a light on feelings that women can have that often aren't portrayed on sitcoms.

Maria Ferrari: The line that "some people are baby people and some people aren't baby people" kind of came from my best friend. Some of us discovered as we were becoming parents that we were really looking forward to when our kids could read books or talk. Some people just weren't into the plant stage of the baby, meaning there's not much to do with them other than feed them, change their diaper, and get them to sleep. My friends took great comfort in being able to say, "Some of these parts are boring." Another thing was, people always say, "Enjoy every minute" when you're with your newborn, and that was maddening to us. Because when you're in the thick of it and when you're sleep-deprived and can't see straight, you feel like you're being tortured. We wanted to articulate that you don't have to feel *any* way. Personally, I did not enjoy being pregnant, which I was three times over the course of the show and I hated it every time. I felt insecure and awkward, like it was the only thing people could notice about me. I'll never forget walking over to the stage one day when a [Warner Bros.] tour bus was driving by—and here I am a producer on a TV show with my script in hand—when one of the tour guides literally said on the speaker, "And over there we have a very, very pregnant lady!" It was such a bummer. I felt conspicuous. So a lot of Bernadette's maternal angst, I just transferred out of my pregnancy angst.

Melissa Rauch: There was such raw honesty in everything that she put into Bernadette. Although I didn't experience the exact anxieties Bernadette did once I became pregnant in real life, I definitely had my fair share. I remember going to a baby store to check out some of the baby gear other parents said I needed, and the clerk was trying to show me how to use everything, like how to fold a stroller, strap on the baby carrier, etc., and

Rauch and Helberg take a break during filming "The Birthday Synchronicity," where Bernadette gives birth to daughter Halley. *Photo courtesy of Kaley Cuoco photo collection*

it was like she was speaking a foreign language. I was on the verge of sheer panic, of "How will I be able to figure all of this out?!" but then I was thinking about what Bernadette had gone through—and granted, I know it's fictionalized, but seeing how in the end none of it mattered and Bernadette was an amazing mother, was comforting. You find your way with your own children, so that was a lesson for me as a mom and something I took from the show.

The lessons extended beyond pregnancy concerns and motherhood. The series was essentially showing how important it was not to assume what anybody else is feeling just because society has told us to.

Kunal Nayyar: I really loved the non-cliché ways in which we really approached relationships and topics, like Bernadette saying, "I don't have a maternal instinct." I think we live in a society where we are supposed to accept our gender roles, but oftentimes what we experience within us are not those roles. So it just feels like everyone's walking around in somebody else's story and not their own, and that's why this was so beautiful to watch. Viewers who related to this moment felt, *Oh, I'm not crazy.* Our harshest voice is our own, so when we realize there are people out there who are embarrassed to admit that they might suck at being a parent, it's like, *All right, I'm not alone.* That's why I love the show.

Melissa Rauch: It was so beautifully done and not in a way that was in your face; it wasn't preachy, it wasn't "A Very Special Episode Of." Our entry in was through humor and comedy, and it gave women permission to have this honesty and this vulnerability around pregnancy. I'm very sensitive to the fact, having gone through it myself, especially as someone for whom pregnancy and birth didn't come easy. So, it felt very hard-fought and very earned, and something that I very much wanted. But then you feel like, "Well, this is something that I wanted and I struggled for, but it's not all sunshine and rainbows when it happens, either." It's uncomfortable! There's fears! There's physical discomfort! And you almost feel like you'd be ungrateful to say anything negative about it when it's something you desperately wanted. But nothing is ever so cut-and-dry. I love that this allowed a conversation about all the different feelings and gray areas of this next chapter, whether it's how expensive it is to have a child, or how to raise a child, or anything. I felt very honored to get to say those words and to be the vessel for that messaging.

Steve Holland: These are stories we couldn't have done in season three or season four. I mean, why wouldn't you want to tell the story of Howard finding the love of his life and becoming a father? So we latched on to those moments, like Bernadette not wanting to be pregnant or feeling like she didn't have a maternal instinct. Or Wolowitz feeling that since he didn't really have a father figure in his life, how would that affect him as a father? Those were real moments and a core we could build around.

At the midpoint in season ten, Bernadette gave birth to a daughter, Halley, and in another deviation from typical TV birthing episodes, the producers decided not to show Bernadette in labor. Molaro told *Glamour* at the time, "That is an area that has been covered so well and so many times on TV shows that I just thought, let's not have her screaming and pushing the baby out....I was more interested in what the gang was talking about in the waiting room while that was happening."

When the show came back with new episodes at the start of 2017, the producers and writers made a commitment to continue to show Bernadette's struggle with parenthood. In "The Holiday Summation," Bernadette is in sweats, covered in spit-up, her hair a mess, and walking around like a zombie thanks to a sleepless Halley. She discovers that the only way to get her to sleep is to climb into the crib and lay beside her.

Maria Ferrari: Since I'm five feet tall, and drop-rail cribs are illegal now, I can't reach into the crib all the way to put my baby in there. If the rail is up to your waist, you have to take your child, who you've been rocking to sleep, and then lower them down. The only way I could do it would be to step in and squat down until the baby was on the mattress, and then climb out of the crib like a ninja, but at any point the baby could wake up. So a lot of times I would just sleep in the crib, which is sad, but it was the only way I could get any sleep. If I left, the floor would squeak, or the baby could sense it was less warm because I would move. It was a piece of parenting I could never figure out, and I remember laying there thinking, *This is really undignified, and I can't believe there's not another option. Here I am, a relatively smart professional person, and yet I'm living in this crib now!*

Melissa Rauch: Maria's got a little height on me, but I had the same experience with these cribs, so I would be doing the same thing. I would put [my daughter in], and then I'd run back to a chair, and then the baby would wake up again. So one night, I climbed in and I slept there. She slept the whole night long, and that was all thanks to Maria and Bernadette. I slept with my baby in the crib more often than not. And I owe that to Bernadette paving the way

Executive producer/writer Maria Ferrari drew on her own experience as a mother to help tell meaningful stories about Bernadette as a new mom. It resonated deeply with Rauch (pictured here), when she gave birth to her own daughter a year later. *Courtesy of Melissa Rauch*

for me. I even have a recollection of being in there and reading the episode for the next day on my phone, laying in a crib, because there was so much time spent there.

Sleeping arrangements weren't the only things that changed. Bernadette's style of cropped cardigans, dresses, and tights were gone after she gave birth to Halley. That was a decision that came directly from Rauch and costume designer Mary T. Quigley.

Melissa Rauch: After Bernadette gave birth, Mary and I talked a lot about Bernadette's wardrobe. I loved the episode when Bernadette was in that purple sweatshirt, thinking what the heck is going on postpartum. It started a conversation because we didn't want to set an unrealistic example of getting back to your pre-mother self right away. I thought it would be doing a disservice to the mothers who watch the show to all the sudden have me back in the tights and fitted cardigans. We made a decision for Bernadette to evolve out of the cardigans and the tights after she became a mother. There's this unrealistic expectation of losing your baby weight and getting your body back right away, and that's just not how it is. We wanted it to feel real, to mirror everything Bernadette was going through and the struggles she was facing as a new mom. She wore loose-fitting, button-down tops, which made it easier to breastfeed. She wore jeans for the first time, which were maternity jeans. And then when I had my own daughter and was breastfeeding during rehearsals and tapings, I remember thinking getting into those tight dresses and cardigans would have been hell for me, so I was very happy to have this new style for Bernadette.

Mary T. Quigley: It was really important to me and her to show, no, you're not a size zero a week after you have a baby. I said, "How about we leave her like this? She doesn't need to get back to the sweaters and the dresses because she's progressed anyway. She's a mother." She still looked great, but we didn't want to always make her look perfect. Sometimes I'd tell the hair department, "Can you please mess her hair up? I don't want her to look like she just got out of the salon."

Melissa Rauch: It was real. That's what you look like.

As Bernadette was becoming a mother for the first time and experiencing the highs and lows of caring for a newborn, no one knew that Rauch and her husband were going through their own journey to parenthood. Rauch became pregnant, and then, as all too common for so many women, had a miscarriage shortly thereafter. She chose not to go public with the news until the summer of 2017, as *Big Bang* was heading into its eleventh season. In an essay for *Glamour* (July 11, 2017), Rauch opened up about the immense sadness she experienced over the previous year, as well as the joy—and apprehension—in announcing that she and her husband were expecting again.

She wrote, "The miscarriage I experienced was one of the most profound sorrows I have ever felt in my life. It kick-started a primal depression that lingered in me. The image of our baby on the ultrasound monitor—without movement, without a heartbeat—after we had seen that same little heart healthy and flickering just two weeks prior completely blindsided us and haunts me to this day. I kept waiting for the sadness to lift...but it *didn't*. Sure, I had happy moments, and life went on, but the heartbreak was always lurking. Inescapable reminders, like the unfulfilled due date, came around like a heavy cloud. A day I had once marked on my calendar with such excitement was now a memorial of a crushed dream."

Melissa Rauch: I felt very vulnerable writing that essay and sharing it with the world, but ultimately it felt like a freedom. I was even hearing from women who experienced this thirty years ago but had never spoken about it. There was something so amazing in that, but the public nature of this job is something I never accounted for. I knew I wanted to be an actor, I knew I loved performing, but I'm super shy and wildly private, and so the feeling of being out there publicly with *anything* is something that was very hard for me. But when I did open up, I was so glad. I was still always scared I would go through a miscarriage again, but by having the article out there, it was like, *OK, everyone knows, and it's OK, and let's talk about this.* I'm so glad it freed up on the conversation. Even now, when someone tells me they're pregnant, they'll often tell me, "and I also had a miscarriage," or "I struggled fertility-wise." And I don't think that conversation would happen so organically if people didn't know that's something I understand or want to talk about, and I'm very grateful for that. Being publicly pregnant, I think that I would have felt, in some way, that it would be inauthentic if I didn't share my experience. I didn't want people to read an article that I was pregnant, and think, *Oh, I bet that was easy for her.* I wanted to be as open as I could.

Before the essay was published, Rauch informed her costars, as well as Lorre, Prady, Molaro, and Holland that she was expecting her first child.

Melissa Rauch: I called everyone individually, and I knew they'd be great about it—which they were—but it was still big news and fragile news. Chuck, Bill, and the Steves are all fathers, so there was just genuine love and excitement. I remember the consensus being *This is the best news you could ever report.* And they said, "We don't know what we'll do with this information, but we're going to make it work. The most important thing is that you take care of yourself."

Steve Holland: I said, "This is nothing to worry about. We'll shoot around it. Don't let that be a single piece of stress, this is great news. It's nothing but exciting." And then it seemed interesting for us to write that Bernadette would get pregnant again, which would be so unexpected and surprising for viewers who saw the character give birth only nine months earlier. There was still a bit of nervousness writing it in, because it was still early in Melissa's pregnancy, and had something gone wrong for Melissa but Bernadette was still pregnant, that would have been really, really terrible. And we had to have that conversation because we wanted to be very sensitive about what she had already been through with her pregnancy loss. We said to her, "We were thinking of this story, but we don't want to put any more pressure on you or make this any more stressful than you need." And she was excited about it. I don't know if she had that thought at the moment, but I was a little bit nervous about going down this path, on the off chance something would happen. But from the character and the show standpoint, it just seemed surprising in a good way. We felt we could do a pregnancy story different from the first time, and we planned to have her on bed rest because we knew she would actually be giving birth earlier than Bernadette and we might need to write around her for a few episodes. But it was important that even those episodes where she was out on maternity leave, we found ways to include Melissa in every show. We preshot a couple scenes, so in the end, I think she's only gone for one episode, but you hear her voice in it. That's the way it needed to be. She's part of our family.

Melissa Rauch: Sitcoms have hidden pregnancies for years, so it's not anything new. But when the season started, I was already majorly pregnant. I remember when they told me they were going to make Bernadette pregnant again, which I honestly didn't think they would, but I loved that. Still, I would be lying if I said I wasn't nervous that something was going to happen to my pregnancy in real life after what I had been through already. I was 100 percent okay that they wrote my pregnancy in, because if something terrible was going to happen it would have been hard regardless if I was pregnant in the show or not. And we'd find a way to deal with it. So the pros really outweighed the cons, and there was a freedom for me in not having to play otherwise. I didn't need to worry about hiding behind counters and laundry baskets, which would have totally been fine, but I think it was such a wise decision that that's how they decided to incorporate it.

And so, in the season eleven premiere—"The Proposal Proposal"—which coincided with Steve Holland's first episode as showrunner, Bernadette tells Howard she's pregnant again. The two do a back and forth of "yes" and "no" that is a master class in comedy.

Steve Holland: Molaro and I kept going back and forth on the no, yes, no, yes. We were like, "How long can we keep that up? How long can we sustain this?" I remember telling Simon and Melissa that each one of these yeses and noes is a different emotion…one is disbelief, one is anger. I said, "We think each one can be a different journey. You're saying the same words, but you're having a conversation that goes beyond these words." And I just love that scene. It seems so simple on the page, but then having them go and imbue each of those yeses and noes with different meaning was really great to watch.

Melissa Rauch: Getting to play that verbal game of tennis with him was just the most fun. He would just hit it back so perfectly and would set me up so there was no way I couldn't hit it back to him.

Simon Helberg: When we did that scene in front of the audience, they laughed the entire time, but we needed the take to be clean and exist without laughs interrupting the dialogue. Mark Sweet, our warm-up guy extraordinaire, would sometimes tell the audience, "We need you to try and hold your laughs through this" because we just needed to get the rhythm right without people laughing over lines. That scene was one where I do believe we had to do that to get the timing right. The reveal of the first baby was so beautifully written, and to nail it again with the second baby is a feat.

It was also another opportunity for the writers to continue to tell meaningful parenthood stories. Originally, Howard's biggest worry was what religion they would raise their child with, or if they were to have a girl (which they did), what would happen if she grew up to look like him. But this time, when the Wolowitzes find out they're expecting a boy, Howard panics that he won't know how to raise a son since his own father walked out on him.

Chuck Lorre: That was a wonderful storyline for Howard, and it wasn't one you necessarily anticipated in a situation comedy. Howard was largely raised by a domineering female figure, and he didn't have a dad to show him what fatherhood looked like or what it could look like or what it should look like. So those stories came out of what was lacking in his childhood, which make for the best stories.

"What do I know about raising a boy?" Howard asks Sheldon, to which Sheldon replies, "Well, what do you know about raising a girl?" Later, Raj provides more support with this anecdote: "You don't know what this little boy is going to be like. Maybe he'll be rough and tumble, or maybe he'll be sweet and sensitive, or maybe he'll be all those things, like me!"

Simon Helberg: Awareness of stereotypes is important. Our show wasn't 100 percent successful in avoiding the pitfalls of stereotypes—no show is—but there was an improvement in that area as we went on, and that has to do with so many factors, from different writers and showrunners and the time we were in. Obviously the times have changed so dramatically even in the last year, let alone since we've been off the air. I don't know if it's the responsibility of television to always reflect the most sanitized or pure versions of people, but awareness is important. I think there are probably a good swath of people who felt upset by certain portrayals of characters or storylines. I'm sure there are things writers would do differently, and I'm sure there are things that were done better than we ever could have hoped for.

> Later that fall, Rauch and her husband gave birth to a healthy daughter. In an Instagram post, Rauch wrote, "Our hearts are bursting at the seams with love for her. I will never take for granted the difficult road it took to get here. To those on that road: I'm sending you so much love today and always." A few weeks later, Rauch returned to work. Actors don't get paid maternity leave, which is why women often want to get back to set as quickly as possible. But knowing that, the producers wanted to make Rauch's return as easy and accommodating as possible.

Melissa Rauch: I was so damn grateful that the producers were so on top of it to know to write in the bed rest for Bernadette. I was like, "Don't worry, I'll be able to get right back into the swing of things after I have the baby!" And Holland, having been through this twice with his wife, as well as Maria and Molaro, were like, "We're writing you on bed rest." And towards the end of my pregnancy, my back just killed me, so thank goodness they knew to do that. They really took care of me, and allowed me to send in a recording on my iPhone for the episode after I gave birth in real life. That way, when I couldn't be on-screen, at least we'd hear Bernadette's voice, because getting my sea legs back for the first time after giving birth was hard. I was still very much learning the ropes of being a new mom. There was so much art imitating life, and it made me realize even more so how they wrote Bernadette's first pregnancy in such a real way. A perfect example was Bernadette's struggle with going back to work. That just reso-nated so deeply once I experienced it for myself. But I remember saying to Holland, Maria, and Molaro a couple of weeks after the baby, "Thank you for knowing what I would need before I even knew it." I'm forever grateful to them.

Chapter 20

THE PAY CUTS, A SET SHAKE-UP, AND THE PROPOSAL THAT BROUGHT THE HOUSE DOWN

In March 2017, CBS renewed *Big Bang* for two more years, which would bring it through season twelve, and what was assumed to be its final season. But this time, instead of salary increases for the cast, the trades and mainstream media were reporting that the five original cast members were actually going to take pay cuts to help Mayim Bialik and Melissa Rauch—who became series regulars in season four and thus were paid significantly less—get paid more.

For years prior, the narrative in Hollywood was shifting more to women's equality—both in on- and off-screen representation and in pay. It became an even bigger movement with the election of President Donald Trump over Secretary of State Hillary Clinton in November 2016. So when word got out that Galecki, Parsons, Cuoco, Helberg, and Nayyar were reportedly taking $100,000 pay cuts from their $1-million-an-episode-salary, the headlines in March 2017 read, "*Big Bang Theory* Actors Take Pay Cut for Women's Equality" (*Business Insider*), "*Big Bang Theory* Leads Taking Pay Cuts So Female Co-stars Can Get Raises" (the *Huffington Post*), "*Big Bang Theory* Stars Give Up $100,000 Each to Help Actresses Making 80% Less" (CNBC).

Not every outlet ran with gender-focused headlines ("*The Big Bang Theory* Stars Mayim Bialik and Melissa Rauch Seek Parity in New Contract," per *Variety*; "*The Big Bang Theory* Original Cast Is Taking a Pay Cut for Their Co-stars," read *Time*), but understandably, it was a feel-good story, especially when women were—and still are—constantly fighting for equal rights.

But something didn't quite add up. *Big Bang* was a money machine because of syndication, reported to have garnered more than $1 billion in revenue for its studio, Warner Bros. It was also the number one comedy on television, and CBS's MVP.

And while taking a $100,000 pay cut doesn't seem like a huge deal when you're already making $1 million an episode, the bigger question was if *Big Bang* was so lucrative, why couldn't the studio and network give Bialik and Rauch something approaching parity without their costars having to take pay cuts?

The cast and the producers have never talked about what really happened—or if they even took pay cuts. The only comment about the situation came a few months later when Mayim Bialik, speaking to *People*, said, "You shouldn't believe everything you read."

Now, for the first time, the original five are confirming that not only did they take pay cuts, but it was because if they wanted the show to continue, major concessions would have to happen, otherwise the future of the show—and that of their costars—would be in jeopardy.

Melissa Rauch: I remember the day it happened because we were told there was going to be a cast meeting in the green room after work. I was about to walk into the room when one of our PAs came running up and said, "Actually, sorry, you're not supposed to be in this meeting." I didn't know what was going on, since we had all been included in every meeting for years up to that point. But I figured it had something to do with negotiations. I didn't find out about what went down until long after.

It was February 2017, when Les Moonves, then chairman and CEO of CBS Corporation, along with Kevin Tsujihara, then chairman and CEO of Warner Bros. Entertainment, called a closed-door meeting to talk to Galecki, Parsons, Cuoco, Helberg, and Nayyar.

Johnny Galecki: Chuck very smartly made the heads of CBS and Warner Bros. talk to us instead of him. He said to them, "I'm not going to be your agent. If you want to talk to the cast, you talk to the cast." And so they flew out from New York, but Chuck wanted to be in the room for it, God bless him.

Chuck Lorre: I made Les Moonves make that speech [about pay cuts]. I was not gonna make that speech. No, no, no! We went into the green room and Les gave them that speech. And they weren't having it! It was not well received. It really fell on deaf ears, and I was really quite shocked, because Les was a formidable, larger-than-life presence in that tiny little green room, and he made this presentation to the cast. Mayim and Melissa were not in the room. And it did not go well. I remember thinking, *Oof, I'm glad that wasn't me!* But after he left the cast was kind of like, "What the f—? It's not my responsibility...!" I was thinking it was going to be this kum-ba-yah, cis-boom-bah, we're all in this together kind of moment, and not even close! [*Laughs*]

Johnny Galecki: [Les and Kevin] basically explained the math to us, which was we were already in syndication, and keeping TBS on the air and their lights on, and if we were going to do more episodes or seasons, we couldn't make more money, especially if we had Melissa and Mayim in the cast. You can't sell it to more platforms at that point. TBS already had 230 episodes of *Big Bang* at the time, and they weren't going to buy more to syndicate. So we took $100,000 pay cuts to pay [Melissa and Mayim more money]. Taking the pay cuts was about keeping the show on the air. There was a lot made about them being women and gender equality, but if they were both men, it still would have been the same case.

Chuck Lorre: It's a very fragile thing. You're talking to people about their income. I didn't want to negotiate on behalf of CBS and Warner Bros. That's not my job. I'm a comedy writer, I'm not a finance guy. And I think perhaps this was a misbegotten thing, but it was clear that the reason that that conversation went directly to the five original cast members was in an effort to bypass all the lawyers and agents and managers and family members who would have a say in this conversation. But it didn't work. It was a noble failure!

Kaley Cuoco: No matter what it was, it's just the way it was presented to us in that meeting that was interesting.

Jim Parsons: Everything Chuck, Johnny, and Kaley are saying is true. I kind of thought nobody would ever talk about it, but maybe that's the way I was brought up. My opinion then, and now, is that there was an absurdity to it…and as much as we all loved and valued each other as members of that cast and friends—and as much as you wouldn't *ever* want to do the show without anybody else there—we were all employees of CBS in this room that were talking to us. So it was an odd thing for them to say, "If you want the show to continue, if you want these other actors to continue, you're gonna have to cough up some money for them." And I've never completely understood that. [*Laughs*] I didn't hire them! What was so weird about them coming to us was that the two people—Mayim and Melissa—they used in front of us were very dear and important to us. Because of that, if you had mixed emotions about what you were being told [by the higher-ups], there was this implication, in my own mind, at least, like you felt sullied in some way because I didn't have any conflict of emotions about my feelings for these two human beings. There's no question in my mind, there's no question in my heart. For me, my deep feelings for them felt like that was exactly what was being preyed upon. Whatever was the truth about the matter of the finances, I have no idea, but the bottom line was, CBS came to us about that because they knew how much we cared about these two people, and that's just kind of ugly. Whether they feel this or not, there was always something that verged on being so disrespectful to Mayim and Melissa about the whole thing. It was sort of a fact hidden from them, because of course it would be.

Melissa Rauch: I just felt so terrible that they were all put in that position. I have a hard time letting a friend treat me to a sandwich, let alone finding out that they were asked to give up part of their salary. I know there are intricacies of this and it's not so cut-and-dry, but the bottom line is, I'm forever grateful to my cast members.

Simon Helberg: [Les Moonves] was a sly [businessman]. Kevin Tsujihara, who was also in the room, somehow managed to disappear with more money than they ever had before. Not for one moment did I actually believe they were going to cancel our show, nor did I ever believe that they were out of money, or that taking a pay cut in any way would benefit the ladies of the show. And I found it to be a very glaring negotiation tactic that felt, to me, to be in poor taste, using women as this human shield, particularly coming from those two fellas. [*Editor's note:* In March 2019, Kevin Tsujihara stepped down as chairman and CEO of Warner Bros. Entertainment amid an ongoing investigation into his past relationship with an aspiring actress who was later cast in two Warner Bros. movies; Tsujihara has denied the allegations of nonconsensual sex. Les Moonves resigned in 2018 after decades of sexual misconduct allegations; he has denied any nonconsensual sexual relations.] So, to me it was 100 percent clear what the motivations of the corporations and the studios behind this were to increase those profit margins. I think that amongst the cast, there were variations . . . in terms of how much each of us did buy into that, who thought the show was actually at risk of being canceled, who felt that it was incumbent upon us to take pay cuts in order to pay out the women on the show, and I think that amongst the cast, there were definitely camps. And some people believed Les Moonves and Kevin Tsujihara more than others. I won't speak for other people; I never felt that my paycheck was directly correlating with other people in the cast's paycheck. That just isn't generally how these things go. It's certainly up for debate, but I think that there's a lovely story that came out of it, which is, you know, the heroes of *Big Bang* fall on their sword to give the women a pay bump, which is not anything that I would've ever put out there, and I don't think there's any actual veracity to that idea. It *sounds* nice, and it sounds convenient [but it wasn't what happened].

Melissa Rauch: I know there's different points of view about it, like would CBS really not have put the money in to keep us on the air? Would our show have really been canceled? I don't know. But it bums me out that it was put on the other cast members to solve that problem.

At the time, *Variety* noted (on February 28, 2017) that while the show was no doubt lucrative, "the way the cable and broadcast syndication deals are structured for long-running shows, *Big Bang* won't generate much incremental revenue from the additional 48 episodes to come in an 11th and 12th seasons." They also added that "CBS' license fee for the show no longer covers all production costs, as it did in earlier seasons. That fee is believed to be in the $6 million–$7 million range under the new deal. The salaries of the five original actors alone take up $5 million of that fee." To make matters more complicated, as the negotiations were happening, Warner Bros.' TV parent company, Time Warner, was in the middle of an $85.4 billion merger agreement with AT&T. "In this environment," *Variety* noted, "spending decisions are being heavily scrutinized. As successful as *Big Bang* has been for the studio, the new episodes won't yield the kind of windfall for the studio that might otherwise grease the wheels for dealmaking in the coming days for Bialik and Rauch."

Johnny Galecki: I just really, really hated that it was [made] public.

Kaley Cuoco: I'm amazed that it stayed as sane as it did. My Cinderella dream was that we would be the *Friends* cast in terms of everyone around the table holding hands, banding together. I didn't want to copy them, but I liked thinking that we could be inspired by them. And because I—as well as Johnny—wanted that, I think that made it look like the two of us were doing our own little thing.

Johnny Galecki: Our goal was to involve everyone equally. Always.

Kaley Cuoco: I'd be the one texting the group saying, "Meet me in my dressing room tonight after we wrap!" I would bring everyone in there, going, "What is going on? What do you want?" I was always trying to do that.

Johnny Galecki: And they'd say, "Well, we have to talk to our reps." Which I understood, too.

Kaley Cuoco: But it was hard. Teams go deep...a lot of people in people's ears. I understand that. But it didn't make it super easy. You get pulled in different directions. It's a tough spot.

Jim Parsons: It was just...an unfortunate way to kick off the final two years for a show that had been such a success and such a gift to so many people—and not just the ones you see on the television. That part of the business I never liked. But I was certainly glad when that part was over and we could move on and just be back at work together. The show in general was so important to us. I know that every single person understood what a gift this opportunity had been and continued to be and you couldn't be so hot-headed or immature to cut off your nose to spite your face, basically. There was a sanity that prevailed on our set for the most part. It was like, *We're in a once-in-a-lifetime situation here, so I'll try to be good to myself and stand up for myself when I see fit*, but also, part of that is understanding the gift I've been given and trying to deal with that in a sane way. And I don't have an ax to grind. Which is not to say everything was always rainbows and roses in the process, but I was personally treated very well by every arm of this production, even the big corporate arms. Was it odd when Les came to talk to us? Yes! I think it was very odd. That said, it was a moment in the twelve-year collaboration.

Mayim Bialik: I credit the five of them for establishing a framework that Melissa and I stepped into, and they welcomed us with open arms into that embrace. It sounds so cheesy to use that metaphor, but they established that for us and allowed us to continue to thrive because of the foundation they established.

In the end, the pay cuts that Galecki, Parsons, Cuoco, Helberg, and Nayyar took helped Bialik and Rauch increase their per-episode salaries from around $200,000 an episode to $450,000. While it was a significant increase, it was still nowhere near what their costars were earning. Given that it was universally acknowledged that the additions of Bialik and Rauch were a major reason for the continuing success of *Big Bang*, it's no surprise that the cast resented Moonves and Tsujihara for bypassing their representation in what felt like a calculated ploy to play one segment of the cast against the other. Would things have been different in today's more transparent climate, and with new leadership? That's the $900,000 question.

But the show must go on—and thanks to the actors and their love for the show and the crew, it did. There were all sorts of changes happening on-screen in season ten that gave new life to the series at a time when it was still firing on all cylinders. After ten years, the producers decided the moment had come to move Sheldon in with Amy, thereby giving Penny and Leonard a chance to have the place to themselves as husband and wife. It started in "The Cohabitation Experimentation," when Amy's apartment flooded, and as an experiment, she and Sheldon moved into Penny's place, and Penny moved full-time into Leonard's. As jarring as it was not to see Rachel live at Monica's apartment on *Friends*, this was even more so because it was technically Sheldon's apartment, and thereby an extension of him.

Jim Parsons: We all had feelings about it. We were like, "How is Sheldon moving?! This makes no sense." And they made it work...but I mostly had to ignore my own feelings, which was, *This is out of whack!* [*Laughs*] At the very least, I couldn't believe it wasn't a two-part very special episode where he ties himself to the kitchen island and won't leave! But that wasn't what they wanted to do. Looking back, I'm still not at peace with it, but when we did it, I basically just chose not to think about it. This is about making bold, decisive choices that some people are going to be unhappy with. And I wasn't unhappy with the result. I loved living over there, actually! I thought Penny's apartment was cute. I was sick of our apartment. But the pathway there, I was like, *Oh, we're just going to do it and get it over with and move on*. I hope that doesn't sound at all judgmental. It's the opposite, if anything. They had so many fucking things to juggle, and sometimes you just gotta move things along.

Steve Holland: Breaking the story wasn't difficult; *deciding* to do it was. But as nervous as Steve and I were, we knew it would give us great stories. We knew one easier option was to keep Sheldon in his apartment and move Leonard into Penny's, but it just felt bigger and more interesting to take Sheldon out of his comfort zone. We wanted the show to grow, but the question was always, how much can you bend it before it breaks? And if you remove Leonard and Sheldon in that apartment, on that couch—which is a vital part of the show's DNA—does the show fall apart? So we didn't go into it lightly, but it felt real. At some point Chuck was like, "You should do it," which gave us the confidence to move ahead, but it was hard. And even when we did it, we built an escape hatch where they were going to do it as a five-week experiment. And if it felt weird and didn't work, we knew we could get out. But it was the best thing we ever did, and opened up a whole new flood of stories. It pushed Sheldon and Amy's relationship forward, as well as taking Leonard and Penny in a new direction.

Chuck Lorre: It was one of those things that just breathed life into the series. It generated so many wonderful stories, because dating someone and living with someone are entirely different things. And certainly neither Sheldon or Amy or Leonard had any skill or experience at cohabitation. Penny had been around, but for the rest of them, it was all brand-new. And it was so fun to watch because we got to watch them learn how to be in relationships.

Steve Molaro: Sheldon's spot was always going to be his. It didn't matter if he lived there or not. It was important that it always felt like *The Big Bang Theory*, and one of the most important things is that the couch is in that living room and that couch is Sheldon's spot. I didn't want that to ever change.

> Once Sheldon and Amy learned they could live together and make it work, the producers could have decided to have Sheldon move back into his place—with Amy—and then have Leonard move into Penny's. It would have been the logical thing to do, but it would have made storytelling even harder.

Steve Molaro: Because in general it was easier to get Sheldon to go see *them*. We wanted home base to still be the set we were using the most, so the amount of times Leonard or Penny would go knock on Sheldon's door were less than Sheldon coming over to them needing someone.

Steve Holland: And as writers, we discussed what the rules would be for Sheldon going forward. Does he have to do his knock, knock, knock when he comes back into his apartment? But maybe if we leave the door cracked to his old apartment, he doesn't have to knock!

> And with Penny and Leonard finally living together by themselves, it allowed them to have meatier stories as a married couple. Over the next few seasons, they had significant conversations about finances, careers, kids, etc., that were intentionally never wrapped up in a single episode.

Kaley Cuoco: I really liked that they talked about real life. The writers made mundane conversations interesting, whether it was talking about money or how Penny doesn't like her job. These are topics that come up in marriages. And then you had Penny tell Leonard she really didn't want kids. I actually wished that they did not, because I loved that message so much. It was cute how the writers did it at the end with Penny's surprise pregnancy, and all in all I'm glad, but I was actually voting for her not to. I loved that she was like, "No, I don't really want them." That's another thing couples go through—maybe one wants to start a family and the other one doesn't. Penny became this career woman, and she was really growing in her job and she loved going out with her friends and she admitted that. She didn't want her life to change, and I loved that she said that. That's a challenge for me, too, in my own life. It was almost mirroring life, in that I understood

Penny because I was almost going through the same thing, of my career's going great and my husband's awesome, but I didn't want anything more to change. I was going through those emotions during those episodes, and being like, *I get it!* And I really wanted to keep that up. I didn't want an episode where all of a sudden she'd say, "No, I want a baby!" Because not everyone wants the life that the next person wants. Not everyone wants kids. Not everyone wants to be married. And I liked that. It didn't need to be a perfect Leonard and Penny ending, but in a way, for them, it was.

Johnny Galecki: Penny wanted to have her career, she wanted to be independent, and I thought that was incredible. Penny grew so much from the first episode to the last episode, and there's certain characters where the writers guide you, and then certain characters where the character guides the writers. And I feel like that was the case with Kaley. I won't comment about how she feels about having children. But she and I have nine. [*Laughs*]

Steve Holland: Steve and I had two reasons for doing the story that Penny doesn't want kids: (1) it seemed really interesting, and (2) we had done pregnancy storylines with Bernadette twice. We really weren't looking for a way to do another pregnancy story. It seemed like an interesting thing to do for the character, and added an interesting friction to Penny and Leonard's relationship. And I know Kaley really liked the storyline. She said it was a storyline that was going on in her home as well. Someone on the writing staff had pitched Penny freezing her eggs as a story on the board, so that was discussed, but I don't remember how much we delved into it. I just know that as characters of a certain age and place in their lives, these were conversations that they might be having.

> There was a running joke that Leonard wore Penny down and got her to marry him, but in reality, as different as they were, she really did love him.

Kaley Cuoco: There were a lot of jokes about that, but there was always an eye roll or a side wink about it. Penny was also sarcastic, and she and Leonard gave each other a hard time. Sometimes they were super buddy-buddy, and other times they were more intimate. Normally, comments like Leonard wearing Penny down would have bothered me, but Penny could get away with things, the same way Sheldon could get away with things. There were things that were earned, and Penny earned those moments. She earned ribbing him, she earned the "Ugh, he wore me down" moments. And it's cute and it's funny, and I think the audience knew what she meant. Penny was completely in love with him.

No matter how much Penny and Leonard ribbed on each other—and facial expressions aside—they were meant to be. Plus, who else could look this cute—and young and fun—dressed up as Cupid? *Courtesy of Kaley Cuoco photo collection*

Tara Hernandez: I really wanted to see Penny's passions ignite, even if that was about her relationship. I really loved episodes where she and Leonard were on the same page, like their Valentine's Day episode where they were trying to have a good time and be carefree. There was often a tension between them, so the fact that they dressed up as Cupid and threw glitter everywhere kind of ignited my heart. Just seeing them together geeking out about something, or her helping Leonard through losing Professor Proton and being at the funeral with him...I liked seeing them on the same page. I didn't want to watch a couple who was miserable, to be honest.

As it turns out, the producers were actually very close to having them break up for good, which was why Penny and Leonard were often seen at odds later in the series.

Steve Holland: We were really close. We talked about it a lot because we didn't want to keep breaking them up and getting them back together. Our initial conception was that these were two people who changed each other's lives and made each other grow, but ultimately didn't end up together. It was that bittersweet thing where we thought their relationship would [eventually end]. And when we talked about it, we were like, "We just need to pick the moment," because there's only so many times you can toy with viewers by having them break up and then get back together. We knew that when we did it, that was going to be it, which meant we had to be careful about when and how. But it became tricky because it begs the question if they can then be in the same room together. And how do you break stories after they break up? I always actually liked them as a couple, so I wasn't rooting for them to break up maybe quite as much, although I did believe that. I believe it felt real that they were these people who came in and changed each other's lives. But I always liked them as a couple.

Kaley Cuoco: These two people have been together a very long time, and even when you know someone so well, it's amazing how communication can totally fail. I loved that they asked those questions of one another and talked about these issues so openly, because to me it showed that they still wanted to be together even though they weren't understanding each other at all. That's just real life. No relationship is perfect. We see a lot of TV ones that are, but this one was not. You know someone so well, but you keep missing, and you sometimes just don't quite know why.

Johnny Galecki: Molaro had a relationship in college with a woman that was akin to what Leonard and Penny had. This woman was out of his league, and they just didn't have a lot in common. So he and I, in private, would talk a lot about how the relationship between Leonard and Penny *should* end. They didn't have enough in common. I felt that was very real, but I think in the end, he, Bill, and Chuck decided that would just be so heartbreaking for the audience, and in hindsight, I agree. At the time, I was very excited about the idea, maybe because it's a little avant-garde for a sitcom and would shock people. But the way that they did it was so much better, with Penny's surprise pregnancy... it was just so beautiful. But I did want to end it on a darker note initially.

Steve Molaro: We thought about how they would still be friends even after they split. We thought about Leonard telling Penny about a girl that he met, and she's happy for him and rooting him on. That's how it was for me and my first girlfriend after we split. We went on to become friends and almost functioned like brother and sister. I understood how that could play out for Leonard and Penny as well.

Steve Holland: But at some point we just realized, audiences are rooting for this couple, and it felt almost a little cruel to break them up because it was what we had assumed we were doing. It was always sort of a joke in the writers room that they didn't have a lot of things in common. They really didn't. And we would talk about that on the show as well. And then going into the last two seasons, we explored conversations where they talked about having kids or not having kids. There were a lot of moments where those conversations felt like it could be the moment where they break up.

And in one of the more bizarre storylines, Leonard considered donating his sperm to Penny's ex-boyfriend, Zack, and his wife, so he could technically still be a father.

Steve Holland: We talked about going down the route where Leonard was the sperm donor for Zack and his wife's child. We were like, "Could Leonard have this child that Penny is ultimately on board with, but it's not theirs?" But the conclusion we came to was that it wouldn't feel OK. People had different opinions about it in the writers room. I don't think anyone was digging in their heels like, *We have to do this*, but I think we felt as a general consensus that it wasn't going to be satisfying, and if we get to the end of this episode and he says yes, it's not going to be what we want it to be.

Kaley Cuoco: Listen, there's a lot of storylines you need if you're going to run twelve years; you're going to hit a doozy once in a while!

Johnny Galecki: I actually loved that. [*Laughs*] I thought that was very Leonard, and beautiful. I just remember thinking that was a great storyline and a very smart mislead on the writers' part.

Tara Hernandez: To be honest, we all love Brian Thomas Smith (Zack), so we were always like, "How do we get this guy back?" I was always tickled by this classic, hulking jock character loving Leonard and thinking Leonard was so smart and cool, so it just ticked a lot of boxes, and that is why that story was there.

In the series finale, Penny and Leonard find out they're expecting, but the way in which the producers got to that reveal is still one of much discussion (more on that later). Meanwhile, the season ten finale—"The Long Distance Dissonance"—was all about Amy and Sheldon and their future. Amy was away at Princeton when Riki Lindhome's Dr. Ramona Nowitzki returned to Caltech after a nearly decade-long absence. Always intrigued by Sheldon, this time she acts on her feelings and makes a move on him, which prompts him to realize that the only person he ever wants to kiss him again is Amy. He immediately flies cross-country, and when a stunned Amy opens the door at the end of the episode, he's down on one knee asking her to marry him.

Tara Hernandez: We wrote that episode in a day. Chuck came in and said, "What are we doing?" and we said, "We're doing the finale; we think we're doing this story." He was like, "Okay, but I feel like we need more conflict for Sheldon to get to the decision [to propose]." So he said, "Let's bring Ramona back." We checked Riki's avail in the morning, and pretty quickly found out that she was going to be available. It also took a lot of audience trust, because she hadn't been on in a while, so we had to understand that some audience members weren't going to know her at all. But we decided to try it and wrote through lunch, through pee breaks, etc. It was total magic, and the episode just had this charge of building to the eventual proposal. That to me is a season finale I cherish the most in addition to the series finale.

Jim Parsons: I distinctly remember when I asked Amy to marry me. My palms were sweating. I can still visualize being on my knee behind the door, but off camera so the audience couldn't see me until she opened it. And I just…you can barely talk! But you have to because that's your job! You're just having that kind of physiological reaction that most of the time in life you can take a Valium or at least get through it quietly. The long kiss in "The Earworm Reverberation" when we get back together was like that, too.

Steve Molaro: The audience went crazy when he proposed. They screamed. I screamed! And then we all got choked up. Kaley could not stop crying. We did it in one take, and we couldn't even be bothered to do it again because the scene was perfect. We loved it.

Chapter 21

LUKE SKYWALKER COMES TO PASADENA

Season eleven started off with a newly engaged couple—Sheldon and Amy; newly expectant parents—Bernadette and Howard; and a new showrunner— Steve Holland. In other words, a hell of a lot of pressure.

Steve Holland: I was sort of Steve [Molaro]'s number two for years, so at the end of season ten, when Steve was getting ready to start up *Young Sheldon*, it was just understood that I was taking over, and Chuck and I just sort of chatted about the upcoming season. But when it was handed off to me in season eleven, it was terrifying because the weight of how beloved the show was wasn't lost on me. I just didn't want to crash this show into a mountain. [*Laughs*] And coming off Chuck doing it, Bill doing it, and Steve doing it, I felt a lot of pressure. I remember the first day in the writers room on season eleven, Chuck popped down just to say hi and stuck his head in the writers room and said, "Just remember, biggest show on TV! Don't fuck it up!" And he walked out. [*Laughs*] It was just a nice tension-breaking moment. But sending him that first script for season eleven, if he hadn't liked it, honestly, it would have been devastating. But he did, and that sort of set the stage and gave me some confidence to go into the rest of the season.

Chuck Lorre: One of the things I learned was by getting out of the way and giving the show to Molaro and then Molaro handing it off to Holland... the show grew, the show expanded. Had I stayed the primary showrunner, I would have strangled it to death. It would have become predictable. Molaro comes along with an entirely different vision and so did Steve Holland. The show expanded and got better, the characters got deeper and richer.

> Although Holland had the support of Lorre and Molaro, looking back he was tasked with two of the biggest episodes of the series under his purview: Amy accepting Sheldon's proposal in the season eleven premiere, and Amy and Sheldon's wedding in the season eleven finale. It was an enormous undertaking, but both episodes turned out to be two of the best in the series.
>
> The season as a whole saw a who's who of prominent guest stars, including Regina King, Bill Gates, Neil Gaiman, Bob Newhart, and Stephen Hawking. But it was the wedding episode—"The Bow Tie Asymmetry"—that set the stage abuzz with Kathy Bates (Amy's mother), Teller (Amy's father), Laurie Metcalf (returning as Sheldon's mother), and Luke Skywalker himself, Mark Hamill.

Mark Hamill: Simon Helberg and my son, Nathan, were close friends, because they were in school from seventh grade to twelfth grade together. And I was friends with his father, Sandy Helberg, because we both lived in Malibu. Simon was always so clever and funny, doing his Al Pacino and Nic Cage impersonations. We were always rooting for him, so when this show happened, we didn't call it *Big Bang Theory*, we called it Simon's show. "Oh, Simon's show is on!" And we watched it early on hoping it would be a success.

Simon Helberg: I tried to get the title changed to "Simon's Show" but nobody would listen. [*Laughs*] But yeah, Nathan, who is Mark's oldest son, was my best friend for most of junior high into high school. And we're still in touch, but we were very, very tight, and one of the ways we bonded is we did these prank calls. We were like a self-declared prank-call duo that recorded them all onto an audiotape, and then copied those audiotapes, and made album art and sold them to kids in our class. I think, like, two albums sold, but we did our best. Mark would sometimes catch us calling people all through the night, because so many nights we were rigging up this contraption to capture all of our comedy. So anyway, there were attempts to get him on *Big Bang* many different times, and I think a couple of those I might've helped out; clearly, I didn't do a good job because he didn't end up coming on until the end of season eleven! But it was a really cool thing to get to do that with my friend's dad. Not to mention that he's one of the most iconic actors ever. But yeah, there was something very cathartic about it, and the whole family was there that night.

Mark Hamill: Yeah, that was really nice. I don't think I told [the writers] that I had a special relationship with Simon, so we were lucky to get that scene.

Viewers had no idea at the time of this episode ("The Bow Tie Asymmetry") that in real life, Mark Hamill has known Simon Helberg for years, and was the reason Hamill and his family watched *Big Bang* to begin with. *Photo™ & © Warner Bros. Entertainment Inc.*

The scene Hamill is speaking of is where Wolowitz rescues a dog, Bark, that turns out to belong to the one-and-only Mark Hamill. When Hamill shows up at his door looking for his dog, Wolowitz—a die-hard *Star Wars* fan—can't believe who's standing in front of him.

Simon Helberg: That's acting. I'm so jaded by Mark Hamill, but I portrayed a character who was very excited. No, it was so spectacular. And I thought they made such good use out of him, too, because I know he's not a huge fan of playing himself. But the way they did it—with Bark Hamill is, of course, a good joke.

Mark Hamill: And the T-shirt I was wearing in that scene—it has a mouse with fangs called Lava Bear—my son designed. That's one of his characters. The *Big Bang* wardrobe department said it was fine to wear on the show. But the dog I was holding was not my dog. My daughter has two small dogs, Millie and Mabel, so either could've played the part of Bark Hamill, but they have certain requirements on set with animals—they need a professional trainer, etc. But people still ask me if that was my dog and is he named Bark. [*Laughs*]

> Given Helberg's relationship with the Hamill family, it would seem like he would have been the easiest of all the *Star Wars* actors to cast, but it took years to get him on the show.

Mark Hamill: I [finally] said, "Let me have a meeting with Chuck Lorre, Bill Prady, and the Steves." I went into their offices and said, "I've played myself before on *The Simpsons*, *3rd Rock from the Sun*, and *Just Shoot Me!* and the disadvantage of playing yourself is it begs the question: Who am I?" But when you're playing a character, you can pretty much do and get away with anything the writers come up with. So I tried to pitch and said, "What if I'm a lookalike that they're trying to pawn off as Mark Hamill?" And what I didn't realize until the drive home—which is always too late—is, *What am I doing? This isn't about me! This is about Sheldon and Amy getting married! They gotta tell these stories in twenty-two minutes!* I guess it was just insecurity on my part because I thought, *I grew up to play anybody but me! I'd love to play somebody's father, or somebody down at the university, or whatever.* But my daughter, Chelsea, said, "Dad, it's not about you, it's about the wedding." I went, "Oh, yeah, okay." [*Laughs*] So I felt a little embarrassed that I had done that. I thought I was only going to be meeting with Chuck and maybe one or two other people in the room, and there must have been fifteen, twenty people in there! I don't know how many writers were on staff, but it was fascinating to me. The whole experience was...like live theater and you get immediate feedback from the audience. And everyone genuinely liked one another, which is amazing eleven seasons in. I've been on shows that were on much less than that and there was tension. But they all had a great sense of camaraderie and spirit. It was nice to see. If you're doing a comedy like that and you're not having fun, there's something seriously wrong. And it was just a really fun four or five days.

Hamill has never given an interview about his experience on *Big Bang*, but now admits he has one regret about his appearance.

Mark Hamill: I didn't really stick with the series early on. Once it became this big hit, I thought, *Well, Simon's set, so we can just move on.* My wife and I don't follow a lot of series anyways, so it was nothing against the show, but where I really sort of rediscovered it was when I was doing *The Last Jedi* in England. I would have to do the treadmill, and I would notice on Saturdays and Sundays, one of the TV stations would air four-hour blocks of *Big Bang*. By that time, there were so many episodes I had not seen, so I would do the treadmill and measure them in, *Well, I'll do one episode's worth on the treadmill.* And then, *Oh, I'll do two episodes' worth on the treadmill*, followed by three. Even then, I probably only saw thirty, forty episodes when I guest-starred, and I wish I had done this in reverse so I knew more about it when I did it, but I was determined to see all of them. It took me months and months and months, but I've seen them all now. I knew they referenced all kinds of pop culture, and the characters loved comic books, science fiction, fantasy, etc., but I had no idea how ingrained it was and how they could be so subversive in their humor. Like, they're planning a day to watch all the movies and they said, "Well, you know, we're starting out with *Phantom Menace* at noon and I'm just wondering if an hour is long enough to schedule for complaints." [*Laughs*] I thought, *Wow, that's a burn! Very clever.* [*Laughs*] Once I knew all of this, it would have really changed my experience. I would have talked to them about when they go to Skywalker Ranch, or ["The Opening Night Excitation"] where it opens with the crawl from [*Star Wars*]. I thought I'd seen plenty when I did my episode, but I became a completist and saw them all. I didn't really become enamored of it to the degree I had become until I had the experience of being on the show. I became obsessed with it.

While he wasn't as well versed with *Big Bang* as he is now, he certainly knew everything there was to know about his costars, which was both charming to some (Wil Wheaton) and surprising to others (Jim Parsons).

Wil Wheaton: Mark Hamill equals a big fucking deal. I normally sat in the same place for the table reads, but I was in a different spot this time. Nikki Lorre came over to me and said, "Hey, I did you a solid," and in the highest-pitched voice, I was like, "Oh my God!" I could not believe I was about to sit next to Mark Hamill. And then in that episode, there is that scene where I say to him, "I'm the guy who you replaced" in the wedding, and Mark Hamill has to say, "I'm sorry, who are you?" It's a very funny beat, so while we're saying these lines at the table read, Mark Hamill says, "I have to stop this for a second." He looks at me and says, "Of course I know who you are. I'm a huge fan." I mean, *what?!* I couldn't believe it. Could not believe it.

Mark Hamill: I know who Wil Wheaton is, from *Star Trek*, and he's had a really solid career. I just had to tell him I knew who he was, since the script called for me to not know. But see, I didn't know that he was so excited to meet me. He's a good enough actor that he acted cool, calm, and collected. I couldn't tell. [*Laughs*]

But Hamill's first meeting with Parsons went a bit differently.

Mark Hamill: Jim Parsons's delivery—it's just magic. I don't know how he does it, and I'm an actor! I played Jim's father in *Elf: Buddy's Musical Christmas*, which was the animated *Elf* musical; I was the James Caan part from the movie, and he was the Will Ferrell part. Now, we never worked together—it was animation, so we recorded separately. I heard his tracks because I was playing his father. So at the *Big Bang* table read, I referenced it and said, "Hello, son!" and it didn't connect! It was really kind of awkward!

Jim Parsons: [*Laughs*] No, I wouldn't have understood what he was referring to, because the thing I would have immediately gone to was "Luke, I'm your father." So for Mark Hamill to say, "Hello, son," I was thinking, *What are you getting at? Are you Darth Vader? No! What's happening?* Hence the confusion. But I just loved him.

Peter Chakos: Mark Hamill is not known for comedy. But he nailed it. He was so funny. You're like, *All right! This is gonna be good!*

The entire week behind the scenes basically turned into one large fan convention.

Mark Hamill: Kathy Bates said to me, "Can I get a selfie?" [*Laughs*] And I had taken my kids to New York when they were still in grade school to see Penn and Teller, so I'm a huge, huge fan of Teller's. People forget that aside from being a brilliant magician he's a wonderful actor as well. And even though Christine Baranski couldn't be there for the wedding, she was just so perfect for Leonard's mother.

Mayim Bialik: Mark Hamill was incredible to have on. He's such an epic personality, and so generous, so having him there was really tremendous. It was the same with Kathy Bates and Teller, but there's definitely a nervous factor when having such prominent and really impressive people guest-star. Kathy gave so much care and attention to the character, which made it feel so significant and important. She's someone I never thought I'd get to meet, so to have her play my mom was really incredible.

Mark Hamill: Mayim Bialik brought her two sons in...what am I gonna say? "No, I don't have time." Are you kidding? That's part of the job! That's part of being able to show your gratitude for how lucky you are. I didn't expect to be remembered for anything! All I wanted was to be able to work in this business and support my family and make a living, so this is a gift. You see these people's faces light up, especially the young ones. So I was just touched that Mayim would go to the trouble to have her boys come in! Of course I did selfies. Even during downtime, I wanted to be out on the floor where all of the action is. You could watch the scenes being rehearsed, so I'd stay out on the floor, which has just become part of what I do over the years. I was happy to do that.

Kevin Sussman: Mark and I occasionally communicate online. And even though we're friendly acquaintances now, it's still always crazy that he is Luke Skywalker.

John Ross Bowie: I still have the call sheet from that episode because it's all hands on deck. Kathy Bates, Laurie Metcalf, Teller, Mark Fucking Hamill. I was raised in the Episcopal Church, and when you get confirmed you have to pick a confirmation name; it has to be the name of a saint. And I picked Luke—but not for the saint. I got to tell Mark Hamill that in person, which was a pretty wonderful thing.

The producers loved that Shamy's wedding afforded them the opportunity to bring more extended family members back to the series, especially Sheldon's twin sister, Missy, who first appeared in season one, episode fifteen's "The Porkchop Intermediacy."

Steve Holland: I was really happy we got to bring Courtney Henggeler ("Missy") back after all that time because even though we could have recast and not many people would know, I don't really like to do that. We had recast Amy's mother, who we had originally seen early on in season four and she was great, but when you can get Kathy Bates for the role, we're not going to say no to that. But I was really happy to get Courtney back for continuity, and because she's really lovely. And Jerry O'Connell (as Sheldon's older brother, "Georgie") is the most energetic person I've ever met in my life. He's got so much enthusiasm, and when we called him to have a conversation about the character, he was so excited and so on board.

The writers crammed a lot of story—and people—into a twenty-two-minute episode, especially for one as monumental as Sheldon and Amy's wedding. In the lead-up to the vows, Mary Cooper visits with Sheldon and tells him she wishes George Sr. could see him now. Sheldon—who has always been sarcastic and critical when it comes to his father—concedes that he misses him, which is a softer approach more in line with the compassionate George Sr. viewers have seen play out on *Young Sheldon*.

Laurie Metcalf: By that point, *Young Sheldon* was on the air, and in our scene on *Big Bang*, Sheldon's father had been gone for many years. But obviously he's alive on *Young Sheldon*. I told Jim it made me sort of emotional in the little scene that we had before he gets married, because it became that much more real. All of a sudden I was really able to lock in the idea of him as a young boy growing up, the way that his character did. I think it hit both of us...and I felt so much more able to identify with our two characters by having known the father on the other show.

Lance Barber (George Cooper, *Young Sheldon*): That chokes me up hearing that. That's incredible. I remember that scene where they say they miss him, which was kind of out of character for both of them given the history of the show prior because he was played as a cartoon-ish redneck slob who had outrageous behaviors. The shift they took with *Young Sheldon* in its tone grounded that and was a fun challenge... in a way that humanized him.

Steve Holland: We knew we wanted to honor Sheldon's relationship with his mom and really find a moment for the two of them, not only because Laurie and Jim are so great together, but also because of Mary's relationship with Sheldon. This was a day she thought was never going to happen. She was always worried—maybe even convinced—that Sheldon would end up alone, and to know that he found someone to spend his life with gave Mary a real great emotional moment to play. We also knew we wanted to give them a moment to acknowledge George Sr. Obviously Sheldon had a complicated relationship with his dad, but one of the things Molaro has talked about a lot with *Young Sheldon* is that as you get older and hit those adult milestones, you're able to look back on your parents and see them in a different, more human light. So it seemed like a great moment for Sheldon to reflect and be a little sad that he never got to know his dad while they were both adults—and a little nod to the George Sr. we see on *Young Sheldon*.

Lance Barber: And at the beginning of the show... I had come up against the challenge of trying to address the memories of Sheldon from *The Big Bang Theory* and how do you make a character that he described [previously], and now make them sympathetic? But the more adult and experienced Sheldon that narrates *The Big Bang Theory* [has a new] perspective on his family, which we all do when we become adults and "see" our parents as human beings for the first time. And certainly one way to deal with the loss of a loved one is to paint a negative picture of them so it doesn't hurt so much.

Meanwhile, only a year prior to Sheldon and Amy's on-screen wedding, Metcalf attended Parsons's real-life wedding to his now husband, Todd Spiewak, with her daughter, Zoe Perry (who plays Sheldon's mom, Mary Cooper, on *Young Sheldon*). How's that for being meta?

Jim Parsons and Laurie Metcalf became so close playing son and mother, respectively, that Metcalf came to Parsons's real-life wedding, and the two still hope to work on another project together. *Courtesy of Kaley Cuoco photo collection*

Judy Parsons: Laurie came to Jim's wedding. It was really something, because she was sitting there, and her daughter, Zoe, was sitting by her, and then there was me. So we had all kinds of mother connections there! Jim speaks so highly of them both. He really loves them.

Laurie Metcalf: It doesn't get much better than that. I guess that kind of sums up how well we hit it off is to be invited to such a personal moment to share with him. But Jim is also such an open and giving person, and very inclusive.

Jim Parsons: For my on-screen wedding, I remember very clearly seeing Mark Hamill, Kathy Bates, Laurie Metcalf. When one of them is in an episode, it's cool. When you start multiplying people you've admired and watched your whole life altogether at once, watching you get married, there is an anxiety and sweetness that is similar to the real event. So I really enjoyed the wedding.

> It was a family affair for Hamill, too, whose own daughter, Chelsea, was an extra in Sheldon and Amy's wedding.

Mark Hamill: She's sitting in the row right behind Laurie Metcalf. And she loved it because she loves the show, too. She was also like my personal assistant on that particular episode.

As with any monumental TV wedding episode, there has to be some conflict, and in true Sheldon and Amy fashion, it came in the discovery of Super Asymmetry, which caused the couple to be late to their own vows.

Steve Holland: My biggest worry going into season twelve was based on the fact that Sheldon and Amy's wedding at the end of season eleven was kind of like the end of your movie. You've taken this character to this point, so where do you go from here? I was really worried we had told this arc and that maybe that's where it needed to end. And then we started talking, and said, "Well, Sheldon being married certainly opens up some things." I pitched to Chuck the breakthrough that they had at the wedding being the thing that leads to the Nobel Prize, but we were always very careful in the series never to break real-world rules. They were never able to come up with a piece of science that didn't exist in physics. We were always really cautious about them living in the real world of science. But, especially when we knew it was the last season, it was like, "We can do this, then. They can come up with this breakthrough that doesn't exist because they don't have to live in this world after this." And then that started getting exciting.

Professor David Saltzberg: The producers told me a year in advance that they were going to need a theory that could win Sheldon and Amy the Nobel Prize. I went, "Oh my God." Normally, they give me a week's notice, so this was a big one. I said to some of my theory friends, "Can you think of a theory which is plausible that might win a Nobel Prize?" And they said, "If I could, I wouldn't tell you!" [*Laughs*] I've grown up during my entire scientific career with this theory called "Super Symmetry." It's a theory about particles. And just about everything we look for at accelerators is based on this theory, but we've never proven it. But there must be twenty thousand articles written about Super Symmetry. And then one day "Super Asymmetry" came to me. There's a server that gives you the titles of all particle physics papers. "Super symmetry" has ten thousand titles. "Super symmetric," which is the adjective, has another ten thousand titles. I typed in "Super

Asymmetry," and zero! And "Super Asymmetric"—zero! I was like, *This is fantastic! Nobody's used it.* So I pitched that title; they liked it. Usually, I give them five or six choices. This time it was the only one I came up with, so thank goodness they liked it. And in case you're wondering, Super Symmetry does exist. But Super Asymmetry is made up.

> **While Sheldon and Amy, are fastidiously at work trying to see if they're on the verge of a breakthrough, Wolowitz attempts to entertain the impatient wedding guests by having Mark Hamill—who is acting as Sheldon and Amy's officiant as thanks to Wolowitz for finding his dog—answer questions about *Star Wars*.**

Steve Holland: I'll credit my son, Aidan, when we were writing that scene and they were peppering Mark Hamill with *Star Wars* questions. I'm a pretty big *Star Wars* fan, but my son is way more, so when Georgie asks why there weren't tires on any *Star Wars* vehicles, I checked with Aidan first. He said, "Well, technically there's no tires, although you could say that the turbo tank had treads, but I wouldn't call them tires." So we put that trivia right into Stuart's mouth in the scene. Stuart wasn't trying at all, but Denise [Stuart's new colleague at the comic book store, played by Lauren Lapkus] found it so hot. [*Laughs*] And the great thing is, you think you can just ask Mark Hamill, but he is the most clueless about all of those technical, in depth topics. At one point he had to ask us how to pronounce Kashyyyk, the Wookiee home planet. He was like, "What do you say? How is that pronounced?"

Mark Hamill: Oh, oh, yeah. Kashyyyk. It's one of those things that's lacking the proper amount of vowels. But again, I didn't know that was the name of the Wookiee planet. Somebody said, "When Chewie graduated from flight school..." I said, "What are you talking about?" "Well, on Kashyyyk." I said, "What's Kashyyyk?" My son, Nathan, said a lot of people are going to be really disappointed that I don't know all this stuff. I said to him, "Do we ever mention that in the movies?" He said, "No, no, no, it's from the..." and they'll name whatever novel it's from. I don't want to disappoint people, but I'm not someone who says, "I want to watch myself in 'X,' 'Y,' or 'Z.'" I'm very self-conscious. I don't really like watching myself. The Stuarts of the world will watch the movies over and over and over, they'll read the novels, they'll play the video games, they'll read the comics, they'll read the spin-off character novels. There's so much ancillary material. Meanwhile, I once flunked a *Star Wars* trivia quiz. The question was "What was Han Solo smuggling?" I'm like, "I don't remember!" [*Laughs*] I mean, I knew he was a smuggler, but who knows exactly what it was?

"That was a cultural, pivotal moment in pop culture," Mark Hamill says of his role as offici-ant at Sheldon and Amy's wedding. "The whole episode was just so effortlessly well done." *Courtesy of Kaley Cuoco photo collection*

While it was certainly funny to see Hamill peppered with *Star Wars* questions, it was Stuart's moment to shine, and therefore the catalyst for his eventual romance with Denise.

Steve Holland: Like everything else, it was *Let's see what happens* with Stuart and Denise. Only a few episodes prior, we introduced the character at the comic book store as the new assistant manager, and Lauren Lapkus was great in the role. But it got tricky because she was in such demand with other projects that we lost her for a big chunk of season twelve. We didn't know if we'd be able to get her back at all. But it was so important to see her character on-screen because we didn't want the comic book store to just be a place where sweaty guys hung out, which is not super accurate to how they are anyway. Having a woman who was in that world was important for us to show, and she was great. And Kevin is hilarious, so seeing Stuart nervous and trying to date was just enjoyable to write.

Maria Ferrari: I'm proud of Denise. There seems to be this perception that the women were more mature than the men, and therefore wouldn't play games, like *D&D*. They always had to be talked into it or complained about it, so that was something I really pushed against. When Denise came into the fold, it was important that she was seen as someone who enjoyed science fiction / fantasy—basically all these things that the guys enjoyed—without making that be her entire schtick. It took us a long time to get there, but I was really pleased with that character. I wanted to be able to show female characters who enjoyed that genre, because many of them do! Amy cracked that a little bit, because she liked historical fiction and the fantasy genre, but I was glad that Denise could take it even further. It was really important to me that she and Stuart were a good couple because they enjoyed the same things; not because she was tolerating his interests. She *shared* his interests. And I really, really wanted that to be something the show said.

> Meanwhile, Amy and Sheldon realized they needed to press pause on their newfound discovery and get married already. It was a moment that Lorre never foresaw ever happening on the show.

Chuck Lorre: If you had said to me when we first introduced Amy that she and Sheldon were going to fall in love and marry, I would have laid down some serious money that that would never happen. I had a very specific attitude as to his character and where it was going, and it was not going into a traditional relationship.

> But it did, and even though Mark Hamill wasn't as well versed in *The Big Bang Theory* at the time as he is now, he certainly knew the importance of his role as Sheldon and Amy's officiant.

Mark Hamill: That was a cultural, pivotal moment in pop culture. I didn't expect the emotion of the moment to happen to me, so when it did, I got choked up. The whole episode was just so effortlessly well done. I love when Sheldon says, "I have four thousand things for you to sign." Jim Parsons is brilliant, but that whole cast, really, is just perfection.

Jim Parsons: It was really nice to have him there. For such a big scene, it was oddly intimate. And you have this person involved in a major moment who you don't know that well and who's never been on the show before, similar to when Stephen Merchant was there to watch me and Mayim kiss at the door. It was a similar situation with Mark. I kind of enjoyed that presence with us. It was beautifully odd!

Speaking of "beautifully odd," the same could be said of Amy's wedding dress, which wasn't Penny and Bernadette's first choice, but it was certainly Amy's. However, it was one of the harder costumes for Mary T. Quigley to design.

Mary T. Quigley: The wedding dress was a challenge. In the story, Sheldon [comments] how she looks like a pile of swans, so for me, that meant a lot of layers and feathers and lightness. Amy's dress needed to be something that was overdone, but not funny. It needed to stay romantic. So that was a big challenge. I took a bunch of different wedding dresses apart to make that dress.

Steve Holland: We were trying to walk that line where it was something that was a little bit over the top and a little bit silly, but also felt very right for Amy. We might have made a couple of small tweaks from what Mary originally showed us, but she really gets her head inside the characters.

Mayim Bialik: It was so ridiculous and awesome, but I could barely sit because the layers were so crazy. I was also many pounds heavier than I wanted to be because it was a particularly stressful time in my life. I got divorced during *Big Bang Theory*. My father died during *Big Bang Theory*. There was a lot of emotional eating, so I wasn't the size I wanted to be in a wedding dress. But I really loved how over the top it was, and how princess-perfect it was for Amy. But being a divorced woman back in a wedding dress was very, very strange.

There were so many moving pieces to the wedding episode that in one early draft of the script, the writers realized—to their horror—that they forgot the most important part of the vows.

Tara Hernandez: We forgot to put the words "I do" in it. We maybe had released a draft and then realized later they hadn't actually said, "I do," because wedding vows are quite long. And by that point, I think we had written three different wedding vows between Bernadette and Howard, and Penny and Leonard, so we knew we had to separate this out for them, and we just forgot. [*Laughs*] We laughed about it later.

Scott London: And I actually had Mark Hamill sign the wedding document when he officiated the wedding. Jim came in and signed it, too, as well as Mayim. And Johnny and Kaley, since Leonard and Penny were members of the wedding party. I have one of those hanging up in my office.

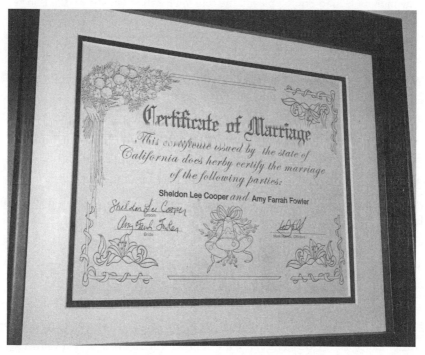

Scott London had Parsons and Bialik sign Sheldon and Amy's marriage certificate, as well as Hamill. This one hangs in Steve Holland's office on the Warner Bros. lot. *Courtesy of Jessica Radloff*

As Sheldon and Amy walk out of the venue as husband and wife, Barry Kripke makes his presence known by singing them off—or trying to, at least— to Etta James's "At Last."

John Ross Bowie: It was actually a wonderful callback because several episodes beforehand, Barry had laid down the law that they can have that particular event room only if he can sing at their wedding because it was originally reserved for his birthday party. But "At Last" is a lovely song. And it's the only thing I do in that episode, which is hilarious.

The episode ran over originally by about twenty script pages, which had to be cut for time constraints. But there were two scenes the producers were able to show fans on *Big Bang*'s social media accounts after the episode aired. One was a message from Sheldon's Meemaw, who wasn't able to travel. Annie Potts, who plays the role on *Young Sheldon*, recorded the message even though June Squibb played the role in an earlier season on *Big Bang*.

Steve Holland: We never wanted to do an hour episode. We all felt that hourlong multicam episodes are never good. I'm sure the network would have given us an hour if we wanted it, but our philosophy was definitely *Better to leave them wanting more than to overstay your welcome*. Even the series finale—which is technically an hour—is really two stand-alone half-hour episodes. There were definitely some things that got cut that I really enjoyed, like with Missy and Georgie, originally, but it was mostly fleshing out the supporting characters. We knew this was Sheldon and Amy's story, and I think the cuts actually kept the episode stronger and more focused. But there were two scenes that were the hardest to cut, and one was Meemaw's phone call to Sheldon. We did that scene mainly to cover the plot hole of her not being at the wedding. We knew if we brought Meemaw back she would have nothing to do but sit there, so we decided that she was too old to travel and would call Sheldon. And at that point, it seemed like the Meemaw that people were more familiar with was Annie Potts. June was terrific, but Annie had really made that character her own on *Young Sheldon*. Ultimately, when we needed to cut time out of the episode, a phone call where we only heard Meemaw's voice seemed like the thing that sadly had to go.

If that wasn't emotional enough, the second scene that got cut was even more profound. Professor Stephen Hawking—who had passed away a couple months earlier—had made arrangements to send Amy and Sheldon a wedding gift. It was a pocket watch that said, "Dear Sheldon, I'm so glad you finally married Amy. It's about 'time.' Haha. Love, Stephen."

Steve Holland: That was in the episode up until the last minute, and we were even considering cutting other things to keep it. The tricky thing about TV shows is you shoot them months ahead of their airing, so sometimes current events happen and you have no way to address them. Professor Hawking was such a friend to the show, his passing was something we definitely wanted to honor, but by the time it happened we were already close to writing the finale. Molaro had the idea that he could have sent a wedding gift before he passed, which seemed so perfect. But again, when we were cutting the episode to time, it seemed so right to leave the episode on Sheldon and Amy walking out of the wedding as husband and wife. But that was a difficult cut to make because it was such a nice way to honor someone who was so important to science and the world and, more personally, to our *Big Bang* family. He was someone who loved poking fun at himself and was always on board for anything we asked him to do.

Jim Parsons: It was the kind of thing that walked a really fine line, and I thought that they landed on the right side of it. I thought the scene was really touching, but the first time I read it, I'm sure there was a cynical part of me that was like, *Oh lord! What is this sentimentality?!* But I know that I completely changed my mind within a few words of reading it where I went, "No, that actually is handled very nicely."

Steve Holland: And although it got cut, we decided to at least put that scene online so fans could see it, and the Hawking estate—who had been very supportive of us—were very understanding.

TIME FOR A HOT BEVERAGE...

Secrets of the Whiteboards

No, Jim Parsons and Johnny Galecki never wrote those equations on the grease boards. They didn't even know what they meant. But the show was damn good at making you think they did.

Professor David Saltzberg: We were not going to have Sheldon write a long equation on the board. It wouldn't look the same from take to take if we did. So, if you look carefully, whenever he's doing an equation, they catch him just as he's writing the final "X" or the final dot and it looks like he's just written an entire equation. Early on, I wrote the equations on the whiteboards, but that would've gotten to be too much to drive out there each time and do it. So when I couldn't, Don Ghio, one of the show's fantastic set dressers, could write in my handwriting! I used to write things on marker on white paper and scan it over.

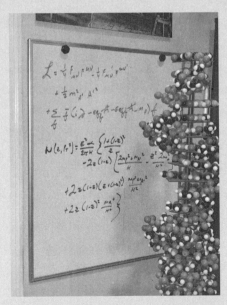

Professor Saltzberg saved nearly all of the whiteboard equations from *Big Bang*'s twelve seasons so he could reference them at any point. *Courtesy of Jessica Radloff*

Chapter 22

BACK TO THE PAST: BRINGING *YOUNG SHELDON* TO LIFE

Spin-offs are a tricky thing. You hope for a *Frasier*, but more often than not you get a *Joey*. If you take an ensemble apart and change its environment, it's always a risky move whether the audience will follow. But *Young Sheldon* wasn't exactly a spin-off; it was a prequel with a very distinct character and a well-established family. There was no guarantee it was going to be successful, but with Steve Molaro and Chuck Lorre at the helm, it certainly had as good a chance as any.

Peter Roth: [In 2016], I got a phone call from Chuck, who said, "I wanna give you an idea that I'm excited about, but I want to reserve my judgment until I hear from you." He pauses. "Young Sheldon. Sheldon at age eight." I remember literally leaping out of my chair and saying, "That is fucking brilliant." CBS had the exact same reaction. It was only later that I was told the idea came from Jim Parsons. I was very surprised and delighted that Jim came up with such a brilliant idea, only because as many other roles as Jim will have—because he's such a gifted actor—he will always be associated with Sheldon. So to have exploited that in a way that is not too taxing but still rewarding is pretty brilliant, I thought.

Chuck Lorre: Jim called me and wanted me to watch an iPhone recording of his nephew, Michael, who is a prodigy. He's like ten years old, living in the Houston area. I watched the video of this little boy explaining a science project he had done, and he was clearly one of those kids, just a genius. [*Laughs*] And Jim asked, "Is there a show in this?" And I thought, if we're going to do a show about a prodigy, we have one! And we already know about his mother and his father and his sister and his brother and his Meemaw; we know about his school, his educational background, we know what kind of character he is. We know so much about Sheldon as a grown-up, why not take this idea and make the show about a character we *already knew*. We didn't have to invent a new show about a brilliant, little boy; we *had* a brilliant, little boy! We just had to do a time-machine show. I called Molaro and said, "What do you think?" and he said, "Yeah, that's a good idea."

Peter Roth: And here's something interesting, but I was probably the most skeptical once we began the process because we did it as a single-camera comedy, which I did not want to do. I wanted to do it as a multicam for a lot of reasons, mostly because I did not want the audience to be thrown out of the picture. I was completely wrong about that. And Chuck argued the exact opposite point. He kept saying, "No, we've got to offer something that's uniquely, distinctively different." And he was right. And the other thing I didn't take into consideration was when you're working with kids, you have rules as to how many hours you can work them.

Jim Parsons: When we first started talking about it, I just assumed Chuck and Steve would do a multicam, and I was astounded when they told me they weren't. I would even say I was borderline disappointed in a weird way. I guess I had assumed I would be able to drop by tapings occasionally and talk to the audience—especially as we're finding our feet. But they wanted it to be its own thing, and filming it as a single cam was part of doing that, which was so smart. And it's allowed Steve to cultivate more heartfelt moments that he's really talented at, especially with these characters that he knows so well.

On December 15, 2016, Lorre and Molaro flew to Houston—along with Parsons and Spiewak—to meet Parsons's nephew and family, and get a taste of their life growing up with a prodigy.

Chuck Lorre: One of the smartest things Steve and I did was go to Houston. We spent time with Jim's nephew, and we used his parents as consultants early on. We paid them for story ideas because they're living and raising this brilliant child and they had things we could never in our wildest dreams come up with. So there was some early stuff that was a result of accessing Jim's sister and brother-in-law telling us about what it's like to raise a prodigy.

The gathering at Judy Parsons's house was nothing short of epic—and essential in bringing *Young Sheldon* to life.

Jim Parsons: She was really excited. I kind of feel bad, because I didn't get it. I was like, "I've been working with these people for eleven years now! You've even seen them at work!" She was just like, "I can't believe they're going to be in my house!" And I was like, "Well, *I'm* in your house, what the hell?!" [*Laughs*] So she was very excited, and she did have plenty of things to snack on, which I don't think anybody touched, because that's the way it goes. But she is a very Southern, hospitable woman.

Judy Parsons: I was a nervous wreck before Chuck and Steve came over. It was the beginning of December, and one of my friends said, "You don't have your Christmas tree up. Do you think you should?" She was over here trying to worry about the Christmas tree, and I was trying to worry about where they were gonna sit and what we were going to do. [*Laughs*] It was another one of those things where I almost had to pinch myself, like, *Is this really happening?* I open my front door and in walks Chuck Lorre and Steve Molaro! And it was a very unreal feeling. But you know what, they walked in and everything was as comfortable and relaxed as it could be. They wanted to meet my grandson, Michael—Jim's sister's oldest son, who is ten. We've always said, "Oh, my gosh, I can't believe he's that smart." He's always been a vessel for knowledge. He just wants to know *everything*. And so many times, when he was growing up I'd say, "That sounds just like what Sheldon would say if Sheldon was little." And Jim would hear it, and Jim would agree. Plus, he resembled Jim a lot. One time we were out shopping and someone stopped me and said, "Your little grandson, he looks just like that person that plays Sheldon on *The Big Bang Theory*." So that's where Jim got the idea to do the show about a young Sheldon. So Chuck and Steve sat there at our house and talked to Michael. At that time, Michael had to do a special project as part of the gifted and talented program, and he chose the brain and Alzheimer's. He and Chuck Lorre got into the biggest discussion about Alzheimer's disease because they had recently watched the same *60 Minutes* show about it. And my younger grandson, Parker, who's three years younger than Michael, is extremely smart, too, but he doesn't quite have that same quest for knowledge that Michael does. But then he started telling them about his project, which was on cows. So we had one kid talking about the brain and the other one talking about cows. He was asking Chuck if he knew how many stomachs a cow has and what a cow uses those stomachs for, and Chuck and Steve were just as kind as they could be. They just sat there and listened to it all.

Chuck Lorre: The one kid is ready to become a world-class scientist, the other kid is probably ready to become a successful rancher! The dichotomy that was Sheldon and George Jr., just a good ol' boy and an eleven-year-old rocket scientist. [*Laughs*]

While Judy Parsons doesn't have any photos from the day Chuck Lorre and Steve Molaro came to her house, she has plenty visiting Sheldon and Leonard's fictional apartment, pictured here with Jim, her daughter, son-in-law, and grandkids. (back row: Nathan Pruski, Judy Parsons; front row, left to right: Michael Pruski, Parker Pruski, Julie Pruski, Jim Parsons) *Courtesy of Judy Parsons*

Judy Parsons: And I had some of Jim's favorite cheese dip—our chili con queso—and chips, plus pico de gallo and some cookies, but they didn't eat hardly anything because they had been to one of our very best restaurants Jim used to love to go to when he was little. But now, every time I have visitors over, I say, "You're sitting in the same chair that Chuck Lorre sat in!" And they'd go, "You're kidding!" It's just crazy to me that I had those two guys in my house.

Lorre and Molaro also visited schools in the Houston area, which would eventually benefit from the *Young Sheldon* STEM Initiative that the Chuck Lorre Family Foundation created.

Chuck Lorre: We visited schools there, which were extremely welcoming, and spent a lot of time with us talking about what it would have been like in 1990. The school administrators were enormously helpful, and eventually the *Young Sheldon* scholarship program made contributions to those high schools over the years, as well as the Burbank School System, which was really wonderful.

Steve Molaro: We also went to a few Baptist churches, and it was shockingly informative. Chuck likes to do this type of research before launching a new show because he says it may open your eyes to a completely different version of the pilot you haven't thought of yet. We also talked to Texas high school principals and teachers and football coaches, we went to restaurants, a megachurch…we packed a lot in. I remember someone at the high school talking about the school's handbook of rules and guidelines and laughing about how they used to have one but no one would ever read it. I remember thinking, *I know exactly who would read it, which would be Sheldon.* And that's a big part of the pilot where Sheldon was ratting people out for not following the rules. And then Principal Petersen at the high school, played by Rex Linn, has his prized paddle that he used to be able to hit the kids with, but then the rules changed, and the teacher said, "I can go get my paddle and show you if you want. We're not allowed to do it anymore, but I still have it." That is literally from one of the principals we spoke to.

Once Lorre and Molaro returned to Los Angeles, casting began a few weeks later in early January 2017. They were prepared for an uphill battle to find the perfect person to play the complex, preteen Sheldon.

Chuck Lorre: We wrote a scene with a monologue, sort of a takeoff on Michael's science fair video explaining his science project. We purposely made it very difficult and long, which is *a lot* to ask of a ten-, eleven-year-old child. We set the bar very high thinking, *No one's going to be able to do this, but if anybody comes close, maybe we can work with them*. And Iain Armitage—who would become our young Sheldon—his mom sent us the home video of him doing it, and it included an impersonation of him doing William Shatner's character from *Star Trek*, Captain Kirk. It actually had a couple of lines where he impersonates Kirk's awkward kind of staccato performances. Iain did those two lines as Shatner would have said them, and it's in the middle of this long, overbloated monologue! We were like, "Uh, can we be this lucky?!" It was really quite wonderful. He got laughs where he was supposed to get laughs, and his confidence and self-assuredness were just astounding. So we flew him out, and he did it for us again in person. Had we not found Iain, there would've been no show. We were not going to try to do this with a little boy who is *kinda* okay. You had to find someone wonderful or you put this project on the back burner until such time as maybe a brilliant, young actor comes along. You cannot do this without the bolt of lightning that is Iain.

Peter Roth: Iain Armitage may be the greatest find of all time. It's one thing to cast an upcoming, relatively unknown Jim Parsons. It's another thing to find the replicant of an eight-year-old version. And Iain is a phenomenon. And of course, the symmetry and beauty of having Laurie Metcalf's daughter, Zoe, playing the role of Mary was so wonderful and so exactly right. But the real hero of *Young Sheldon* is Steve Molaro. That's his baby. My first boss in the business, Perry Lafferty, told me, "Ideas are the trash of the business. Execution is everything." I've quoted that thousands of times over my career. It was one of the smartest, most prophetic things I ever learned.

Chuck Lorre: Steve and I had understood early on that we couldn't ask Iain to carry the show entirely on his shoulders; it had to be an ensemble show. I think it's really very clear that the depth of that ensemble is the result of Steve Molaro. I've stepped aside to some extent, and I'm just a consultant these last couple of seasons. Steve sends me scripts, and I go, "Wow. This is great. I'm jealous." [*Laughs*] It's so good that my response is this dark jeal-ousy of "Wow, this is great writing! I wish I was part of this!"

Lance Barber, who plays George Sr., Sheldon's dad on *Young Sheldon*, actu-ally guest-starred on *The Big Bang Theory* as a bully of Leonard's from high school in "The Speckerman Recurrence" in season five.

Steve Molaro: I've been friends with Lance since 2002 because we had a mutual friend. He was actually super close to getting the role of Mike in *Mike & Molly*. It was down to him and Billy Gardell. And it killed Chuck to have to pick one of them, because he thought they were both amazing. So, when we were looking for Sheldon's dad on *Young Sheldon*, I tossed Lance's name out there and Chuck lit up. He was like, "Oh, my God, you know he was almost Mike. That guy's great. Get him in here!" and that's how that happened.

Lance Barber: Billy and I are similar big, blue-collar-type guys. So we've been in the trenches in the audition room for a really long time. He's just a wonderful guy, so I was thrilled for him [when he got the role of Mike]. But when this audition for George came around, I was already aware in the back of my mind that I was getting into the room because of the history I had with Chuck. But that being said, when you're an actor in LA for twenty years, I was appropriately cautious. I've gotten that close one hundred times. But I felt akin to the role because it had familiarity in the writing. My father passed away when I was a year old, so I never knew him. The two father fig-ures in my life were my grandfathers. They were different men from different areas, but similar men of a certain time, a certain culture, and so I brought what I had to them into the role of George. I feel like I hit the jackpot in so many different ways with this job, and so much about it has been a dream come true.

And what can one possibly say about the casting of Zoe Perry—Laurie Met-calf's real-life daughter—other than the casting stars aligning?

Jim Parsons: The funniest part is that all three of us—me, Laurie, and Zoe—were all thirty-three when we got the roles in the multicam shows that really affected our trajectories. All of us. And when they were casting

Mary in *Young Sheldon*, it was really Todd who said, "They should look at Zoe." We had seen her onstage and knew she was a very good actor, not to mention she has a lot of similarities to Laurie that could work in the role. But when we suggested it to Chuck, his original reaction was like, *That's outlandish! She's a child.* Because he really only knew Zoe from when Laurie would bring her to the set of *Roseanne* when she was a baby. But that was thirty years ago!

Laurie Metcalf: When Zoe told me she was going in to audition, I was excited for her, but I knew it certainly wasn't going to be handed to her. I was nervous about how she would audition, and she came to me a little bit beforehand to ask me to help her. And then we quickly decided, "No, no no, that's not a good idea at all." Because it's a dangerous thing to get into the head of another actor. I didn't want to do anything to her confidence before she went in the room.

Zoe Perry (Mary Cooper, *Young Sheldon*): It's funny because even prior to my audition, I remember my mom mentioning that the show might even exist, just from a conversation [she had] with Jim. They had to cast young Sheldon first, and even the way Chuck and Steve talked about it, it all hinged on *Can we find an actor who can really pull this off?* And they struck gold with Iain. Once that was established, I think it became possible to flesh out the rest of the cast. And I just remember my mom saying, "You have to audition for this!" And I would laugh [because] I don't have control over whether or not I get seen, or whether or not I get cast, all those things. But she was like, "You have to go in!"

Chuck Lorre: As curious as it was that Zoe came in and read, it was meaningless if she was not, in fact, the best choice to play that part. She's a gifted, remarkable actress, and while the connection is cool, it was not the reason to hire her. "Cool" doesn't get it, not when you're working with people day in and day out, hopefully for years. Zoe just knocked it out of the park the first time she read for the part. We were like, "Okay, we got Sheldon's mom!"

Laurie Metcalf: It's still funny to me that I'll see somebody write about how they think that the mom on *Young Sheldon* is so well cast because she can do a good impression of me. They don't assume that we're related, but a lot of people tell me that we really do sound alike. I'm happy that she got the part, but also in that it makes it just a little tiny layer deeper for the show. It looks like it really could be the same woman, thirty years earlier. And I don't think it's happened that there are relatives that have played the same character decades apart on currently running shows, before *Big Bang* went off the air.

Zoe Perry: It's completely surreal. I felt like I won the lottery when I booked the part. It's my grandma's favorite thing I've ever done and she tells me if she doesn't like something! [*Laughs*]

(left to right) Zoe Perry, Laurie Metcalf, Chuck Lorre, and Annie Potts at the Critics Choice Awards in 2019. Perry plays Mary Cooper on *Young Sheldon*, which is the same role her mother, Laurie Metcalf, played on *The Big Bang Theory*. Annie Potts plays Meemaw on *Young Sheldon*, who is the mother of Zoe's Mary Cooper, but actor June Squibb played Meemaw on *Big Bang*, even though Potts once did a voice mail voice-over as Meemaw for *Big Bang*. Got that? *Courtesy of Zoe Perry*

The cast was rounded out with the extraordinary young talents of Raegan Revord as Sheldon's twin sister, Missy, and Montana Jordan as older brother Georgie, along with Sheldon's Meemaw, played by the iconic Annie Potts. Lorre and Molaro also brought in *Big Bang* fan favorites like Professor Proton. And at least this time Bob Newhart could easily slip back into Proton's lab coat and not have to struggle with his Obi-Wan costume.

Bob Newhart: Chuck called me as they were about to do the pilot for *Young Sheldon*, and I went in. Oddly enough, the first episode was directed by Jon Favreau, who directed *Elf*, which I was in. And now sometimes they'll call me and I'll go in and do more appearances. They make me look younger for that though. Sheldon is thirty years younger. I only get to look ten years younger. [*Laughs*]

The spin-off was ordered to series in March 2017 for the 2017–2018 season. In August 2017, Steve Holland was promoted to showrunner for *Big Bang*'s eleventh season so Molaro could launch *Young Sheldon*.

Steve Molaro: Working on both shows at the same time was definitely an experience. The days were just nonstop. Filming on *Young Sheldon* starts fairly early in the morning, so then I'd scoot off to a *Big Bang* table read or a runthrough, then back to the *Sheldon* stage. Then I'd edit or go to other meetings during the lunch breaks, edit on the weekends, and then there was

Young Sheldon cocreator Steve Molaro poses with the cast in season one: (left to right) Montana Jordan (Georgie), Molaro, Iain Armitage (Sheldon), Lance Barber (George Sr.), Raegan Revord (Missy), and Zoe Perry (Mary). *Courtesy of Ansley Rix*

still *Big Bang* tape nights on Tuesday. It was wild, but I'm grateful I was able to go off on that new adventure while still being able to participate on the last two seasons of *Bang*. Any new show comes with pressure, but I think Chuck and I felt extra levels of it since it was an offshoot of such a successful program and a beloved character. Plus we were very invested in it feeling like its own thing, which came with its own learning curve. *Young Sheldon* is a single-camera show, which is like shooting a mini-movie each week. It takes us six days to shoot one episode of *Young Sheldon*. The scenes are shot many, many times from many different angles to cover all the characters. We would shoot an entire episode of *Big Bang* in the time it takes us to shoot one family dinner scene on *Sheldon*.

The story behind the Young Sheldon *theme song…*

Steve Molaro: I had been on the hunt for a theme song for *Young Sheldon* and it was an especially daunting task, since the *Big Bang* theme song was so well-known and universally loved. Since the *Big Bang* song is pop, I thought maybe some kind of guitar anthem might be a good way to go. I was sifting through music looking for something that might work and suddenly remembered an obscure song I loved from the early 2000s that was written and performed by [original *Blue's Clues* host] Steve Burns called "Mighty Little Man." I knew immediately that was the one. While I worked at Nickelodeon in New York during the height of *Blue's Clues,* I didn't know Steve. I went through a few old friends there and managed to get his email. I think he thought I was joking when I told him I wanted his sixteen-year-old song to be the theme song. I still love it every time I hear it. It's perfect.

Young Sheldon premiered on Monday, September 25, 2017, following *The Big Bang Theory*'s eleventh season premiere. Reviews were strong, but the audience response was even better: It was the most-watched comedy debut in fifteen years. The series was given a second-season renewal in January 2018, followed by a two-season renewal in February 2019.

The success of *Young Sheldon* only fueled interest from critics and fans as to whether there would be a crossover episode with *Big Bang* before it wrapped its twelve-season run. The two shows overlapped by only two years, but there was never a concrete plan to do such an episode. Not to mention, both shows exist in entirely different decades. But then the perfect opportunity presented itself in "The VCR Illumination": Amy and Sheldon got the devastating news that their research on Super Asymmetry wasn't going to move forward, thereby diminishing their chances of winning the Nobel. In a moment of despair, Leonard reminds Sheldon that he made a pep talk to himself when he was younger on VHS tape should such a scenario ever present itself.

Steve Holland: We never really planned on a *Young Sheldon* crossover. The timeline made it pretty tricky. We had done a few small things, like the episode where we meet adult Tam and find out what happened to him, but we really weren't planning on using the *Young Sheldon* cast, until we hit on this idea of Sheldon needing advice from the only person he truly respected—himself. We really wanted to bring Sheldon to a low point regarding his and Amy's breakthrough and who could buck him back up. We had the thought that he had recorded an emergency video of himself when he was younger and that seemed like a fun way to show a glimpse of Iain and to have the two Sheldons share a scene together. In fact, the initial thought was just that we see young Sheldon on the tape and then it's taped over by one of his dad's football games.

But it's his late father's halftime speech—urging the team not to give up—that gives Sheldon the kick in the pants that he needs. "If we do lose, you need to know that doesn't make you losers," George Sr. says. "You learn as much about who you are and what you're made of from failing as you do from success. Maybe more. So you can spend the next half feeling sorry for yourselves, or you can get out there and give 'em hell." Sheldon pauses the tape on his dad's face at the exact frame where George Sr. seems to be looking at the video camera, and Sheldon says, "Thanks, Dad." The sentimental moment instantly bridged the two shows.

Steve Holland: One of our writers, Andy Gordon, pitched that his dad's halftime pep talk could be on the tape and that could be the thing that gets Sheldon over his crisis. It seemed so perfect that it's surprising that that wasn't the idea all along. It seemed like such an emotional moment for Sheldon to get the advice he needs from his father who is no longer alive. And initially at the end, Sheldon took the VHS tape out and said, "Thanks, Dad" to the tape. At the runthrough, Chuck had the idea for him to pause it and say the line directly to the image of his dad, which was so much better.

Jim Parsons: I personally felt very meaningful and grateful that we got to have that little moment. What really resonates for me—and probably anyone who has ever lost a loved one—is that feeling that the lessons to be learned and gleaned from that person aren't gone just because they are. You never know when a memory, or in this case a video—so much later in life, so many years after the event—will help you again. I have a very specific view on fathers and children, having lost my dad in 2001. Not that it has anything to do with mine specifically, but sometimes things can be too sentimental and it makes me take a step from them, but that wasn't that. I thought there was a simplicity to the moment, coupled with a really inspired use of cross-over stuff, as it were. I think one of the reasons this was not gimmicky is that there was no need for it. It wasn't the type of thing where the producers were like, *Oh, we gotta get people interested in* Young Sheldon. It had nothing to do with that. It was just a really smart, thoughtful use of these characters and storylines.

Steve Molaro: And Lance was adorably nervous doing the performance for the tape, because he really wanted to get it right. He was like, "Did that work for you? I'm not a sports guy! You need to tell me!"

Lance Barber: Steve was right. I did get all anxious about it. I was a big kid growing up who was always asked to play football, and I'd say, "I'm too busy singing show tunes in my bedroom." Luckily that was the path I chose and it's worked out better than athletics, which I had no prowess for what-soever. But I was anxious about that feeling real in the speech in the locker room, but it played out beautifully.

In the years since, there's been plenty of other *Big Bang* Easter eggs on *Young Sheldon*, from "Soft Kitty" to the appearances of young Leonard, young Penny, young Amy, young Howard, young Raj, and young Bernadette.

But perhaps the most special was the season four premiere tag which featured a surprise Mayim Bialik voice-over cameo as Amy, and later again in season five. In a quick exchange with husband Sheldon, it's revealed that they have a son named Leonard Cooper. Sheldon says he wanted to name his son Leonard Nimoy Cooper, but Amy says she's lucky she let him have the Leonard name.

Steve Holland: Their son is named for both Leonard Hofstadter and Leonard Nimoy, but more so Hofstadter. Steve reached out to Mayim and she said, "Absolutely!" Sheldon had already said via a voice-over on *Young Sheldon* that he and Amy had kids as he talked about the things he wished he had said to his dad and thinks about now, because he has his own kids. And in this weird, sort of small way, we realized we kind of get to keep telling the story of *Big Bang Theory* in these little asides. We don't want to undo anything we've done, but...sometimes the reason Sheldon's family seems sweeter on *Young Sheldon* than on *Big Bang Theory* is these are stories being told by an older Sheldon who has kids of his own, and it gives him a greater appreciation of his dad through a different lens. We're still trying to adhere to tentpole canon, but it gave us some wiggle room to tell these stories in a slightly different way as we move forward. And we've never said how old Sheldon is as the narrator in *Young Sheldon*, but we figure he has a couple of kids who are probably the age he is in *Young Sheldon*, who are probably ten or eleven, which means he's probably in his fifties. We've never said canonically, but that's sort of in our head.

Mayim Bialik: It was so lovely to do. We did it during COVID, so I recorded it by myself, with Steve Molaro on FaceTime from the other room. [*Laughs*] It was such a sweet little endnote to my time on *Big Bang*. I miss all those people and I miss telling those stories, so to get to be involved, even in a small way, was really exciting.

A year later, in the show's fifth season, Molaro emailed Simon Helberg to gauge his interest in reviving Howard Wolowitz for a surprise voice-over where he and Sheldon argue over engineering—and Sheldon's constant need to wear his Nobel medal everywhere. It was an instant yes, so over Zoom, Helberg and Parsons came together to record new scenes as Howard and Sheldon.

Jim Parsons: When we did that scene, there were two things immediately evident again: One was how easy it is to work with Simon. There's a human comfortability factor I feel with him. But the second thing was there was a shocking, internal familiarity with the way we talk to each other as those two characters, which is in no way reminiscent of the way we talk to each other in real life. And to do this scene with Simon, even though it was future selves, they were very much in a relationship that was still very rooted in the *Big Bang* relationship. They had not advanced at all, apparently. [*Laughs*] But when we were recording the scene together over Zoom, I realized that it was sort of like seeing someone who you thought was dead all over again. It was like, *Oh my God! I never thought I'd see you again!* And that's really dramatic, I know. But it kind of felt that way in a weird way, like, *I thought these conversations between these characters were literally deceased, and here we are having another one of them!* [*Laughs*] *Bickering at each other.* It was delightful. It really was.

Steve Molaro: How could we do an episode about engineering and it not have something to do with Wolowitz? And what a joy from beginning to end. I don't think Simon had been on the Warner Bros. lot since the night *Big Bang* ended, so it was lovely and surreal for all of us. Even though Jim was in New York and Simon was on a soundstage in Burbank and we were in our offices on Zoom, it was an emotional and hilarious experience.

Jim Parsons: And I loved finding out that Sheldon wears his Nobel medal all the time. That was probably the funniest thing to me. [*Laughs*] So obnoxious of him to wear that everywhere! That was the best part because it echoed those best, absurd qualities...like, no one would do that, except Sheldon would do that! And so that was fun to get to say, "Look how shiny it is!"

By this time, *Young Sheldon* had earned a three-season renewal (as well as a lucrative syndication deal) guaranteeing the show would run at least seven seasons. It also gives the producers ample time to fully explore Sheldon's adolescence before George Sr.'s eventual fatal heart attack when Sheldon is fourteen. But it also begs the question of whether they'll plan additional *Big Bang* character cameos, or perhaps an entire cast reunion.

Steve Holland: You never say never. It would be exciting. I would love to be around them all again, but I don't want to take anything away from the magnificent cast of *Young Sheldon* by leaning on the *Big Bang* cast. That show and those actors have earned their mark, and while it would be a very fun nostalgia play, I don't think it would be fair to them or the show.

But regardless, the purpose of *Young Sheldon* has always been about looking to the past to inform our future, perhaps with a new, more understanding, compassionate lens.

Nikki Lorre: There's things I think a lot of people that were popular growing up take for granted, such as how much it means to have a friend, and how much it means to have a community of people that support and love you. Especially going back and watching *Young Sheldon* now, you understand how hard it must be growing up in a place like East Texas in the early '90s with a religious family when you're different. Because they were coddled so much from a generation that didn't know how to deal with them and their social anxieties, they're kind of hard to deal with as adults because they weren't given the proper tools to learn how to interact and engage with people that are more socially astute. Watching *Big Bang* now, it's easy to roll your eyes at Sheldon, but this is a person that was just trying to navigate a world where everyone's speaking a different language. And that is really relatable to people.

And for Parsons, it's a chance to revisit the role that changed his life and further proof of how much Sheldon Cooper still means to him.

Jim Parsons: Even though I walked away from the mothership, I narrate every single episode of *Young Sheldon*. I do like four episodes in an hour or two. But to drop in and talk like Sheldon for a little bit here and there is interesting. It's kind of sweet. It revisits a specific type of fun that I don't have anymore.

It also means that by the time *Young Sheldon* completes season seven in 2024, Parsons will have played the role of Sheldon Cooper for seventeen years.

Jim Parsons: It's kind of shocking to know that statistic. The only thing that strikes me as very normal about it is that it's what I grew up understanding working a job meant. You didn't bop around a lot, you had one good job and it paid the bills and you stuck with it! And so it sounds like that, but it's nothing like that. [*Laughs*] On many levels! But it's interesting…I'm glad that that time is extending through voice-over work. I don't know that I'd be a pleasant person to be around if I kept playing the same character five days a week in person, fighting with Wolowitz or whatever. [*Laughs*] But seventeen is a surprising number. If I knew [I'd have this kind of longevity in one role] leading up to the initial audition for this, I think I would have passed out if you said that number to me then. I would have been like, *Baaahhh!* And you just can't conceive of it, even if you wouldn't have wanted to run from it. I think I would have understood that's going to be an insane blessing, but at the same time, it's just so inconceivable. It's still sort of inconceivable.

Chapter 23

THE LORRE LEGACY

The power of television can keep us company in our darkest hours, connect us with a stranger, or inspire major life changes. And if you're lucky enough to work in the medium and become successful at it, you have the power to actually make a difference.

When Chuck Lorre and Bill Prady created *The Big Bang Theory*, they weren't thinking about inspiring the next generation of scientists; they just wanted to make a successful TV show. But with success comes great responsibility, and when it was becoming obvious that the likes of Sheldon, Leonard, Raj, and Howard were inspiring an interest in the sciences, it took a powerhouse like Lorre to push through the logistical paperwork to do something to capitalize on it. And so, in 2015, the *Big Bang Theory* Scholarship Endowment at UCLA—with additional funding from Warner Bros. and CBS—was launched to ensure undergraduate students in need of financial aid could pursue a degree in the fields of Science, Technology, Engineering, and Mathematics (STEM) without tuition debt. And then, in 2018, the Chuck Lorre Family Foundation—which actually began two decades earlier in the late '90s—created the *Young Sheldon* STEM Initiative, which as of this writing has provided nearly $2 million in funding to fifty-five public schools in Southern California and East Texas. This was followed by the *Big Bang Theory* Graduate Fellowship Fund in 2019, which provides dedicated scholarships for *Big Bang*–UCLA scholars who have been accepted into a STEM-focused graduate or PhD program.

It's not unusual for a TV series to inspire someone's career, be it a journalist like Murphy Brown, a surgeon like Dr. Cristina Yang, or an SVU advocate

like Olivia Benson, but it is very rare for a producer to take matters into their own hands to make a very costly field of study a little more attainable. But leave it to Lorre to put it simply: "That was an easy decision to decide to do something to make those goals a reality."

Chuck Lorre: The mission statement for the foundation was based on my own life to provide health care for people who didn't have access to health care. And the *Big Bang* scholarship came about as a result of hearing there was an increase in students pursuing STEM fields in high school and college because they were watching *The Big Bang Theory* and it looked fun and cool to be a physicist or a mathematician or an engineer. Students were choosing to go into technological fields that they otherwise would have ignored as boring or dry or dull. I started it with a few million dollars, and then went to everybody I could and said, "Do you want to participate?" We generated a considerable amount of money that was earmarked for an ongoing scholarship at UCLA. Professor David Saltzberg was instrumental in helping us set it up because we wanted to find students who needed the financial assistance to pursue chemistry, biology, physics, math, engineering, etc., *and* were also good students capable of doing something with the assistance and making it effective. It started off with twenty-one or twenty-two students, and four years later, twenty of those students graduated. And then we expanded the scholarship availability to kids staying within the California system to help subsidize masters programs. UCLA was chosen because we wanted to be able to participate. These students were coming to the set, meeting the actors, hanging out, and meeting the actual folks behind the program. My running joke when they graduate has always been, "We don't ask much of you other than to change the world. For the better! We don't want to grow the next generation of super villains. Do good!" And there is no greater feeling of happiness than seeing the joy on these kids' faces when they enter the scholarship program and then when they graduate. God damn it, we're making scientists!

Peter Roth: The generosity with which Chuck is giving away so much money is really remarkable. It's the thing about Chuck that I think I love the most. The Foundation and what it represents is who he really is, because

Dear Mr.Lorre and the Chuck Lorre Foundation,

Thank you for the Big Bang Theory scholarship! I am extremely grateful for your support, the community, and the impact that both will make on my four years at UCLA.

I am a part of the class of 2025, from San Diego, California and am so excited to begin my studies at UCLA. As an undeclared engineering major who is still largely unsure of her future, this scholarship will allow me to explore all the possibilities UCLA has to offer. In my Engineering 96G class, I am working on building a fully functional go-kart where I can practice applications of mechanical engineering. I chose engineering because of my childhood in underdeveloped regions. I hope to use my degree to implement infrastructure or develop solutions that will improve the standard of living for the underprivileged. Because of this, I joined Engineers Without Borders at UCLA and am working on the Uganda project to build a reliable water source for the Bukonko community. I also am a member of SLAM at UCLA where I can continue my passion for music by mentoring kids in local schools.

I've been wanting to get an iPad since the beginning of the quarter but was concerned about the cost so I held off. It's made note-taking so much easier and more efficient. I haven't met the rest of the Big Bang Theory scholars yet in person, but we do have a planned social event at the Marina that I'm really looking forward to. I am very excited to be a part of such a special community. With all my academic and extracurricular endeavors, the scholarship has relieved the additional financial pressure, allowing me to make the most of my time here. Especially since I am from a single-parent household, I feel proud to not have to burden my mom. I am thankful for this scholarship and plan to reciprocate your generosity through my future work.

Sincerely,

Sundi

Just one of the many letters that Lorre and the Chuck Lorre Family Foundation received on behalf of the students benefiting from the generosity of the *Big Bang Theory* Scholarship Endowment. *Courtesy of Sundi Win and the Chuck Lorre Family Foundation*

once you get past that hard shell, God, he is a good man. I love him like my brother. For me, the show has always given to its audience. Now, Chuck and the Foundation are giving to the next great thinkers of our time, and hopefully can be the next Nobel Prize winners.

Steve Holland: When my younger son was touring high schools around the Los Angeles area, the tour guides were talking about how a lot of interest was in their STEM program, and they called it the *Big Bang* effect. Now, mind you, they didn't know what I did or where I worked when they said that. But they relayed that there was a whole generation of kids who said science seemed fun and cool because of *The Big Bang Theory*. It was amazing to hear that. So much of this job is sitting in a room with eight other writers trying to make each other laugh, so to realize that what we were doing was touching people in a bigger way was really humbling, and it was something that we never took for granted. We would get letters from people all the time saying they had decided to become a scientist or go into the sciences because of *Big Bang*. And then to meet the kids who were part of the *Big Bang Theory* Scholarship Program who were now graduating was really powerful.

Chuck Lorre: We never heard of anyone wanting to become a jingle writer because of *Two and a Half Men*. Chiropractors did not suddenly become a hot profession watching that show. [*Laughs*] But listen, one of the most wonderful things about the scholarship fund is the handwritten letters I've gotten along the way from the students. It's also nice to see cursive alive and well. [*Laughs*] The subsidizing that we've been doing has allowed them to just focus on their schooling. They didn't have to wash dishes in the cafeteria or sit in a toll booth in a parking lot while studying. They could just study. You get a lot of satisfaction out of the success of the show, but it's an entirely different level of happiness when you see these kids crying with joy that their financial crisis is over. Even though *Big Bang* is no longer coming out with new episodes, the scholarship is not only continuing to go forward, but we're going to expand it.

Thank you so much!
Josselyne
Aerospace Engineering

Lorre loves all the letters he has received, but has a soft spot for the handwritten notes (stickers are always a plus!). *Courtesy of Josselyne Berrios and the Chuck Lorre Family Foundation*

In fact, in November 2021, in celebration of both *Young Sheldon*'s fifth season and the work of public school teachers across the United States, the Chuck Lorre Family Foundation partnered with top education nonprofit DonorsChoose to support teachers and STEM education with a $1,500,000 commitment to support schools in low-income communities. This was in addition to a $200,000 pledge, which originally began in 2019.

Chuck Lorre: We created a pool of money for Van Nuys High School, which was immeasurably helpful to us in using their facilities. When Molaro and I went to East Texas before we wrote the pilot for *Young Sheldon*, we met with school administrators at a lot of different high schools around Houston, so some of the money has also been going there to supplement programs and buy equipment. It's not a lot to make sure that the high school has a music teacher. It's not a million dollars to make sure there's instruments so when kids decide they want to join the band, they can get their hands on a flugelhorn. And the fact that California can't do it and these public schools are stretched so tight, it's kind of heartbreaking but easily fixed.

Kunal Nayyar: Inspired by Chuck's example, I started scholarships at Temple University and the University of Portland. I wanted to help actors who cannot complete their education due to lack of finances. Chuck always said to me, "None of this is worth it if you don't have humility. None of this is worth it if you don't give back. None of this is worth it if you don't have a platform to do something bigger and better for the world."

Simon Helberg: To see all these young kids coming to the set and hearing someone wanted to become an engineer because of Howard, or someone wanted to become an astrophysicist because of Raj, was pretty incredible. It was a pretty wild thing to see these kids' dreams come true, and that was because of what Chuck did. It's not something you would foresee going into a sitcom, not to diminish what the value of a sitcom is, but the show did other things besides just make people laugh.

Kevin Sussman: I get told a lot by people that the show piqued their interests in the sciences, in physics. *Big Bang* always had its detractors—people that don't like mainstream, multicam comedy. And oftentimes, when something is so popular, people just want to shit on it. But being able to make a show accessible to such a wide array of people of all ages, of all different cultural backgrounds, of all different classes…that's really, really hard to do.

Melissa Rauch: I truly believe each of those brilliant minds are going to change our world for the better. I remember one day I was asking one of the students what they were up to, how school was, and she was telling me all about it and then said, "I have midterms tomorrow, so I need to study after we get home from this." And I was like, "Don't waste your time talking to me. I barely passed Chemistry. I'm going to shut my yapper, so you can get back to the dorm and start saving the world!"

Mayim Bialik: To see the faces of these kids whose lives were being changed, by what Chuck had established, was really, really powerful.

Watching Lorre's generosity over the years inspired the cast to give back in their own way, whether it was starting their own charities, or by making time for special visitors on set from various organizations.

Johnny Galecki: Sunshine Kids was one of the first charities we were involved in. It's a nonprofit for kids with cancer, so sometimes thirty or forty kids would come to set and we would spend time together. Those were always very emotional days for me when you have these kids there, fighting a very serious disease, who just want to ask you questions about your character and look through the set. Years before I was on *Big Bang*, I volunteered for a bit as a clown at a children's hospital in Chicago, and learned how important it was to give a child a sense of power, because they are often talked about in relation to their disease and not as a person. So it's important to just kind of let them be the boss for a while. Those were days that meant a lot, and after they left, I'd run up to my dressing room and cry it out a little bit. You just feel so fortunate to be a special part of somebody's day like that.

Kaley Cuoco: One of my little EB [epidermolysis bullosa, a rare genetic skin disorder] kids, Isaiah Zarate, had a seat every episode the last two seasons. And he could bring whoever he wanted with him. To me, the best thing that came out of our show and the moments I remember are the Make-a-Wish nights. And it was never long enough for me. To think someone's last wish was to come meet us? You can't even know. I remember one sweet little girl who was there one of the nights we were doing a flash mob

Sunshine Kid recipient Jasmine Love spent time with Johnny Galecki during her visit to the *Big Bang* set. Love, who is from North Carolina, is currently doing well. *Courtesy of The Sunshine Kids*

dance rehearsal actually joined us. Her mom wrote a letter later to say it was the best moment of her daughter's life, but it was also one of the best moments of our lives. It always puts things into perspective for us.

Nikki Lorre: Even though the cast had so much stuff to learn and new pages would be coming down from the writers room to memorize, they would spend so much genuine, quality time with these kids. Especially Kaley. She just knew how to speak their language because often they were kids with disabilities and it was hard for them to move or speak. She always wanted to make sure it was a memorable, intimate experience for them. With all the pressure they had coming up in an hour, they could switch roles and be the kindest, most genuine human beings for someone else. It was such a beautiful gift.

Anthony Rich: The [cast would always] drop *everything*. They went above and beyond. And with the Make-a-Wish kids, the cast would sit down and ask them, "What's your favorite episode?" Sometimes kids would start to stutter and didn't know how to talk to them, or they'd start crying, and the cast was so very comforting in those situations. And other times you'd have kids who would be like, *Oh, no, I belong here!* [*Laughs*] It was just all very moving. The most beautiful moments.

Jim Parsons: It was always very emotional... and at some level, that was the most important work that we could do. [*Choking up*] There's so many people that have had their lives touched by the show, but it's hard to find a comparison to those visits, and being chosen by them for their wish. And then being there with their families... there's an appreciation there that helps color your own appreciation for what you've been given.

Simon Helberg: It was an incredible reminder of the power of storytelling, whether it's television or pop culture or films or any kind of creative field. It could be a matter of putting on *Friends* at night to go to sleep to that rhythm, or watching it in the hospital to get you through a tough time. And then when you get to meet people who tell you that... it takes the wind out of you in a really powerful way. I was always, *always* moved by it.

Kunal Nayyar: The impact of the show goes beyond just popularity. There's a friend of my brother's whose father was ailing in the hospital from cancer. I remember him writing to me and saying, "In the last few days that I could spend with my father, the greatest joy was having *Big Bang* on in the hospital." And then he said, "As a goodbye to my father, I'd like to come and watch a live taping just as an homage to how much this show had meant to him." I remember him sitting in the audience, just crying the whole time, because it was that connection between him and his father. That's just a small example of a personal relationship with someone. I was recently in New Delhi and the amount of kids who came up to me and said, "I watched this show with every single meal," or "Because of you, I want to study astrophysics." So yes, the show was immensely popular, but I think the emotional impact it's had on the youth is what really touches my heart. Truly. I do not take that lightly.

Melissa Rauch: A family from Ireland, Yavanna and Lar Keogh, reached out to tell me their beautiful son, Oscar, was a huge fan of the show and he referred to Bernadette as his girlfriend. Oscar had recently been diagnosed with diffuse intrinsic pontine glioma, an aggressive form of pediatric cancer. I fell in love with him and his family, and the cast was so wonderful and recorded a video for him. Oscar tragically passed away the July after *Big Bang* ended. To honor his life, my husband and I joined forces with his amazing parents to form Oscar's Kids, a charity that endeavors to fund pediatric cancer research with a focus on DIPG as well as helping other families navigating similar diagnoses. Not only will Oscar's magic live on, but he will always be a tremendous part of *Big Bang*'s legacy as well.

Chapter 24

THE DECISION TO END THE SHOW

On Wednesday, August 22, 2018, Warner Bros. released a statement to the press with the subject line: "WBTV Release: *The Big Bang Theory* to End in 2019 as Longest-Running Multi-Cam Comedy Series in TV History." It was both shocking *and* expected. When the cast signed new contracts in March 2017 for two more seasons, *Deadline* reported that "it would likely be the sitcom's final chapter." But just three weeks prior to the press release announcing the conclusion of the series, the *Hollywood Reporter* ran a story saying, "*Big Bang Theory* Season 13 Renewal Talks Underway," with CBS Entertainment president Kelly Kahl telling reporters at the Television Critics Association press tour that "we don't believe it's the final year. We are in preliminary discussions to renew the show with Warner Bros."

Depending on who you talked to, it was the perfect time to bring the show to a conclusion, yet also puzzling. Streaming was already dominating the zeitgeist, and viewership was eroding for the broadcast networks. So when you have a show as successful and popular as *Big Bang* still was, it would seem like the network and studio would do everything to keep it on the air.

It took only a few hours after the news broke for *Entertainment Weekly* to report that *Big Bang* was ending because "Jim Parsons was ready to leave." Although Parsons posted on Instagram the following day that it was hard—"nearly impossible, actually"—to accept that they had only one season left, and that he would "miss all of you...more than I can say and more than I can know at this time," fans were devastated and confused. They wondered why anyone would walk away from what they assumed would be nearly $50 million if Parsons signed on for two more seasons.

To make matters more complicated, Kaley Cuoco and Johnny Galecki were quoted as saying they felt "blindsided" by the decision to end the show, while Mayim Bialik later said the series ended for "reasons the public doesn't know about." Chuck Lorre told *USA Today* that he was "grief-stricken" as the end approached, and based on the amount of tears and sadness from the cast over the course of the final season, it fueled more questions than answers.

Jim Parsons: I was in New York that summer doing a play on Broadway when my dog, Otis, died at the age of fourteen. Todd and I had had him since he was eight weeks old. Otis was this emblem, basically representative of me and Todd, our time together, and all these major life events. It was the end of an era, and his passing brought a sense of clarity for me. I don't think there was a part of me that actually thought I would do more seasons after the twelfth, but I was ready to . . . get out of the security of the show to fully find out what was next for me. I was ready to move back to New York full-time.

Simon Helberg: I was aware that Jim felt ready to move on from the show, and we did talk about it. I felt the same. We felt like season twelve was the end of the run. Now, that didn't mean that we, in *any* way, expected that the show would certainly end or that there wouldn't be any kind of attempt from the producers or the studio or the network to keep the show running, whether or not we were involved. Or that there wouldn't be an attempt to keep us involved. But the feeling to move on from the show for both Jim and myself was totally genuine.

Jim Parsons: That's completely true. There was very little going on in my life in general that Simon, more than anybody else that was employed on this show, wouldn't have known about just because we were that close. I had to talk to him before anything like that happened. It has nothing to do with the respect level or love that I feel for other people on the show, but he was in my dressing room more than he was in his own. There are so few other people on this planet we could talk to [about our situation], and even if

Jennifer Aniston and David Schwimmer walked in the room, they wouldn't completely understand because each show is different and unique.

Simon Helberg: But I expected with the show being such a success for the studio and network, that they would really make an effort to, in one way or another, keep it on, or keep us there, or at least bring up the conversation, but they never did. So by the time we were about to start season twelve, and the studio was talking about continuing the run, Jim and I were like, "This is so weird."

Jim Parsons: In August, we went back for that first read-through of the new season. At the time, nothing had come up about contracts. The one thing I knew was, if this was going to be the final season, or at least the final season for my character, the writers needed to know sooner rather than later. I was very frightened and anxious about having to do it, but I knew I had to. I felt like a liar at that table read, because I knew that at the end of these next twenty-four episodes, that was it for me. So I asked Chuck and Steve if we could talk.

Steve Molaro: Jim had sent me and Chuck an email on a Wednesday afternoon asking to have a meeting with the two of us, so we made a plan to have him come into Chuck's office that next morning. I read the email a few times, and got the sense from the way it was worded that something like his future on the show might be why he wanted to meet...and that this was going to be the end for him.

Chuck Lorre: When he came by, he just jumped right into it. I certainly didn't see it coming. I said, "*Oh*. OK. Well, this is kind of a big conversation. A big conversation that impacts hundreds of people. Not just the actors but the crew." I didn't try to talk him out of it, like, *Oh, let's stop and think about this.*

Jim Parsons: Before I told Chuck and Steve the news, I did think of how I would respond to a scenario in which I was asked to be in like six episodes or something if the show continued, but I knew that was not appealing to me. It's not like I had another job lined up and couldn't do it, but this was a life move I was making, and dropping in for big moments if the show continued was not the full break I was aiming for. But had they continued without me, I did think, *My God, what would you do with Amy?! Would they* *have to kill me? In a train accident? And then they could carry on sensibly?* But on *Young Sheldon* they already revealed we had kids, so they couldn't kill Sheldon! These were the things I thought about.

Steve Molaro: I wasn't completely shocked when he said it, but obviously you can be prepared for something and still feel totally unprepared for the gravity of the moment once it happens. And when he told us, Chuck and I understood why he wanted to move on. There was never a question about continuing on without him. The show was this ensemble and the thought of doing some strange version without him didn't seem right.

Jim Parsons: There was no pressure from them, and they were very sweet and kind. But I had a part of me that was hopeful that if other people wanted to keep doing it, that they would find a way to do that. I didn't feel possessive about it, in that, just because I didn't want to continue, I didn't want anyone else to, either. I didn't feel that at all. I mean, look, I'm not an idiot, I understood you'd be dealing with a very different show if I was gone. *Two and a Half Men* carried on without Charlie Sheen, albeit with some major changes. *The Office* carried on when Steve Carell left. I didn't necessarily think they would continue our show once I left, but I knew it was not out of the realm of possibility.

Lee Aronsohn: I'll tell you, without Jim Parsons, there is no twelve years of *Big Bang Theory*. Not to take anything away from the rest of the cast, but... the show couldn't have lasted as long as it did without him. The ensemble together was a '61 Yankees of comedy. Losing any one of them would have been an incredible loss, but Sheldon was irreplaceable—that character *and* the actor.

> **Parsons had only told Helberg about his plans prior to his meeting with Lorre and Molaro. Nothing was spoken about officially with any other cast members, as they were mainly waiting to see what the studio and/or network might say first.**

Jim Parsons: Every situation had its particulars. And from all things we've heard and read over the years, it's very clear that *Friends* was a different situation as far as a level of communication about those types of business decisions. It is simply not how we ran. So, if I had been more torn with my decision, like, I have to change something in my life and I'm not sure if it's this or that, then I could see more of a group conversation with the cast, perhaps. But being sure of my knowledge of what I needed to do for myself, it would have been one unending difficult conversation after another. I fully understand the feeling, and I would feel the exact same way [that Johnny and Kaley did] about not hearing the news or being consulted until the hammer dropped, but going by how we ran things around there, I didn't think it was my responsibility. Also, I wasn't ever purposely suggesting this show needs to wrap up. It was completely personal and so, to tell them ahead of time, what would have happened? Would it have been like I was asking them to come to a conclusion? I can't imagine what that would have been like, if suddenly people wanted to keep doing it. It sounds like a mess, which is probably why nobody talked to anybody before these conversations.

Melissa Rauch: I know everyone had their own personal feelings about whether they wanted to do more or not, so it was loosely discussed in that way. I was sort of under the impression that if there were going to be future seasons we would hear from the decision-makers with offers or a formal notice of another season happening and then those talks would start. I thought everyone was just waiting to see if the powers that be were going to greenlight a thirteenth, and then we'd get into it.

Jim Parsons: Even though I was ready to move on, I did think that we would be approached with an offer for something, and that would be my chance to say, "I'm done." But there was no offer on the table. With that said, it was impossible not to imagine that a show doing *that* well, *still* at this age, that the network wasn't going to fight for it. And maybe other people don't agree with this next statement or maybe it sounds risque, but all the trouble for CBS and Les Moonves happened right around then [*Ed. note:* A few weeks after the decision to end *Big Bang* was announced, Moonves resigned amid sexual misconduct allegations, which he has denied], so there was never a battle once they found out I didn't want to do it anymore. And I was grateful for that, because I didn't want to have hard conversation after hard conversation and get some offer you can't refuse. I didn't want to deal with any of that, and I didn't. But I can't help but think there were a *lot* of major distractions going on for that network at that point in time. And maybe that wouldn't have changed anything, but those are just the facts of the situation.

Steve Molaro: This is true. Jim's people had made it clear that this was happening, and said, "Please don't try to undo this, it's already hard enough," which was honored.

Jim Parsons: I know somebody from Warner Bros. eventually called my agent and said, "At the very least, doing our due diligence, is there any way, any sliver of…" and he was able to tell them, "No. This isn't a ploy, nor is he on the fence about it." So it's not like nobody did anything in that way. I hope I don't sound scandalous to have my guesses of why I think more wasn't done to pressure that situation, and maybe it was just simply that they were being respectful of me. I have no idea, but I really am eternally grateful that that part of it was fairly clean.

Chuck Lorre: Ultimately at the end of the day, it didn't matter how much money might have been on the table, Jim was done. I really think he deserves a tremendous amount of credit. He turned his back on what would have [probably] been an absolute fortune for creative reasons. He wanted to pursue his art, and in order to do that, it would be an act of financial courage to walk away from a truckload of money. Which I think should be applauded. I don't think the others wanted to keep doing it for money, either. We just loved doing it. We were still having fun! But for Jim in particular, he kind of hit a wall creatively and wanted to do other things. And I don't know if he's gotten enough credit for it.

Peter Roth: I'll never forget that moment when I got a phone call from Chuck. He asked what I was doing; I told him I was driving and he said, "Pull over." I did and that's when he said, "Jim wants to leave the show." My first thought was, *What do we have to do to convince him to stay? Surely there's something we can do. What about a reduction in the number of episodes? Is it about money? What's it about?* And Chuck, in that phone call, said to me: "This is it." I clearly heard the tone of Chuck's voice that this was a fait accompli; this was a decision that had been made. And then I had to keep it quiet for the weekend. My first thought was to tell my boss (then Warner Bros. chairman and CEO Kevin Tsujihara), but I swore to Chuck that I wouldn't tell anybody, and I didn't. So I sat with it for a Saturday afternoon and all Sunday. I spoke to Chuck a number of times Sunday asking if there was any change of mind, which there wasn't. And then we had to very, very carefully orchestrate the phone calls; Chuck to CBS, me to my team and to my boss. It was not pleasant. We were so terrified that the story would leak, so it had to be so carefully coordinated. But especially now with some distance and retrospect, I don't think there's anybody that doesn't agree that it was a wise decision.

Steve Molaro: Our big concern was how do we inform the cast without it being leaked to the press in two seconds? Everyone knew that was going to happen. But it was tough because for now, only the three of us knew, and I couldn't say anything until it was public. A few days after Jim came to me and Chuck, I woke up at 5 a.m. on a Saturday and the reality of it had finally sunk in. I sobbed uncontrollably for about forty-five minutes, shaking in bed, crying, as the reality that it was ending really was starting to sink in for the first time. And it was the first day of many, many tear-filled sessions regarding *Big Bang Theory* coming to a close.

> Over the weekend, Lorre and Molaro decided that on the coming Wednesday, after the morning table read, they would gather the full cast, along with showrunner Steve Holland, in Lorre's office, to tell them the news. Once the meeting was adjourned, they would have a press release sent out.

Jim Parsons: There was a lag of days between my talking to Chuck and Steve and the cast getting together, and I can't remember the specifics exactly, but I know there was some consternation on Chuck's part about what best to do, meaning when to gather everyone, what to talk about, whatever. And I know that he was very concerned about press leaks. Ideally I would've loved to have had the rest of the cast be able to talk about their feelings on it, and what their wishes had been, or if they had thoughts about it. And that didn't really happen.

Steve Molaro: Was [that meeting] the best way to do it? I don't know. Was there a best way to do it? Probably not. It was an attempt to let everybody know without any of those people finding out through the press, which would have been not great.

Nikki Lorre: I had to go and tell everyone not to leave after the table read because [Chuck and Steve] wanted to have a meeting. Seeing them all happy riding in a golf cart [to the production offices] for this meeting was not the way to deal with this. It was just going to explode in everyone's face, because it just got dropped on them.

Eddie Gorodetsky: There's a small conference room across the hall from Chuck's office, and we were writing the pilot of *Bob Hearts Abishola*, when Chuck—the master of understatement—says, "I got the cast of *Big Bang* coming up for a meeting, so you guys will have to write a little bit without me." As the cast walked by, we said, "Hi, how are you," etc. Their meeting seemed to go on longer than expected.

> Once the cast gathered in Lorre's office, they sat in a circle—some in chairs, others on the sofa. Normally, meetings would happen on the stage in the green room, so being sent over in golf carts to the office was a rare occasion, and at least half the cast walked in thinking it was going to be a discussion about coming back for more episodes following season twelve. But while everyone was in a good mood as they took their seats, there was also a sense that something was different. There was no small talk, no banter. Lorre briefly welcomed everyone before turning the floor over to a surprised Parsons.

Chuck Lorre: I've often wondered if I misstepped, because I said, "You probably wondered why we all called you here," and I think I started off by saying, "OK, well, Jim . . . you have the floor." I got the feeling he was upset with me because maybe he thought I was going to lay out the future, but I didn't think it was my place to do that. So he explained to them that he was ready to say goodbye at the end of season twelve. And then I said I didn't see a path forward without Sheldon, and frankly I didn't want to see a path forward with anybody leaving the show. I said, "Let's go out on top as the wonderful show that we've been blessed to do for twelve years." But there was a lot of crying in the room. Kaley, in particular. It was a blow. And there was no way to soften it by giving them a heads-up. I didn't know any other way to do it.

Jim Parsons: I don't know if Chuck misstepped or not. The only thing that felt bad for me was that by me going first, it put some responsibility on me in a weird way for ending the show since I knew that that's how Chuck and I, and I guess Steve as well, felt about my decision, which was its own personal thing. And again, I didn't overly assume they would carry on without me, but I guess selfishly I want to make sure everyone knew that the fate of the show was not ultimately my decision. Whether I had spoken first or not, it would've been difficult to be in that room. The feeling in the pit of the stomach when you know the information the rest of the group is about to get is pretty terrible. I'm not sure how it should've been handled. There is no blueprint. I've gone back and forth about it, and ultimately I think I did the right thing; I know I did the right thing for myself. I think I did a decent version of the right thing in general, which was going to Chuck and Steve as opposed to telling the rest of the cast first. I don't know. Everyone was in a no-win situation. And that includes Chuck.

Simon Helberg: In terms of the actual, I guess what you could call the cancellation of the show, that occurred in [that] meeting, where we were informed by Chuck that the show was done. That's what I found to be the most upsetting. Jim didn't cancel our show. Jim just finished the run of our show as we all did, contractually, and no one ever asked us to continue doing the show. That is not an exaggeration. No one ever said, *Would you guys like to keep doing the show?* Or, *Is there any version of this show that could carry on where Jim would come back?* Or, *Is there a version without Jim?* Or, *Is there any kind of scenario where we can figure out some way to do the show?* There was never one conversation that was *ever* had one time with any single person that I am aware of in the cast. Jim was not in charge of canceling our show or renewing contracts or discussing the future, and I felt that was an unfair burden on him. But that's my two cents.

Jim Parsons: I was uncomfortable with how shocking the moment was. When I talked to Chuck and Steve about it, and there was back-and-forth about when to get the group together, I did not really understand until we got in there, that it was going to be quite as definitive as it was. I didn't know that no one was going to ask anybody, "How do you feel?" Not that I thought it should be my responsibility...since it wasn't going to involve me [should the show have gone forward]. And I would never have assumed that I had the power, frankly, to open a discussion like that.

Kaley Cuoco: The shock of *Oh my God, what is next?* was scary. I mean, we cried for hours that day. We thought we were going to do another year, so all of the sudden your life kind of flashes before your eyes. I looked at Chuck and said, "What are we going to do?" I couldn't breathe. It just felt like a death, but also a new horizon for everybody as well.

Johnny Galecki: I was shocked. We were just blindsided that day. And not necessarily shocked by Jim's decision, but that he hadn't had that conversation with his castmates first to prepare us. So yes, it could have been handled better. We're a family; have a conversation. And I don't even disagree with how Jim felt, because in many ways, I felt the same way. I just disagreed with how it was managed. We thought we were going into Chuck's office to talk about renegotiating, and then Chuck tossed the baton to Jim. And Jim was shocked and obviously caught off guard. I remember him trying to find the words to explain his feelings. I was sitting next to him and I hugged him, and I said, "I totally understand." But at the same time, I was kind of losing it as I saw my castmates emotionally crumble upon hearing the news. There was a part of me that almost stood up and said I'm not going to sit here and watch the people I love be so hurt. But I stopped myself from doing so and I hugged him instead. Still, that's what literally went through my mind because it was tearing me to shreds watching Kaley break down and see the tears from everyone. I'd almost only ever seen this group of people laughing together. I think that was in large part what caused my reaction. But I don't think I could have performed in the way I wanted to, or would want to, if we did continue. I was done myself, I think. I didn't really know how to serve the character or the great writing anymore. But none of us—the actors, writers—were comfortable with doing the show without one of us. And we absolutely would not continue on without Jim.

Melissa Rauch: There were a lot of tears. It was such a vulnerable moment for Jim...he was emotional. As someone who I love and care about, I saw how difficult it was for him as he was telling us how he felt. But Jim was so sweet about it and spoke from the heart, and it was totally understandable that he was ready to move on. It was twelve years of his life. He was ready to start a new chapter and I completely got that.

Steve Molaro: It's such a blur...that meeting is like being in a car crash in slow motion. We were all crying, it was uncontrollable.

Nikki Lorre: It was easy for emotions to run wild and seem like it was Jim's [choice to end the show], which was not true. A lot of people made Jim the villain, and it was way more nuanced than that. Everyone has their own opinions, but there's only one truth to that story and it's not so black-and-white. These things end in much more complicated ways than just someone pulling the plug.

Judy Parsons: I hated when all these things came out that said, "*Big Bang* is over because Jim Parsons no longer wants to do this," or "Jim Parsons is the reason that *Big Bang* is over." Those headlines really did crush me... but he didn't make a rash decision to move on. He's the kind of person that thinks things out *completely*. But *The Big Bang Theory* had become such an integral part of our whole family's life that when it was over, it was depressing to me! It took me a while to get over it. It was like a part of my life was over. I'm fine now. But it was hard.

Peter Roth: Here's the deal: Jim was the catalyst for the decision. But with time and distance and perspective, he should have no blame. There should be no blame at all. Because it was fortuitous. It was the right thing at the right time. It was never about the decision. It was about the process. I think that's where Jim took his lumps.

Nikki Lorre: I completely understood Jim's mindset, where it's kind of insane to walk away from a show that is *this* successful and making people this much money, but when you've been doing it for twelve years, you have to take a step back and be like, *What, we do two more, and then where's my life?* As much fun and as much joy as the show brought, I think a lot of people, myself included, felt stuck in time, like, how is my career going to take off and go in different directions when I only have this credit? Because I've only worked on this show with these people for twelve years, so even though I was terrified and filled with emotions about having to take that next step, whatever that would mean, I was relieved that I knew when it was happening.

Melissa Rauch: It was the right decision, but of course there would be no time you could possibly break that news where l wouldn't have felt it viscer-ally. No matter when the time came, a cry was going to be had. Which I did as we were sitting in that circle, and it was an ugly cry at that. But listen, I was the kid who didn't want to leave someone's house even though my mom said it was time to go. So I'm grateful I had that call made for me.

Kunal Nayyar: When the words were spoken that we were not going to be coming back, I had a very physical reaction in my body. It's something I've only experienced once before. I felt a giant weight had been lifted off my shoulders. I don't mean this in a positive or a negative way. I mean this in an absolute honest way, that something within me was released. At that moment I said goodbye. I had no resistance. I was ready to spend more time with my family. I was ready to start again. And yes, it was sad and I cried, but there was no resistance from me. I was ready to say goodbye.

Mayim Bialik: I take inspiration from Kunal in that everything happens the way it's supposed to, and everything unfolds the way it's supposed to according to a plan that we can't know. I really tried to be in acceptance of that. Life is enormous, and my life in the years on *Big Bang Theory* were some of the most grief-heavy, complicated years for me personally. It was kind of like, *OK, what next?* [*Laughs*] That had to be my attitude, and it still is. But I had nowhere else I would rather be, and I would have been happy to be there until people weren't watching anymore.

Simon Helberg: I get the love of the show and people not wanting it to go away, but I find it funny to be part of the longest-running multicam show ever, and people still probably thought, *How selfish you would end after almost three hundred episodes!* I guess it's ultimately a compliment, but I find it funny that there would be any—if there is any—resentment. But you can't have a head full of gray hair and be wearing *The Flash* T-shirts and putting on fluorescent skinny jeans. At a certain point, wearing a Nintendo belt buckle becomes just creepy. [*Laughs*] Now, with that said, I have that Nintendo belt. You bet I took it! I'm no fool! I don't wear it. It's just in a box.

Steve Molaro: We knew at some point the series had to come to an end. And while it was a challenge then, I think creatively it ended up being the best for the series. My personal feeling was the show stayed good until the end. I think it's remarkable that a show could go twelve seasons and maintain some semblance of quality. Would season thirteen have been good? I don't know. It's possible. I also feel like it was very possible that we might not have been able to hold it together that well. So, from a creative standpoint, ending it after twelve years was the right thing to do. And it gave us a place to write to, which we didn't do often. It allowed us to leave on what I hope was a classy note.

Jim Parsons: It's impossible to know how many other people were maybe equally as ready and just didn't want to be the one to say it. Or didn't feel it was their job to say. I don't know. But I definitely had a sense of that, too. [*Laughs*] I didn't know who exactly, but I guarantee there are plenty of other people who were like, *This may have gone long enough.*

Johnny Galecki: In hindsight, it was the way to go and the best idea. I'm so proud of all that we did, and I really truly do think that it was the right time to end it all. Kaley and I actually were thinking of ending the show a few years before, around season ten. I didn't feel like I was earning my keep, honestly. When you do something long enough and you feel like you can do it in your pajamas every day... that's how I was starting to feel. I still cared very much about the show and the character, but it just became a little too easy, which happens when you've done something for so long. But then I thought, *Oh man, we're still number one and we have a good thing going and we're employing a lot of people.* We started to feel differently, and we decided not to say anything, because we really were still enjoying it. But yes, we had talked about ending it two years prior because you want to go out on top.

Kaley Cuoco: Anything in regards to that big of a change is scary. But I think the best part about this and the blessing was...we had an entire season to make memorable. It wasn't like we ended and realized we weren't coming back. That's when I wanted to do the big flash mob again and a big dance and have fun days on set. And it was cool because I didn't take a moment of it for granted.

But at the end of the meeting, with the news now online, the cast and producers immediately needed to tell the crew, as well as the writing staff.

Steve Molaro: When we were starting to leave, Kaley asked Chuck, "Well, what happens now?" and Chuck said, "We have the unfortunate task of going downstairs and letting the writers know." To watch the cast be told,

and then let all the writers know...it was just horrendous. It was like letting people know that a death had occurred. But when Chuck said we were
going to tell the writers...oh gosh, I'm going to cry...Kaley's immediate
response was, "I want to come." And Johnny said, "I want to come, too, I
want to thank them." Jim came, too, as well as Melissa and Simon. Kunal
had an appointment and Mayim had a press commitment, but when we told
them [*Chokes up*], everyone started crying again, uncontrollably. We couldn't
work, so some of us went back to my office, and we just talked and had a drink
and cried. It was like a funeral. Later, our assistant said, "Hey, Johnny's on the
phone. He wants to know what you guys are doing." I said, "We're just sitting
in my office, tell him to come by." So he and Kaley came by, and we hung out
and talked and cried some more, and then at about four o'clock, Holland said,
"Oh shit, we still have to do a rewrite from the script this morning!" I was like,
"Who's left in the building? We sent the writers home!" And we were all in my
office drinking! So whoever was left, we went back—not in the mood to do a
rewrite—but it ended up being a really great rewrite. It was therapeutic in a
way in that it gave us something productive to try and focus on.

After the news became public that *Big Bang*'s twelfth season would be its last, Johnny Galecki captured this photo of Kaley Cuoco and Steve Molaro consoling each other. *Courtesy
of Steve Molaro*

Johnny Galecki: And then Kaley, Mary Quigley, Mark Cendrowski, and I immediately got into my wine fridge in my dressing room.

Jim Parsons: I'm sure after I went home I drank that night, too. I had broken down in that meeting... [my decision] had been brewing and brewing and brewing and then suddenly just happened, and I think that I just, or at least looking back now, the feeling that's coming over me is, I was just so tired.

At the time, there were a lot of hard feelings between Parsons, and Galecki and Cuoco, who weren't privy to everything that had unfolded leading up to the decision to end the show with season twelve, or unaware why they weren't brought into the fold sooner. Understandably, the next day at work—which was a Thursday runthrough—was fraught with tension.

Steve Molaro: That was tough. I got a text that morning from Kaley saying she didn't know if she could work that day because she was still really upset. Upset with Jim. She said, "Do we have to do this runthrough today?" I called Chuck at 8:30 a.m., and said, "Kaley's upset," and Chuck's response was, "I'm on the phone with Johnny right now. You handle Kaley. Good luck!" [*Laughs*] I asked if we could cancel the runthrough but we couldn't.

Johnny Galecki: I wasn't coming from a place of wanting to shut down the runthrough because we still had a show to do. And I probably don't recall much, because I was probably a bit hungover. That next day might be a little hazy to me. [*Laughs*]

Steve Molaro: I texted Kaley back and said, "I understand everything you're feeling. Chuck is talking with Johnny. It's already a shortened week, so it's not going to be a good idea if we cancel it. I'll do anything you need, but do you think there's a world where you can just make it through the runthrough today, and then we'll regroup if we need to make any other changes in the week?" She said yes. Now, that first runthrough back was kind of icy and none of them were talking between scenes, but everyone was professional.

Steve Holland: Kaley could barely make eye contact with Jim during the runthrough, but they got through it. That gave them three days before they had to be back at work together.

Steve Molaro: And then, by the next runthrough, pretty quickly I saw Kaley and Jim talking between scenes and laughing, and thought, *OK, tensions have come down a little bit.* They seemed to be able to be around each other and not just want to get into their cars and leave immediately afterward. So, yes, while the day after that meeting was tough, they all found a way to start talking about and get to what seemed like a better place to me, really fast.

Steve Holland: When they came back on Monday, everyone was back to normal. I remember Kaley saying later that they loved the show so much and it was such a special place and such a big part of their lives, that they didn't want it to end ugly. If this was going to be the last season, they were going to put aside their anger and frustration and differences and enjoy every moment of it. And that's what they did. But that came from them; they made a choice not to end the show on a bad note. That really set the tone for the last season, and everyone treated it like senior year of high school. We all knew it was ending and we were all going our separate ways, but that's part of what made that last season so special.

Jim Parsons: After the shocking moment of [that meeting], things eventually began to fall into place, and got peaceful moving towards the finale. The older you get, you just have to do what you need to do for you, and you're not always going to do it perfectly well. So much of life is like this situation, in which there is no playbook. It was just time for me to move on in my life, and see what else I was going to do. It was still complete gratitude [to the character of Sheldon and the show]. And technically I'm still playing him in narration form for *Young Sheldon*. It really had more to do with just where I wanted to be location-wise. It's why I always refer to Otis passing away at the start of that last season...everything pointed toward the beginning of a new chapter.

Chuck Lorre: And quite frankly, the media would have lambasted us if we had continued past season twelve, saying we don't know when to quit. We would have gotten heat, and we would have gotten derogatory things written about the show, saying things like we're a bunch of money-grubbing assholes who don't know they've gone past their peak, and now we have to tolerate this horrible show that should have been stopped years ago. We would have been clobbered no matter what. [*Laughs*]

Melissa Rauch: All good things come to an end, and in this case, all great things come to an end. It ended when it absolutely should have, and I am even more sure of that now.

In the days after the announcement, fans wondered what the odds were that there might be an eventual spin-off (unlike *Young Sheldon*, which is a prequel) to continue the story of one of the main characters or supporting players.

Simon Helberg: I, personally, wouldn't have been interested in doing it. At the same time, it was never discussed in any real substantial way. I think if Melissa and I wanted to try and come up with something, or felt really strongly about it, I'm sure we could have gone to someone. Outside of meeting Howard's dad, I personally felt that I told all the stories as Wolowitz that I wanted to tell. And there was something to me that was very clean and poetic about ending the run of our show as we did. There's a luxury and an anomaly to get to play the same character for twelve years, and letting that character grow in real time, but for me it's always been about telling different stories and playing different people.

Melissa Rauch: The possibility of a spin-off kept being mentioned to me by everyone except the creative forces behind the show. [*Laughs*] I think so many people were just hopeful to keep this world going in some way, but we all knew these characters thrived best together. If you take any element out, it's just not the same. And I never entertained it, because the way we went out, and the bow they put on Howard and Bernadette and their family, with getting to see those kids, was perfectly done. I wouldn't want to unwrap that bow and that present.

Wil Wheaton: I gently pitched the idea of a Professor Proton spin-off as a legitimate educational show where I played the Professor Proton character and we do the show as it exists. And I decided that Wil Wheaton hires Amy as his science adviser, so it would be me and Mayim. We walked over to Chuck and were like, "Hey! We have an idea." We got a little bit of interest and then no interest, but we knew if it wasn't going to get past Chuck, it wasn't going to go anywhere. But it's a character that I love. And even though I really only played Professor Proton for two episodes, just having that opportunity and getting to share a character with Bob fucking Newhart was pretty awesome.

Kevin Sussman: After the series went off the air, I mentioned it to Chuck…but he didn't really see Stuart carrying a show. He thought Stuart worked better as an ancillary character. But if he changes his mind, I would do it! Still, spin-offs are always really risky, and when you don't have the entire cast, it's hard for people to accept that the tone is different.

Steve Holland: Nothing was talked about in a serious way. I think we felt there was no winning with something like that. *Big Bang* was this magical thing that we captured, and then to recapture it with any version of them that wasn't the whole cast wasn't something we really wanted to do. We joked about in the room, and people would toss out ideas, but it wasn't seriously given consideration.

Chapter 25

THE FINAL GOODBYE

On April 30, 2019, *The Big Bang Theory* filmed its final episode on stage 25. The writers never planned storylines too far in advance, but this was different—they had been preparing for the better part of nine months. The one-hour finale (which was actually two episodes; the first called "The Change Constant" and the other "The Stockholm Syndrome") aired May 16 on CBS. Out of 279 episodes, it is that last one that is understandably the hardest for the actors and producers to talk about, given the finality of what it represents.

Jim Parsons: It was emotional just driving to the studio. It was emotional the night before when I was going to sleep. I've never been through a final day which was so similar to a first day, which is like, *Oh Jesus, how is this going to go?* Especially when you consider all the times we had done this exact routine over and over. I remember saying to Simon and probably Mayim as well, that I was kind of counting the episode before the last one as the finale. Because I knew experience-wise, all bets are off after this. The second-to-last episode was the last time it was going to be us doing an episode in the way that we've done the other 277-plus episodes. And even though I knew it was the right time to say goodbye, it's such a complicated, heavy emotion. There's nothing more challenging than doing your job that you're used to doing but suddenly everyone's telling you, *This is a very special time to do it!*, and it's like, *Wait, what?! OK. Do I change something?* So that's kind of weird. One of the joys of being an actor, at least for me, is the ability to get in these places without all that extra help. It can depersonalize it. I think I was making efforts to keep myself... as unsentimental about it as possible...because it was way too much to kind of take in. So much life had happened in those twelve years.

Simon Helberg: Emotion was really encouraged during that final week, but not everybody experiences it in a wallowing, pool-of-tears way. And sometimes it was uncomfortable because it can kind of rob people of their own individual experience when there's camera crews and tissue boxes on every table. I'm generally a super-emotional person, and I was constantly rocked back on my heels throughout that whole week, both in unexpected ways and in ways I really didn't want to give in to. There's this weird expectation of getting these raw moments immortalized and gimme-all-you-got tear ducts. But it gets you. And I thought that the ending of the show, both creatively and on a personal level, was all that I had really hoped it would be.

Peter Roth: It was one of the most satisfying finales I've ever been a part of. I vividly remember being at the last episode of *Friends*, but I'd only been involved with *Friends* for five years instead of the entire run (Roth joined Warner Bros. Television in 1999). But this was probably the finale that moved me the most.

Chuck Lorre: I was very proud. Very, very proud. Steve Molaro said, "The show can say goodbye, but the characters shouldn't." We had the conclusion of the Nobel storyline, but these people will continue leading these lives we're leaving. We're leaving them; they're not leaving. I thought that was brilliant, and it made the whole process of writing the finale really joyful because there wasn't so much plot to try and figure out how to end everything.

Steve Holland: In the world of these characters, the next day they're still getting up and going to work and living across the hall. While we wouldn't be seeing those stories anymore, they're still going on, and that was really how we wanted to leave the show.

Jim Parsons: The writers were under tremendous pressure. I remember telling them, "You can't win! Someone is going to hate the way you've ended it. Is there any peace in that for you?" But I thought they did a great job.

Steve Holland: Class rings were given out, but one of the things I remember most about the finale was we had heard there were all these fans in a

The cast in their street clothes as they rehearse for the last scene in the series. (left to right) Melissa Rauch, Simon Helberg, Johnny Galecki, Kaley Cuoco, Jim Parsons, Mayim Bialik and Kunal Nayyar. *Courtesy of Steve Molaro*

standby line for tickets to the finale outside of the Warner Bros. parking garage across the street from the lot. About one thousand people were there and most of those people who'd been camping out all night weren't gonna get in. Kaley said, "Can we go say hi to them?" We had a slight break between the runthrough and the live show, and we were like, "Yes!" Kaley, Johnny, Simon, Kunal, myself, Steve, and some of the other writers took golf carts over there. As the golf carts pulled into the parking lot, you just heard this enormous roar of the people. Kaley, Johnny, Simon, and Kunal stood up on this bench and said hello and thanked them and signed autographs and took pictures. I almost think those people in the standby line got a better experience. I mean, to see the finale was amazing, but they sort of got to be there one-on-one and see the cast up close and talk to them. It was really, really moving.

The first episode in the two-part finale opened with a one-minute, forty-five-second recap of the previous 277 episodes, until we see Sheldon, Amy,

Kaley Cuoco, Simon Helberg, Johnny Galecki, Kunal Nayyar, Steve Molaro, and Steve Holland went to meet the fans who were in the Warner Bros. "holding area" hoping to snag a last-minute seat to the *Big Bang* series finale taping. *Courtesy of Steve Molaro*

Penny, and Leonard waiting impatiently for a potential phone call from the Nobel committee to determine if Super Asymmetry will win the prize for Physics. It was the first of many moments that the writers considered moving around within the episode.

Steve Holland: The phone call that Sheldon and Amy won the Nobel came in the very beginning of the two-part finale, but at one point there was a thought that it would come at the end of the first part of the finale, so the end of episode twenty-three ("The Change Constant"). What we always knew was that the Nobel speech would be the second-to-last scene, and the last scene would be them on the couch.

When Sheldon and Amy finally get the call that they've won, Sheldon is so shocked, Leonard feels no choice but to slap him out of his state of disbelief.

Johnny Galecki: One of my favorite moments. [*Laughs*] I felt like that was a gift that the writers were giving Leonard before the show ended. Like, it's time to throw a punch already of Leonard being exasperated with Sheldon.

Jim Parsons: Johnny didn't actually slap me, but that was an example of my very favorite kind of comedy, especially in a multicam format. I love being slapped like that, I really do! It's so much fun to be a part of those moments.

Anthony Rich: I got drafted into doing the slap off camera. We couldn't get a proper slap sound, so we had to do an old theater trick where I'm standing offstage and as Johnny goes to slap Jim, I am the one that actually slaps my hands together. And it's seamless! That's my claim to fame. The video of me doing the slap is actually on my IMDb page.

Jim Parsons: I was just so happy for Amy and Sheldon in that scene when they found out they won. I had been twelve years as Sheldon talking about how much the Nobel Prize meant to him, and it's one of the few things I proffered up early on of what I'd like to see happen for Sheldon. Years ago I said, "I would like to see him win the Nobel. He really wants one." And then just to have it . . . as far as the storyline goes, that was so satisfying.

> Later in the episode, Raj overhears Amy sobbing in a Caltech restroom. She tells him her picture is all over the internet now that she and Sheldon have won the Nobel, and she thinks she looks terrible. When she asks Raj if she's really that frumpy-looking, he assures her she's a beautiful woman, but if she's not happy with the pictures, she should make some changes. In the next scene, she has a new shoulder-length haircut and is wearing form-fitting clothes with heels, a stark departure from the Amy viewers have come to know and love. Sheldon tells her he likes her better "the way you were." Opinions were just as split behind the scenes, particularly for Bialik.

Mayim Bialik: This is a case where I don't know that I agreed with our writers, but also I have ultimate faith in them, and that's part of being a team player on a show. I loved that I got to wear some nicer clothes, and it was really a thrill to have my hair cut after having the same [style] for all those years. It was straightened [all those years], which damaged my hair in ways it may never recover from, which is fine, because now I have short hair and I've stopped trying to see if it can ever be healthy again. [*Laughs*] But honestly, it was so exciting that I didn't have to wear it straight anymore, and I could have some more character to my hair and my face. So it felt really good that people could see me that way, but in some ways, it did feel like a betrayal of *our* Amy. We didn't go crazy and have her dressing in ways that completely didn't look like her. She still wore kind of sensible things— like what'd you get at Loehmann's. She had an old-lady Loehmann's shopping trip! But it was definitely something I had conflict about...I thought it would be, *Let's dress Amy up and take her out for the night!* I didn't think it would be like, here's her new normal!

Steve Holland: I think this was one of those moments where the story in the script wasn't exactly the way Mayim had pictured it. We felt that the storyline was really honest, because oftentimes, when people see themselves on TV or in pictures all the time, it can make you really self-conscious. It felt real in a way that we thought was interesting, but I don't know if Mayim ever completely came to terms with that storyline. We were honest about where we were coming from and why it was okay that Amy can be complicated and not really care about her appearance that much, but on some level, it was something that we had talked about as writers who are not on camera a lot; you go to things like the Emmys and you start getting pictures taken and it makes you have another respect for actors who have to see themselves all the time. You get very self-conscious about things you've never thought of before. Like, I don't care what I look like—I'm wearing a T-shirt and jeans! Doesn't matter. And then I see pictures, and I'm like, "Why didn't I put on a nicer shirt?!" So it felt very human and real to us for Amy. But to Mayim's credit, even though I don't think she 100 percent agreed, never for a second was she like, "Well, I don't want to do it." She voiced her opinion and we had a discussion about it, and she was like, "Okay, here we go."

Also, the scene where Koothrappali finds Amy crying in the bathroom originally had some jokes in there that veered on the mean side, and Mayim accurately pointed that out. We were like, "You're right, those are too mean. We're gonna cut those out." Sometimes you can get lost; you're in a writers room, you're trying to get a joke, it gets a big laugh, and sometimes that can blind you to the fact that until you see it onstage. We tried to be good safeguards to that and the cast, who were also really protective of their characters, as they should be.

Whatever your thoughts on Amy's makeover, there's no denying that Sheldon's reaction to it set up one of the greatest reveals not only on *Big Bang*, but also in the history of television. Just as he storms out of the apartment and tells Leonard that Amy was the one constant in his life and now she's changing, there's a ding, and with that, the elevator, which had been broken for twelve years and was the onus for countless jokes, opens on an amused Penny who says, "Can you believe it? They finally fixed the elevator!"

Kaley Cuoco: Anthony Rich got the script sooner [than we did], so I said, "Tell me something! Tell me something!" because I'm the girl that reads the last page first of every book. He said, "I don't want to ruin it for you, but you get to do something very special." And all week I kept thinking, *I wonder what it is, I wonder what it is*, and when I found out I got to be in the elevator, that was *it* for me. I was so excited. I could not wait to do it in front of the audience. In front of our producer runthrough, it killed! People were screaming for all the reasons that you would.

Back where it all started for Galecki and Cuoco. *Courtesy of Kaley Cuoco photo collection*

Steve Molaro: Chuck always thought the elevator finally opening should maybe be the final scene, but as we got closer, I think you could feel people expecting it. We wanted to do it, but we wanted to try and catch people off guard.

Steve Holland: There was one version of it where they were all walking up the stairs after having gotten back from the airport and their trip to Stockholm, and just as they got to the fourth floor, the elevator would ding and it would open. There was a talk about a moment in which Sheldon and Amy say, "It's crazy; we won the Nobel Prize and in some ways, everything's exactly the same," and then the elevator opens, and that would have been the end of the show. The tag still would have still been them sitting on the couch, but as we were breaking the story, we thought about two things: the moment where Sheldon was freaking out because Amy had gotten the haircut; and the Nobel Prize, it was like the straw that broke the camel's back. So it seemed right for the elevator to open then, and also, I just thought it would be much less expected to have it happen so much earlier in the episode.

It also provided a sweet gag joke later in the next episode in which all the characters pile their luggage inside the elevator for their trip to Sweden instead of fumbling down the stairs.

Jim Parsons: That was a lot of fun, but also a pain in the ass. [*Laughs*] It's a lot of cooks trying to figure out how to get in there, but I thought it worked really well. You had to fake certain things, because it wasn't as cramped as it looked, but it was fun to look like you were suffering!

Steve Molaro: My favorite part was Melissa being stuck in it.

Melissa Rauch: That was so fun. I love a physical comedy bit so much. When they piled the luggage up, I needed a boost over it to get out. I'm four foot eleven, but I have to say, I did grow on the show, because when I started, I was four foot ten and a half. And another crazy fun fact is my shoe size is six point five, but the shoes I wore as Bernadette were always a six. Go figure.

The second episode began with a two-month time jump in which Sheldon and Leonard are re-gluing (well, more Leonard than Sheldon) the molecular

DNA structure that's been a constant staple in the apartment. Leonard says that was a "very pleasurable 139½ hours."

Johnny Galecki: It was the total number of hours of television we had produced. I think we were all so full of emotion, I don't remember specifically…but I certainly didn't put that structure back together after each take. Thank God we had prop masters because that would have been a pain in the ass. [*Laughs*]

Minutes later, Penny and Amy come back from dress shopping for the Nobel ceremony, where Amy comments that the tailor had to let Penny's dress out a bit. It's then revealed in a private moment between Leonard and Penny that she's pregnant. Although the reveal goes against Penny's wishes not to have kids, the writers chose to have her get pregnant as a way to pay off the line from the pilot where Leonard, in a moment of wishful—and maybe delusional— thinking, says to Sheldon, "Our babies will be smart and beautiful." But many viewers and critics had a problem with Penny's surprise pregnancy, including *Vulture*'s Kathryn VanArendonk who wrote at the time (May 17, 2019), "There are several reasons why this makes me want to rip my hair out…This was always Leonard's vision, but never Penny's," and "In an otherwise heartwarming finale…it's infuriating and unfortunate that *The Big Bang Theory* would essentially erase a woman's right to choose from her own narrative."

Steve Holland: I wish we had earned it a little bit more, getting to that reveal. Some people called us out, and maybe rightly so, that Penny made the decision not to have kids and was OK with it, and then ended up pregnant. People were like, "Why does she have to? Why can't she be okay without kids?" And those are perfectly legitimate feelings. It sort of comes with the time jump we did in the finale, but we talked about whether there were other ways to do it, like what if she had a pregnancy scare that turned out to be false and she was disappointed. We talked about ways to get her to that moment that didn't feel quite so abrupt. I wish we had Penny take one more step before we got to the finale. The way the last episodes broke out, we just didn't get there. But with that said, I do think it was a great landing place for them. We really wanted to honor that relationship, as well as the

"Our babies will be smart and beautiful" line from the pilot as a way to tie it back together.

Steve Molaro: It was such an early structural piece of the entire series. At the same time, we still tried to honor her feelings about having been against it earlier in the season since [the pregnancy] wasn't planned.

Speaking of reveals, the producers also decided to introduce Bernadette and Howard's kids, Halley and Michael, who had previously been unseen and only heard.

Simon Helberg: It was a very surreal experience in every way, finishing the run, meeting the kids. They were lovely, but it is a whole new game if you haven't done it for twelve years. It was that little extra heart-wrenching, sweet moment that feels so teed up and also surprising at the same time.

Melissa Rauch: I remember Simon walking in holding the hand of Sailah, who played Halley, and I started getting choked up. As Bernadette and as Halley's mother, I have seen Halley all the time since she was born, so there's no reason I should get emotional about seeing her walk in, but I, as Melissa, knew it was such a big moment, so seeing that image of Simon hand-in-hand with her as our series was coming to an end was just more than I was ready for. I had a lump in my throat, and I get choked up thinking about it now. But at the time, I was like, *This is not the right reaction! Bernadette has seen her daughter every day!* I'll never forget standing near the crib with the young boy who plays Michael, and turning to the wall between takes to not let that emotion affect the scene.

Steve Holland: When we were originally writing Bernadette's pregnancy, we had the idea that the baby being heard but never seen could be our nod to Mrs. Wolowitz. But once we got to the finale, we were like, "We won't have to deal with kids on set ever again, so it's okay to do it!" And I do think it was a great moment. They were both sweet kids, but the little boy just kept wandering everywhere. He would not stay in one place! It made us very grateful for our decision not to see the kids before now, because we had this two-year-old who would squirm when he was being held, and roam everywhere! But it was cute, and it was a fun Easter egg to pay off.

Peter Chakos: When we finally see the kids in the finale, I thought the reaction would be much bigger. I was actually arguing with Chuck onstage when we were shooting, saying "You've got to give me a shot to play the reaction," but he said something to the effect of, "It's just a kid, nobody cares." And he was right. The audience didn't react like I thought they would. I left too much room for a reaction that never came.

Bill Prady: I liked that we showed the Wolowitz children in the finale, but I would have disagreed with Peter, because what I would've said is, "If we'd done our job well along the way, and made you not feel weird about not seeing the babies, then seeing them won't be a treat."

But the audience was filled with more friends and family than usual, as opposed to die-hard fans who would have realized the gravity of the moment.

Melissa Rauch: It's so true because if you put all die-hard fans in the audience for that episode, you do get audible gasps, for sure. The feedback I got from people after the taping was, "Oh my gosh, I can't believe we saw them!"

While the Wolowitz family got a sweet ending, a lot of viewers were disappointed that Raj remained single. *Buzzfeed* said Raj deserved a better ending, noting he "deserved to have a happy love life, but he ended up being the token representation character in the finale."

Peter Roth: I wish that Raj found the woman of his dreams. He's the only one that didn't at the end of the show.

Kunal Nayyar: I thought it was very astute that the one person who wanted love so badly realizes maybe he needs to love himself first. It doesn't have to come through someone else, and that's a very lovely way to end a character's storyline. He grew so much those last few seasons as a character, and you saw him become less and less dependent on all the things he thought he needed, which is very beautiful.

Steve Molaro: This show started as five single people and I always liked that there was one character that still hadn't found themselves in a permanent relationship to represent those that haven't found that person. And so rather than saying, "Oh, look, everybody did what they were supposed to do and got married and found themselves in a relationship," I was like, "Well, that's not exactly how it has to end. That's not necessarily the best way."

Still, Raj was able to take Sarah Michelle Gellar, who he met on the flight to Stockholm, as his date to the Nobel ceremony. But Gellar almost wasn't cast in the cameo.

Steve Holland: Sandra Bullock was actually our first go-to because of Koothrappali's long love of her. We were really excited about it, but we got a polite decline because she was shooting a movie and wasn't available. But we were very excited Sarah was available to come on. And we had mentioned *Buffy* before in the series, where Leonard was going to show *Buffy* to Penny. We were also big *Buffy* fans in the writers room, so it really worked out well.

Kunal Nayyar: If there's any storyline I wish could have played out, it's that I really wish Raj and Lucy could have worked out. I really enjoyed working with Kate Micucci but also just from a character perspective, I loved that this was someone Raj could take care of. There was something very sweet about their chemistry; it was very gentle and loving. If there was anyone that he could have ended up with, and this is nothing against any of the wonderful actors that came on as potential love interests, I think Raj and Lucy would have made a really sweet couple.

Steve Holland: We didn't have a grand plan, and it wasn't like Raj was not going to find anybody. We talked about him and Anu getting married at the end. We had talked about that relationship being a love story out of order where they got engaged, and *then* they got to know each other. Nothing against Rati Gupta, who was terrific as Anu, but it never quite clicked in the way that we wanted it to, and we never felt like we had to write to an ending. There were definitely times where we had on the board in the writers room: "Raj and Anu's wedding in India." That was something we were going to do, but it just didn't feel right. A lot of the way we approached this was kind of just going by our gut, so when they broke up, the thought that his rom-com movie ending is Wolowitz running to the airport felt right. That friendship as Raj's most important relationship felt right. And it didn't feel right or fair to cram him into a new relationship in the end. Plus, everyone doesn't have to be with somebody. Raj is a romantic, and I think he ends up with somebody eventually, but the thought of just doing it to make it a happy ending for all the characters felt false.

Steve Molaro: I'm glad we didn't go that route. There's a sad irony to the fact that he's the one who remained on his own through to the end when arguably his character wanted love the most. Maybe he wanted it so much it affected his pursuit of it and made it more difficult, but I don't think there's any shame in being single. Doing it this way felt more realistic and a nicer way to end it.

Chuck Lorre made an impromptu decision to slate (i.e., introduce) the final scene filmed in front of the studio audience, which featured Penny and Leonard in their Stockholm hotel room as they ordered room service.

Chuck Lorre: I just realized this was the last scene that we were gonna shoot on the stage. I don't know quite how it worked out that that was the last scene, because we'd preshot the Nobel awards ceremony the day before since it was so elaborate with the crowd. So I said, "Gimme the slate. I wanna do it." It was very much an impulse decision. I wanted to be able to be a part of it. I didn't want to be on camera, but I wanted to be a part of it. And I certainly did not anticipate choking up, as I am now just thinking about it. They gave me the slate, and I keep it in my office to this day.

Lorre stepped in to slate the last scene that was filmed live in front of the studio audience on April 30, 2019. *Courtesy of Steve Molaro*

The finale built toward Amy and Sheldon accepting the Nobel Prize in Physics at the awards ceremony, and while it was one of the highlights of the episode, the most moving part of the scene actually happened during the table read the week prior.

Steve Holland: I got to announce, "This is the final table read of *The Big Bang Theory*," which was really emotional. And then when they were reading the scene where Sheldon calls each one of the gang out by name at the Nobel, Kunal decided to stand up when Jim called out Raj's name. That wasn't planned, but they all decided to stand up as their names were called. The tears were already flowing, but this just opened the floodgates.

Steve Molaro: We wondered if they might stand up during the table read in that scene, but it was also fine if they didn't. When Kunal did, it was... yeah...just a layer of emotion on top of another twenty-eight layers that were already happening.

Simon Helberg: That scene during the table read was probably the most profound moment of the end of the show for me. It felt like we were ending this life-changing chapter that we all began together. It was the end of that era, and it just embodied all of that in that moment.

Jim Parsons: It was absolutely inevitable you were going to have all that emotion, which is why I was like, "Let's get through this and get me out of here." But I didn't know they were going to stand up during the table read.

Kunal Nayyar: I knew Raj's name was being called first by Sheldon, so I stood at the table read, not for effect, but as a sign of respect for all the table reads we had done before. People don't realize that the success of our show was how prepared we were for the table read, [meaning] our entire series was shaped by the first time we would read the script together. Me standing up was an homage to that sacred institution called the "table read." It was a sign of respect to all 279 episodes; it just felt right.

And the scene itself was less about Sheldon winning the Nobel and more about the growth and significance of the moment for the character.

Chuck Lorre: We began the series with a character—Sheldon—who was very isolated, couldn't touch or be touched, and was very difficult to be

How do you possibly say goodbye to a twelve-year experience? The truth is, you really can't; you just hope to get through it, as evidenced by everyone at the final table read. *Courtesy of Steve Molaro*

around. And he remained so for many years. So to then have him recognize how his accomplishments couldn't have happened without the support and affection of his friends and his wife was a very wonderful experience for me, both in the writing of it, and watching Jim's performance. It was beautiful and restrained, never erring on the side of treacle and schmaltzy.

Jim Parsons: Specifically, I felt apprehensive that [the writers] wanted some breakdown or something from Sheldon at the Nobel ceremony. Nobody told me that, but it was a fear of mine. But all those fears went away as soon as we started working on it...and it felt well-balanced to me. There was a real moment of humanity...and it was really lovely. I was able to see the cast members from the podium as I spoke, and Mayim was right there next to me. It was something that I went into being apprehensive about, and in the end, it was a very memorable moment that will stick with me.

Steve Holland: Sheldon was such a unique, specific character, and I think he dominated what people thought of the show, but to us it was always an ensemble, and we wanted the last episode to acknowledge that. Sheldon giving that speech at the Nobel ceremony was somewhat meta because it was a chance to thank and pay tribute to the team that was with him through it all.

Andy Gordon (co-executive producer): The writing of the finale was like nothing I'd ever experienced. Chuck, who is an incredibly fast and focused writer, joined us. Without realizing it, we were only a few scenes from the end, and I started to get a lump in my throat. I think others started having the same realization, because almost everyone started choking back tears. When Sheldon told his friends he loved them in his Nobel speech, those of us in the writers room lost it.

The scene was also a chance to celebrate women's achievements in the field of science, and offer encouragement. Amy says, "I would just like to take this moment to say to all the young girls out there who dream about science as a profession: Go for it. It is the greatest job in the world. If anybody tells you you can't, don't listen."

Chuck Lorre: We discovered just how many remarkable, powerful, impactful women scientists there are and have been for generations; they haven't gotten the attention. So many pioneers in this field are women who had to fight for recognition and for their position because of the bias.

Steve Holland: It was important for us for Amy to get her moment, too, because it would have been easy to make it just Sheldon. It also felt like a moment for us to say something real and honest. We were going to get to some jokes, but she could actually take that moment to deliver something real and impassioned. And when we were talking and researching the Nobel, we realized there had only been a couple of female Nobel prize winners in physics, *ever*. Madam Curie was one of them, so it had been a long time. Not to mention the amount of pressure that could be put on Amy, who also hopes to inspire another generation of women. So it was nice to highlight her achievements, and also, in the moments where she was freaking out in an earlier episode [season twelve, episode nineteen's "The Inspiration Deprivation"], Sheldon could be the one who comforted her instead of the other way around.

Mayim Bialik: I still hear from fans that our show got them interested in the sciences, which is unbelievable. You can't even wrap your head around that, and if any way our show made science cool or more acceptable or more relatable, I think that's such a tremendous thing to be able to say the number one comedy in America, oh, PS, also did *that*.

Jim Parsons: And now, any time I hear about a Nobel being announced, I imagine the anxiety and excitement of what the recipients must go through. Having gone through that scene where Sheldon finds out he and Amy won, and then the ceremony, it changes the way I look at how those people receiving those Nobels must feel.

In fact, on October 8, 2019, some five months after *Big Bang*'s finale aired, the Secretary General of the Royal Swedish Academy of Sciences, Goran Hannson, praised the show during the announcement for the real-life Nobel prize winners in physics. He said *The Big Bang Theory* was "a fantastic achievement" for bringing "the world of science to laptops and living rooms around the world," and name-checked Sheldon and Amy, as well as quoted the show's theme song.

Jim Parsons: It's kind of crazy. It's beyond crazy, actually. There were a few of those through the years, just shocking mentions. And the Nobel is the ultimate.

Bill Prady: *Big Bang Theory* was a lot of journeys, among them was that our love of science and scientists would come across respectfully. We got a glimmer of this when the show was the first sitcom to ever be reviewed by *Science.* And it was further validated by the number of world-class scientists who visited us during production, but having the series name-checked by the Nobel Prize committee is, well, the Nobel Prize of name checks.

Mary T. Quigley incorporated some secrets into the formal looks for the Nobel ceremony even though fans would never see them.

Mary T. Quigley: I incorporated Penny Blossoms in Penny's dress...slightly hidden in the cummerbund, if you will—in that hot pink sash. It's a secret that Kaley and I knew. We both got teary when we were in the fitting, because we got to do Penny Blossoms again. And everybody else had adjustments in their clothes as their lives moved forward, but not Sheldon. He was in the tux in the finale, and wore Flash socks even though nobody saw them. I knew that's what Sheldon would do.

The last scene that aired in the finale was not played back for the audience at the final taping. That was a surprise that was left for the version that aired on May 16. It featured the seven main characters sitting around the couch eating Chinese food as an acoustic version of the theme song by the Barenaked Ladies played over their dialogue.

Chuck Lorre: That last moment was everything I had hoped to end the show in a meaningful way.

Jim Parsons: Usually you don't hear the music until it's added later. I kind of hoped they would have let us shoot it without having us listen to the music, because we can't play the music in our acting, which would go against the entire point of this...we're sadly having our last meal? No, no, we're not. None of us are dying. But I didn't get my wish on that. [*Laughs*]

Cuoco (in the same shirt she wore in the pilot episode and in the 100th) captures one last memory of the epic Chinese food spread that Scott London and his team prepared for the last episode's final scene. *Courtesy of Steve Molaro*

Kaley Cuoco: To end the show around the table eating Chinese food the same way we started our show...was unbelievable. I loved that I got to wear the aqua-and-purple shirt that I wore in the pilot—and the one hundredth—again for that moment. It was so Penny. So to then end it like that, [this time] sitting next to Leonard and him touching Penny's stomach...it was the perfect cap. I wouldn't have wanted it any other way.

Johnny Galecki: That was mirroring what my life was at that point, too, with my hand on Kaley's stomach in the last scene of the show. That was a little something for my son, [Avery] Orbison, who wasn't born yet, to see a little later in his life. I asked Kaley if it was OK if I did that, and she smiled at me, knowing exactly why I was doing that, because that's a little salute to him that will be forever.

Andy Gordon: And when we were writing that last scene in the writers room, I remember thinking the writer's assistant shouldn't type the final "Fade Out," but rather Chuck or Molaro. I started to say this, but had trouble getting the words out. Finally I did, and Chuck went to the keyboard to type those two final words. And that was it.

Lorre typed the last words in the script in the writers room. *Courtesy of Andy Gordon*

After the finale taping was over, plenty of cast and crew stuck around for photos and goodbyes, while others just needed to escape the emotional pressure cooker that had been building to a crescendo all night.

Kunal Nayyar: I cried a lot at the curtain call. I cried when I realized it was the last words I was ever gonna say as Raj. I was pretty overwhelmed.

The cast greets the studio audience—which included plenty of family and friends—one final time before filming their final scenes as Amy, Howard, Bernadette, Raj, Leonard, Penny, and Sheldon. *Courtesy of Ansley Rix*

Chuck Lorre: It was just too much. It was very emotional to be part of this thing for twelve years and to end it. So I got in my car and went home. It just was sort of an overwhelming experience, and the best way for me to handle it was to just go. Because what more was there for me to do?

Jim Parsons: I had family with me, so that was different, having the distraction of other people instead of coming home just to Todd and the dogs. The next day we had the handprint ceremony at the Chinese Theatre, and then Todd and I left for New York.

The morning after the last taping, the cast gathered in front of the TCL Chinese Theatre in Hollywood to put their handprints in cement.

Johnny Galecki: That was a thrill. It was such an iconic event to be invited to. I don't even know where they are because I've never looked at them since we put our hands in the cement, but it was surreal.

Steve Molaro: The biggest help was Johnny quoting Winnie the Pooh at the handprint ceremony. It was so great and poignant and helpful because the quote was "How lucky I am to have something that makes saying good-bye so hard." Yeah. [*Pauses*] The simple act of Johnny pulling that quote out really helped me personally to keep it in perspective.

Jim Parsons: Before we went outside, we were in the lobby and they had these little boxes of concrete to practice our signatures, and I remember thinking, *This is fucking amazing*. That was really neat. But there was a certain heaviness hanging over everything…not sadness, but just the heaviness…because you see literal, physical manifestations of a ripple effect of this experience through other people's lives and their families, and you're like, *Oh God, it's a much grander tree than I can see from the few branches that we occupy here.*

The day after they taped the last episode, the cast had their handprint ceremony at the TCL Chinese Theatre in Hollywood. *Courtesy of Andy Gordon*

Two weeks later, the cast gathered for the last time to appear on *The Late Show with Stephen Colbert* after the finale aired. But the night before, they all had dinner at Ralph Lauren's famed New York City restaurant, the Polo Bar.

Johnny Galecki: Kaley and I were sitting next to each other and we were basically just gossiping about our romantic relationships. She had better things to say than I did! But otherwise, we as a cast didn't really know how to close it down. How do you close such a thing down? I don't know if there is a way.

Kunal Nayyar: It was really a fun evening. I think all of us were dreading that one moment when we had to say goodbye. It wasn't the last day of shooting, it wasn't the wrap party, it wasn't on *Colbert*. And it wasn't really the night of the Polo Bar. It didn't have the finality of it, maybe because it's just too difficult and everyone processes these things differently. I remember personally having a great time, but in the back of my mind feeling like, *Is this it? Could this be the last time we were all together like this?*

Steve Molaro: That was really nice. It wasn't too often that all of us could be together like that, and I'm really glad that it could happen. It was another helpful way to say goodbye to this thing. The other great part of that dinner was that Kunal ordered an extremely expensive hot dog.

Kunal Nayyar: Kunal also paid for dinner... [*Laughs*]

Jim Parsons: I didn't remember Kunal paid, I'm embarrassed to admit! It was nice to see everybody, as I knew it would be, but there was also an odd energy to it because this came a few weeks after the last taping, so there was that feeling of *Oh my God, how many times are we saying goodbye?!* Not literally from each other's lives, but in the aspect of the final this and the final that. Now, there was something special about when we got to *Colbert* because we knew it was airing that night, so there was a literal end about to happen that made it very official. But I do remember at that dinner feeling like we had been walking through goodbye purgatory for about a month now, and it's a very weird feeling. But the Polo Bar is always very good. There's nothing I don't like there, from the pigs in a blanket to the caviar and fingerling potatoes. Oh my God, it's *so* good.

There's nothing quite like a dinner at Ralph Lauren's Polo Bar in New York City, and it has remained a favorite of the cast's (and this author's) long after they all gathered for their final dinner on Tuesday, May 14, 2019, while promoting the finale (which aired two days later). *Courtesy of Steve Molaro*

Kunal Nayyar: And the day that the finale aired we were in New York, we had done *The Late Show with Stephen Colbert*, and my wife, Neha, was with me as we ran back to the hotel to watch the finale. It was just me and her in the hotel room. And when the last frame aired, I really wept for a couple of minutes. And then it was a sense of, *Okay, I'm ready*. We went to this French bistro and had a couple of martinis and ate some food and it was a really special moment. Because as much as someone thinks fame is some really glamorous, fulfilling thing…fame is a very, very lonely experience. It just is. And social media makes it seem otherwise. But ultimately, it's just an acceptance and a true surrender to realize ultimately you are just alone. Like, when it comes down to it, there's only two or three people. And it was a real sense of "We did it, this chapter of my life is done, and I didn't fuck it up."

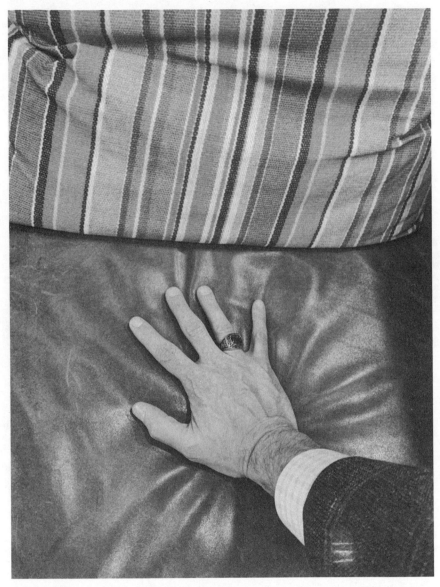

Steve Molaro—wearing his class ring, inscribed with the year *Big Bang* premiered and the year it ended—commemorated the last night of taping by paying homage to Sheldon's spot on the couch. *Courtesy of Steve Molaro*

EPILOGUE

In an age of reboots and reunions, stage 25 wasn't even dismantled before fans and press started asking the cast if they'd do a reunion. Three years later, it's still a topic of discussion in nearly every interview the actors do, specifically after the success of the *Friends* reunion—which, keep in mind, happened seventeen years after the finale episode aired.

Kunal Nayyar: I would do a reunion if it made sense creatively...where time had passed and we did it as an homage to the fans, that could be a possibility. I just think it still feels too soon to jump back into it. It's like breaking up with the love of your life when you know nothing is wrong, but it's just time. And that's what this feels like. I ran into Steve Molaro recently and almost started crying. It's so difficult.

Jim Parsons: I think it's impossible to imagine getting together to do any other acting version of [the show]. I mean...never say never, only because I don't know how I'm going to feel sometimes day to day, never mind seven to ten years from now. That being said, I just don't feel like I'm going to get older and want more to go back into character in that way. It's really hard for me to imagine. There's certain things that should be left alone. And even with a TV reunion, like *Friends*, there's a time limit. Here, in this capacity, I have time to expand upon it in a way that I might feel like it was a land mine if in front of the rest of the cast.

Simon Helberg: I can't say I have a tremendous desire to actually reboot anything, but in terms of getting together or celebrating a milestone, that's exciting to me. But I don't think I'm going to age into the wardrobe that Howard wore in any more graceful way that I left it.

Johnny Galecki: Maybe after the amount of time that the *Friends* cast had, but one of the reasons I kind of have been staying out from in front of the camera is I'm still kind of bleeding Leonard out of my system. Because these characters…they stay with you for a while. Once I am able to start from a clean canvas again, I'm not really interested in performing…so not for a very long time, if at all. But this book is a reunion. It's an emotional reunion.

Kaley Cuoco: Jess, are you going to host our reunion show in twenty years, [because] you're already hired!

Chuck Lorre: It's foolish to say "No, never," but at the same time I love where we left things, and I wouldn't want to do anything that diminishes what we did. Certainly if there was a time and place where it just felt right to do something? Of course! For the very simple reason it'd be wonderful to hang out with everybody again. Just for that reason alone, to spend some time with people that I spent so many years with and came to cherish. The fact that we did 279 episodes, and for the most part, really enjoyed doing them, and everyone got along and cared for one another is amazing. Listen, any human endeavor over twelve years has its bumps. That's inevitable. If I were to tell you that, "Oh, everyone got along *famously* for twelve years and there was never an argument," that's ridiculous. We would not be human beings. But for the most part, we did, and that is something to be grateful for. It made going to work *fun*.

Mayim Bialik: I've never had a better job and I've never wanted to have another job besides that one. I'm just a media whore. I'm here for what anyone wants me for. [*Laughs*]

Maria Ferrari: It was a dream. It's the absolute reason to be a writer. It's the best drug. You never stop chasing it. And it never gets old.

Melissa Rauch: Looking back now I'm just struck by how damn special it was, and I'm sure if you ask me in ten years that feeling will be even stronger. There wasn't a day that I drove onto that lot where I wasn't aware of how lucky I was, but I think it's hard to fully process the layers of something when you are living it day to day and you are occupied with the work itself. Now getting to see it as a whole it feels like a dream.

Steve Molaro: There were so many incredible aspects to working on the show, such as the family that was the writers room and getting to work with such insanely talented comedic actors. It was such a surreal, amazing chapter in all of our lives. I would say I miss all of it, but I don't know if *miss* is accurate. I'm just deeply grateful to have had the experience. As time goes on I keep appreciating more and more about it.

Jim Parsons: I get it. I really do. That's why for my mom, I don't know how much she missed new episodes each week—although that was part of it—but the bigger thing was, it was a really fun conversation for her with her friends. And as rare as it is for an actor to find a job that goes on that long, it is even more rare for the parent of somebody who has this as a career and to have their child be a part of something that is so beloved. Most jobs don't offer that.

Chuck Lorre: Every once in a while, I'll turn on the TV and stumble across one of the episodes, and I'm watching 'em like I've never seen them before. There was magic that happened thanks to the extraordinary, magical confluence of events of getting Jim, Johnny, Kaley, Simon, Kunal, then Kunal getting fired while I was in a plane going to New York, and then rehired when I landed in New York. [*Laughs*] It was a perfect ensemble. And later down the road adding Kevin, Melissa, Mayim, and having Laurie Metcalf and Christine Baranski. And what can you say about a situation comedy where Stephen Hawking and Nobel Prize–winning physicists are watching and want to participate? Where Bill Gates comes on and Steve Wozniak? It was a part of my life and career that I'm deeply grateful for. And the fact that it has some continuity, and people are still enjoying it? That's everything to me. I dreamt of being a musician and songwriter as a child, and what was magical about that was that a song has the ability to traverse time. I always wanted to do something, to be a part of something that had the ability to withstand time. And *The Big Bang Theory* does.

ACKNOWLEDGMENTS

In the season four premiere of *Young Sheldon,* Sheldon Cooper invokes the rare wisdom from his twin sister, Missy, when giving his valedictorian speech. "It's okay to be scared," he tells his fellow graduating class. "We just have to do it anyway."

I relied on that advice often throughout the last two years. In fact, while I had plenty of wonderful—even exhilarating—moments while writing this book, for the most part I was in a constant state of anxiety and fear. Now, I know what you're all thinking: You've worked at *Glamour* for over a decade and you're writing a book about one of your favorite TV shows—what on earth is there to be scared about? (Honestly, when I put it that way, not much!). But I also believe that the reason I've achieved what I have in my career is because of that fear and pressure. (I should also say I'm sure I could get by with a lot less of it.) Regardless, it's never lost on me that what I get to do is a great privilege, and with that privilege comes even greater responsibility.

In the case of *The Big Bang Theory*—a show that's so beloved, both to those who were a part of bringing it to your screens every week and those watching it at home—the pressure I put on myself with this book was more than I've ever experienced. One of the first things I said to executive producer/showrunner Steve Molaro when I first discussed the possibility of a book was that if I was going to embark on this journey, I needed (aside from his and Chuck Lorre's blessing and participation) to know that there was plenty of new and interesting stories to tell that would make even the most diehard fan feel they were learning something new. (Obviously that answer was a resounding *yes.*)

So there was that pressure to deliver to you, the reader, but also to the producers, writers, cast, and more. Most of them spent the better part of twelve years calling stage 25 home, and by spending hours talking to me, they trusted me to tell their legacy. They cried with me and laughed with me, and they told me deeply personal stories that they had never discussed before. That, combined with an intense deadline to deliver this book to my editor in time for the show's fifteenth anniversary, nearly drove me to the edge. (In fact, I'm now on a cholesterol-lowering medication and have new prescription glasses after straining my eyes looking at a computer screen. I really took this over-achieving thing too far.)

I will never forget the night before Grand Central Publishing came to me with their offer in early February 2021. I very seriously said to my parents, "I'm really scared. I don't know how I'm going to manage to do both *Glamour* and write this book on deadline, especially knowing the lengths I'll go to make this as perfect as I can." They didn't try to brush off my concerns or tell me "You got this" (a phrase I've come to truly dislike for both how trendy it's become and its generic-ness). Instead, they said, "We know," followed by, "We'll do whatever we can to help you along the way. And we will get through it." Much like Missy's advice to Sheldon, it was exactly what I needed to hear, when I needed to hear it. In fact, I often joked that this book was going to come with a disclaimer saying, "Kids, don't try this at home." I also joked that I understood why there's so much time between when you turn the manuscript in versus when the book is published, and it's only to give yourself time to recover and try to look like a normal human being again. But I also would do it again in a heartbeat, because as scared as I was, the trust of the cast and creative team was truly the greatest gift I've been given in my career.

And that brings me to the people who helped get me to this point. In early May 2020, a few weeks before the launch of HBO Max (*Big Bang*'s streaming home), I did a *Glamour* feature with Molaro and fellow executive producer / showrunner Steve Holland about the twelve best episodes of the show and the stories behind them. What was supposed to be only a thirty- or forty-five-minute chat turned into three times that length, as we reminisced and laughed about the greatest hits. It was so much fun that we started to devise ways to keep doing more of these, whether it be the twelve most emotional episodes or the twelve funniest scenes. If there was ever a show I missed covering once it went off the air, it was this one.

And then, nearly five months later, fate intervened. On a late August afternoon, Lesley Goldberg, the West Coast TV editor for the *Hollywood Reporter*, called me to say she'd been approached by a well-known literary agent in New York who was interested in exploring a possible *Big Bang* oral history. She was interested, but she also knew that she didn't have the bandwidth to take on such a project given her already insane work schedule. And so, in the ultimate example of support, she said to me, "I actually think you'd be the best person to write this." My heart dropped in the moment—again, there's that anxiety—because I knew she was probably right. And that was terrifying.

That led to an email introduction from Lesley to Rick Richter, who is now my wonderful literary agent at Aevitas Management. He's an honorary Radloff as far as I'm concerned, and he guided me through a world that was completely foreign to me when we started. Rick, I can't thank you enough for your support, your knowledge, your compassion, and for being my North Star. There's truly no one like you, and I will forever be your biggest fan. And Lesley, thank you for introducing me to Rick and being my fervent supporter. You're amazing.

From the beginning, I told Rick that the only way I was going to proceed with an oral history was if Chuck Lorre and Steve Molaro were on board. If they weren't, then neither was I. So for them to not only give me their blessing but to do so enthusiastically was something for which I will forever be grateful.

Steve, I don't know anyone who puts their heart and soul into everything like you do. I thank you for your trust, your honesty, and, above all, your friendship. Thank you for answering every single question and encouraging me to never stop bugging you when I needed something. Thank you for giving up hours of your Sundays for interviews. Thank you for being your stubborn, hilarious, heartfelt, hard-working self. You were the first one to say yes to this, and I'll never forget that, *ever*. For the record, you are also an expert bread maker and super smoker and Shappy pretzel lover. That's just an added reason why I know you'll be in my life forever. I love you and your family so much.

Chuck, three things in particular (among many!) stand out during our ten hours of Zoom interviews. One, I'll always remember when you told me the story of coming back from the writers strike in 2008 and being relentless about not letting this "thing" (as in *Big Bang*) fail. That's how I felt about this book. I knew it wouldn't "fail," but I expected perfection out of myself and had a relentless drive to deliver. Two, you told me how fortunate you felt to become friends with Norman Lear in your career and soak in his wisdom. I have felt—and will continue to feel—that way about you. And three, you may not remember this now, but you gave me one of the biggest compliments I think I'll ever hear. I know you never say anything unless you mean it, and it's something I will cherish always. Thank you for that gift, and so many others. You mean the world to me.

I had so many incredible publisher meetings for this book, but it was that first meeting that changed my life. As I talked about the show's impact, and specifically about the impetus for the coupling of Sheldon and Amy, I noticed everyone tearing up. I noticed that I—someone who does not cry in public—was beginning to get watery-eyed. It was at that moment that I knew I had found my home with Hachette and its Grand Central Publishing imprint. I wanted this book to have heart, to have emotion, and I felt that so strongly in that meeting. And so, to Grand Central Publishing's executive editor Suzanne O'Neil—otherwise known as *my* editor extraordinaire—thank you for believing in me and this show. Thank you for giving me the freedom to write the book that I wanted to write, and for championing me from day one. And to Jacqueline Young, Staci Burt, Tiffany Porcelli, and the entire Grand Central and Hachette team: thank you for being on my side.

Now, in order of my interviews... Thank you, Simon Helberg, for going first in the cast interviews and doing numerous sessions while you were in the middle of a move and also work and travel. You opened up about some deeply difficult days on the set, and I thank you for your trust, but also for talking so candidly about your anxiety. I related to that so much, and I know you'll help so many others feel less alone. Also, your sarcasm and one-liners made me laugh out loud constantly; I personally think they are some of the true gems in this book. I adore you.

To casting directors Ken Miller and Nikki Valko: Thank you for opening up in such detail about the audition process and casting stories. You are truly exceptional at what you do, and thank goodness you never gave up on getting the actors we now know and love to say yes.

To Jim Parsons: I never told you this, but I was the most nervous ahead of our first interview. I had prepared so many questions for you that my biggest fear was how on earth I was going to get through them all. Also, after rewatching all 279 episodes again (plus the unaired pilot), I had an even greater appreciation for your already exponential level of talent and was just so scared I wouldn't have enough time to dig deep with you. The fact that you gave me more than twenty hours of your time and opened up in such a heartfelt, honest, and in-depth way was a gift beyond measure. I already had tremendous respect for you as an actor, but your heart and who you are at your core is even more impressive. You are my favorite dodo bird, always!

To Wil Wheaton: I'll never forget when you told me how much you love oral histories and were so excited to be a part of this one. We only spent an hour and fourteen minutes on the phone, but you packed so much in and are such a compelling story teller. Thank you for your authenticity and enthusiasm.

To Kevin Sussman: You dropped the biggest bombshell on me when you revealed you booked the role of Wolowitz first, then bowled me over with your thoughtfulness when you explained why you never told Simon. You are so incredible, and you bring so much heart to everything you do.

To Kunal Nayyar: Thank you for Zooming with me from all over the world, and even letting my parents and sister crash several of our interviews. (They can't wait to host you in St. Louis one of these days.) Thank you for your tremendous advice throughout this process. As a fellow author, you told me what to fight for, what to let go of, and how to be kinder to myself in the process. I'll never forget that.

To Melissa Rauch: There is simply no one like you. You have been my guiding light, my therapist, and my greatest support. Your talent is boundless and your heart is enormous. You are my soul sister, period.

To Johnny "Not Just a Piece of Meat" Galecki: I have so much love for you. I'll never forget when you said, "Fuck you, Radloff," when I caused you to cry for the first time after bringing up a very emotional scene. (For the record, "Fuck you, Radloff" is now my second favorite thing you've ever said to me.) That's because months into our interviews, you confided that you were probably the most nervous about opening up, but now it was the greatest gift and you couldn't shut up. I am so grateful for your candidness on literally every subject in this book. You made me laugh harder than I ever have before, and I promise to bring you all the unicorn balloons next time I see you.

To Mark Cendrowski: There is a reason everyone loves you. Thank you for all your insight and wisdom and details. Now whenever anyone asks me about the stairs, I'll just point them to your portion of the book so they can understand just how brilliant you are.

To Nina Tassler and Wendi Trilling: Thank you for giving this show the second chance it so deserved and the reason we're all here today talking about it. You both really are the fairy godmothers of *Big Bang,* and it was such a joy to hear about those early days from an entirely new perspective.

To Bob Newhart: What a thrill it was to just listen to you for forty minutes. Your comedic timing was on full display, and I just love how much *Big Bang* meant to you personally and to your career. "It was damp" will forever be my favorite line from our interview, and I'm still working on getting that standing ovation recording from the Emmys for you.

To Peter Roth: You're a mensch, and I have never loved talking to someone more about television. For years I heard how much everyone just adored you, not just as an executive but as a friend and mentor, and after several hours of interviews, I feel that same way. Thank you for being such a champion of wonderful television and people.

To Mayim Bialik: I don't know how you juggled *Jeopardy!, Call Me Kat,* directing/writing your movie *As They See Us, and* talking to me for the book, but you did. Thank you for Zooming with me, leaving me voice memos, and telling *Variety* that I'm the reason you wanted to do this book. I've never cried at my desk, but reading that article did it, and I can't think of a better reason why. Thank you for giving us your Amy and being one of the most important characters I'll ever see on television.

To Kaley Cuoco: Where do I even begin? From inviting me over to go through all your Polaroids to scheduling all our interviews on your own (and then even taking charge of Johnny's schedule for the Zooms we did as a trio), you are something else. You love this show with every ounce of your being, and it was on full display in every interview. Thank you for your memory *and* memories, as well as your candor. It's no secret that one of my favorite parts of the book is your romance and friendship with Johnny, and it's because you have such a zest for life and you celebrate the people who mean the most to you. You are a magical unicorn, and I adore you. And yes, I will host the TV reunion... just tell me when.

To Bill Prady: These characters exist because of *you*. Thank you for embracing what makes us different and special. Thank you for telling such meaningful stories that help illustrate why these characters needed a place on mainstream TV and making so many of us feel less alone in the process. And thank you always for making me feel so at home on the *Big Bang Theory* Stage. I'll never forget at the series finale taping when you called me down to the railing to hear what *I* thought, and I was like, *Wait, what?* He wants to hear from *me*? I will always value that.

To Lee Aronsohn: You were such an important part of getting this show off the ground and establishing its foundation. Your impact can't be overstated. Thank you so much for being such an integral voice in this book. I truly loved our chat.

To Eddie Gorodetsky: You kept me on my toes during our interview, and the photo we took on Zoom still scares me a bit, but you are a big teddy bear and I love your anecdotes and perspective on the legacy of *Big Bang*. I know you aren't a fan of interviews, but if I had to go out on a limb, I'd say you had a pretty good time during ours.

To Peter Chakos: I can say that breakfast at More Than Waffles in Encino while watching old episodes on HBO Max on my laptop is the best way to start one's day. Thank you for all your insight, and for being such a brilliant editor. There's a reason why you have so many Emmys.

To Professor David Saltzberg: Thank you for all your incredible contributions both as an educator and as a TV science consultant. You made the science community proud with your accuracy, your passion, and your joy. I've never been so captivated talking to anyone about Super Asymmetry, and that's because of you.

To Mary T. Quigley: Your vision is simply beyond, and your thoughtfulness into the world of each character is so profound. It will live on forever, and our world is more colorful for it.

To Steve Holland: I adore you. Technically you were my first interview, since we did one for the sample chapter before I sold the book. So one, thank you for being in the trenches with me since very early on. Two, thank you for being one of the most honest, compassionate, thoughtful people I've ever met in my life. And three, thank you also for inviting me over to your house to look through photos and do interviews. I know I can talk to you about anything, and I am so lucky to have your friendship.

To Judy Parsons: Thank you for being so game to sit down for an interview when I asked Jim if you'd be a part of this book. You are the voice for all of us, having a front-row seat to a once-in-a-lifetime experience, but also having such an insightful perspective. I can't wait to eventually meet you in person (though Zoom was lovely!) and give you the biggest hug. Thank you for raising an incredible son in Jim, but also for being such an amazing woman yourself.

To Mark Hamill: I still can't believe I got to talk to you for ninety minutes about *The Big Bang Theory*. You love television so much, and that curiosity and knowledge came through tenfold. As soon as we got off the phone, I texted Molaro and Holland to tell them you were the best—and to send you *Big Bang* swag immediately. They have assured me you received it, but let me know, and if not, I'm sure they'll open up the Warner Bros. Studio Store for you and pay for anything you want.

To Maria Ferrari: Thank you for making time as you plowed away on *United States of Al*. Your stories are essential to the book and your contributions to *Big Bang* can't be overstated. Thank you for telling stories that we hadn't seen on TV before in a way that made so many of us feel seen. You are a true rock star.

To Amanda Walsh: Thank you from the bottom of my heart for saying yes to your first big interview about your experience playing Katie/Penny on the first pilot of *Big Bang*. Your story is such an important life lesson regardless of the business you're in, and I know it will resonate with so many. You're a class act.

To Scott London: I have never been more hungry after doing an interview.

You are a genius for what you created on *Big Bang*, and the fact that you gave me Penny's driver's license, résumé, bills, et cetera, to tell the story of her *many* last names is something I am still giddy over. Thank you for being a true superstar and just a really wonderful human being. Also, I can't wait to come over to your house for Chinese food and brisket. That's still okay, right?

To Adam Nimoy: I've never had anyone come prepared with sheets of paper detailing their love of *The Big Bang Theory*, but you did, and it was the most sincere gesture ever. I'm so glad you loved—and continue to love—this show as much as I do. Thank you for not only sharing your memories, but providing a voice for your dad's experience on the show. Live long and prosper, indeed, my friend.

To Nikki Lorre: Your perspective on *Big Bang* can't be overstated, and I hope you know how much I adore you. Your insight is second to none, and your honesty is so appreciated. You are so beyond talented, and just like your dad, I am so impressed with all you've accomplished and all that you'll continue to do.

To Anthony Rich: Poor WiFi connection be damned, I loved our choppy Zoom so much. You radiate joy and passion for what you do, and I'm so glad Nikki connected us. Thank you for everything!

To Eric Kaplan: I still have no idea half of what we talked about while you were walking the streets of New York during our interview, but it was hilarious. You are a good one, EK, and even if none of the pictures you sent me made it into this book, just know I received them all with much love and appreciation.

To James Burrows: You are a legend, and I am so thankful you are part of the legacy of *Big Bang*. You gave us an iconic pilot episode, not to mention the gift of so many incredible episodes of television in general, and it was and will always be an honor to talk to you.

To Tara Hernandez: Apologies if I made you late getting back to the writers room on your new show, *Mrs. Davis*; you just had so many great anecdotes and memories to share that I couldn't get enough. And I'll never forget the support you showed me when I was feeling so stressed and anxious on mile 24 of this process. You always had my back, and I have yours.

To Laurie Metcalf: Thank you for making time to chat during a busy filming schedule on *The Connors*. You may have only appeared in a little more than a dozen episodes of *Big Bang*, but your mark is on the whole series. You are an icon.

To Christine Baranski: I will never forget when your amazing daughter (and also incredible actor), Lily Cowles, first put us in touch, and then I accidentally FaceTimed you on a Sunday morning while I was still half asleep and panicked that you might pick up while on holiday in Italy. But the fact that you did call me from your Tuscan villa the next evening to wax poetic about the show while drinking a glass of wine was just beyond. You're a legend, and I'm never deleting your phone number from my contacts.

To Andy Gordon: Thank you for your amazing photography skills and for never hesitating to dig up an old photo when I asked, "Do you have this one?" You were my secret weapon, and I'm so glad Steve Holland introduced us!

To Zoe Perry: I don't think there's ever been a more perfect casting than you as Mary Cooper on *Young Sheldon*. You are simply so damn good at what you do, and you radiate kindness to all who know you.

To Lance Barber: Who would have thought we'd love George Sr. so much given how Sheldon often talked about him on *Big Bang*, but you have made him so compassionate and human. Everyone who works with you says you have a heart of gold, and they are right.

To John Ross Bowie: Given your last-minute casting stories, I guess it made perfect sense that you were my last interview. In a way, I am so glad that it happened like that (although apologies for any unnecessary anxiety!). Your audition story will forever be one of my favorites, and I'm so glad "Kripke" is represented.

To my *Glamour* family, starting with editor-in-chief Samantha Barry and business manager Eilish Morley: Thank you for giving me the green light to pursue this endeavor all the way back in September 2020. And to deputy editor Anna Moeslein and digital director Perrie Samotin: I would never have been able to take this on without your support and understanding. Thank you all for helping make it a reality.

To (in alphabetical order) Alex Ayers, Heather Besignano, Maria Candida, Trisha Cardoso and the Chuck Lorre Family Foundation, Dave Goetsch,

Marilou Hamill, Ansley Rix, Andy Sacks, Jillian Roscoe, Jeff Tobler, and Warner Bros. Television's Rebecca Marks, Robert Pietranton, Kristy Chan, Yong Kim, Greg Khach, Josh Anderson, and more: Thank you for your incredible support. So many of you helped make so many things happen for this book, from interviews to scheduling to photo approvals and more. I am so beyond appreciative.

To Melody Chiu, Scott Radloff, Mandy Moore, Rachel Brosnahan, Sheryl Anderson, Chris Rosa, Caitlin Brody, Jenny Singer, Rick "Tensor" Kopp, Rina and Hoang Yoon, Jill Kaplan, Nathalie Kirsheh, Cara Buono, and Lauren Davis Brody: Thank you for cheering me on and always asking me how I was holding up. I am so incredibly lucky for your friendship and love.

To Niko Mason: Thank you for helping support my Panera coffee addiction, and reminding me to simply breathe when "I'm freaking the f–k out" became my go-to line. Thank you for making everything a million times easier and having my back, but also knowing exactly the right thing to say and exactly when to say it.

To Jeff Giles: Thank you for helping guide me through this process and provide me with a sense of calm when I needed it most. Your insight and advice—which truly was tailored to me—was such a gift. And for all the times where I said, "No, I can't meet you for brunch this weekend, I have to work on the book," I realize I owe you like three hundred breakfast burritos now.

To Marc Klein: Thank you for being my sounding board constantly. You didn't want to be thanked, but I wouldn't hear of it. You made me better and made me think about things that I normally wouldn't have. You also might have freaked me out more as a result, but I'll let it slide. (Kidding!) Thank you for never getting sick of me—and if you did, for never showing it—and for being my best advocate. Ten years of friendship, and I feel so damn lucky. I love you.

To Melissa: I know I've already thanked you, but let me thank you more here, as one of my best friends in life and throughout this process. I couldn't have done it without you, plain and simple. You are so remarkable as an actor, but even more so as a human being, mom, wife, and friend. I'm in awe of you constantly, and you truly were a life raft for me. We never end our texts without at least three "I love you"'s, so I'm going to make it four for the book: I love you so much, I love you so much, I love you so much, I love you so much.

To Chris Kaspers: I promise your copy of the book will come with your picture as the main image in this section. Thank you for being my body-guard, my fellow burger and ribs lover, and looking out for me always. You helped make me laugh when I wanted to do anything but. Thank you for your enthusiasm and support, and, most important, for reminding me to see in myself what you see in me. I love you.

To Britney Young: The fact that you're one of my closest friends *and* you love this show? I hit the jackpot. You were always trying to find a way to make things easier—and you did. From airport pickups to chapter feedback, I am forever grateful. You listened to every freak-out, every "win," and every "what does this mean?" with the patience usually reserved for a therapist. I love you.

To B-Rad and Livi: Thank you for the endless comfort, love, and snug-gles. After pulling eighteen-hour days for the last two years without a day off, you helped keep me from falling apart. I also hope you can come on my book tour as the "Soft Kitty" stand-ins.

To my sister, Laura Radloff, who was the only person I trusted with help-ing me to transcribe hundreds of hours of interviews. Laura meticulously went through everything with me (don't worry, I paid her!). She also did this while starting her first year as a teacher, and I can't thank her enough. Laura, we may fight over the dumbest things, but I love you more than you'll ever know.

Most important, thank you to my parents, Barb and Stuart Radloff. Everything I am and everything I've learned is because of you. You were there every step of the way, *every day*, and are truly the only ones who saw up close what it took to bring this book to life. You were there to celebrate with me, feel anxious for me, and experience every emotion in between. You're my compass and my heart, not just over the last few years, but always. The greatest gift in this life is having you as my mom and dad, and I celebrate this book with you and for you. I love you forever.

INDEX

ABOUT THE AUTHOR

Jessica Radloff joined *Glamour* in 2011 as the West Coast entertainment correspondent, becoming West Coast editor in 2018, and then senior West Coast editor in 2022. She regularly appears on *Access Hollywood*, in addition to *The Talk, Good Morning America, Today*, and more on behalf of the brand. She also frequently moderates panels for shows such as *The Crown, Stranger Things, Outlander, The Flight Attendant, Emily in Paris*, and *This Is Us*, and she moderated *The Big Bang Theory* and *Young Sheldon*'s PaleyFest panels in 2018.

Prior to *Glamour*, she wrote for AOL, the *Huffington Post, Modern Luxury Media, WHERE Los Angeles*, and Major League Baseball's St. Louis Cardinals *GameDay* magazine. She is a member of the Television Critics Association, the Critics Choice Association, and the Screen Actors Guild. She is also an associate member of the Television Academy.

A native of St. Louis and a graduate of the University of Arizona, Jessica resides in Los Angeles.